P9-CDX-057

LATIN AMERICA

McGRAW-HILL SERIES IN INTERNATIONAL DEVELOPMENT

ALDERFER · *Local Government in Developing Countries*
BRYCE · *Industrial Development: A Guide for Accelerating Economic Growth*
DUNN · *International Handbook of Advertising*
EICHER AND WITT · *Agriculture in Economic Development*
HARBISON AND MYERS · *Education, Manpower, and Economic Growth: Strategies of Human Resource Development*
POWELSON · *Latin America: Today's Economic and Social Revolution*
WALINSKY · *The Planning and Execution of Economic Development: A Nontechnical Guide for Policy Makers and Administrators*

LATIN AMERICA

Today's Economic and Social Revolution

JOHN P. POWELSON
Johns Hopkins University and
Centro de Estudios Monetarios Latinoamericanos

McGRAW-HILL BOOK COMPANY
New York Toronto London

II

LATIN AMERICA

 Library of Congress Catalog Card Number 63–20719

50579

Este libro lo dedico con todo mi afecto
a los alumnos del quinto curso, Año 1960,
de la Facultad de Ciencias Económicas de la
Universidad Mayor de San Andrés con un
fuerte abrazo de su antiguo profesor

Preface

THIS BOOK stems from my association with economics students in Latin America. It covers the topics we talked about—what they said to me and what I said to them. Its purpose is to help establish communication where it is most wanted, and yet most wanting: between intellectuals in both halves of the hemisphere. It is addressed to Latin American students but intended for North Americans as well. We in the United States do not always know which issues are most on their minds.

Classroom sessions with these students are highly rewarding. I have found in them—particularly the most Marxist—an eagerness, almost thirst, to share their opinions with "Yankees," to debate, to argue, to listen, and to learn. In Bolivia, as in Mexico, discussions with university students extended long beyond the hour for dismissal, and they continued in restaurants, or as we were walking along the street or meeting in small groups. The subject matter was too urgent to be put aside merely because a bell had rung.

Let no one suppose that these contacts were not friendly, or not punctuated with laughter, or not conducted with mutual esteem. The respect for academic freedom in both Latin America and the United States makes it easy for students from one and teacher from the other to meet with no vested interest other than in honest intellectuality. There is nothing inconsistent, in the mind of a Marxist student, between shouting epithets at the American Embassy one day and sitting down in friendly fashion with an American college teacher the next.

I shall occasionally describe economic institutions, such as the hacienda system, with which my readers are already familiar. There are two reasons. One is that my own comprehension of Latin American economics is tempered by the fact that I am not Latin American. It may be incomplete or offer a new vantage point, and this should be made clear before discussion begins. The other is my hope that North Americans also will read this book.

In order to minimize my errors in interpreting student opinion, I have quoted liberally from papers written in my classes. These quotations are identified only as "by a Latin American student." Most originated in the University of San Andrés, La Paz, Bolivia, in 1960. I did not label them specifically "Bolivian" because I have heard the same opinions with much frequency elsewhere. The only difference is that other students did not write so many papers for me to cite.

One truism must be borne in mind. Any North American who criticizes his own government abroad plays a dangerous game. His attempts to be objective, freely citing what he considers the weak and strong qualities of his government, often result in his audience's hearing only the faults. The virtues fail to register, and he has merely confirmed the ugly sentiments already held. Particularly is this likely in countries where the political structure is monolithic, where one is either for or against, friend or foe, loyalist or traitor—in short, where the pluralistic society from which the North American comes is not understood.

The easy solution would have been not to write this book.

JOHN P. POWELSON

Acknowledgments

I AM indebted to Louise Dudley, Richard Wood, José Epstein, and John P. Clark for reading the entire manuscript and offering valuable comments. Thomas Carroll, John Delaplaine, David Hartzog, William Waylett, and Theodore Tibbutt read various parts of it and offered comments within their fields of specialization. My mother, Mary S. Powelson, also made some useful suggestions. Participants in the Institute for International Development and students in the School of Advanced International Studies of the Johns Hopkins University read the manuscript as part of their course materials, and I have benefited much from their classroom discussions. Research undertaken by S.A.I.S. students Rita Kahn, Robert Bell, Nicholas Rey, and George Schuyler yielded material that I have used at various points.

I am also indebted to students at the University of San Andrés, La Paz, Bolivia, to *becarios* from the *Centro de Estudios Monetarios Latinoamericanos* in Mexico City, and to various staff members of the Inter-American Development Bank and the International Monetary Fund from whom I obtained innumerable thoughts and ideas in the course of conversations and informal discussions.

I am also indebted to my wife, Alice R. Powelson, for her assistance in proofreading, to Miss Elvira Bagares for typing the entire manuscript, and to Miss Graciela Echaury for secretarial help.

J.P.P.

Contents

1 The Economic Revolution

"The Alliance for Progress," a Latin American student once told me, "is but a cunning shift in the strategy of the United States. Your fundamental purpose is still economic domination in our hemisphere. But you do sense that a revolution is in the making and that it is too strong to be quelled by the blunt weapons of the past. So your only recourse is to board it and dilute it from the inside."

TO SAY THAT there is a dichotomy in Latin American thinking toward the Alliance for Progress would be an understatement. On the one hand, there are those who argue that the decade of the sixties marks a fundamental change in the official attitude of the United States toward Latin America. Previously, they say, it followed a bumbling policy, neither consistent nor well conceived, composed daily according to circumstances, and designed to meet crises only after they had occurred. The coming of the Alliance, this group argues, marks an about-face, and a new comprehension of the social and political problems to which Washington earlier was officially blind.

John Dreier, former United States Ambassador to the Organization of American States, acted as spokesman for this group when he wrote that ". . . the people of the hemisphere [have] begun to sense the deeper implications of the change in policy and attitude that is involved—a change of tidal character that may best be likened to that which, about thirty years ago, marked the transition from the United States' policy of intervention in Latin America to the policy of the Good Neighbor." [1]

The other group consists of those who, like my student friend, feel that the policy of the United States has many faces, but that nothing will alter its basic disposition. Whatever methods are used—military intervention, the Good Neighbor policy, the inter-American conference table, or the Alliance for Progress—are only different shades of strategy whose unalterable design is to keep Latin America weak. A spokesman for this group wrote the following: [2]

> Imperialism has used, and continues to use, different means depending on circumstances of time and space. Sometimes military occupation is employed to subjugate a territory. At other times the objective, which is always economic domination, is achieved through treaties, pacts, the creation of regional organizations, and the like. Sometimes such agreements are plotted by the large powers, even though representatives of the region to be subjugated may participate in the discussions. Frequently imperialism is imposed through blackmail or bribery of whoever holds the power in the country to be made subservient. At other times it is inflicted through puppet governments, composed of politicians who will throw themselves into the arms of the capitalists in exchange for a few crumbs.

Many students and intellectuals in Latin America have always felt that the relationship between their governments and the United States was in the nature of an alliance. This alliance, in their thinking, is one of the rich against the poor, the strong against the weak. In country after country the rulers have traditionally been a small military or wealthy civilian clique who monopolize industry, income, wealth, votes, cultural advancement, and all the amenities of urban living. In sharp contrast to the wealthy classes, masses of peasants, often in economic slavery to landowners, eke out a bare living on subsistence farms or in the mines and petroleum fields.

Dominance by the wealthy has been possible, they argue, only because of financial support from North American investors. Armed with dollars and often backed by the guns of the United States Marines or private filibusterers, Yankee investors have traded wealth for more wealth. They have received land and mineral claims that Latin governments, not freely and fairly elected by their people, had no moral right to assign away from their people. Thus Porfirio Diaz, the "tyrant of Mexico," welcomed foreign capital to build railroads and mines, while he used not only his share of

[1] John Dreier, *The Alliance for Progress,* The Johns Hopkins Press, Baltimore, 1962, p. xiii.

[2] Editorial written by a second-year law student, University of San Andrés, La Paz, Bolivia, August, 1960.

the funds but also lands confiscated from the hapless Indians to buy military support from *caudillos* he was unable to beat. Thus Juan Vicente Gómez carved up the rich oil lands of Venezuela and handed them to foreign interests (who themselves drafted the nation's petroleum legislation), while he in his turn received the financial sustenance necessary to remain dictator and "lord high everything else."

The divergence of opinion on the turnabout in United States policy hinges on whether the interests of the two parts of our hemisphere are in fact complementary or necessarily at loggerheads. No one—aside from a few idealists—expects the United States and Latin America to reach a *rapprochement* for motives vaguely associated with the brotherhood of man or the biblical dictum on loving your neighbor. Nations become good neighbors not for the sole sake of so being but only if their mutual interests conform sufficiently to produce this result. Some economists, politicians, and sociologists have argued that not only is the brotherhood of man in the Western Hemisphere possible but history is resolutely leading us in this direction. Many Latin American intellectuals and students, however, contend that no conciliation is possible, because what is good for one side is inherently not good for the other.

The United States is a large industrial power, and the Latin American countries are suppliers of raw materials. Is this a complementary relationship advantageous to *both* parties? Many would argue that it is to the interest of the United States, but not of Latin America, to preserve the *status quo*. "The loss of your markets in our part of the hemisphere causes the United States to oppose our economic development," one of my students wrote. "If we were a developed continent, then you would export only machinery and capital goods to us, and you would lose vast markets for consumer goods together with the profits attached to them."

Echoing this belief, another Latin American student wrote that ". . . the United States wants only an economic development that benefits its own interests and not those of Latin America. Think what would happen if our continent should become *more* developed than the United States! Surely this would not please the North Americans, and they would not permit it. The United States wants simply to develop raw-material industries here, so as to obtain higher productivity, lower costs of production, and hence lower prices (to be paid by the United States)."

If one is convinced, as these students are, that whatever manner in which the United States participates in Latin American economic development bodes no good for the Latin nations, then one is bound to believe also that the Alliance for Progress represents no change of heart on the part of the United States, but simply a continuance of past imperialism with a new strategy. If North Americans are dissatisfied with the old-style imperialism, if they (now) disapprove of the behavior of the Marines before the Good Neighbor policy, it is only (this school believes) because the old policy did not work or because it embroiled the United States in present problems more delicate and more difficult than the ones it solved in an earlier decade.

But my purpose is not to argue the Good Neighbor policy. The present version of the controversy centers on the Alliance for Progress, and the United States attitude toward agrarian reform, business investment, the prices of primary products, inflation, economic integration, foreign aid, and national planning. North American policy in all these areas has undergone significant change with, or since, the Alliance for Progress. Many Latin American students are asking whether these changes reflect a genuine turnabout in United States attitudes toward Latin America. Or are they just a new strategy in the same old game of economic conquest?

CONFLICTS OF OPINION

Conflicts of opinion divide the Latin American student world on each of the issues listed above. It would be impossible here to enumerate all the shades of sentiment that make their way into conversations, the classroom, and articles in the learned journals. But a general impression of the area of controversy can be gained by examining opposite pairs of extreme positions.

Two sample opinions are cited below on each issue. The first set (opinions numbered 1) are held mainly in the United States, but they are also seconded by some Latin Americans, including civil servants, businessmen, and students. The second (opinions numbered 2) are heard primarily in Latin America, although a few North Americans would endorse them. They represent the group that distrusts the United States in varying degrees or believes it is mistaken in official policies. Holders of these views in their most anti-United States version, such as some students and professors in the economics and law faculties of the universities, believe most strongly that North American participation in the Alliance for Progress constitutes a revision of strategy, not a change of heart.

On agrarian reform

Opinion 1. Apathetic for many years, the United States has at last awakened to the urgency of agrarian reform. Its interest stems in part from genuine concern for the welfare of the masses. But, mainly, it is aware that social justice is a requisite for avoiding repetition in other countries of the Communist inroads into Cuba. Only if peasants own their own land will they have a personal stake in maintenance of political and economic institutions.

Opinion 2. The United States has never favored agrarian reform and never will. North Americans are prominent among the powerful owners whose pocketbooks will be compromised if land is confiscated. But Washington is aware that the revolutionary winds are becoming more intense, and it is no longer possible to suppress them by the traditional means. The most rational strategy is to pretend to be in favor of agrarian reform, to infiltrate the movement, and to gain control. Then it can be diverted into "painless" programs of resettlement on public lands, minor tax revisions, and a few confiscations of generally unproductive land, where the impact on the landlords will be minimal.

On the market mechanism

Opinion 1. With rare exceptions, market prices are the most rational way of selecting goods and services to be produced and the people who will buy them. They respond to the desires of the people and predict the exhaustion of scarce resources. They distinguish successful ventures from failures. Any subsidies for the latter become aboveboard, and they are measured. Price ceilings and artificial or multiple exchange rates, on the other hand, not only pervert the rational use of resources but inevitably fail in their objectives. Over the long run, even the most pervasive controls can be avoided in a democratic society.

Opinion 2. Complete freedom of pricing favors the wealthy and injures the poor. Since income is a factor in determining demand, the unhampered operation of the laws of supply and demand will satisfy the whims of the wealthy while subsistence needs of the poor go unattended. Prices of basic goods and services such as transportation, electricity, fuel, food, and water must be kept low, for these are the consumption of the poor. Any foreign enterprises interfering with this *sine qua non* must be nationalized. Exchange controls are necessary for increased imports of capital goods to promote the nation's development.

On foreign investment

Opinion 1. Investment by United States and European companies contributes to the economic development of Latin America. Foreign companies bring foreign exchange, which provides essential imports. Through their taxes, they often supply a significant percentage of the government's revenue. They share technical knowledge, train workers, and frequently pay higher wages than are earned elsewhere in the economy. They also require supplies from local companies, thus increasing demand and creating employment. Some companies have promoted Latin Americans into top management positions and have appointed them to boards of directors. Many have built schools, hospitals, and housing for their workers that are far superior to what they would otherwise have had.

Opinion 2. Foreign enterprise in Latin America has been largely of the extractive type. For whatever values it has contributed, it has taken more away. Foreign companies have acquired vast concessions in oil fields and other mineral deposits by bribing local dictators not elected by the people. They have followed repressive labor policies, often calling on the dictator to use troops against strikers, spilling their blood. Many companies do not promote Latin Americans into top positions, and when a Latin American and North American hold similar jobs, the latter often earns a higher salary than the former. Sometimes the foreign companies are more powerful than the government. They have exerted tremendous pressure to influence legislation, oppose agrarian reform, and keep their taxes low, and have even overthrown governments.

On the prices of primary products

Opinion 1. It has never been proved that long-run changes in the terms of trade are adverse to Latin America. World demand for manufactured goods is increasing in proportion to that for primary products, but the absolute demand for both is rising. Commodity agreements to hold prices of primary products high are dangerous to the supplier, because buyers will seek synthetic substitutes or other ways of economizing. Furthermore, artificial prices will promote inefficient production, since mining companies and farmers will not be forced by competition to use less costly techniques.

Opinion 2. The prices of the goods that Latin America sells and the prices of the goods she buys are both set in the United States by large monopolies. Over the years the terms of trade have been turning against Latin America, so that a given quantity of raw-material exports buys much less in manufactured goods than it did in the nineteenth century. Fluctuations in the prices of primary products make it difficult for Latin American countries to plan their economic development or even balance their national budgets. The United States should pay a fair price for the raw materials it buys, and this should be established by intergovernmental agreement.

On inflation

Opinion 1. Inflation is caused by irresponsible monetary and fiscal management by governments. It discourages saving and impairs the quality of investment, by channeling funds into speculative rather than productive capital. It causes irrational choices of economic activity. It leads to price and exchange controls that suppress agriculture and encourage the domestic production of luxury goods whose import has been forbidden. It causes a drain on the balance of payments and leads the country into hopeless foreign debt.

Opinion 2. While runaway inflation is disastrous, nevertheless a conscious policy of mild inflation will encourage economic growth. It is, in fact, the inevitable consequence of growth, since some sectors of the economy will expand more rapidly than others, and prices will necessarily rise in the latter. But the growth of the former would be suppressed if overall price stability is required. Some say the United States discourages inflation because it wants to impede Latin American growth; the International Monetary Fund is a "lackey of the imperialists," whose objective is to strangle the forward movement of the economy.

On economic integration

Opinion 1. Attempts to integrate the economies of Latin America and to establish common tariffs are bound to arrest economic growth. Less than 10 per cent of Latin American imports and exports are with other countries in the area. The bulk of trade is with the United States and Europe. Costs will be higher if Latin American countries are forced to buy from each other rather than traditional suppliers. Thus real incomes will be lower, and ability to save for capital formation correspondingly impaired. Similarly, the formation of a payments union does not justify the effort and expense. With world currencies increasingly convertible, Latin America will be just as well off settling intra-area accounts in dollars or other currencies traditionally used for this purpose.

Opinion 2. The small size of markets is a principal reason for underdevelopment in Latin America. If each of the twenty republics fosters growth of the same industries, none will become large enough to enjoy cost reductions on account of scale. Granted that the countries do not now trade with each other very much, nevertheless this need not be so in the future. Through international conferences, Latin American countries will determine which will specialize in which industry. Despite the liberalization of currencies, Latin America still suffers from a dollar shortage, and a payments union—similar to the one that was so successful in Europe—is desirable.

The United States has long opposed integration in Latin America because she did not wish to lose her export markets. Her present, mildly favorable attitude does not stem from conviction but from a resigned acceptance that integration is inevitable.

On foreign aid

Opinion 1. The United States extends foreign aid to Latin America partly from a genuine desire to help a neighbor. But more importantly, it is widely believed that foreign aid will help combat communism. This is so not only because poor people are susceptible to demagoguery but because the proper kind of aid, extended under the right conditions, can encourage growth along democratic channels. If the latter is to occur, however, certain reforms must be undertaken by the Latin Americans themselves, and aid should be made contingent upon them.

Another basis for foreign aid relates more to the self-interest of the United States. Economists have observed that high-income nations are the best customers for each other. North Americans want to promote Latin American economic growth, because they know the Latins will then buy more United States exports, thus promoting mutual prosperity.

Opinion 2. To comprehend the reasons for foreign aid, one must first understand that the United States is opposed to economic growth in Latin America. Wages would rise, and the consequent increased prices of raw materials would be detrimental to North American industry. Furthermore, the development of consumer goods industries in Latin America would deprive the United States of markets.

Foreign aid is a means of disposing of capitalist surpluses, which arise as part of the final stage of capitalism, before its inevitable demise. In particular the agricultural surpluses shipped by the United States are intended to compete with Latin American farmers and to retard the increase in their productivity. In other programs, the United States *gives* industrial commodities (primarily consumer goods) to politicians, who *sell* them to the people and pocket the proceeds. Thus aid strengthens the compact between the imperialists and the oligarchy and rarely filters down to the people who need it most.

Finally, foreign aid is part of the overall strategy of the United States to maintain its economic domination over Latin America. Instead of (or in addition to) United States businessmen's bribing corrupt politicians, the United States government is now doing so.

On national economic planning

Opinion 1. National planning is essential to economic growth in Latin America. Unfortunately, the country plans currently formulated are too heavily weighted toward a macro-, or overall, approach. They make elaborate projections of gross national product, investment by sectors, saving, taxes, and other data interesting to the intellectually curious. Such an overall plan may create a false sense of security, making development strategists feel comfortable even though they have not undertaken the less precise, more difficult, but vital tasks of seeking out and analyzing sufficient projects. Furthermore, planning may distort the government's statistical machinery. Scarce talent will be used to collect macro-type data, relating to total output, consumption, and saving. But there is a limited usefulness in analyzing the overall national economy, as opposed to studying the technical, economic, and marketing feasibility of specific projects. Statisticians would serve better by ferreting out more fundamental information, such as industrial statistics, on the basis of which entrepreneurial decisions are made.

Opinion 2. Overall national planning is vital to rapid development. Latin America has neither the time nor the resources to make the mistakes undergone by the United States in its haphazard growth. These are evidenced by the number of business failures, with consequent loss in resources. The individual entrepreneur, unguided by national policy, will consider only the effect of his decisions upon himself, and not how they fit into a total picture of economic growth. If development is slow, as it was in the United States in the nineteenth century, the errors of such individualism are minimized, for the external conditions on which the entrepreneur bases his decision are not much changed for many years. If growth is fast, as is contemplated for Latin America, an entrepreneur who bases his calculations on what he sees about him at the moment is apt to be fooled some years hence. He will not realize what potential competitors, suppliers, or customers are simultaneously doing. But if his enterprise fits into the framework of a national plan, those entrusted with the overall direction of the economy will already have taken these factors into account.

Beginning in Chapter 3, these opinions and their variations will be discussed in a series of issues relating to economic development in Latin America. They will be documented by citations from student papers, journal articles, and books. With freedom of thought guaranteed in both Latin America and the United States, any one of these opinions might be held by an American from either part of the hemisphere. But I believe that the first set is found more predominantly in the United States, and the second in Latin America.

Adherents to extreme versions of the second set of opinions interpret United States policy as intent on economic domination. Weak agrarian reforms, strict adherence to market prices and exchange rates, large-scale foreign investment, only occasional commodity agreements, monetary stabilization, free trade, foreign aid, and economic planning—all are weapons in the struggle for control of the Latin economies. The papers cited from my students in Latin America argue this case persuasively, and it is not always easy for a North American to reply.

But the dichotomy is not confined to the extremes. Many Latin American intellectuals, friends of the United States, argue that North American policy has not distinguished between the economics of nineteenth-century development and what is appropriate to the revolutionary vigor of modern Latin America. New theories of growth are in vogue, with new perspectives on the law of comparative advantage, the marginal laws, inflation, and other economic matters.

These groups recognize that the United States sincerely wants to help Latin America, but they believe it is like an eighty-year-old grandfather who does not understand the modern generation. To them, the International Monetary Fund is not a "lackey of the imperialists." Rather, it is a gentlemen's club, populated by well-intentioned but old-fashioned conservatives.

Are economic laws immutable, unchangeable over time and space? Virtually every economist would answer "no"; the economic history of the West has shown formidable changes since the days of Adam Smith. But on the other hand, are economic laws on one continent so vastly different from those on another, or in one era from those in another, that they must be scrapped as one moves in time and space? Again virtually every economist would answer "no"; for there is a consistency to economics that gives it doctrinal body and soul. The question is, *how* changeable is economics? To what extent, for instance, is Keynesian theory valid in a Latin American context? I have a feeling—and it is only that—that if all Latin American opinions were added up, they would weigh in favor of changeable doctrines far more than those in Europe and the United States.

Why is it, one is then tempted to ask, that *objective* economists, who sincerely want to divorce themselves from chauvinism and see the truth *as it is,* nevertheless tend to divide along lines that belie their geographic origin? Are interests of Latin America and the United States really in conflict, and do economists unconsciously rationalize those of their own country into "immutable" laws? Or apart from conflict or harmony, do different laws apply to different places, and are we so limited in vision that our intellectual concepts do not extend beyond the environment in which we were raised?

It is in search of answers to these questions that this book is written.

2 Individual and Collective Approaches to Development

"WE NEED MUCH more contact with North Americans," the student at the University of San Simón [1] told me. "This is the first time I can recall an economist from the United States coming to this campus to talk with us about North American imperialism." He was telling me, in a polite way, that he wanted most of all to know what North American capitalists *think* as they exploit Latin American workers. Do they sense any shame for the low wages and denial of civil rights, for favoring United States citizens over Latin Americans in management positions, for keeping autocratic governments in power by their financial support, and above all for wielding monopoly powers to control the prices of both what they buy and what they sell? Or are their minds so warped that they are beyond any feeling of empathy for their victims?

There is no simple answer, at least unless one grants without reservation the hypotheses of the question. Even without internal uniformity within each continent, the gulf between Latin Americans and North Americans on questions of business enterprise, the government's role in economic development, labor relations, prices, and similar matters is so great that it is hard even to verbalize questions for discussion. Before the student from San Simón and I could come to grips with them, we would have had to spade the ground and construct a common launching pad. This chapter covers only the launching pad; the issues come later.

Let me start with the hypothesis that Latin Americans are more prone, *in general,* to seek collective solutions to economic problems (in which the government plays a significant role), whereas North Americans, *in*

[1] Cochabamba, Bolivia, June, 1960.

general, prefer to solve their conflicts in an arena where individual (business or person) deals with individual. This is a sweeping generalization to which there are many exceptions, and its truth lies only in the fact that it is stated relatively—that there is a greater preponderance of Latin American opinion on the collective end of the scale, while North Americans gravitate more toward the individual end.

One wishing to pass judgment on collectivism versus individualism could find arguments in favor of each, with a strong feeling that neither is good in the extreme. Collectivism has its virtues because man is a social creature, who finds satisfaction in joint endeavors with his fellow men. I am confident that President Cárdenas of Mexico favors communal villages (*ejidos*) as an instrument of agrarian reform not solely for their economic advantages, but also because he thinks this is the way people *ought* to live. North American farmers, by contrast, have laid more stress on self-reliance as a moral virtue. The cooperative movement in the United States has often been dubbed a reaction to excessive individualism.

A point that both peoples have in common is their fear of large power concentrations. I venture, however, that each tends to feel that his side alone has this fear and the other is oblivious of it. This is because they differ in their definition of power concentration. Latin Americans, of both right and left, look askance at the intrusion of foreign enterprise. The large oil companies in Venezuela, the fruit companies in Central America and Ecuador, the tin companies (now nationalized) in Bolivia, and the copper companies in Chile all represent the specter of power. Some have resources equal to, or greater than, those of the government. They are accused of being monopolies, of paying unduly low prices for raw materials, and of acting as sources of national political power. Rightists in Latin America view them as challengers to national enterprise and the growth of local capitalist classes. From Mexico to the Southern tip of Chile, if there is one common ground on which left and right can stand together, it is their aversion to the power of foreign enterprise.

North Americans also are wary of power concentration, but they do not (in general) place the business corporation in this class. Rather, to them a strong, central government constitutes a dangerous focus of authority likely to intrude on personal freedoms. President Eisenhower characterized government enterprise (such as the Tennessee Valley Authority) as "creeping socialism" (a derogatory term). Government regulation has come into many fields, by force of necessity, but it is basically distasteful to most people. The sentiment is strong that the more the government does for the people, the less they will do for themselves—they will become fat and lazy, and private initiative will end.

This sentiment is reflected in the political system, which contrasts with all Latin American countries (except perhaps Brazil) in the division of authority between local and central governments. Government in the United States is based on the theory that political authority should be decentralized as far as possible. The tiniest village should do as much for itself as it possibly can, and only where its actions might infringe on the rights of a neighboring village does it become subject to a higher power, that of the county or state. The Federal Constitution defines a specific list of powers that belong to the national government (in Washington), and declares that *all others* are reserved for the states.

Thus Latin Americans and North Americans each tend to feel that the other does not protect its people sufficiently from the infringement of concentrated power. North Americans view the nationalization of electricity in Mexico and telephones in Rio Grande do Sul as an aggrandizement of political authority in the hands of the rulers, and not as vesting wealth in the people. They are uneasy about labor-union dependence on political support in the struggle for social justice. They shudder at government regulations requiring businesses to provide employee housing and schools—not because these are not deserved, but because in North American eyes schools and housing should be created by community initiative and designed by community choice, rather than bestowed by paternalistic dispensation. North Americans note with alarm Latin American price and exchange controls, allocation of resources, licenses, discriminatory tax systems, and subsidies, which (they argue) will "hobble" the initiative of the individual and unduly subject him to central authority.

Many Latin Americans, on the other hand, are disturbed by the concentration of private power in the United States, which appears to them undiluted by any rules or government-applied code of fair conduct. Business is big and wields tremendous power over consumers and foreigners. If labor unions assert their individuality more in the United States than in Latin America, it is because they too are large and powerful. Interlocking directorates, pyramided corporate structures, informal relationships among corporation officers, concentration of the money supply in a few private banks all present the aspect of conspiracy by a few powerful blocs. From this vantage point, it is not difficult to conclude that Wall Street dominates Washington.

Certain historical developments, whose treatment is beyond the scope of this book, have tended to make Latin Americans more collective-minded and North Americans more individual-minded. One of these is that England was a modern nation at the time of New World conquest, but Spain and Portugal were still feudal. Another is the fact that the industrial revolution occurred first on the British islands and not on the Iberian peninsula. The type of conquest and manner in which independence was achieved, as well as the history of land expansion (affected by geography) and the development of labor unions, the military, and political institutions—all are interrelated historical influences. If we were to debate whether history occurred as it did because different types of people carried it out or because of the physical factors and accidents they encountered, we would debate forever.

Out of our divergent histories have come differing degrees of acceptance of the Marxist and capitalist ethics in Latin America and the United States. Not all who endorse the Marxist ethic are Marxists, just as those who support the capitalist ethic are not necessarily capitalists. Adherence to each is relative. In my own subjective view—not empirically tested and possibly biased by my greater contacts with the student and intellectual world than with businessmen—there is far greater acceptance of the Marxist ethic in Latin America than in the United States. Likewise, the capitalist ethic wins the popularity polls north of the Rio Grande. If this is so, it is a condition worthy of analysis.

CAPITAL AND THE MARXIST ETHIC

That economic development depends absolutely on capital formation and cannot take place without it is accepted in the writings of many economists, both Latin and North American. While recognizing that other factors, such as technology, education, governmental processes, and labor skills, are essential to growth, nevertheless many authors place capital in central focus. The accumulation of capital, wrote Celso Furtado of Brazil, "is the basis of what is called economic development." [2] The late Ragnar Nurkse states that ". . . capital formation lies at the very centre of the problem of development in economically backward countries." [3] In a footnote in his *Economic Development*, Professor Kindleberger cites several other authors whose works support the primacy of capital in the development process.[4]

If observation is the main analytical tool, this conclusion is readily understandable. In virtually every country where development has occurred, capital is omnipresent. Even in high-income agricultural societies, little touched by the intrusion of heavy industry, the use of combination harvesters, heavy-duty tractors, and other tools is patent, and the relationship between capital and productivity cannot be denied. More so is this true in industrial countries, where giant blast furnaces, power plants, and thousands of miles of railroad tracks stand as testimony to

[2] Celso Furtado, "Ensayo de interpretación histórico-analítica del desarrollo económico," *El Trimestre Económico*, vol. 23, no. 90, p. 151, April–June, 1956.

[3] Ragnar Nurkse, *Problems of Capital Formation in Underdeveloped Countries*, Oxford University Press, Fair Lawn, N.J., 1953, p. 1.

[4] Charles P. Kindleberger, *Economic Development*, McGraw-Hill Book Company, Inc., New York, 1958, p. 35.

the capitalistic nature of enterprise. The visitor from a less developed land need only look about him, and he will see that the high-income countries are ringed with steel girders and roll on power-driven wheels.

The importance of capital is bound to be stressed in any Marxist analysis of development. Although Marx contended that all value emanates from labor, nevertheless capital is, he argued, the principal agent through which labor productivity is increased. First, it is through capital that labor is accumulated in one spot to take advantage of the economies of large-scale production. In the second place, the use of power machinery enables laborers to produce an output far greater than their capabilities as unequipped individuals.[5]

True enough, Marx qualified the central role of capital when he doubted that certain machinery really reduced the labor requirement of production by any more than that necessary to produce the capital goods themselves.[6] But we must remember that in his day power manufacturing was a phenomenon of only the preceding century. It was not totally evident—as it is today—that the power applied in capitalistic methods not only increases labor productivity enormously but permits scientific wonders that would be impossible without man-made, physical requisites.

In Marxist terms, the central role of capital lies not only in its ability to increase labor productivity but more importantly in the opportunity for exploitation of labor that it bestows upon the capitalist. Indeed, the two work hand in hand, for it is through the creation of "surplus value," which Marx avows has been stolen from the laborer, that capital begets capital and the capitalist is able to concentrate the wealth of the world in his hands.

Marxist students are ever alive to the implications of surplus value and the exploitation of labor. To them, the Western Hemisphere is divided into the rich and the poor, and it does not much matter whether the rich are from the United States or Latin America. North American capital, they argue, was accumulated from two sources. Some came from England and Europe, and was compounded over the centuries by the reinvestment of surplus value. More was ground from the Negro slave by Southern plantation owners in the later eighteenth and early nineteenth centuries. Capital from both sources joins hand in glove with the riches that Spanish *caudillos* carved from the back of the enslaved Indian, to create further surplus value by paying no more than subsistence wages to Latin American workers. In Marxist terms, the capital created from exploitation of the Negro and Indian is known as "primitive accumulation," whereas that brought from England and Europe, and compounded in profits in the

[5] Karl Marx, *Capital,* Charles H. Kerr & Co., Chicago, 1908, vol. I, chap. 13.
[6] *Ibid.,* vol. II, chap. 15.

United States and Latin America, is called "capital acquired through surplus value."

The distinction between the two origins of capital is not always appreciated by North Americans, but it is important to Latin American students. In the early chapters of *Capital,* Marx treats so extensively the manner in which wealth begets wealth (surplus-value capital) that he postpones discussion of how the world's initial stock was created. Yet the question is a natural one, for if capital comes from capital, how did the process start? Marx is conscious of the omission, for he later returns to the analysis of primitive accumulation.

"The starting-point of the development that gave rise to the wage-labourer as well as to the capitalist," wrote Marx, "was the servitude of the labourer." [7] Thus slavery is an important element in the system. Only by appropriating for himself a portion of the product of someone else (according to Marx) may a capitalist gain the resources to initiate the continuous process by which capital produces profits and profits produce capital. Marx's illustrations were drawn primarily from the history of England and its feudal system. He insisted that economic servitude continued even after the breakup of feudal estates, for these divisions served only to concentrate land, century after century, in the hands of small numbers of large holders, leaving their former serfs helpless except in so far as they were willing (or forced) to sell their labor for the pittance that the "master" offered.

The concept of primitive accumulation is not solely of historic interest. Modern Marxists do not consider that, even today, all capital formation comes by way of surplus value. Many Latin American students argue that primitive accumulation still takes place alongside surplus value, that both add to the wealth of the capitalist, and that both play a central role in modern economic development. Capitalism is a process, developing and running its course at different historical eras in different parts of the world, and is only beginning in some sections of Latin America where wealthy landowners are practicing primitive accumulation as they exploit Indian, Negro, and mestizo peasants.

It is perhaps a curious aspect of Marxism that it has made a greater intellectual impression on economics curricula in Latin American universities than it has in the United States. Whether he espouses Marxism or not, the Latin American student tends to look upon it as current doctrine, of present-day importance in understanding events that are now occurring. In many universities it is discussed not only in courses on the history of economic thought but as an integral part of today's economic theory.

In the United States the opposite is true. A student majoring in economics may pass his courses with honors and receive his degree with only

[7] *Ibid.,* vol. II, chap. 26, p. 787.

a vague notion of who Marx was. His curriculum may have been so crowded with other subjects that he did not study the history of economic thought or take courses in political theory, and the faculty regulations may not have required him to do so. His economic theory course might make only passing mention of Marx, if any at all, since the professor of theory would not want to impinge on the area of the professors of history and comparative government.

Why is this? Why is Marx considered a political theorist by North Americans and an economist by Latin Americans? Extremists among my Latin American friends have sometimes argued that the university is not free in the United States and professors are not at liberty to discuss doctrine at variance with official government directives or adverse to the interests of Wall Street sponsors. They have argued that universities are private, often endowed by wealthy people and big businesses, that they hold stocks in large corporations and limit education to the few who can afford to pay tuition.

This explanation must be rejected summarily, for virtually anyone closely familiar with United States universities will agree that academic freedom is as strong there, and as well defended, as it is in Latin America. Six regional bodies, independent and apolitical, are responsible for certifying that universities maintain high academic standards and are not using their positions to proselytize in favor of any political doctrine. The penalty would be withdrawal of accreditation, and public disgrace.

In addition, it is not true that all universities are privately endowed. Each of the fifty states maintains its own university, and most of them have several, supported by public funds. They charge either no tuition or very nominal rates, thus providing education to the masses in much the same way as Latin American institutions.

The failure of Marxism to make much headway in the United States is not confined to the university. In labor unions, where its greatest support might have been expected, Marxist influence is minimal. Time and again workers have rejected it in free, secret elections. Thus the same groups—labor and the university—that have been the bastion of Marxist support in Latin America, have been either apathetic or opposed in the United States.

Some have argued that the degree of development, the high national income and especially its more egalitarian distribution (than in Latin America), explain Marxism's failure to capture the imagination of the North American people. This feeling is especially common among those who equate low incomes with susceptibility to communism. Upon hearing that more and more workers in the United States are buying stocks of corporations, one Latin American student cynically wrote: "Maybe it is the intention of North American workers to become capitalists themselves and to convert the people of the less developed world, including Latin Americans, into workers who produce raw materials for them."

It is obvious that workers, students, and others who enjoy high incomes derived from a capitalist system will tend to call that system successful and not be easily converted to another. But this is not the only, and I believe not the principal, factor explaining lack of Marxist support. I shall argue that—despite the writings of some economists—North Americans *in general* are not convinced that capital lies at the core of economic development. The capitalist ethic implies that success and wealth do *not* come from the exploitation of others, do *not* arise through ownership of inherited wealth, are *not* the result of gambling and speculation—in short, do *not* come primarily from holding capital at all. Rather, success (and with it capital accumulation) is the result of ingenuity, hard work, and the discovery of new ways to produce that are of benefit to mankind.

It is, of course, a question of relative emphasis. No rational person will deny the role of capital in production, or the ability of an ingenious person with capital to produce more than an ingenious person alone. North Americans, however, tend to emphasize the "ingenious person," whereas Marxists stress the capital. The greatest prestige and admiration in the United States are reserved for the "penniless immigrant" (of which there have been many) who, by his own efforts, skills, and providence, accumulated a fortune. (Of these, there have been a few.)

This ethic underlies the writings of Horatio Alger and Benjamin Franklin; it is blessed as "rugged individualism"; it appears in North American folklore, and in the doctrines of the Protestant (or Puritan, or religious) ethic. It accounts in large part for the North American admiration of wealth and respect for people who have gained it. It helps explain why North Americans extol private property and the market economy, and why they have long resisted agrarian reform. It is the antithesis of Marxism, but like Marxism, it is neither altogether true nor altogether false; it is partly rationalization. It explains much when applied to United States thinking but causes misunderstanding, fear, and hatred when North Americans misapply it where it does not belong, or when they assume that all others are equally influenced by it. Above all, it behooves any Latin American who wants to understand the inner mechanism of his North American neighbors to spend a few moments in attempting to absorb their mysticism.

THE CAPITALIST ETHIC

For a Latin American student to understand the capitalist ethic as it is believed in the United States, he must first bear in mind certain factors. One is that North Americans do not live in a feudal society. Most of them have never set eyes on a Latin American *latifundio,* nor heard the term "economic slavery." A second factor is that North American business is far more competitive in the United States than the few examples of it to which Latin American students have (in general) been exposed. While North Americans look upon monopoly as one of many economic problems, within their experience it is by no means serious. A third is that incomes are more evenly distributed in the United States than in Latin America, and few North Americans have ever seen anyone living on the verge of starvation. In short, United States economic life is far different to most North Americans from the view that Latin American students have of it, and this difference affects their sense of social proportions.

This is not to argue, however, that capitalist ethic is entirely myth. Nor is it to agree with those Latin Americans who insist it would founder if once extended beyond the boundaries of a wealthy, developed nation. Far from it. Much of it is truth, and a few of its truths are universal.

An important essential of the capitalist ethic is that capital is not the *sine qua non* of economic development. Professor Schumpeter voiced this belief in the following way: [8]

> That rudiment of a pure economic theory of development which is implied in the traditional doctrine of the formation of capital always refers merely to saving and to the investment of the small but yearly increase attributable to it. In this it asserts nothing false, but it entirely overlooks much more essential things. The slow and continuous increase in time of the national supply of productive means and of savings is obviously an important factor in explaining the course of economic development, but it is completely overshadowed by the fact that *development consists primarily in employing existing resources in a different way, in doing new things with them, irrespective of whether these resources increase or not.* In the treatment of shorter epochs, moreover, this is true in a more tangible sense. Different methods of employment, and not saving and increases in the available quantity of labor, have changed the face of the economic world in the last fifty years.

If the focus of economic development is not on capital, then where does it reside? It lies, according to the capitalist ethic, in individual personalities, in perceptiveness and rationalization, and in a certain set of values. The earliest form of this ethic (that I know of) was described in 1904 and 1905 by Max Weber in a work entitled *The Protestant Ethic and the Spirit of Capitalism.*[9] Weber's thesis is that religious dogma, initially

[8] Joseph Schumpeter, *The Theory of Economic Development,* Harvard University Press, Cambridge, Mass., 1934, p. 68. (Italics added.)

[9] Orginially published in German, in the *Archiv für Sozialwissenschaft und Sozialpolitik,* vols. 20 and 21, for 1904–1905. The first English translation was published in England in 1930. The latest and most readily available edition is a translation into English by Talcott Parsons, published by Charles Scribner's Sons, New York, in 1958.

associated with protestantism, compelled its adherents to forgo earthly pleasures in order to accumulate capital and to produce. But capital accumulation was only a part of the total philosophy, which consisted more importantly of a drive for achievement, for the development of business acumen and the rationalization of one's surroundings and one's calculations. Man's duty is to control his environment, to make it serve him better, and in so doing he magnifies the glory of God.

> It is one of the fundamental characteristics of an individualistic capitalistic economy that it is rationalized on the basis of rigorous calculation, directed with foresight and caution toward the economic success which is sought in sharp contrast to the hand-to-mouth existence of the peasant, and to the privileged traditionalism of the guild craftsman and of the adventurer's capitalism, oriented to the exploitation of political opportunities and irrational speculation.[10]

This quotation distinguishes not only between capitalism and precapitalist (peasant or guild) societies, but also between "true" capitalism and that of the adventurer. "True" capitalism is based on production and a sense of responsibility for society. Its basic motivation is to produce a better product for the community, to do so more efficiently through greater rationalization of the means of production, and to sell it for a price that covers cost and a reasonable profit.

At several points Weber sharpens the contrast between "true" capitalism and that of the adventurer. The adventurer desires quick return with little effort; he wants to find gold and silver, to capture and enslave, to achieve power through political position and wealth through bribery or by depleting a national treasury entrusted to him as the people's "representative." He uses his wealth primarily for display, for conspicuous consumption, and to establish prestige. He is to be distinguished from the capitalist driven by religious or other personal motives better to serve his country and his people through more efficient production. "The ideal type of the capitalist entrepreneur," wrote Weber, "as it has been represented even in Germany by occasional outstanding examples, has no relation to such more or less refined climbers. He avoids ostentation and unnecessary expenditure, as well as conscious employment of his power, and is embarrassed by the outward signs of the social recognition which he receives."[11]

I shall now venture that most North Americans who read the preceding paragraph will feel they recognize the "true" capitalist. Many will find among their acquaintances (or among "pillars of the community") in-

[10] Max Weber, *The Protestant Ethic and the Spirit of Capitalism,* translated by Talcott Parsons, Charles Scribner's Sons, New York, 1958, p. 76.

[11] *Ibid.*, p. 71.

dividuals who fit the description, and they will agree that the distinction between him and the adventurer is accurate. I shall venture further that many (not all) Latin American students of economics will find the distinction spurious, will argue that most (if not all) capitalists are of the adventurer type, and will be able to cite specific businessmen (both Latin American and from the United States) who fall in that category.

If I am correct in these guesses, let me hasten to add my opinion that businessmen in the United States are not to be blessed as the epitome of "true" capitalism, productive beyond measure, and serving only the interests of God and mankind. Nor are businessmen in Latin America necessarily restricted to the adventurer type. The description is of extremes, and in practice the same businessman may be to some extent adventurer and to some extent "true" capitalist. If North Americans and Latin American students polarize their opinions, it is because they tend to exaggerate into an extreme what may, however, in fact be the skew pattern for their respective geographic regions.

Weber cites the concern of religious leaders that hard work, ingenuity, and restraint in spending leads naturally to accumulation, which in its turn brings the very temptations of the flesh that the religious man initially spurned. He quotes John Wesley, for example, as follows: [12]

> I fear, wherever riches have increased, the essence of religion has decreased in the same proportion. Therefore I do not see how it is possible, in the nature of things, for any revival of true religion to continue long. For religion must necessarily produce both industry and frugality, and these cannot but produce riches. But as riches increase, so will pride, anger, and love of the world in all its branches. How then is it possible that Methodism, that is, a religion of the heart, though it flourishes now as a green bay tree, should continue in this state? For the Methodists in every place grow diligent and frugal; consequently they increase in goods. Hence they proportionately increase in pride, in anger, in the desire of the flesh, the desire of the eyes, and the pride of life. So, although the form of religion remains, the spirit is swiftly vanishing away. Is there no way to prevent this—this continual decay of pure religion? We ought not to prevent people from being diligent and frugal; *we must exhort all Christians to gain all they can, and to save all they can; that is, in effect, to grow rich.*

Others have declared that the Protestant ethic is not really protestant, that it is found in other religions as well (Hagen cites it as being an ingredient of Catholicism as practiced in certain areas of Colombia),[13] and

[12] *Ibid.*, p. 175. Quoted from Southey, *Life of Wesley*, second American edition, vol. II, chap. 19, p. 308. (Italics are Weber's.)

[13] Everett E. Hagen, *On the Theory of Social Change*, Dorsey Press, Homewood, Ill., 1962, p. 370.

still others have denied that it is, in fact, a religious matter at all. The "work ethic," it is argued, can be found in people with no necessary religious affiliation.

Marx was acquainted with the ethic of frugality. His method of attack was first to ridicule it (without necessarily disproving it) and then to demonstrate that much capital accumulation had occurred through robbery, violence, and other forms of appropriation of the rightful belongings of others.

> This Primitive accumulation plays in Political Economy about the same part as original sin in theology. Adam bit the apple, and thereupon sin fell on the human race. Its origin is supposed to be explained when it is told as an anecdote of the past. In times long gone by there were two sorts of people; one, the diligent, intelligent, and, above all, frugal elite; the other, lazy rascals, spending their substance, and more, in riotous living. Thus it came to pass that the former sort accumulated wealth, and the latter sort had at last nothing to sell except their own skins. And from this original sin dates the poverty of the great majority that, despite all its labour, has up to now nothing to sell but itself, and the wealth of the few that increases constantly although they have long since ceased to work. In actual history it is notorious that conquest, enslavement, robbery, murder, briefly force, play the great part. In the tender annals of Political Economy, the idyllic reigns from time immemorial. Right and "labour" were from all times the sole means of enrichment, the present year of course always excepted. As a matter of fact, the methods of primitive accumulation are anything but idyllic.[14]

The schism between the Marxist and capitalist ethics boils down, finally, to a question of price. At what price does the laborer sell his services to the capitalist, and at what price does the capitalist in turn sell his product back to the laborer, and to others? Ricardo and Marx both argued that the wage of labor was no more than necessary to keep the worker alive and to raise his children until they reached a productive age. The laborer was constantly living on the verge of starvation, and because of his sheer numbers and the competition for scarce jobs, he was apt to remain so for a long time to come.

The Marxist conditions fit many Latin American countries perfectly. There are systems of land tenure in which a worker is deprived of all incentive to increase his output. Economic stringencies, such as debt servitude to his feudal lord, prevent him from moving to other employment. Political pressures or the police may keep him where he is, or sheer ignorance (and illiteracy) prevent him from moving to the city to look for a job. Finally, even if land reform has taken place (as in Bolivia),

[14] Marx, *op. cit.*, vol. II, chap. 26, pp. 784–785.

alternative employment may not be available to the masses of workers, because of a low national level of development.

So the price of labor is the principal bone of contention between Marxists and non-Marxists. The very existence of this issue presupposes a separation between laborer and capitalist. They cannot be the same person, since no one can rationally exploit himself. "The capitalist system," wrote Marx, "presupposes the complete separation of the labourers from all property in the means by which they can realise their labour. As soon as capitalist production is once on its own legs, it not only maintains this separation, but reproduces it on a continually extending scale." [15]

Celso Furtado added his assent to this separation when he wrote that ". . . accumulation begins with slavery; that is, with the total or partial appropriation *by one group* of the surplus production *created by another.*" [16] Indeed, if one has observed Latin American land patterns carefully, and even employment in certain industries, it is most improbable that he could arrive at any other conclusion.

Yet to assume that capital can be accumulated *only* if there is complete separation between the capitalist and the laborer is to deny other empirical observation. Ashton cites numerous entrepreneurs in early England whose capital arose entirely from family labor. He writes about the industrial revolution as follows: [17]

> In the early years of the period many of the industrial units were small family concerns or partnerships of two or three friends. In most industries the fixed capital required was not more than a domestic manufacturer, or even a workman, could supply from his earnings. If a profit were made it was possible to use it to extend the plant: "ploughing back" is not, as some have supposed, a transatlantic discovery of the twentieth century. The early stages of accumulation can be illustrated by quotations from the diary of Samuel Walker of Rotherham:
>
> > 1741. In or about October or November of the same year, Saml. and Aaron Walker built an Air Furnace in the old nailer's smithy, on the backside of Saml. Walker's cottage at Grenoside, making some small additions thereto, and another little hutt or two, slating with sods, etc., with a small Garth walled in: and after rebuilding the chimney or stacks once, and the furnace once or more, began to proceed a little, Saml. Walker teaching the school at Grenoside, and Aaron Walker making nails and mowing and shearing, etc., part of his time.
> >
> > 1743. Aaron Walker now began to be pretty much imploy'd, and had 4 shillings a week to live upon. . . .

[15] *Ibid.*, pp. 785–786.

[16] Furtado, *loc. cit.* (Italics added.)

[17] Thomas S. Ashton, *The Industrial Revolution, 1760–1830,* Oxford University Press, Fair Lawn, N.J., 1948, pp. 95–96.

1745. This year Saml. Walker, finding business increase, was obliged to give up his school, and built himself a house at the end of the old cottage, then thought he was fixed for life; then we allowed ourselves ten shillings a week each for wages and to maintain our families.

At this time the value of the concern was put at £400. But in the following year £100 was added by Jonathan Walker (a brother of Samuel and Aaron), £50 by John Crawshaw (who had previously been employed "as much as we could, at 12 pence per day"), and £50 by Samuel himself. Thus equipped, the partners set up at Masborough first a casting house and then, in 1748, a steel furnace. The story that Samuel Walker rose to fortune by stealing from Huntsman the secret of crucible steel has no foundation: it was not by such methods, but by unremitting labor, thrift and integrity that success was achieved.

The burden of my proposition is that capital can be formed *either* by robbery and appropriation *or* by diligence, ingenuity, and hard labor. In some eras and in some places it has been accumulated more in one way than in another. The Spanish conquistador who expropriated land from the Incas, the Mayas, the Aztecs, and others, did it in a manner more accurately described by Marx's primitive accumulation. So also has capital been stolen in African slave raids, by the colonial practices of some of the most modern and "upright" nations, and in the Southern plantations of my own country.

But not all capital originated in this manner. Marx's cleavage between labor and the ownership of capital is historically false, for there is abundant evidence of the ingenuity and thrift of individual entrepreneurs *who constructed capital equipment with their own hands and who never employed a laborer outside their own family.* That many of these entrepreneurs were motivated by the protestant (or religious) ethic is substantiated by both Ashton and Hagen.

In the seventeenth century the congregation of Puritans gathered about Richard Baxter at Kidderminster included the Foleys, the Crowleys, and the Hanburys, who were to set up great establishments in places as far afield as Staffordshire, Durham, and South Wales. In the following century members of the Society of Friends played a prominent part in the development of corn-milling, brewing, pharmacy, and banking; and the Quaker families of the Darbys, Reynolds, Lloyds, and Huntsmans came to direct the destinies of the iron and steel industries at a period of rapid change. There were Baptists, like Thomas Newcomen, and Presbyterians, like James Watt, in engineering; Independents, like John Roebuck and Joseph Dawson, alongside the Quakers, in iron-smelting; and Unitarians, including the M'Connels and the Gregs, in cotton-spinning.[18]

[18] *Ibid.*, p. 18.

In an exhaustive inquiry into the lives of ninety-two innovators of the seventeenth and eighteenth centuries in Britain, Hagen has concluded that by far the majority had devout religious convictions.[19] His theory, which is well worth reading, is that the most important ingredient of economic development is a certain psychological approach, instilled from earliest childhood, whose characteristics are inquisitiveness, curiosity about one's surroundings, lack of inhibitions against change, and an unrelenting urge to achieve.

Both the time (seventeenth and eighteenth centuries) and place (England) treated by Ashton were also the subject of Marx's theory of primitive accumulation. If it is true that small entrepreneurs were legion, gathering capital and building their enterprises by their own efforts, how could Marx have failed to observe this?

A likely answer is that Marx, living in the nineteenth century, saw the industrial revolution as it had just evolved. There is no denying that injustice occurred. Land enclosures had taken place with little regard for peasant rights that had been established by centuries of tradition but not by legal form. Labor was abundant, wages were low (although city workers earned more than they had earlier on the farms), working conditions atrocious, and people were poor. The cleavage between the rich and the poor was all too distinct, and the rich were becoming richer on the basis of their earnings. What setting could be more appropriate for the theory of capital accumulation through surplus value?

Furthermore, Marx (like so many of us) was an extremist. He would have been more accurate (but perhaps less effective) had he expounded his theory of value as a limiting rather than universal condition. He assumed, for example, that the low wages of the industrial revolution were the minimum necessary to keep a worker alive and replace himself with a son; he also supposed that the large supply of cheap labor came from the workers driven off the land with the enclosure movement.

Less extremist students of the industrial revolution have argued that the labor supply was not suddenly dumped on the market by enclosures, even though these may have contributed to the worker's decision to go to the city. Ashton writes that ". . . there is, indeed, no evidence of any mass exodus from the English countryside to the industrial towns, and it seems likely that the redistribution of labour took place in less abrupt ways."[20] His studies also show that wages in English factories were higher than in the countryside during the early nineteenth century, and that workers were attracted all the way from Ireland. Amid working conditions which by present-day standards were unthinkable, there grew

[19] Hagen, *op. cit.*, pp. 305–308.
[20] Ashton, *op. cit.*, p. 125.

up a sensitive labor market, with new skills and a mobility (from job to job) never before achieved in English history.

> Some agricultural workers, there is no doubt, migrated to nearby towns; but that they were attracted to manufacture, rather than repelled from agriculture, is indicated by the relatively high level of farm wages in the neighbourhood of the industrial centres. The fact that no single county of England registered a decline of population between 1801 and 1851 suggests that there was no widespread depeopling of the countryside at this time.[21]

ATTITUDES TOWARD WEALTH AND POVERTY

Subscribers to the Marxist and capitalist ethics are distinguished most notably in their attitudes toward wealth. In the moral code of each, robbery and other forceful appropriation are disapproved, while ingenuity and hard work are esteemed. To the Marxist, private wealth is immoral because it is the product of theft and slavery. Its expropriation and vesting in the hands of the people (through their government) would be simple justice.

Believers in the capitalistic ethic, however, hold that wealth is (in the main) accumulated through ingenuity and labor, which are virtues. It is therefore to be admired. The millionaire is revered, not because he has a million dollars, but for the contribution he must have made to society to obtain it. Perhaps he (or his ancestors) invented a new productive process, engineered a new railroad construction, made a scientific discovery, or wrote a best-selling novel. North Americans are often accused of crass materialism, of craving wealth for its own sake. Clearly material well-being brings its satisfactions, but much of the so-called materialism is rooted in admiration for the accomplishments of those who have acquired wealth.

I have already contended that in the long continuum between the Marxist and capitalist poles, there is a greater relative concentration of Latin Americans toward the Marxist end while North Americans tend to congregate on the other side. A possible reason might be that wealth in Latin America *has* been gained more by expropriation and slavery, while in the United States it has been more frequently associated with positive qualities. One Latin American student expressed this position in the following words:

> Latin America was not for the Spanish what North America was for the English. Our dark land represented for our conquerors an inexhaustible supply of precious metals to be exploited and exported to the Metropole.

[21] *Ibid.*, p. 61.

> The Spanish soldiery was composed of adventurers who came to seek their fortune and then go away. They did not bring their whole families to colonize the conquered land, and thus they did not leave investments in capital goods in the New World. Furthermore, the monopoly over trade and industry imposed by the Contract House of Seville did not permit the development of industry or of trade relations with any country other than Spain. The exploitation of mines did not leave any real profit in the colonies, either in the colonial period or in the republic. Instead, human capital was pitifully exploited. A fact on which many authors are agreed is that the indigenous population diminished alarmingly during the colonial period.
>
> The wars of independence provided no more than a simple political change without economic repercussions. There were no transformations in agriculture, only an encouragement of concentration of landholding in few hands. Completely forgotten was their true owner, the indigenous population.

No position in which Latin America and the United States are polarized, or associated uniquely with one type of occurrence, is correct. The Latin American student who wrote the above probably was not aware of the struggles by British colonists against the monopolies of the crown, and he failed to mention—what most Latin American Marxists do not easily forget—the epoch of slavery in the United States. He also ignored the growing middle class in many Latin American countries, and the small entrepreneurs who are currently contributing to capital growth in Mexico City, Lima, Buenos Aires, São Paulo, and many other urban centers.

Despite these omissions and qualifications, it can hardly be denied that the attitudes of Latin Americans toward private capitalism, and of North Americans toward socialism, are largely explained by their different experiences. Nineteenth-century capitalism succeeded in making the United States an industrial and high-income country, while it failed miserably to do so in Latin America. Even those who have not fared so well in the United States nevertheless tend to look upon it as the "land of opportunity," an expression whose validity in Latin America is sometimes said to be restricted to opportunists.

The approach to individual (versus collective) responsibility is partly a corollary to this historical division. The Marxist argues that poverty is the result of oppression so strong that, no matter what he does or how hard he tries, the victim is unable to overcome it. The peon on a feudal hacienda or the laborer whose attempts to unionize are quashed by Federal troops are typical Latin American examples. It follows that individual initiative is useless, for ultimate redemption lies only in collective action, and even that will be successful (wrote Marx) only when capitalism has run its course and come afoul of its inevitable historical weaknesses.

But poverty is the fault of the poor, argues the supporter of capitalism.

Every man, no matter where he is or what his station, has innate resources, and poverty is the punishment for not using them properly. Christ's parable of the talents observes that these resources are not divided equally and stresses that the greater wrong lies in not using to full advantage what one has. Thus the responsibility for conquering poverty falls on the individual or—if individuals so prefer—in small-group or community action.

Proponents of capitalism call on their own history to defend their approach. When subjected to religious persecution in Europe, they fled to North America, establishing new communities. This was no mean feat, for both the land and its native populations were hostile. While Marxists would argue that taking land from the Indians was oppressive, the settlers contended—in accordance with their "protestant ethic"—that the land belonged to those who used it most rationally. The Indians were hunters, and the settlers were farmers. If the Indians would only adopt more modern agricultural methods, they would be able to provide amply for themselves. Indeed, in North America there was enough land for everyone.

It is a puzzle to most North Americans that land should be a problem in Latin America, where it is also abundant. As they needed more land, the people of the United States moved to the West, where more land was. Such moves were an individual responsibility,[22] although travelers cooperated in small groups. It is generally believed in Latin America that the terrain made this colonization easy, because there were no jungles, swamps, or malaria (except in the Southern United States). North Americans, however, refer to it as an epic undertaking, in which many died of thirst and hunger or were killed by the Indians. Much of the Western land was desert, mountainous, and little explored. Those who went did not always know what they would encounter, but they went nevertheless. That North Americans now take a romantic pride in the heroic achievement of early settlers is evidenced by the novels, movies, and television programs—known as "westerns"—that emphasize the courage of the people and hardships of the era. What is there about Latin Americans, they argue, that prevents them from doing the same *without the government's having to plan it for them?*

[22] Some may dispute this contention on the ground that the Homestead Act contributed government sponsorship to the settlement of the West. Actually, the Homestead Act came fairly late in North American history (1862) and was largely a political gesture to expand Northern influence in the Civil War. Its only economic contribution was to provide free land which would otherwise have cost from a few cents to a dollar or so per acre. The real cost of settling the West was not the land itself but the blood, sweat, and tears of physical movement, building homes, and planting new crops.

SOCIAL CHANGE IN THE UNITED STATES

When Grau San Martín became President of Cuba in 1933, the U.S. State Department was aghast. Here was a leader who stood for the "rights" of the peasants, permitted workers to seize sugar mills, and was an outspoken proponent of Cuban nationalism. United States Ambassador Sumner Welles dubbed him as "ultraradical," with ideas that were "frankly communistic." [23] The North American response was to refuse recognition and to work consistently toward his overthrow, an achievement realized early in 1934 with the help of a military officer named Batista.

When Fidel Castro became head of the Cuban government in 1959, the United States was equally disturbed. Diplomatic relations were established but then broken. Even before the Russian buildup in Cuba, the government in Washington initiated economic sanctions and aided an invasion by anti-Castro Cuban refugees. To those who remembered the days of Grau, the response to Castro seemed like an old phonograph record.

But there was one emphatic difference: the United States did not counter with an Alliance for Progress in 1933. In those days Washington evinced no official concern for the lot of the peasant, no attempt to "beat the communists at their own game" by promoting an economic revolution. Castro has taken credit for United States aid to Latin America, and rightly so. But an all-too-neglected question is: how had the North American character changed by 1959, to evoke a response that was unheard of in 1933?

For students who believe the shift in United States policy is one of strategy and not fundamental intent, this difference has little meaning. To them, the Alliance for Progress is but a modern phase of dollar diplomacy. Fifty years ago the State Department called on private businesses and banks to lend money to sagging Latin governments. Then as now, one of the conditions was fiscal reform that would balance budgets and enable obligations to be met when due. There was no discrimination between democratic and dictatorial administrations, so long as they would protect United States property, keep out European powers, and quell revolutions.

But the Alliance for Progress is far different from dollar diplomacy. The reforms under the Alliance are more pervasive than simply balancing the budget and keeping law and order. The Social Progress Trust Fund, with hundreds of millions of dollars to spend on low-cost housing, public water, hospitals, sanitation, and schools, is far more than a sop to keep

[23] Robert F. Smith, *The United States and Cuba*, Bookman Associates, New York, 1960, p. 149.

the peasant contented. Has anything happened to awaken the conscience of the North American people toward social injustice?

In 1933, the year Grau came to power in Cuba, the United States was suffering the worst depression it had ever known. Previously all "lapses from full employment" (in Pigou's words) had been corrected in short order; the usual depression lasted only a few months. We believed in Say's law and thought a depression was automatically accompanied by its own redemptive forces. It was like bad weather. Just shrug your shoulders and wait.

Imbued with the capitalist ethic, we had supposed that if a man couldn't find a job, there was something lacking in him. The enterprising could always be successful. The poor deserved charity, but certainly not understanding. Yet in 1930 an amazing thing happened. There was a depression that was not over in 1930. It wasn't over in 1931. Or in 1932 either. Or 1933. Not even in 1934, 1935, or 1936. At its depth in 1933, about one-third of the United States work force was unemployed. It gradually began to dawn on us that a large part of our population was facing poverty that was conclusively and undeniably *not* the fault of the poor.

To those who have lived in Latin America, this revelation may appear commonplace. Yet our historical experience had been one of almost certain success for the provident. Persistence and hard work had always been rewarded, and there was always opportunity for the diligent. Except that in 1933 there wasn't. And this came as a great shock to us.

The Depression shook the capitalist ethic and the sanctity of individualism as they have never been shaken before. It began an unprecedented social revolution that changed the face of the United States economy and made government a far stronger force than it had ever been. Union activity and collective bargaining were strengthened through the Wagner Act. The government supplied low-cost housing, guaranteeing and buying private mortgages. It introduced old-age benefits, government-financed unemployment insurance, and minimum wages for industry in general. It established the Securities and Exchange Commission to suppress stock-market abuses and conducted investigations of monopoly and concentrated industrial power. Large enterprises have been prosecuted and broken up, and their officials imprisoned for abuses of power.

The social revolution also brought government assistance to depressed areas at home. Coal mining has long been suffering under the competition of new fuels, and unemployment in the coal districts is chronically high. Before the Depression the United States government took little note of this, but now there are persistent efforts to retrain miners and move them to more productive occupations. Assistance to farmers and other primary producers has also become an accepted function of government. The

Negro became recognized as a social sector repressed for reasons beyond his fault, and a sweep of legal and executive orders promoted integration in schools, transportation, and restaurants, and equality of political rights and job opportunities. The war for racial equality is not over, but some important battles have been won.

With the Full Employment Law of 1946, Congress officially recognized that everyone has the right to a job. There is no guarantee, but it is accepted that the government bears a responsibility if unemployment is high. New weapons of monetary and fiscal policy were sharpened, and even budgetary deficits became acceptable (within limits) to create funds for employment. All these events were a framework of planning for economic growth.

Social change takes place at home before it finds its mark abroad. By the mid-fifties the United States had not yet adapted its foreign policy to include the trends that had already taken shape in domestic affairs. Yet it was against the backdrop of accomplished change in the United States that Fidel Castro appeared 90 miles south of Florida. The shift in policy toward Latin America was precipitated by Castro, but it was built on a profound domestic revolution.

The new climate at home made it easy for the United States to incorporate planning for economic development in its foreign-assistance program. Low-cost housing, tax reform, promotion of sanitation and water supplies, and construction of health facilities all received fresh impetus, because they had all occurred earlier at home.

The Alliance for Progress is far more than "mere changes in strategy to counter a growing revolution in Latin America." It is distinguished from dollar diplomacy by a pronounced revision in (or departure from?) the capitalist ethic and a greater willingness to assume collective responsibility. Business as an arm of foreign policy has been replaced by government. Fifty years ago the United States relied on J. P. Morgan and the National City Bank to carry out its foreign lending. Now the foreign-aid program is funded by the United States Treasury and the Agency for International Development (Point Four).

Has the capitalist ethic been destroyed, and is individualism dead in the United States? Far from it. Marxists argue that the Great Depression was the beginning of the end for capitalism. But to most North Americans, it was a challenge to promote individualism by collective authority rather than destroy it. The social changes of the New Deal and thereafter were intended to remove obstacles to private initiative rather than to subject it to rigorous control by government.

The distinction is subtle, but vital to an understanding of the way North Americans look upon the Alliance for Progress.

3 Agrarian Reform

La tierra es de todos, como el aire, el agua, la luz, y el calor del sol. (Inscription carved above the entrance to the Secretaría de Educación, Mexico City.)

LAND IS LIKE air, like water, like light, like the heat of the sun. It was bestowed upon mankind by whatever superior being we believe in (if any), and it belongs to everyone. It would be unthinkable for any man to shut off the supply of air or water, so that his fellow beings could not breathe or drink. Likewise it would be inhuman to deprive any man of light or the heat of the sun. So also must man not be alienated from land, or from its products.

These ideas were penned by a Mexican. Another Mexican, as chairman of a conference on agrarian reform in Washington in 1959, observed that the United States showed no active interest in assisting concrete plans proposed by Latin Americans for expropriating lands or financing their redistribution among peasants. Wrote Dr. Mendieta y Nuñez: [1]

> The representative of the United States of North America did not approve one single proposal that might signify the expropriation of land, because he was thinking of the enormous *latifundios* exploited in Latin America by businesses and private persons of his country. Nor did he

[1] Lucio Mendieta y Nuñez, *La reforma agraria de la América Latina en Washington,* Instituto de Investigaciones Sociales de la Universidad Nacional Autónoma de México, Mexico City, 1960, pp. 107–108. Report on a conference held in Washington, D.C., October, 1959.

> approve the creation of an Inter-American Agrarian Bank, because he understood that an institution of this nature would be, as indeed it would, a constant invitation to all the peoples of Latin America to accelerate or undertake their respective agrarian reforms. Such an occurrence would constitute a menace to the territorial interests of North Americans. It would endanger the relations of the Government of the United States with those of various Latin American countries, for it would alarm the agrarian bourgeois of these countries who own the *latifundios* and who either themselves hold power or else influence those that do.

In August, 1961, less than two years after the conference to which Dr. Mendieta referred, representatives of the United States assumed a leading role in encouraging the Latin American republics to sign the Charter of Punta del Este, giving birth to the Alliance for Progress. Title I, Section 6, of this charter lists among the fundamental goals toward which the American republics agreed to work during the succeeding decade:

> To encourage, in accordance with the characteristics of each country, programs of comprehensive agrarian reform leading to the effective transformation, where required, of unjust structures and systems of land tenure and use, with a view to replacing latifundia and dwarf holdings by an equitable system of land tenure so that, with the help of timely and adequate credit, technical assistance and facilities for the marketing and distribution of products, the land will become for the man who works it the basis of his economic stability, the foundation of his increasing welfare, and the guarantee of his freedom and dignity.

Latin Americans have every right to view this high-sounding statement with skepticism. For years the United States has shied away from encouraging agrarian reform, and for years North American nationals have owned large sugar, cattle, and other properties in Latin America. Almost overnight there is a complete turnabout. Is it not—many ask—simply a change in strategy, a move designed to catch the defenses of revolution off their guard? If the "imperialists" discover that agrarian reform is gaining more and more momentum, is not their shrewdest tactic to climb aboard the movement and, once having gained control, to head it off?

On the answer to this question may well hinge the success or failure of the Alliance for Progress. Economic development in Latin America will mean nothing if it leaves the numerically dominant rural populations untouched. Land tenure is the keystone of agriculture, and if the stone itself is rotten, the structure will not stand. It is therefore on this battleground that the serious intentions of the United States, and the heads of Latin American governments, will meet their most critical challenge.

So that the reader will better follow the line ot argument, I shall present my general conclusions in advance. Stemming from the social revolution that has taken place in the United States since the thirties, a gradual awareness of Latin American land problems has dawned upon educated and influential North Americans. Combined with this has been a growing sense of leadership in world affairs, which requires more responsible decisions than those based solely in the interests of one's own nationals. Certain events in recent years—such as the Cuban revolution—have focused the problem more clearly, but focus was possible only because the camera was already aimed. The answer is that there *has* been a genuine change in United States policy on agrarian reform. The change itself has been gradual, but the awareness of it—both by those responsible for it and by those who view it from a distance—has been sudden.

What is meant by the growing sense of leadership? It is no secret that the United States government is concerned over communist activity in Latin America and the possibility that the Soviet Union will come to dominate part of the Western Hemisphere, both economically and politically. It has also become clear that *change is inevitable* in land tenure systems, and there are two general directions in which it can go. One is toward private holdings of more moderate size, avoiding the extremes of *minifundio* and *latifundio,* together with a more equitable distribution of the fruits of labor. The other is toward a conversion of *latifundios* into state-controlled farms modeled after those of the Soviet Union. The government in Washington would like to have some influence over the choice and is aware it will not be listened to if it does no more than cling stubbornly to a crumbling structure whose age was yesterday.

Unfortunately, the very real change in United States thinking toward agrarian reform is not generally understood in Latin America, *either by the Marxists or by the ruling cliques.* Marxists would obviously proclaim that the United States has only changed its colors and not its shape. What is unfortunate is that in several countries those responsible for government also believe this is so. All protestations by Washington to the contrary, they blindly fancy that they *still* have the support of the United States government in anachronistic agrarian structures. Venezuela is perhaps an exception, as are those Alliance members—Bolivia and Mexico—whose reforms were initiated earlier. There are, however, governments that *do* take for granted that espousal of agrarian reform is simply a maneuver to capture the movement and sidetrack it. In this respect they are bound to come into conflict with the aims of the Alliance as understood by the United States.

Before developing this argument, it is essential to discuss land tenure in Latin America and its relationship to economic development.

LATIFUNDIOS [2]

Economic development can be aggressively promoted, or seriously retarded, by the astute choice of agrarian systems. Particularly is this so in Latin America, where the agricultural sector is predominant. Here extremes are the norm. Few are the family-size farms both large enough to support the family living on them and not so large as to entail unwieldy management problems. While agricultural statistics are notoriously deficient, nevertheless the accompanying table gives some indication of the vast estates (*latifundios*) side by side with tiny plots (*minifundios*).

The origin of *latifundios* lies principally in grants by the kings of Spain and Portugal (or their representatives) to conquistadors or other royal favorites. In Indian-populated territories, these were principally in the form of encomiendas, which carried rights of taxation and paternalistic supervision over large territories and the Indians living upon them. Gradually the encomiendas became what they were not intended to be from the start, the personal property of descendants of the original encomenderos, and the Indians upon them became "economic," if not legal, slaves.

Other forms of land grants occurred as well. There is also evidence that the kings of Spain from time to time had real concern over the welfare of the Indians and attempted to establish legal equality between Indian and creole, with moderate-sized agricultural units. But law and reality

TABLE OF LANDHOLDINGS IN LATIN AMERICA

Country	*Latifundio*	*Minifundio*
Argentina (1950)	2% of farms on 60% of land	42% of farms on 1% of land.
Bolivia (1950)		75% of rural population with no rights to land.
Brazil (1950)	1.6% of farms on over 50% of land	22% of farms on 0.5% of land.
Chile (1955)	3,250 farms over 1,000 hectares each, on 75% of land	37% of farms on 0.3% of land.
Colombia (latifundio 1958, minifundio 1955)	0.9% of farms on 40% of land	70% of farms on less than 7% of land.
Costa Rica (1955)	1.3% of farms on 42.5% of land	38% of farms on 2.1% of land.
Cuba (1946)	1.5% of farms on 46% of land	70% of farms on 12% of land.
Dominican Republic (1960)	221 farms of more than 500 hectares	388,583 farms of less than 5 hectares.

[2] Landholding of a large size. The singular is *latifundio* and the plural properly *latifundia*, although *latifundios* is also common in Latin America.

TABLE OF LANDHOLDINGS IN LATIN AMERICA *(Continued)*

Country	*Latifundio*	*Minifundio*
Ecuador	Statistics inadequate; hacienda system predominates	
El Salvador (1950)	1% of farms on 50% of land	80% of farms have less than 5 hectares.
Guatemala (1958)	Less than 1% of farms on more than 40% of land	76% of farms on 9% of land.
Haiti (1950)	Only a few large properties, mostly sugar cane and sisal	93% of farms less than 1 *carreau* (1.23 hectares); only 3.6% have more than 20 *carreaux.*
Honduras (1952)	1.8% of farms on 46% of land	65% of farms have 1–9 hectares.
Mexico, *ejidos* (1961)		Average plot 3.9 hectares.
Mexico, private lands (1950)	Less than 1% of farms on almost 50% of land	82.5% of farms less than 5 hectares.
Nicaragua (1952)	5% of farms on 57% of land	35% of farms have less than 20 hectares.
Panama (1950)	Few large estates	52% of farms are 1–5 hectares.
Paraguay (1946)	11 farms on 35% of land	44% of farms have less than 5 hectares (1956).
Peru, coastal areas (1961)	2% of farms on 75% of land	
Peru, jungle (1961)	2% of farms have 92% of land	61% of farms are dwarf holdings, many without title.
Peru, mountains (1961)	1.26% of farms on over 50% of land	82.4% of farms have less than 10 hectares.
Uruguay (1951)	4.2% of farms on 56.5% of land	13% of land covered by farms of 1–5 hectares.
Venezuela (1956)	2.5% of farms on 82% of land	

SOURCE: Data on all countries except the Dominican Republic and Cuba are from Inter-American Development Bank, Social Progress Trust Fund, First Annual Report, 1961. Dominican Republic data from the Dominican census, and Cuba data from Lucio Mendieta y Nuñez, *La reforma agraria de la América Latina en Washington,* Instituto de Investigaciones Sociales de la Universidad Nacional Autónoma de México, Mexico City, 1960.

NOTE: The word "land" in every case refers to land in production.

were far apart, just as Madrid was a long way from Mexico City and Lima. Three factors militated against the growth of family farming. One was the feudal structure in Spain and Portugal, to which the conquerors of the new world were already accustomed. A second was the nature of the conquistador. He had come to Latin America to gain wealth, and only secondarily to settle. There was a dichotomy in his mind between obedience and loyalty (*obedezco pero no cumplo*), and laws made from across the Atlantic withered before his avarice and were melted by his opportunities. Finally, there was the nature of the Indian himself. The Incas, who dominated Western South America, had established communal land tenure and were unacquainted with the freeholding system of the Spanish. Weak and ignorant, they were easy prey to speculative landgrabbers whose cleverness in twisting the law was rivaled only by their ability to change it ex post facto.

Latifundios vary in size, character, and relative importance in different Latin American countries. No one has defined their minimum dimensions, but they range roughly from 500 up to 100,000 hectares or more.[3] In a few countries, such as Haiti and the Dominican Republic, *latifundios* are few in relation to total land area, while in others, such as Peru and Chile, they dominate the rural economy, politics, and social organization.

The character of a *latifundio* depends on where it is and whether the country has a large Indian population. In Uruguay and Argentina (except in the North), where the white man found few Indians but favorable soil and climate, *latifundios* have developed into large cattle ranches, some of them operating efficiently and contributing significantly to the nation's output and income. In the Caribbean islands, where the Indian population was wiped out by the conquerors, *latifundios* were resolved into sugar plantations and cattle ranches. Where sugar and tobacco land was plentiful, as in Cuba, the system remained until upset by revolution. But in the Dominican Republic the country is mountainous, and sugar is confined largely to a few highly productive coastal areas. Except for sugar and some cattle, the *latifundios* have been gradually divided (by inheritance) into small farms of subfamily size. In three countries—Mexico, Bolivia, and Cuba—twentieth-century agrarian reforms have either abolished or seriously shaken the *latifundio* structure.

THE HACIENDA SYSTEM

In countries where the Indian predominates, *latifundios* have been associated with a feudal form of agriculture known as the "hacienda[4] system." Indians initially subject to encomiendas gradually became servants (peons) of the master who owned their lands and met their obligations to him through labor and sharecropping. The importation of Negro slaves made the hacienda possible in some Indian-scarce areas, such as Northeastern Brazil. In Chile, where the Araucanians were never fully defeated by the white man, the system exists, but master and peon are not separated by racial lines.

[3] A hectare is roughly 2.4 acres.
[4] In Portuguese the word is *fazenda.*

The hacienda system has been described in much literature in both the United States and Latin America. Here it will suffice, therefore, to outline it only briefly. Although haciendas differ according to time and place, their framework is essentially the same. They dominated rural society and urban politics in prerevolutionary Mexico and Bolivia, and still preponderate in Ecuador, Peru, Chile, and certain sections of Brazil. They are also to be contended with in Central America and in Panama, Colombia, and Venezuela, although their relative poltical power varies from country to country.

Life on the hacienda revolves around the person known as the *hacendado* (in his capacity as controller of the economy) or *latifundista* (in his capacity as large landowner). Since not all *latifundistas* are *hacendados,* I shall confine myself to the latter term in order to be explicit. Typically, the *hacendado* does not live on his estate. His home is in Lima, Santiago, Bogotá, Recife, or one of the other large cities of his country. He entrusts the operation of the hacienda to a major-domo, or resident manager.

The richest lands of each *latifundio* are usually assigned to the hacienda itself; that is, their product belongs 100 per cent to the *hacendado.* In Andean countries, where the *latifundio* covers mountains and valleys alike, the bottom lands are typically cultivated for the *hacendado,* since they are more easily irrigated or contain fertile soil eroded from above. The peon will be assigned other lands, usually up on the slope where cultivation is more difficult, land less fertile, and water scarcer. Often there are gradations of peons, as in a caste system, those with more land carrying greater prestige.

The peon and his family are required to perform certain obligations to the *hacendado.* The women will be servants in the manor house for so many days a week. Once a week (or at other intervals) the peons will be called in general assembly, where the major-domo assigns them their tasks. A frequent pattern is for the peon to work three days on hacienda lands and three days on his own. There may be a small cash wage in connection with some of or all this work, and sometimes payments are made in food or drink.

Many haciendas are economies unto themselves, with their own currencies. Transactions with outsiders are confined to the sale of the product of hacienda land, from which the *hacendado* gains his income, and to the purchase of manufactured goods for consumption by the *hacendado* and his major-domo. Often the peons are unaware of any other nationality than that of the hacienda. When agrarian reform occurred in Bolivia in 1953, peasants from as far away as Cuzco went to La Paz to apply for land, unaware that they were Peruvians, and that Bolivia was another country.

The closed nature of the hacienda has given rise to debt servitude. Typically, the *hacendado* will operate a store where products of the community are exchanged, and occasionally some goods from the outside. The peon has the right to buy at the store, and often will be granted credit. Since the major-domo keeps the accounts and the peon is illiterate, there is no way of knowing whether the debts are accurately recorded or not. In some countries, debts of the father have been inherited by the son, and no peon was allowed to leave the hacienda for other employment until his debts were paid.

Hereditary debt servitude, which was important to Mexican history, has been legally abolished in many countries. Nevertheless, the ability of the peon to leave the hacienda for better economic opportunities has been circumscribed in various ways. Most importantly, he is ignorant. One can slash sugar with a machete or dig potatoes without being literate, and the hacienda is therefore not noted for excellence in primary education. We who can read are frequently oblivious of the limitations imposed on others by their illiteracy. The peon often cannot leave the hacienda simply because he knows of nothing else.

But it does not "just happen" that the peon is ignorant. It is to the interest of the *hacendado* to keep him so, to forbid him to travel far from the hacienda, and above all not to allow him to drive the truck that takes the crop to the city for sale. More than anything else, the hacienda system depends for its survival on the immobility of labor and denial of alternative opportunities.

This dependence comes from the fact that the hacienda is an inefficient, anachronistic agricultural system. Its principal factor of production is the peon, yet the peon has no incentive to improve his output. Theoretically, he might employ more modern techniques on the land assigned to him (if he knew what they were) and retain a greater crop. His experience, however, has been that any intensification of effort leads only to a greater share for the *hacendado.* So long as the peon's income does not depend on his production, he takes no interest in efficient or more productive farming.

This observation was underlined by a team of social scientists from Cornell University who conducted an experiment in agrarian reform on an hacienda called Vicos, in Central Peru during the 1950s. The provision of technical advice was not at first found a sufficient factor, in and of itself, to persuade the Indians to adopt new methods of cultivation. Only when they were permitted to make decisions in local government and share in the proceeds of increased production were they willing to undertake new methods. And then their potato yields increased up to 400 per cent, so much so that one of the professors wrote that ". . . the *sierra* of Peru no longer stands out as the area of poor resources that it has always been considered."[5]

THE DECLINE AND FALL OF THE HACIENDA

The hacienda is not just an economic system; it is steeped in history, culture, and politics. But economics is not separate from the other social sciences anyway. The day of the hacienda is in twilight, and the reasons lie in all branches: economic, social, and political.

The chief economic reason is its inefficiency. Given the same factors of production (land, labor, and capital) and probably even with little or no change in technology, other agrarian systems are capable of producing a higher output than the hacienda. Here it is that economics blends with the cultural. The objective of the *hacendado* is more the prestige of landowning than the economy of his venture. He does not concern himself with the latest technology; indeed, he does not consider himself a farmer at all.

The major-domo, whose responsibility it is to operate the farm, is often not acquainted with the latest techniques, nor is he given incentive to learn them. Like the peon, he is underpaid, and any improvement in output would not redound to his benefit. Nor does the peon share in the proceeds of increased output. So long as these conditions exist, the hacienda system will act as a drag on the nation's economic development. Food supplies will not keep pace with higher demand emanating from urban growth.

In progressive urban centers (such as Lima, Medellín, and São Paulo) there is growing recognition that the hacienda system conflicts with the interests of a rising middle class. Higher food costs lead to higher costs of production, and money wages are increased without a corresponding rise in the real share (and hence the satisfaction) of the worker. Furthermore, the more astute industrialist realizes that his welfare lies in expanding markets in rural areas, which are severely restricted by low living standards on the haciendas.

Shifting politics stemming from these considerations made possible the São Paulo agrarian-revision law of 1961, providing for both subdivision and resettlement of underproductive lands, as well as graduated taxes intended to encourage more rational use. Unfortunately the politics of the rest of Brazil were not so advanced as those of São Paulo, and the attempt fell beneath the crushing weight of Federal authority.

[5] Allan R. Holmberg, "Changing Community Attitudes and Values in Peru," in Council on Foreign Relations, *Social Change in Latin America Today*, Harper & Row Publishers, Incorporated, New York, 1960.

The economic decline of the hacienda lies not only in the political opposition of growing middle classes but in the alternative opportunities that urban development provides for rural labor. We have already observed that the *hacendado* does his best to keep his labor immobile, ignorant of the outside world. There is good reason, for the system hinges on "slave" labor. Once this labor is attracted away by something better in the city—a phenomenon that can be seen virtually everywhere in Latin America—the system begins to crumble.

Thus the hacienda died in Mexico. For years (1876–1910) Porfirio Diaz, the tyrant of Mexico, had consolidated his power by bringing large landowners into his camp. He paid for political patronage in land and money. The land he grabbed from the Indians, or from *caudillos* too weak to withstand him. (They were despatched with a shot in the head and heard from no more.) The money came from foreigners (in Europe and the United States) who invested principally in mining and railroads. As was typical of foreign investment in that era, the investor received magnificent concessions and the ruler a handsome "tax." The power of the Presidency lay in foreign investors and in landowners not strong enough to challenge Diaz, but with enough strength so that he had to buy their support.

But the very practices that built Diaz also brought his downfall. Foreign investment, no matter how extractive and how export-oriented, *does* contribute, over the long run, to a nation's economic growth. When Diaz became President, the only railroad ran from Mexico City to Tampico. By the time he resigned, Mexico was crisscrossed by almost 15,000 miles of rails. Mining and transportation had led to a steel industry in Monterrey (in 1903), which along with Mexico City was a growing industrial center. Workers on the hacienda found they could hop a freight train, melt into the security of the city or darkness of the mines, and no one (from the hacienda) would ever hear of them again.

By the time the revolution began in 1910, the haciendas were bankrupt. Agricultural output had been languishing for years, and many properties were mortgaged to the hilt. More immediate economic and natural forces helped fix the timing. A financial panic in 1907, emanating from New York, squeezed the balance sheets of the *hacendados,* along with a freeze in 1909 that destroyed their harvests. When Francisco Madero, motivated by the political consideration that a President should not succeed himself, assumed the reins of the revolution, Diaz's structural support was already so eaten away that there was nothing for the tyrant to do but pack his bags and leave.

Some argue that the peon has long chafed under the dominance of his master and for centuries has been anxious to overthrow his oppressive burden. If this were so, it is hard to believe that he would not have done it before now. Most Indians, and particularly the Incas, were living in paternalistic, communal societies before the white man arrived. The *hacendado* and major-domo simply supplanted the Inca or other rulers. They were not entirely objects of hatred, for they provided comfort in time of illness and death, food when there was hunger, and spiritual guidance when it was needed. Only the peon can say whether his lot has been bearable, but I suspect it was at least that.

The *hacendado,* of course, acquired inordinate political power. The Iberian tradition (in sharp contrast to the United States) has always accorded prestige to landowning, and the landed of Latin America have been the principal focus of power. The scale has been turned against them only with the aid of economic events strong enough to transcend a cultural heritage, or at least transform it into some sort of accommodation with the irresistible. The tragedy is that so many of them refuse to recognize the irresistible.

But this is not the only tragedy. Another lies in the revolutionaries themselves. Equally oblivious to these economic forces, they too suppose the landlords are powerful enough to stem the relentless march of history. Their own role is thus to implement it by bloodshed. Quite the contrary! The greatest challenge to today's revolutionary—which is far harder than sniping at a president or blowing up an oil line—is that of guiding the process of change into those forms and with those instruments that will most contribute to orderly economic and political growth.

LANDOWNING IN THE UNITED STATES

The Latin American wanting to comprehend the attitude of the United States toward agrarian reform and struggling to distinguish between Yankee intervention, on the one hand, and material aid and comfort, on the other, ought to know something of the landholding pattern in the United States. Four important facts must be understood. The first is that the United States is primarily not an agrarian economy. Only 36 per cent of the population (less than in any Latin American country) is rural, and even most of these are engaged in occupations other than farming. In fact, in 1960 only 8.7 per cent of the total population in the United States lived on farms. The rest of the rural inhabitants are employed in such pursuits as small-scale manufacturing, services, and retailing.

Contrast this with Latin America. In only four countries (Argentina, Chile, Colombia, and Venezuela) is the rural population less than half the total. The percentage is lowest in Argentina (37.5 per cent), which exceeds only slightly that of the United States. In Haiti it is highest, at 87.8 per cent, and in three countries (Ecuador, Guatemala, and the Dominican Republic) it is between 70 and 80 per cent. In all other Latin American countries, the rural population is between 60 and 70 per cent of the total.[6] Furthermore, in contrast to the United States, most rural people are engaged in agriculture.

A second important fact is that the size of holdings in the United States is more moderate than in Latin America. In 1959 only 6.5 per cent of total farms were under 10 acres (roughly 4 hectares), and only 9.1 per cent were over 500 acres (roughly 210 hectares). The remainder, or 84.4 per cent, consisted of farms between 10 and 500 acres (or between 4 and 210 hectares). In this middle group, 39.7 per cent of all farms were from 10 to 99 acres, 20.9 per cent from 100 to 179 acres, and 23.8 per cent from 180 to 499 acres.[7] The extremes of *latifundio* and *minifundio* are simply absent in the United States.

A third important fact is that—contrary to the belief of many of my Latin American friends—land in the United States was *not* stolen from sedentary, agricultural Indians. In the first place, when English and French settlers landed in North America, the number of Indians in what is now the United States was far smaller than in Latin America (only 846,000 as compared to 19 million).[8] In the second place, the Indians of North America were primarily nomadic, in contrast to the Incas, Mayas, and Aztecs, who had settled cultures. In both Mexico and Peru, the Indian cultures were based on the need to organize irrigation systems around which sedentary agriculture developed. But in North America the Indians were hunters and fishers, and did not depend on crops. The white man *did* invade their hunting grounds and *did* convert them into farms. There were harsh wars and a history of broken agreements of which we in the United States cannot now be proud. But the white man taking the land used it more productively than the Indians, and *to him* this was justification. The same was not true of the *latifundios* in Latin America.

The fourth point is a corollary of the third. Since there were no Indian laborers, the hacienda system never developed. An important exception is the plantation system of the South, based on Negro slavery. I shall not dodge this issue but shall freely admit my country's shame where it is

[6] All data in this and the preceding paragraph are from *América en Cifras, 1960*, published jointly by the Pan American Union and the Inter-American Institute of Statistics, vol. 1, pp. 11–13, except the percentage of United States population living on farms, which is from the *Statistical Abstract of the United States*, U.S. Department of Commerce, 1961, p. 613.

[7] *Statistical Abstract of the United States*, U.S. Department of Commerce, 1961, p. 619.

[8] Obviously no one counted the Indians in the fifteenth century. These educated guesses by authorities do, however, provide a rough approximation of relative numbers. The United States figure is from J. B. Mooney, "Population," *Handbook of American Indians North of Mexico*, Bureau of American Ethnology, Bulletin 30, vol. 2, Washington, D.C., 1901. The Latin American figure was estimated by Angel Rosenblat in *Indigenous Peoples*, International Labor Office, Studies and Reports, New Series, no. 35, pp. 30–31, Geneva, 1953.

deserved. I shall postpone discussing it until Chapter 5, however, where it is more appropriately related to the problem of primary products (i.e., cotton). At the moment I am talking about farming as it is today and as it developed in the nonslave, Western states.

This farming is virtually all of a family nature. In 1959 there were 5,223,000 persons engaged in agriculture in the United States, of whom 2,097,000 were employees and the rest owners.[9] The total number of individual farms was 3,710,503.[10] The "typical" farm is thus one of moderate size, owned and operated by the farmer who lives on it, and averaging less than one employee. Many farms are family enterprises entirely: a man and his wife, plus a son or two, with no hired help.

North Americans are proud of their agricultural system. It is the most efficient in the world, combining capital and modern science to produce a high output at the lowest ratio of man to land anywhere. Furthermore, productivity is rapidly increasing. In 1960 one man, on a given amount of land, could produce 3½ times as much cotton as he could in 1930, 5½ times as much grain, and 1½ times as many fruits, vegetables, and nuts.

In sharp contrast to the hacienda system of Latin America, there has been no Marxist exploitation of labor on Western United States farms. The people who moved to the plains were not the same ones who had held slaves in the South. They went in covered wagons, with no other capital than a horse to pull them and their personal possessions. They staked out lands that were not previously cultivated, although they had to ward off attacks by Indians who resented intrusion in their hunting grounds. They also fought among themselves, and efforts by a few to monopolize the land were put down by the guns of the many. Is it any wonder that Marxism has not gained a foothold in the North American agricultural community?

Quite the contrary, North Americans are convinced that family farming is by far the most satisfactory system of land tenure. It is politically stable. Each family is content with the *status quo* and in fact has a stake in its perpetuation. The few farm workers who are landless are generally agreed that wages are satisfactory. There is no need for revolution fanned by discontentment, for of that there is a minimum. The system is sociologically satisfactory. Land prices are not exorbitant, and those who work hard (in accordance with the capitalist ethic) are successful; landless become landowners. Prestige is not related to land; hired hands and farm owners are social equals. Income is related to ability and effort, a condition not present in the hacienda system. Finally, family farming in the United States is economically sound, as measured by its performance. The government played a strong role in experimentation and provision of

[9] *Survey of Current Business,* U.S. Department of Commerce, July, 1962, p. 29.
[10] *1959 Census of Agriculture,* U.S. Bureau of the Census, vol. 2, chap. 1.

new techniques, but these would not have been applied had not the agricultural community been receptive to them.

Many Latin Americans of my acquaintance have misread the political structure of the United States by assuming that farmland owners have the same dominating voice that they have in Latin America. One of my students expressed this by writing: "The government of the United States has been directed, and continues to be directed, by men who possess colossal fortunes, *who are owners of large, landed properties,* and stockholders in the large corporations." [11] In the next chapter I shall show that he is wrong about the stockholders in large corporations; I trust I have shown in the present one that the "owners of large, landed properties" do not exist.

We are now prepared to make some generalizations on North American attitudes toward agrarian reform. The first is that most North Americans do not liken land to air, water, light, and the heat of the sun, as the *sine qua non* of existence. To them it is more like a machine, an instrument of production. They have discovered that it is quite possible to live well (in the United States) without owning farmland, for the bulk of the population does it every day. Conditions are vastly different in Latin America, but most North Americans do not know that.

In the second place, *most* North Americans are not acquainted with the manner in which *some* North Americans obtained land and concessions in Latin America. Cubans, for example, have objected to the consolidation of sugar lands under North American banking hegemony in the administrations of Zayas and Machado. Concessions and land rights granted to foreigners by Diaz of Mexico, Leguía of Peru, Gómez of Venezuela, and others of equal infamy are not widely publicized in the United States. Rather, North Americans tend to think that land is *always* acquired and used as *they* have acquired and used it. If this is so, they consider expropriation unjust.

Fifty years ago United States foreign policy assiduously protected North American investments abroad, not because (as many Latin Americans believe) these investors were a strong political force, but because they had no domestic opposition. However large or small they were, foreign investors were voters in the United States, and there was no constituency to vote against them (since Latin Americans do not participate in United States elections). Hence the politician had all to gain and nothing to lose by supporting them.

But times are changing, and reasons for the change are complex. Surely they relate to the social revolution that the United States has experienced since the Great Depression (as mentioned in Chapter 2). But there is also a growing awareness in the government of the United States that *the time for change has come in Latin America* and that if it does not take one

[11] Italics added.

form, it will take another. The hacienda system is doomed, and two choices (or a combination of them) lie ahead. One is toward moderate-sized family farms, and the other toward state control and collectivization.

It is obvious that the United States feels it has a stake in the answer and that this stake far outweighs the interests of United States private investors in Latin American land. It is equally clear that many Latin Americans feel the choice is no business of the United States but should be made by them and them alone. Before taking up the question of intervention, however, let us consider the relative merits of family farming versus collective farming.

FAMILY VERSUS COLLECTIVE FARMS

Out of many gradations of difference in land tenure systems, two stand out as principal contenders in the race to supplant the *latifundio* and *minifundio* of Latin America. These are private family farms, the model for which lies in the United States, and collective farms, the model for which is found in the Soviet Union. Latin America does not need to follow either model implicitly, and modern revolutions have demonstrated a praiseworthy effort to find a new combination that is peculiarly Latin American. Mexico has instituted a combination of both *ejido* and private farm, and even in Castro's Cuba the agrarian reform left well over half the cultivated surface in private hands, while simultaneously establishing cooperatives and state farms (although the former were eventually converted into the latter). Even so, we would be deceiving ourselves to suppose that the choice of system has not become an issue of the cold war.

Being author of this book poses a dilemma. As an economist who has some acquaintance with Latin America, I believe the family-farm system will contribute far more to that continent's development than collective farming, both because it is economically sounder and because it will provide a more satisfactory sociological experience. I shall outline my reasons below. On the other hand, I regret that this has become an issue of the cold war, which I do not want to fight in these pages. The countries of Latin America should select their land tenure systems themselves, without interference by either the Soviet Union or the United States. My dilemma will be solved only if I can convince my Latin American friends that I speak as an independent university professor, and not as spokesman for my government.

The Soviet Union

Agriculture is the admitted Achilles' heel of Communist economies. In 1953, shortly after the death of Stalin, Nikita Khrushchev reported to the Central Committee of the Communist Party that agricultural output was inadequate in the Soviet Union, and he attributed the shortcoming to lack of incentives.[12] The similarity of collective farming to the hacienda system is striking. So long as the peasant is not a decision-making unit, sharing in the benefits of his wise choices and suffering from his mistakes, he will not fully exert himself.

A principal problem of collective farming has been not only lack of incentives but also that of persuading the peasant to trade his product in the city for manufactured goods. The distribution of real income between urban and rural groups is a matter for central decision, implemented mainly through the prices of agricultural output. Historically, Communist countries have emphasized manufacturing and heavy industry, and have resisted the transfer of resources to the country as incentive to produce more and sell more.

Some capitalist ideologists argue that the problem is inherent in collective farming, and hence incapable of ultimate solution short of abandoning the system. That this *may* not be so is evidenced by the relative success of measures taken by Khrushchev since 1953. Prices of Soviet agricultural goods have been increased. Furthermore, a sort of "private farming" has been encouraged within the collective framework. Agricultural quotas that collective farms must pay to the State have been reduced, thus allowing farmers to sell a larger part of their output at free-market prices. The traditional exodus from country to city has thus been reversed, and more urban workers are being attracted to the farms.

Nevertheless, farm productivity in the Soviet Union is far behind that of the United States. Based on a study made in 1938 (but written in 1945), Naum Jasny concluded that ". . . the productivity per person of farm population in USA was more than four times that in USSR; the difference was still substantially greater in the productivity per person engaged in farm work." Specifically, he found that in 1937 ". . . more than six times more labor was used per 100 pounds of milk in USSR than USA. The figures on pork production are even more striking . . . perhaps 7 days per 100 pounds of hogs (live weight) as against 3.2 hours, the average for American farms." [13] Jasny concluded that the principal reason for low productivity in the Soviet Union was the low pay scale.

In the summer of 1957, Professor Gardner Clark of Cornell University visited several collective farms in the Soviet Union to determine whether Jasny's conclusions of 1938 were still applicable. During this visit Clark

[12] N. S. Khrushchev, *Measures for the Further Development of Agriculture in the U.S.S.R.*, Foreign Languages Publishing House, Moscow, 1954, p. 9.

[13] N. Jasny, "Labor Productivity in Agriculture in USSR and USA," *Journal of Farm Economics,* May, 1945, pp. 420, 430, 431. Quoted by M. Gardner Clark in "Productivity and Incomes on a Soviet Dairy Farm," *ILR Research,* New York State School of Industrial and Labor Relations, Cornell University, Fall, 1958, p. 9.

selected two dairy farms, one in the Soviet Union and one in the United States, that were as similar as possible in size and type of operation, climate, and soil fertility. Each had roughly the same amount of cattle and the same mechanization. The Soviet farm produced and sold more milk than the North American farm, but the latter had higher output in meat and wool. Although the farms were not identical, Clark felt that the advantages of one probably offset those of the other (the Soviet farm had a few more tractors, trucks, and horses, and the United States farm enjoyed slightly better soil conditions). The outstanding difference, however, was that the Soviet farm used 211 workers (51 men and 160 women) compared to 7 (all men) on the North American farm. The North American farm thus produced twenty times as much milk per worker as its Soviet counterpart. Based on his visits to other collective farms, Clark felt that his model was typical and that even though the worker's standard of living has been improving on Soviet farms, still the output per farm worker is "incredibly low." [14]

Cuba

Similar problems of material incentive have been encountered in the Cuban revolution. The initial direction of agrarian reform was toward a combination of private, cooperative, and collective farming, and early indications are that the reform was successful in increasing certain agricultural output in 1959 and 1960. Beginning in 1961, however, the system began to be strained, and it was clear that farm deliveries to the city were lagging. The revolutionary government at first attributed this condition to higher incomes in the country and the desire of the peasants to consume the fruits of their increased productivity themselves. Later on, however, it was disclosed that farm output itself was diminishing.

Land tenure was one of the principal sources of dissatisfaction before the Cuban revolution. Cuba's comparative advantage in sugar was so high that (except for some tobacco and rice) it became virtually a one-crop economy. Within the sugar belt, which covers most of the Eastern half of the country, almost any land could be more productive in sugar than in anything else. Furthermore, world demand for sugar has been rising, and the companies controlling the land have been looking forward to increased sales.[15]

The prospects of increased markets led to land monopolization. Sugar producers were accustomed to keep idle land in cattle ranches, partly to serve as additional sources when the market grew and partly for rotation.

[14] *Ibid.*, pp. 6–9.

[15] In this there may be disappointment. While world demand is rising, so also is world supply, with some countries becoming self-sufficient. As world consumption has increased, therefore, international trade in sugar has been declining.

Juan Noyola, a Mexican whose sympathies for the Cuban revolution were not concealed, charged that the prerevolutionary landowners followed a system of extensive ranching, in which cattle fend for themselves and eat whatever is available. Considering the rich, agricultural lands of Cuba, it would be far more economic to engage in intensive ranching, where pasture lands would be planted and more cattle produced per hectare.

But, complained Noyola, the principal purpose of the ranching was not cattle per se but to hold the land as excess capacity in case of future need. "In excellent tropical lands," he wrote, "in pasture lands as good as, or better than, our own in Tabasco or southern Veracruz, the average density is one head of cattle for each four or five hectares. In other words, these lands were not being used." [16] The existence of unused land side by side with hungry people was an anomaly that the Cuban revolutionaries found impossible to accept.

One of the earliest objectives of the agrarian reform was to cut down the size of large private holdings, and especially the cattle ranches. All holdings above 402.6 hectares were confiscated. Sugar-producing lands were converted into cooperatives, and the remainder were either parceled into private ownership or organized in cooperatives or state farms (*granjas del pueblo*). By 1961, 59 per cent of agricultural land was in private ownership, 28 per cent in 300 state farms, and 13 per cent in 630 cooperatives.[17]

AGRICULTURAL OUTPUT IN CUBA, 1958–1962
(*Thousands of metric tons*)

Commodity	1958	1959	1960	1961	1962
Sugar	5,781	5,965	5,865	6,870	4,800
Tobacco	26.0	26.4	26.3	22.0	
Rice	170	140	162	150	
Corn	170	147	195	190	
Beans	23	35	34	28	
Meat (beef, veal, pork, lamb, mutton, goat)	221	240	207	161	

SOURCE: John D. Powell, *The State of the Cuban Economy in 1962*, Library of Congress Legislative Reference Service, 1962. Similar data are reported by Jacques Chonchol, "Análisis crítico de la reforma agraria cubana," *El Trimestre Económico*, January–March, 1963, p. 137.

[16] Juan F. Noyola, "La Revolución Cubana y sus efectos en el desarrollo económico," *El Trimestre Económico*, July–September, 1961, p. 409. Noyola was killed in an air crash near Lima, Peru, in 1962.

[17] Data released by the Cuban National Agrarian Reform Institute and cited in John D. Powell, *The State of the Cuban Economy in 1962*, Library of Congress Legislative Reference Service, 1962.

Indications are that output of several agricultural products increased in the early years of the revolution (1959–1960). Tobacco, rice, corn, and beans all improved. The most important single reason appears to be the conversion of cattle land into crops for domestic consumption. Sugar production increased phenomenally from 1958 to 1961. Thereafter, however, output across the board declined. Sugar production fell disastrously from 6,870,000 tons in 1961 to 4,800,000 in 1962, with indications that the 1963 crop will be similar. Meat output began to fall as early as 1960, and it is reported that many reproducing cattle (such as prize stud bulls) have been sacrificed to the growing consumer demand.

The Cuban regime has not hesitated to criticize the operation of cooperatives and state farms, and to blame the food shortage largely on their inadequacies. In February, 1962, the Havana radio broadcast that ". . . many farm administrators, many persons in charge of cultivation and livestock have acted in accordance with the patterns of the past. They proceeded a little at random and promised to achieve targets for which they did not prepare themselves, nor did they properly prepare the necessary objective conditions. The unfavorable results of this are evident to all of us." [18]

The worker on Cuban cooperatives and state farms has been paid a flat wage per hour, regardless of his output, and hence has had little incentive to work harder. Castro has justified this procedure on grounds of equity ("equal pay for equal work") and perhaps on the (Marxist) theory that the value of any product is determined by the socially necessary labor that it embodies. Specifically, Castro has pointed out that workers in some cooperatives or state farms that have poorer soil or lower water tables will have an inferior yield to those on better soil and with better irrigation. Why, he argues, should some receive less than others because of the accident of their geography? [19] His concept of equity is to be admired, but unfortunately a system of equal pay regardless of output also reduces the willingness of workers to perform. This defect was recognized by President Dorticós in September, 1962, when he announced plans to tie industrial wages to output. At the time of writing, however, the development of agricultural incentives is still uncertain.

The development most disastrous to Cuban agriculture has been the decline in sugar output. *Hoy*, the official Communist organ of Cuba, has attributed this to the shortage of workers. Many have been siphoned off into the armed forces, and others have just drifted away from the farms. Some observers believe that workers cut cane until they have earned enough money to buy their food ration, and then, because they can buy no more, they work no more. Volunteer brigades, including women and

[18] *The New York Times*, Feb. 25, 1962.

[19] Speech by Castro in Havana, Mar. 6, 1961.

students, have been brought in from the cities, but their net effect has probably been harmful. If sugar is cut below the lowest nodule, the cane will not reproduce itself the following season. Many canes were lost through inexperienced cutting by volunteers.

The response of the authorities has been to clamp a tighter control from Havana. In 1961 greater direction was imposed on private farms, as they were organized into a National Association of Small Farmers, and in August, 1962, all remaining cooperatives were converted into state farms. Workers would then be required to live on the farms, instead of in homes of their own choosing elsewhere in the neighborhood, and would be subject to greater discipline by the farm director.

In August, 1962, Dr. Carlos Rodriguez, director of the National Agrarian Reform Institute (and a leader in the Cuban Communist movement since the 1930s) set the stage for ultimate take-over of private farms, with the following words: [20]

> We do not believe it proper for individual workers to till separate bits of land. . . . Life will have to convince these comrades of the impracticability of that parcel of land. It will be the growth of the economic force of socialism that will demonstrate to them that such things are no longer necessary . . . the fact that by working on the state farms they will have more than if they cultivated small parcels of land. Through discussions with their comrades they will arrive at the conclusion that a thing that obstructs our agriculture and sometimes interferes with our planting is of no benefit to them. . . . However, we are not going to tell the farmers officially that they have to get rid of that land or that they have no right to that land. . . . It is a problem of conscience, or persuasion.

Mexico

The experience of the Mexican agrarian reform also carries some lessons on collective farming. The constitution of 1917 provided that each peasant had the "right to land." The *latifundios* would be broken up, land stolen by Diaz returned to Indian communal villages (*ejidos*), and other lands parceled out in family-sized farms. Each *ejido* was to cover 7 kilometers radius from center, in which plots would be assigned for individual use. The *ejidatario* (member of the *ejido*) was rigidly tied to his tiny lot. He could not sell his rights, but if he did not cultivate his land for two years, they might be forfeit. Since his land could be neither sold nor bought, legally its size remained unchanged, regardless of innovations in agricultural techniques. The *ejidatario* had little incentive to invest in improvements, for they would belong to land which was not legally his.

Ejidatarios were not selected necessarily for their farming prowess.

[20] Speech on Havana Radio Rebelde, Aug. 17, 1962, cited in Powell, *op. cit.*, p. 19.

Some have decided they would prefer to work in the city, where they have foreseen greater opportunities. Others have wanted larger parcels of land, which could be farmed more economically with newer techniques. The result has been an almost irresistible force in favor of illegal land-right sales, and these have occurred *de facto* if not *de jure*, by one means or another. Sometimes lands are consolidated within the *ejido*, and sometimes they are attached to adjacent private lands.

This development has caused serious debate among Mexicans. Some see it as a betrayal of the revolution and a tendency toward the restoration of the old *latifundios*. Others argue it is simply the result of normal, technological progress, in both agriculture and industry. Among the latter is Ramón Fernandez y Fernandez, who has proposed a "reform of the reform," to include regrouping of *ejido* properties according to family size and introduce a limited right of sale (but only to other *ejidatarios*). Fernandez does not want to see the *ejido* extinguished through unlimited sales to those with private property.[21]

Conclusions

What conclusions can one draw from the experiences of the United States, the Soviet Union, Cuba, and Mexico, on the relative merits of collective versus family farming? In the first place, the Mexican *ejido* should not be classified as a collective farm, since the private plots demonstrate many of the characteristics of family farming. In the second place, it would appear that incentives are all important. Collective farms suffer from some of the same ills as the hacienda system, in that individual workers lack material incentives. Some argue that it is possible to introduce these while leaving the system fundamentally unchanged. The Soviets and Cubans have made motions in this direction, and some Mexicans have proposed new systems of incentives for the *ejidos*.

There is, however, a positive dimension to family farming that does not relate to incentives as they are normally understood (i.e., greater return for greater effort). Rather it is the pride of achievement and ownership. The family farmer forms a personal attachment to his farm. He sings about his cattle as if they were his friends or family. When the cow is about to have a calf, he will sleep in the barn to see that all goes well in case the birth should occur at night. Many is the farm wife who has jokingly complained that her husband loves the cows as much as he does her. The land is part of him, and him personally. He put the fertilizer in it, he ran the soil through his fingers to see how sandy it was, and he knows every row of corn and every acre of wheat as well as he does his own son (and sometimes better). States and localities have fairs in which

[21] Ramón Fernandez y Fernandez, "La reforma agraria mexicana: logros y problemas derivados," *El Trimestre Económico*, April–June, 1957, p. 15.

farmers show off their cattle and hogs—not to sell them (necessarily), but just to show how big they are. *There is personal pride of achievement, because the farm is the farmer's and what comes from it is what he has done.*

I believe, along with most North Americans, that this pride in, and association with, the land explains much about the high productivity of United States agriculture. It is a factor *x*, too big to be described as incentive, impossible to measure, with direct relationship to output unproved, but decidedly there. No system other than family farming can induce it. It is found in many countries other than the United States, and explains why the peasants in Russia resisted collectivization so compulsively. North Americans often associate it erroneously with *any* private ownership, but it does not belong in privately owned *latifundios*. The *hacendado* never knew factor *x*, because he has always been too far removed from the land.

Perhaps factor *x* cannot be transferred from one culture to another. Maybe the Andean Indian—whose farming was communal before the conquistadors came—can never know it, because it is beyond his experience. This I do not know. Maybe the Soviet farmer is too far removed temporally from the era of family farming, and maybe family farming never really had a chance in Russia, because farm sizes in the latter half of the nineteenth century were too small. This also I do not know. Maybe collective farms can introduce all the incentives that man can provide, and maybe the spirit of the collectivity—comradery with one's neighbor—will prove to be a factor *y* in socialist countries that we of the capitalist ethic could never know.

Maybe it will, but it hasn't yet.

THE DIRECTION OF AGRARIAN REFORM

Bolivia

Except in Cuba, agrarian reform in Latin America is tending toward the family farm. The Bolivian reform of 1953 has gone far toward the division of old haciendas into family units. The first years were retarded by an empty national treasury, an inflation that played havoc with credit systems, and an inability to survey for land titles or adequately provide technology. At first the peon tended to rely on his old *haciendado* for grain and marketing; and because he could do nothing else, he repaid in services, much according to the former pattern.

Statistics are not fully reliable, but every indication is that Bolivian agricultural output declined in the mid-fifties, at least on the Altiplano. Some of the drop was offset by new plantings of sugar, rice, and cotton in the Santa Cruz area. There is convincing evidence, however, that even on the Altiplano farm product is now increasing.

What to me is most exciting about agrarian reform in Bolivia is a phenomenon that most would consider mundane. This is the number of trucks crossing the Altiplano or climbing the steep road from the Yungas Valley into La Paz. These trucks are filled with Indians in their colorful costumes, who stand as testimony to the new mobility introduced by reform. The very fact that they are going to market means an exchange economy is being developed. It is not necessary to have sophisticated data on gross national product to know what is going on; one can simply count the increasing number of trucks. The government in La Paz points with pride to the fact that the Indian farmer is no longer called *Indio,* but *campesino,* a term that apparently carries more prestige. But it is a pity this is so, for the Indians have a heritage of which they should be proud.

Guatemala

Only in Mexico, Bolivia, and Cuba have agrarian reforms encompassed thorough expropriation of *latifundios.* A notable attempt was made in Guatemala under the Arbenz government (1951–1954), however. The reform law of 1952 was based on the constitution of 1945, introduced after the overthrow of the dictator Ubico (1931–1944) and the restoration of popular government. The agrarian law provided for the liquidation of feudal properties, prohibition of all forms of servitude, and distribution of land to the landless. It was no more radical than what would be acceptable today under the Alliance for Progress.

Unfortunately, the Arbenz government became so influenced by Communist elements that much concern was felt in Washington. It was finally overthrown by Guatemalans, although many believe with the assistance of the United States. This was before the Alliance for Progress, and Washington's official position in favor of agrarian reform had not yet solidified. Probably Washington was more upset by the infiltration of communism than it was by agrarian reform. Still, reform was set back when the new government (of Castillo Armas) assumed power. The whole incident is extremely unfortunate for those who—like myself—try to convince Latin Americans that the change in United States attitude toward agrarian reform is, in fact, sincere.

Reform was not completely stopped in Guatemala, however, Instead, it assumed a new, more moderate character. In a resettlement program carried out since 1954, 20,000 families have received farms of their own.[22] A "rural development program" was begun, including supervised credit for small and medium farmers (carried out with assistance from the United States government).

These measures are not nearly so pervasive as the reform contemplated

[22] *Second Annual Report,* Inter-American Development Bank, Social Progress Trust Fund, p. 290, Washington, D.C., 1963.

by the Arbenz administration. There are approximately 370,000 rural families [23] in Guatemala, a country of extreme *latifundio-minifundio,* in which 76 per cent of the farms are on 9 per cent of the land. According to the Inter-American Bank, some 40 per cent of all farms are operated by tenant farmers, sharecroppers, and squatters. One can well imagine that resettling 20,000 families is only a small bite into a tremendous cake of molasses, and the government of Guatemala should be humbly aware of this. Critics of the government, however, should remember that it *is* a start, and a successful one.

Resettlement versus expropriation: experiences in Bolivia, Peru, and the United States

All governments in Latin America that are signatories to the Alliance for Progress have an obligation to carry out programs of agrarian reform. Most have already introduced legislation, and in many the laws have been passed. Scope and implementation vary from early achievement in Venezuela to foot dragging in Brazil, Chile, and Peru. A country-by-country summary of progress is sketched in the annual reports by the Social Progress Trust Fund of the Inter-American Development Bank, so I shall not outline it in that manner here.

Two types of changes in land tenure are contemplated: resettlement on public lands and redistribution of private lands (breaking up of *latifundios* into family-sized farms and/or regrouping of *minifundios*). Obviously, resettlement is the politically easier. Public lands are scarcely populated, and no vested interests are upset. Often their fertility presents excellent opportunities for migrant families. Time and again (in the United States, for example) countries have solved their demographic pressures by moving into new, unoccupied lands. Latin America is fortunate to have such a resource in a world where cultivable land is generally a scarce commodity.

Government assistance can spark the opening of new lands. Some countries have discovered that the army can at long last be put to productive use. Instead of simply consuming an inordinate portion of a pressurized budget, it can start to contribute to the national economy. In Bolivia army construction battalions have opened new roads, and the people are urged to migrate. Likewise the Brazilian army has encouraged colonization of the interior and undertaken a study of natural resources. Colombia, the Dominican Republic, El Salvador, Guatemala, and Chile have other economic development programs in which the military is used. The adequacy of the military for such tasks is, however, limited by its

[23] Based on statistics of legally married women in Guatemala (157,421) plus women in common-law marriages (335,476), multiplied by 75 per cent, the overall ratio of rural to urban population. Data from *América en Cifras, 1960, op. cit.,* vol. 2, pp. 12, 16–17.

traditional lack of popularity. In Colombia there are rural areas where a man in uniform would be shot on sight.

While resettlement must be tried where promising, nevertheless its limitations preclude it as the principal implement of reform. In the first place, its strongest asset—that it is politically easy—is also a liability. In the minds of many Latin Americans, the primary objective of agrarian reform is to break the political stranglehold of parasitic landowners. Presumably they contribute little to the national economy, and their power lies not in achievement but in the military prowess and chicanery of their ancestors. To avoid breaking up their lands would leave one of the leading objectives of agrarian reform unresolved.

In the second place, settlement should never be undertaken without extensive studies of the land, its fertility, topography, and soil type. Fertile land is available, but its amount tends to be exaggerated. Many suppose that jungles have high productive potential, since presumably they have long been gathering the humus formed by decomposition of unharvested vegetable matter. In fact, however, tropical soil is usually so leached by heavy and persistent rainfall that all the fertility is removed. To suppose that the vast hinterland promises to be for Latin America what the wheat belt was for the United States is a serious error.

In the third place, settlement has its economic limitations. To move large numbers into the Eastern jungles of Colombia, Ecuador, Peru, and Bolivia, or the interior of Brazil, would be to create isolated subsistence villages as poverty-stricken as the communities from which the peasants came. The history of Peru is replete with examples of failure to establish successful colonies in the interior simply because they were so far removed from markets, and the mountains too steep and costly to cross.[24]

[24] Preston James writes of one of these experiments as follows (in *Latin America*, 3d ed., The Odyssey Press, Inc., New York, 1959, p. 186):

In 1858 the Peruvian government undertook to bring in immigrant colonists from Germany to start a movement into these eastern border valleys. There were 50 families, 174 people, from Bavaria—all experienced farmers and all Catholics. Unfortunately by the time the immigrants reached Peru the government had been changed and support for the venture had evaporated. Nevertheless the Germans were determined to reach the lands that had been promised to them. It took two years for the group to cross the Andes and reach the middle Huancabamba valley where they established the town of Pozuzu. Each colonist had his own farm and did his own work. Visitors to Pozuzu in the early twentieth century brought back reports of the neatness of the European style homes, the attractiveness of the people and the efficiency of their methods of farming. Yet there was no prosperity. For a time coca leaves were used for the production of cocaine, which was valuable enough to stand the high costs of shipment. When this was prohibited, the settlers had to fall back on unprocessed coca leaves and brandy . . . the Pozuzu colony has expanded but little beyond its original area. Its population is still about 2,000. The colonists must send out their products by a three- or four-day muleback journey to the end of the new highway near Oxapampa.

A further problem in the resettlement of Andean Indians is their cultural reluctance to move. For centuries the Peruvian cordilleras and Bolivian Altiplano have been their home. Their village *fiestas* are related to specific geographic landmarks. The Incas loved the mountains and feared the lowlands; they established penal colonies in the Eastern jungles, and sent exiles there. Eastern Peru was to them what Siberia is to Russia. Furthermore, they are adjusted temperamentally and healthwise to higher altitudes. Bolivian Indians drained off the Altiplano to fight the Paraguayans in the Chaco War died like flies in the steaming jungle, many without ever seeing the whites of the eyes of the enemy.

Efforts to resettle Bolivian Indians on a mass basis in the province of Santa Cruz have not been successful, even though it has a thriving economy and a paved road back over the mountains to Cochabamba. Colonies of Okinawans and Mennonites have been established there, and individual Indians have moved from the Altiplano, but little more. By contrast, when the government started a penetration road through the Yungas Valley which will ultimately connect Bolivian roads with the Eastern river system at Rurrenabaque, the Indians moved in so fast that they were squatting on land some miles ahead of the road, waiting for it to reach them. But the Yungas is much closer to the Altiplano, and they could return overnight to the *fiestas* of their home towns. Also, the altitude is greater than that of Santa Cruz.

Despite the cultural, economic, and physical difficulties, in 1961 and 1962 the Peruvian government relied on resettlement as a principal arm of its agrarian reform under the Alliance for Progress. In April, 1961, it established the Institute of Agrarian Reform and Land Settlement, which is currently carrying out two projects, one in the Piura Department on the Northern coast (adjacent to Ecuador), and the other in the Apurímac Department in the forest region of the South.[25]

There is strong sentiment in the United States (much of it based on misinformation) that the bulk of agrarian reform can be carried out in Latin America through means short of expropriation. Resettlement is one of the alternatives, tax policies another. Here North Americans erroneously envisage a repetition of United States history, in which our nineteenth-century land problems were solved by a westward movement, referred to in earlier chapters. In Chapter 2 (page 28) I mentioned that many North Americans wonder why Latin Americans cannot solve their agrarian problems by spontaneously moving where the new land is.

What these North Americans forget is that our westward movement was based on high incomes in the South and East, and strong demand for foodstuffs. Throughout most of the nineteenth century the Southeastern

[25] Inter-American Development Bank, *Second Annual Report*, Social Progress Trust Fund, p. 374, Washington, D.C., 1963.

states produced high-value cotton and "imported" their wheat from the West. Settlers in newly opened lands of Iowa, Kansas, and Nebraska shipped their wheat and other crops down the Mississippi to Southern ports. Other outlets were the Great Lakes route, and ultimately the Erie Canal, to feed New York and the Northeast. Except for occasional mavericks, the settlers never cut their commercial ties. Many lived in isolated homesteads, but trading posts were nearby. The secret was that economic development was occurring and incomes rising, in the lands from which they had come. There was a pony express, transportation routes were not too onerous, and the basis for trade was there.

Herein lies both a similarity between our respective economic developments and a lesson for Latin America. This is that *interior settlement on a massive scale will not take place without simultaneous development of population centers on the coast and in the mountains. There must be good transportation routes, and never must the frontier push beyond the economic possibilities of commerce. Otherwise, the movement will fail.*

There is evidence that before 1963 the Peruvian government did not appreciate this. Before the fall of the Beltrán administration the Mexican news magazine *Tiempo* wrote as follows about Peruvian agrarian reform: [26]

> In 1961, a commission that had in fact been created five years earlier, drew up a bill devoid of practicality. The Peruvian "agrarian reform" escapes confronting the system of landed properties. Nor could one expect any other attitude by the governments that until now have held power in Lima, given the social stratum from which they have come.
>
> The minister who drew up the bill was Pedro Beltrán, whose idea it was to relieve the overpopulated zones of the highlands, sending their inhabitants into practically virgin regions in the east, where land rotation would be much more economical than irrigation of new desert areas by the coast. There would be a double benefit: expenditures on currently-depressed areas would be diminished, and new territory would be opened. There would even be a third advantage, for it would avoid the painful decisions of an agrarian reform which would inevitably clash with the current landholding pattern.

Upon its access in 1963, the Balaunde government in Peru announced a radical change in land policies and began the expropriation of *latifundios* and their distribution among Indian peasants. At the time of writing, it is uncertain how successful or widespread this new program will be.

Taxation as an instrument of agrarian reform

Some have proposed that—if resettlement is uneconomic and expropriation politically impractical—taxation should be used as a weapon of

[26] *Tiempo*, May 21, 1962.

agrarian reform. Landowners are notorious for their ability to prevent tax increases from being passed and to avoid payment of those that have. Land tax rates in Latin America are, in general, far lower than they are in the United States. Agrarian reform legislation in several countries includes tax schedules designed to promote more intensive utilization of land.

One method is to tax idle land at a rate higher than productive land. A major difficulty, however, is the definition of productive land. How much of a crop does a landowner have to plant in order to avoid the high idle-land rate? Will a few stalks of corn scattered here and there be enough? If so, the introduction of this tax would soon lead to the extinction of all land registered as idle but might not cause much increase in production. This problem should not be minimized by the suggestion of certain criteria and controls. They will have to be pervasive, and rigid inspection will be necessary to see that lands are properly categorized. Often the difference between idle and productive will be a matter of opinion, and underpaid tax assessors may be susceptible to monetary persuasion.

It must also be remembered that increased taxes on land are economically akin to expropriation. The capitalized value of land is based on its earnings; an increase in taxes decreases earnings and precipitates a fall in value. Market value is different from capitalized value because land is bought for reasons other than earnings, but they rise or fall together. Landowners who are influential politicians may be just as adamant about tax measures as they are about expropriation.

Finally, the implementation of a land tax will be no better than the tax machinery with which the country is equipped. So long as the tradition of taxpaying is not established, land surveys not made, books and records not adequately kept, and officials subject to bribery, taxation will not be an effective instrument of agrarian reform.

This is not, however, an argument that it should not be tried. Tax systems must be strengthened as a requisite for development, and land taxes must fit into the pattern. The purpose of the present section is only to stress that taxation must not be considered an alternative to expropriation because of political obstacles to the latter. In fact, the obstacles to both are formidable.

CONTRASTING EXPERIENCES: VENEZUELA AND CHILE

Venezuela

Venezuela has the only government in Latin America that has introduced serious land expropriation without violent upheaval. Here the richest agriculture is in the highlands bordering the Caribbean, where Caracas and Valencia, the foci of political power, are located. Passage of the agrarian reform law, providing for both expropriation (with compensation) and settlement, induced peasants to demand hacienda properties. Most of the initiative was carried out by the farmers' union, with threats (and a few actual occurrences) that the peasants would take over the land if it weren't expropriated. In September, 1962, *The New York Times* reported that about 40 per cent of all land distributed to peasants had been taken from large landowners, and the remaining 60 per cent was public land deeded by the State.

Territory outside the central highlands offers varying possibilities of settlement. There is much State land in the plains extending southward toward the Orinoco River, some with high fertility. Rains are variable, however, becoming less reliable the farther south one goes. An irrigation project on the Guárico River has made possible the settlement of over 100 plots (500 more are contemplated) of some 160 to 240 hectares each. The World Bank has criticized this project because of high unit costs and poor internal drainage. The Bank feels that good land not requiring irrigation is abundant and other areas (such as south of Lake Maracaibo) would bring greater yields per bolivar invested in irrigation.[27] Two of my students (from the United States) who visited the Guárico project, however, found it successful from the point of view of the individual farmer. Farms are profitable and wages high.[28]

Chile

Chile is a country of much talk, and—many charge—little action on agrarian reform. Some emphasis has been placed on resettlement, but unfortunately the possibilities of migration are limited by geography. The most fertile land lies in the central plains, hemmed in by the Andes on the east and the coastal plateau on the west. North of the central plains is desert, whose principal products are copper and nitrates, not agriculture. The South is cold, rainy, and forested. A large part of the land assets of the Settlement Fund lies in the Southern province of Magallanes, just northwest of Tierra del Fuego and the tip of South America.

Chilean agriculture has been languishing, partly because of the inefficiencies of the hacienda system and partly because inflation has entailed credit problems and price controls discouraging to farmers. Chile used to be self-sufficient in foodstuffs but now falls about 20 per cent

[27] *The Economic Development of Venezuela,* International Bank for Reconstruction and Development, Washington, D.C., 1961, p. 57.

[28] John P. Clark and John D. Powell, *To Struggle Is My Destiny,* Washington, D.C., 1961, p. 21. A three-month study of Venezuelan agrarian reform. (Multilith; copy in the library of the School of Advanced International Studies, Johns Hopkins University.)

short, thus finding it necessary to spend some $100 million a year of valuable foreign exchange on agricultural imports.

The long, almost interminable discussions on expropriation and payment have led some to question the sincerity of the Chilean government in its promises for agrarian reform. There has been much controversy over the maximum permissible acreage to be retained, the sizes of plots to be distributed, and the method of compensation. Some see a conflict between the most efficient sizes and those that will satisfy all peasant demand. If the smaller sizes are adopted, more land will be distributed, but (they say) agricultural output will be decreased.

Opposition spokesmen in Chile have charged that the Agrarian Reform Law of 1962 is too little and too late. It calls for 5,000 new small landowners, one pointed out, while farm population is rising at the rate of 60,000 a year. "Nothing significant in the way of reforms can be expected," he said, "from a Government made up in large part of wealthy landowners and businessmen who would have to make sacrifices." [29]

SIZE OF HOLDINGS AND AGRICULTURAL EFFICIENCY

There is much conflicting opinion on the relationship of agricultural efficiency to the size of landholdings. For example, there is no agreement on whether plantation farming—bananas, sugar, coffee, and the like—must be carried on as a large-scale business to attain low unit costs. Plantations are neither family farms nor haciendas. Often incorporated, they are organized like manufacturing enterprises with hired laborers and foremen, and produce principally for the market (usually export). Their purpose is more profit than ownership prestige.

North Americans acquainted with agrarian problems in Latin America usually distinguish between plantations and haciendas. Many see the rationale of reforming the tenure of haciendas but fear loss of efficiency if plantation lands are confiscated. Latin American reformists, who don't make the same distinction, interpret (or misinterpret?) the North American position as political, since some of the largest plantations (bananas in Central America and sugar in Cuba) have been owned by North American companies. The quotation by Dr. Mendieta at the beginning of this chapter is a case in point.

The case for plantation efficiency is based on the type of agriculture. It is argued that plantation crops demand heavy investment, sometimes in machinery (tractors, harvesters, and spraying equipment) and sometimes in other requisites such as fertilizer, pesticides, and seed. Harvesting is performed by many workers, with limited requirements in skill, but supervised by a foreman acquainted with planting and harvesting tech-

[29] *The New York Times*, Oct. 28, 1962.

niques. He in turn is subject to a management skilled in scientific farming principles.

A study of the United Fruit Company made by the National Planning Association (United States) illustrates the argument for large-scale operations. The authors state that ". . . disease incidence, natural disasters, and the exceptionally demanding logistics of banana distribution promise to keep the pattern in this field one in which large-scale, vertically integrated operators predominate."[30] Bananas suffer from three formidable blights: Panama disease, sigatoka, and moko. The control of sigatoka requires elaborate spraying equipment, usually installed in a network of pipes with access to every banana plant. Unlike sigatoka, Panama disease is carried through the ground. There is no known cure, but it can be held in check by periodic flooding of attacked lands, an operation requiring considerable capital and skill.

The transportation system is another argument for large-scale, integrated operation. Bananas are not salable unless they reach the grocery store in peak condition, which lasts only a few days. Where they are exported from Central America, Panama, Colombia, and Ecuador to the United States, careful calculation must determine the exact date for shipment from particular ports. But the exact moment when bananas will be ready for harvesting is not known much in advance. United Fruit continuously has ships in the Caribbean, many with exact destination unknown, to be informed by radio where they should go to pick up the bananas that have just reached the shipping point. How else could this service be performed but in an integrated operation?

Despite all this, however, in recent years United Fruit has been selling much of its Central American property to private farmers. There are several reasons. One is that land has been abandoned because of Panama disease and turned over to other types of cultivation. But even banana land is increasingly farmed by individual owners. Probably the company has become more alert to the likelihood of expropriation under agrarian reforms. In addition, as operations have expanded southward into Ecuador where private farms are the rule, it has discovered that integrated growing and marketing are not so necessary to efficiency as previously believed. So long as the company provides the requisites (disease control, etc.), there is no reason why it cannot buy from individual producers and sell in the United States just as efficiently as it could on its own plantations.

This may well be true of all large-scale, corporate farming. Individual family farms may buy the requisites (current capital and services of fixed capital) from supplying corporations, which may or may not be the same

[30] Stacy May and Galo Plaza, *The United Fruit Company in Latin America*, National Planning Association, Washington, D.C., 1958, p. 139.

ones to whom they sell their output. Many agricultural economists have argued that farming—unlike industry—does not require management units larger than the family for most efficient operation. Among these is Ervin Long, who wrote as follows: [31]

> Contrary to popular belief—and to the interpretation often given to farm management research data—there is no strong indication that given amounts of land, labor, water, capital, managerial skills, and other resources are more efficient, under most conditions, when combined in larger than what are normally thought of as "family" units. . . . As I have pointed out elsewhere, using Indian data, efficiency in the use of a given resource is, if anything, inversely related to the size of the farm. These same relationships are borne out in data I have observed from several other countries, including Germany, Chile, Formosa, and Japan. Obviously, the quantum of resources per man should be as high as possible; but this is not achieved by the mere aggregation of resources into larger conglomerates.

One must be clear, of course, on how family farms are defined. There has been a recent tendency in the United States to consolidate farmland, as some sell to others and move to the city to find jobs in industry. Those who remain can operate large units more economically by mechanization that substitutes for costly labor. But these are still family farms.

This approach to economic size bears on those countries which, like Chile, must decide between dividing land into smaller sizes to accommodate all the landless or larger sizes to achieve allegedly higher efficiency. The answer is that, apart from a shortage of management skills, large-sized farm units *do not* enjoy advantages of scale in places where labor is abundant and has no alternative opportunities.

Much misunderstanding of this fact comes from the erroneous belief that machinery can increase output and that once farms are mechanized, unit costs will diminish with larger scale. Therefore, it is argued, efficiency will be sacrificed if large units are divided among peasants and mechanization becomes impractical.

But mechanization is already impractical, for other reasons. Unlike industry, agricultural machines do not perform feats of power that man could not do with rudimentary tools.[32] Put enough men (with hand tools) on a given piece of land, and they can plough, seed, fertilize, and reap a harvest as great as any machine can accomplish. In lands where labor

[31] Ervin J. Long, "The Economic Basis of Land Reform in Underdeveloped Economies," *Land Economics*, May, 1961, pp. 113–123.

[32] Except in drilling wells or building irrigation systems. But the importance of irrigation to general agricultural development is often exaggerated. Experts have estimated that potential irrigation could increase the world's supply of agricultural land by only about 1 per cent.

is plentiful and has no other possible employment, the mechanization argument for leaving some without land is simply not valid.

The argument against dividing up efficient agricultural operations rests more firmly on the loss of management skills. Peasants may not know *how* to plant, cultivate, reap, and market in order to yield the greatest return. More than any other factor, lack of management ability explains the decrease in output that often occurs after agrarian reforms. But will a peasant learn the skills more rapidly if he continues to be employed on a plantation or if he is put on his own land, with incentives of his own, and provided with the best technical assistance the government can supply?

AGRARIAN REFORM AND AGRICULTURAL DEVELOPMENT

To many persons, agrarian reform extends far beyond land tenure, to include agricultural credit and marketing, tax systems, and the provision of technology and other services to rural areas. In 1951, the United Nations defined agrarian structure in the following way: [33]

> It includes, in the first place, land tenure, the legal or customary system under which land is owned; the distribution of ownership of farm property between large estates and peasant farms or among peasant farms of various sizes; land tenancy, the system under which land is operated and its product divided between operator and owner; the organization of credit, production and marketing; the mechanism through which agriculture is financed; the burdens imposed on rural populations by governments in the form of taxation; and the services supplied by governments to rural populations, such as technical advice and educational facilities, health services, water supply and communications.

The emphasis I have placed on land tenure in this chapter has not resulted from a feeling that the other aspects of agrarian reform are not important. Indeed, they are vital. This book, however, is intended to concentrate on controversial issues, and there is little controversy over the need to provide extension services and agricultural credit. There is some dispute over community development as a means of providing technical assistance, but it does not involve international issues of the same magnitude as land tenure. I shall leave discussion of the most satisfactory methods of dispensing agricultural knowledge to those more skilled in the field than I.

I should, however, like to make a few points. One is that it is scarcely possible to carry out any change in land tenure without adverse effects on production. The Mexican and Bolivian experiences have shown this,

[33] *Land Reform*, United Nations, New York, 1951, p. 5.

and now Cuba is added to the list. In Mexico the expropriation (or threat of it) of haciendas caused much agricultural capital, such as irrigation systems, to fall into disuse, and from 1910 to the mid-1920s output was probably below the prerevolutionary average. From then on, however, the government vigorously promoted new irrigation, rural education, and extension services, and established an agricultural bank. In Bolivia farm output fell after the reform but appears to be on the mend in more recent years. The upheavals of an agrarian reform are such that farmers must grit their teeth and expect early losses.

Opponents of agrarian reform should refrain from criticism based solely on its initial deleterious effects unless they can substantiate that they will be more harmful than continuance of an archaic structure. In Cuba, where output increased in the first two years of revolution, its subsequent decline can be traced directly to the withdrawal of material incentives and the independence of the farmer. It is regrettable that Havana's solution lies in the direction of intensifying the cause. In Mexico and Bolivia, decreased output was caused by a rupture of supply of requisites and marketing systems, which were subsequently restored and improved.

A second point is that simply providing technology will not persuade the farmer to use it. More important than pure education is the development of a mentality toward change, of a willingness to experiment with new methods. It may be necessary to hire peasants to carry on experiments on their own farms (even though the results are already known), so that they can experience learning for themselves that new ways are better. Ofter there are farmers of different capabilities in the same community, and the first step toward improvement is to persuade the poorer ones to experiment with the methods already in use by their neighbors.

A final comment is on the problem of *minifundios.* Many reformers feel that these must be regrouped into larger-sized units, each one the vital minimum to provide for a family. Surely this should be done, provided, however, there is enough land for everyone (or else that those who are excluded can readily be settled elsewhere). If *latifundios* are simultaneously being divided, and if the supply of land thus generated is more than necessary to provide for the liberated peons, there will be some left on which to settle the surplus *minifundistas.*

In the Dominican Republic and Haiti there is not enough land for all the *minifundistas* and currently landless peasants. Agrarian reforms here should not consolidate the *minifundios,* but—through education and extension—should try to improve farming practices to increase the income on existing plots. No traction, either mechanical or animal, should be introduced as long as labor is plentiful. Oxen would not increase the output available for human consumption but might even reduce it by preempting pasture lands that would otherwise be available for truck farming.

THE ALLIANCE FOR PROGRESS AND INTERVENTION

The Alliance for Progress is an inter-American program. It was drafted in a conference at Punta del Este, Uruguay, in August, 1961, attended by representatives of all the American republics. Some say its origins lie in President Kubitschek's proposal for an "Operación Panamericana" three years earlier, and some even carry it back to Bolivar's attempt to unify the continent. Still, the term was first employed by President Kennedy, and many consider it to be a North American idea, because money is coming from the United States. Kennedy has disclaimed any credit, possibly because he does not want it to be thought of as Yankee intervention.

Yet the simple fact is that just as in the days of dollar diplomacy, the United States is providing money contingent on certain performance by Latin American countries. Washington has made it clear that the funds promised under the Alliance for Progress will not be paid in full unless the Latin American governments undertake serious agrarian reforms.

Often I have asked my Latin American friends whether in their opposition to North American intervention they distinguish as to its quality. This question, which employs generalities, usually evokes a negative answer. The Latin countries should resolve their affairs for themselves, they argue, and there is no such thing as good intervention. When I have posed the question in specific terms, regarding the aid programs, I have sometimes been told that financial assistance is an obligation of the United States, partly to make amends for its former support to the landed aristocracy and partly to compensate for low prices paid for primary products.

We have reached a historical era in which the United States is convinced that, for its own political and international security, there must be a change in the agrarian structure of Latin countries. We would be blind not to recognize that Washington is motivated by a desire to avoid Communist upheavals and the growth of socialist organisms such as the collective farm. The new position adopted in Washington has been facilitated by the social revolution in the United States during the last thirty years. Agrarian reform is still not popular with North American businesses that own land in Latin America, but the government in Washington—based on broad, popular support—has ceased to cater to their interests.

In Latin America, on the other hand, there are certain governments that obviously feel the Alliance for Progress is a device to capture the agrarian revolution and head it off. Influencial officials of these governments do not look upon the Indian as a full human being, to be accorded the same dignity as the white man. Many of them have no intention of giving up their lands. Laws introduced in the legislature may satisfy the words of the Alliance, but there is a world of difference between passing an agrarian law and carrying it out. Some government officials, like the Marxists, are unaware of how serious the United States is in its determination to see that reform is implemented.

We have now reached the crucial question. The United States government is bound to come in conflict with these governments soon or late. Shall it continue to use the pressure of Alliance funds, and threaten to cut them off, if reforms are not made? Should it continue to provide assistance to recalcitrant governments on the ground that it has an obligation to do so? Or should it withdraw entirely and let matters take their course? *Which one of these possibilities, if any, constitutes intervention, and which one, if any, does not?*

When a Latin American government is dominated by landowning interests adamant against expropriating their own holdings or taxing themselves into a willingness to sell at lower capitalized values, what forces will bring about a change? One very powerful force is economic development. We have already seen a conflict between the interests of new industrialists—the growing middle class so evident in urban centers like Mexico City, Medellín, Lima, and São Paulo—and those of the traditional landowning aristocracy. Will this struggle be resolved by ballots as new distributions of economic strength cause shifts in political power?

Or will it happen by blood, as it did in the only three countries with agrarian reforms worthy of the name before the Alliance for Progress—in Mexico, Bolivia, and Cuba? Venezuela, Brazil (in the Northeast), Chile, and Peru are the most critical countries in the tests of the next few years. Venezuela has demonstrated that reforms *may* be implemented by peaceful methods, although even the Betancourt government has faced pressure by leftists who want to carry out the program faster.

Are we all agreed that it is better to solve the problem by constitutional processes than by blood? Or are constitutional processes too torpid, and a little blood not an excessive sacrifice? Pressure by the United States will be in the direction of solution through votes and political decision, not bullets. Do Latin Americans find this method deliberate and plodding, or reprehensible if done with pressure from abroad? I ask these questions in all earnestness, because I do not know the answers. They will not be found in this book. Only Latin Americans can answer them, by writing the history of years to come.

4 Monopoly

The economy of the United States displays pronounced monopolistic traits. The large enterprise is the typical economic unit of the present era in the American union. Groups of two, three, or four big companies dominate the most important activities. Their power does not derive from the fact that there are no other enterprises operating in each activity, but to the great magnitude of the "small group" in charge of each branch's operations. Thus the economy of the United States is characterized by a concentration of giants in each important activity.

THE CRITIC of the North American economy whose work is quoted above is José Luis Ceceña, a Mexican, writing in *Siempre* on May 30, 1962. He is not alone in his opinions. The conviction is widely held in Latin America that both the economy and the government of the United States are dominated by monopolies. Indeed, many attribute Latin America's state of underdevelopment to powerful enterprises from the North. These companies have committed (so it is charged) a systematic plunder of natural wealth both through their political domination and by their ability to set prices.

Time and again my students in Latin America have told me it is useless to talk of economic development until the stranglehold of the monopolies is broken. So long as they exploit resources and export profits for investment abroad, these students argue that Latin America will be deprived of the capital it badly needs for growth. "The economy of the United

States is one of imperfect competition," wrote one of them. "It is dominated by trusts and large corporations that monopolize markets, determine prices, decisively influence the government, and control all spheres of social organization. . . . These monopolies are the greatest enemies of our colonial, semicolonial, and dependent territories, for they systematically sack our natural resources and subject our peoples to the severest kind of exploitation."

The problem of monopolies is so important to Latin American students that three chapters will be devoted to it. In the present one, the impact of power concentrations on trade and development will be outlined. The next chapter will treat the role of primary products in developing economies, since producers of these are said to be the victims of monopolies. Thereafter we shall turn to specific commodities, dealing with their recent history and the extent to which trade channels are monopolized.

A curious aspect of monopolies is the divergent opinions of them in Latin American and North American universities. North Americans accept that monopolies are a problem of economic organization, but not a compelling one. Upon visiting economics faculties in Latin America, students from the United States are generally shocked and surprised by the attention focused on monopolies, which they believe to be all out of proportion to the magnitude of the problem.

This dichotomy has two possible explanations: *either* monopolies affect Latin Americans more adversely than North Americans, *or* Latin American students are wrong in their assessment of monopoly power. I rule out the possibility that the North American students are wrong, since they live in the shadow of the enterprises under attack, and it is hard to suppose they would suffer harm and not be aware of it.

It is, however, quite conceivable that monopolies in the United States affect Latin America adversely in a way that the North American students, with limited experience abroad, do not comprehend. In fact, I believe the truth lies in *both* explanations. Large enterprises in the United States do affect Latin Americans differently from the way they affect North Americans, and less favorably. At the same time, many monopoly-hating Latin Americans have incorrectly assessed their economic and political power.

Before proceeding with this argument, let us define our words. Latin American students—at least the ones in my classes—often use the term "monopoly" to mean any large, powerful enterprise, whether it is unique in its field or not. "The steel industry in the United States is under the control of eight monopolies," one of them wrote, "which in 1953 controlled 83% of the nation's potential output." I am accustomed to define monopoly according to its etymology, as the sole producer or seller of a given product. Under this definition, United States Steel does not qualify.

But what is important is ideas, not words, so let us compromise on semantics and proceed with the discussion. I have labeled the chapter "Monopoly," but I shall hereafter refer to "big business" or "concentrations of power" unless I mean a monopoly in its pure sense.

POWER CONCENTRATIONS AND THE FRUITS OF TECHNOLOGY

Latin Americans often charge that the price and wage policies of big business in the United States preclude less developed countries from sharing in the fruits of technological progress. According to this argument, big businesses that reduce their costs do not lower prices but instead raise wages and profits. Hence the classical doctrine, by which international trade and the price mechanism were alleged to pass on the benefits of new technology from the innovating country to others, does not work in a noncompetitive world.

Classical economists, of course, did not insist that this happy event was inevitable. Particular countries under particular circumstances might well suffer from the impact of technology. For example, if scientists in the United States should perfect a synthetic coffee, cheap enough to undersell the natural product, half of Latin America would be the losers. A technological improvement of this nature is referred to as "import-biased" (from the point of view of the innovating country), since it involves an import substitute. Import-biased innovations usually turn the terms of trade (ratio of export to import prices) in favor of the innovating country.

The United States has made many import-biased innovations that have adversely affected the incomes of primary-producing countries. Rayon, nylon, and other synthetic fibers have reduced imports of wool from Uruguay and Argentina (as well as silk from Japan). More messages are sent on a copper wire than before, aluminum is substituting for tin in cans, and a given number of beans will make more instant coffee than regular grind. We will return to these innovations in the next chapter, when we take up the problems of primary products. All we need to point out here is that they have probably not improved the economic prospects of Latin America.

It is through "export-biased," or at least "neutral" innovations that one country presumably passes on to others the benefits of its technological advance. An export-biased innovation is one that lowers the cost of production or improves the quality of goods produced for export. Neutral innovations are those that improve the quality of labor or other factors of production in such a way as to affect export- and import-substitute goods alike.

For years the United States and Europe have been centers of technological innovation, far more so than Latin America, Asia, and Africa. Advancing technology has been indiscriminately export-biased, import-biased, and neutral. The engineers and scientists who make the inventions are not concerned whether the impact will fall on their own countries or on others, or whether one will benefit more than another. They are scientists; they ply their trade and let the chips fall where they may.

If Latin America is to benefit from an export-biased innovation in the United States, it can do so only through changes in price and quality. For example, when a North American engineer invents a process for producing refrigerators cheaper (with, we shall assume, no change in quality), Latin Americans (as importers) will benefit only if the result is a price reduction. If refrigerators sell at the same price as before and all the fruits of the new technology are distributed to North Americans as profits to the producer or higher wages to the laborers, then no gain will be passed on to Latin America.

This is the picture that many Latin Americans have of power concentrations in the United States. Technology is not working in their favor, they say. Big business (monopoly?) in the United States makes export-biased, neutral, and import-biased innovations. Latin America does not gain from the export-biased and neutral ones, because resulting benefits are all distributed to North American laborers and capitalists. On the other hand, she loses from import-biased innovations, which undercut the markets for primary output.

Nor does the disadvantage end here. Many Latin Americans have charged that benefits from export-biased innovations on their own continent also tend to be passed on to the United States. To the extent that producers are large and integrated (as in petroleum, copper, and Central American bananas), the benefits may be distributed either as price reductions to importing North American firms or as profits to North American stockholders. Less often do they accrue as wages to Latin American workers, and then only after social upheavals or bloody strikes. Where producers are competitive (as in coffee, meat, wool, and Ecuadorian bananas), the buyers—presumed to be monopolists—set the price, and the competitors must comply. The benefits are therefore passed on to the foreigner and do not remain for the Latin American worker.

This thesis is generally credited to Raúl Prebisch, one of the foremost economists of Latin America and formerly director of the United Nations' Economic Commission for Latin America. It is spelled out in a document published by ECLA in 1950.[1]

North Americans have not accepted these arguments unchallenged. Their replies have been along three lines. In the first place, they say the

[1] *The Economic Development of Latin America,* United Nations Economic Commission for Latin America, E/CN.12/Rev. 1, Apr. 27, 1950.

Latin American position has never been substantiated through proper interpretation of terms-of-trade data. I shall discuss this in the next paragraph. In the second place, they insist that even where prices do move to the disadvantage of Latin America, the statistics do not disclose all distribution of benefits but exclude quality changes. Suppose engineers in the United States design a better refrigerator that sells for the same price. Latin Americans, as buyers, benefit even though they pay no less than before. Finally North Americans point out that their integrated enterprises in Latin America do pay high wages and taxes. Oil companies contribute some two-thirds of their profit to the Venezuelan government, and the proportion for copper company taxes in Chile has risen to between 60 and 80 per cent. Furthermore, wages paid by these enterprises are significantly higher than the general level in the market. This has not always been so, but it is now.

Those of us who are not statisticians tend to suppose the question of prices can be easily resolved. We have had export and import price data for almost one hundred years, so why not just look at them to see what has happened? More sophisticated technicians realize the answer is not so easy, for several reasons. One is: whose export and whose import prices do we look at? Sometimes prices of the same goods go up according to continental European data while they are declining in Britain or the United States. Another is: which products do we measure? Schultz notes that from 1929 to 1955 the prices of metal, lumber, and wood products were increasing, while those of farm products and fuels were falling.[2] All are important exports for Latin America.

A further reason why statistics are inadequate is the change in types of goods and services consumed. What does it mean to say that export prices in England have changed in a certain manner since 1870? Are we talking about horse-drawn carriages and kerosene lanterns or about automobiles and electric light bulbs? Exception is taken not only for quality but for completely new products.

Despite statistical inadequacies, recorded data may present a general impression of direction, and several studies have been made. In one completed in 1949, the United Nations came to the following conclusions: [3]

> Such general statistical data as are available indicate that from the latter part of the nineteenth century to the eve of the Second World War, a period of well over half a century, there was a secular downward trend in the prices of primary goods relative to the prices of manufactured

[2] Theodore Schultz, "Economic Prospects of Primary Products," in H. S. Ellis and H. C. Wallich (eds.), *Economic Development for Latin America,* St Martin's Press, Inc., New York, 1961.

[3] *Relative Prices of Exports and Imports of Underdeveloped Countries,* United Nations Document 1949.II.B.3, New York, 1949.

goods. On an average, a given quantity of primary exports would pay, at the end of this period, for only 60% of the quantity of manufactured goods which it could buy at the beginning of the period.

These results have been criticized not only because the "quantity of manufactured goods" consisted of different products in the later years from those in the earlier but also because the United Nations used British trade data for its comparisons. British imports are valued c.i.f., that is, including transportation and insurance. Technological improvements in transportation reduced shipping costs greatly in that period, and Ellsworth has shown that the price paid to the raw-material exporting country was higher and the c.i.f. import price in Britain lower at the same time.[4]

In a study based on European data, Professor Kindleberger concluded that terms of trade were not necessarily moving in favor of manufactured goods or away from primary products. He did report, however, that ". . . there is evidence . . . to suggest that . . . the terms of trade seem to favor developed and run against underdeveloped countries."[5] The explanation is that prices of raw materials produced in more developed countries have not fallen like those from less developed countries. While primary prices *as a whole* probably did not suffer in relation to manufactured goods, those of less developed countries probably did. Kindleberger does not attribute this to monopolies, however. Rather, he argues that more developed countries have more elastic supply schedules. Some of their primary products may be in continuous depression (such as coal in the United States), but the price impact is minimized by the existence of alternative opportunities to which capital and labor can shift. Thus when less coal is demanded, less is produced. In less developed countries other opportunities are not so readily found; hence, adverse shifts in demand tend to have a greater impact on price.

This reasoning would imply that it is not monopolies but unfavorable demand changes coupled with absence of alternative opportunity that causes a shift in the terms of trade against less developed countries. We shall have more to say about this in the next chapter. At present we are confined to two conclusions. One is that the terms of trade are a matter of opinion depending on how one interprets the statistics but that there is a strong probability that they have turned against the less developed countries. The other is that there are many causes, including big units

[4] P. T. Ellsworth, "The Terms of Trade between Primary Producing and Industrial Countries," *Inter-American Economic Affairs*, Summer, 1956, pp. 47–65.

[5] Charles P. Kindleberger, *Economic Development*, McGraw-Hill Book Company, Inc., New York, 1958, p. 241. See also Charles P. Kindleberger, *The Terms of Trade*, The Technology Press of the Massachusetts Institute of Technology, Cambridge, Mass., and John Wiley & Sons, Inc., New York, 1956.

of production in the United States (discussed in this chapter) and shifts in relative demand (which will be treated in the next). It is impossible for anyone to judge definitively how the responsibility is to be allocated. It does seem to me, however, that North American economists should not discount the Latin American position as much as they have in the past.

If Prebisch's thesis has substance and if Latin Americans do suffer from the ill effects of concentrated enterprise in the United States, how is it that North American laborers and farmers, who might also be expected to suffer, are willing to tolerate such conditions? Why do they not threaten revolution? The answer is—*must be*—that virtually all North Americans share the benefits of big business. The economy of the United States is not dominated by any single group but by many whose bargaining with each other assures a relatively egalitarian distribution—at least to North Americans—of its product.

This thesis has been developed by Professor Galbraith, who dubs the system one of "countervailing power." The economy of the United States is indeed characterized by bigness, Galbraith contends, but one bloc tends to counteract another.[6] Amalgamated labor unions offset the power of large corporations, demanding that the fruits of technology be distributed more widely than to stockholders. Large retail chains confront large producers of electric appliances and other goods. Galbraith cites how the A. & P. (retail food chain) was able to bargain down the price of corn-flakes, because it was a powerful buyer. But the seller also had to be powerful in order to have the margin by which to be bargained down.

Countervailing power did not just happen, Galbraith contends. He writes: [7]

> The fact that a seller enjoys a measure of monopoly power means that there is an inducement to those firms from whom he buys or those to whom he sells to develop the power with which they can defend themselves against exploitation. It means that there is a reward to them, in the form of a share of the gains of their opponents' market power, if they are able to do so. In this way the existence of market power creates an incentive to the organization of another position of power that neutralizes it.

The differing views of Latin American and North American students on big business stem in large part from their different vantage points with respect to countervailing power. Virtually all North Americans participate in one or more economic blocs that will protect their interests. They belong to labor unions, many of them own shares of stock, and

[6] J. Kenneth Galbraith, *American Capitalism*, rev. ed., Houghton Mifflin Company, Boston, 1956, especially chap. 9.

[7] *Ibid.*, pp. 111–112.

some (like farmers) depend on political pressures. Even consumers benefit from the power of retailers, who do compete among each other but who are nevertheless large enough to bargain down the prices of suppliers.

But woe unto those few who are outside the power blocs! Latin Americans consider themselves outside, and this feeling largely explains their eagerness to form blocs of their own, as through commodity agreements, the Latin American Free Trade Area, and the Central American Common Market.

The Latin American position should not be stated quite so forcefully, however. Latin American consumers of United States manufactures also benefit from the efforts of organized retailers in the United States to keep prices down. Probably the greatest anomaly in Latin American opposition to big business is that it appears to have two poles. On the one hand, one hears that the power combines unite to keep their prices high for Latin American buyers. On the other hand, it is also argued that the low costs (and, of course, low prices) of large, integrated corporations in the United States make it difficult for incipient Latin American firms to compete against them without protection (a question to be developed in Chapter 8). One can hardly help being struck by a certain inconsistency between the two attacks.

THE ECONOMIC POWER OF CONCENTRATED ENTERPRISE

If power blocs survive in the United States only because North Americans are able to counteract their disadvantages, then they are a negative blessing. Why tolerate them at all? Cannot perfect competition be restored by a breakup of large enterprise and a return to the world of Adam Smith? We are led to the question of whether bigness in business historically contributes to, or subtracts from, the real income of all other groups (including labor, farmers, consumers, and foreigners) taken as a whole.

Whenever I have put this question to Latin American students, the answer has invariably been that monopoly leads to reduction of output, higher profits, and a concentration of wealth among the monopolists. If a society were to change overnight from being competitive to being monopolistic (they argue), the result would be a shift in real income away from all other groups and in favor of owners of enterprise.

Much static economic theory is on the side of this answer. These students cite the sloping demand curves of Marshall and Chamberlin, the intersection of marginal cost with marginal revenue to the left of the lowest point on the average cost curve, and all the other trappings that indicate that, *other things being equal and considering today's economics alone*, monopolies will tend to restrict output as compared to competitive business.

The same students have not been persuaded by the following paragraph by Schumpeter, which Samuelson considers important enough to quote in his text on fundamentals of economics (a Spanish translation of which is used in Latin America): [8]

> The modern standard of life of the masses evolved during the period of relatively unfettered "big business." If we list the items that enter the modern workman's budget and from 1899 on observe the course of their prices not in terms of money but in terms of the hours of labor that will buy them—i.e., each year's money prices divided by each year's hourly wage rates, we cannot fail to be struck by the rate of advance which, considering the spectacular improvement in qualities, seems to have been greater and not smaller than it ever was before. . . . Nor is this all. As soon as we go into details and inquire into the individual items in which progress was most conspicuous, the trail leads not to the doors of those firms that work under conditions of comparatively free competition but precisely to the doors of the large concerns—which, as in the case of agricultural machinery, also account for much of the progress in the competitive sector—and a shocking suspicion dawns upon us that big business may have had more to do with creating that standard of life than keeping it down.

North Americans tend to look upon large enterprises *not* primarily as companies that keep prices high (although some may do this) but as those that lower costs, raise wages, improve quality, and provide a high standard of living. The Du Pont Company has vast laboratories constantly experimenting on new products and ways of producing old ones with increased efficiency. Likewise, Sears, Roebuck has been an innovator in giant retailing, introducing greater efficiency in handling materials and so bringing them to the customer at lower cost.

Many enterprises have become large to take advantage of economies of scale. Often they consider themselves forced by competition to do so. For example, companies A, B, and C may be competing for the same market. Suppose company A, by dint of better management or greater efficiency in producing and selling, grows more rapidly than B or C. A then finds it can produce at lower unit costs because of its large size. Companies B and C observe this, so they merge to obtain the same advantage for themselves. There remain two larger corporations instead of three smaller ones. But efficiency has been enhanced and wages probably increased. Prices may well be lower, or at least not any higher.

[8] J. A. Schumpeter, *Capitalism, Socialism, and Democracy*, Harper & Row, Publishers, Incorporated, New York, 1942, cited in Paul A. Samuelson, *Economics*, 5th ed., McGraw-Hill Book Company, Inc., New York, 1961, p. 97.

An editorial in *The Washington Post* commented on such mergers as follows: [9]

> The tendency of the giants to grow through merger and acquisition has not precluded the establishment of a large number of small and very profitable firms in the chemical, electronics and specialized service industries. But once established they too grow large, frequently by the merger route, *because greater size permits them to survive in a fiercely competitive world* where access to financial resources, production economies and ability to innovate are essential.

From the foregoing it should be clear that labor, consumer, and investor all feel they share in the fruits of economic progress in the United States. But these are not the only economic groups. What about purveyors of services, such as retailers, servants, and professional people (doctors, lawyers, accountants, and the like)? What about farmers?

Purveyors of services are clearly beneficiaries of increased productivity. Fees charged by professional men tend to rise along with the wages of labor and profits of business. As labor becomes more expensive in industry, more also must be paid for services. If it were not, those who perform them would move to better opportunities. Fifty years ago the more affluent households in the United States had one or more servants, much as in Latin America today. Now servants have virtually disappeared, for two interrelated reasons. One is that they can earn such high wages in industry that middle-class households can no longer afford to pay for a maid or a cook. The other is that households are becoming mechanized, with automatic washing machines, dryers, dishwashers, and vacuum cleaners. Surely this is an indication that the fruits of progress are shared more evenly than before.

Farmers also are the gainers, but whether they would be in the absence of government assistance is another question. We have already mentioned (in Chapter 3) the amazing technological progress on farms in the United States, which has both reduced costs and increased output. Other sectors of the North American economy have not been able to absorb the vast quantity of foodstuffs that agriculture can grow, and without government assistance farmers would have faced disastrous losses. But they *have* received help from Washington through price supports, credits, and government purchases of their output. Income of all farmers has been falling within the last decade, but (because the number of farmers has diminished) per capita income has been rising, although not by the same percentage as industrial wages.

Just as many sectors share in the diffusion of income, so also is the distribution of wealth becoming more egalitarian. While the percentage

[9] Editorial in *The Washington Post*, Nov. 13, 1962. (Italics added.)

of millionaires is not much changed since the turn of the century, nevertheless the remainder of the population has increased in wealth and, with it, relative political and economic power. Despite mergers and the growth of giants, the number of small firms is actually increasing. There were 3 million business enterprises in the United States in 1929, and now there are close to 5 million, or one for every eleven families.[10]

As incomes rise and inheritance taxes make it harder to pass on wealth, the big businesses have become more and more popularly owned. Only 14 per cent of households held stock in 1960, but the trend is upward. In 1959, for example, there were 12,490,000 shareholders, compared to only 6,490,000 in 1952.[11] The United Fruit Company has 72,860 different owners.[12] Furthermore, many North American workers own stock indirectly, through pension funds and mutual insurance companies. In commenting on this, a Marxist student in Latin America wrote that perhaps ". . . there will come a time when all Americans hold shares in the same quantity, and thus they will all be converted into capitalists. Does it not seem that if this happened, all capital would theoretically be socialized, and the capitalism of today would disappear?"

These various forces lead North Americans to conclude that bigness in business promotes technological progress, efficiency, and economic growth in general, and that furthermore the people as a whole share in the benefits. But of what significance is this to Latin Americans? I have already agreed that Latin Americans (for whom this book is intended) do not share these bounties equally with North Americans. What is it to them that increased incomes in the United States are diffused and not concentrated in a few owners of industry?

It makes this difference: that many Latin American students are convinced that Wall Street capitalists dominate the government in Washington. Whether or not this is so depends partly on their relative economic power. It is to this question that we now turn.

THE POLITICAL POWER OF CONCENTRATED ENTERPRISE

"Do you know anyone in my country?" the Ecuadorian gentleman to whom I had just been introduced asked in friendly fashion.

"Yes, I do," I replied, "I have some good friends in Ecuador."

[10] In 1961 there were 4,717,000 businesses and 53,021 million families. In 1929 the number of businesses was 3,029,000, which dropped to 2,782,100 in 1933 (the midst of the Depression) but has been increasing steadily since. *Statistical Abstract of the United States*, U.S. Department of Commerce, 1961, pp. 37 and 480.

[11] *Ibid.*, pp. 465–466.

[12] Stacy May and Galo Plaza, *The United Fruit Company in Latin America*, National Planning Association, Washington, D.C., 1958, p. 115.

"Who are they?" he asked. "I probably know them, because I know everyone in Ecuador."

Although I knew right away what he meant, nevertheless the thought flashed in my mind that, if taken literally, here was a gentleman who knew every *huasipunguero* in every hacienda and every Indian in every small village throughout the coastal, mountain, and jungle regions of his country. Of course, he meant he knew all the people that counted, and Indians don't count.

Political power in Latin America has long been concentrated among those who count—not only the landowners, but a few businessmen often characterized as monopolists. A major reason for this concentration is the lack of widespread markets, not so much in geographic size (for Brazil and Argentina cover vast areas), but in people with sufficient incomes to buy. There may be room for only one firm in a field, so it becomes a monopoly.

It has not been difficult for landowning-business interests to enrich themselves through political power in Latin America. A license granting exclusive control over this trade channel or that, a special permit to import supplies, a word of caution to a potential competitor or failure to maintain the road to his place of business, a "gentlemen's" agreement to stay out of my market while I stay out of yours—all and many more are ways to assure monopoly control. They are easy where the economy is small and power is concentrated in a few.

It is understandable that Latin American students, observing the statistical size of corporations in the United States, impute the same conditions there. These impressions are often confirmed by observation of North American businessmen in Latin America, who have sometimes demonstrated amazing flexibility in adapting to local customs and aligning themselves with the proper people. But in the United States itself, the wide diffusion of economic power tempers the influence of those very groups which in a Latin American context might be all-powerful.

The banking system—an illustration

José Luis Ceceña, whose article is quoted at the beginning of this chapter, falls into this very pitfall. In this same article, he comments as follows on the concentration of banking resources in the United States:

> The bulk of these enormous resources and deposits, however, is managed by a small group of large banks, that play a decisive role in the control of the financial resources of the nation. Thus the twenty-five largest banks, all with resources greater than a billion dollars, together manage \$81 billion, or 33% of total deposits. These twenty-five largest banks earn profits of \$702 million, or 56% of the total profits of banks. That is

to say that only twenty-five banks, or 0.4% of the total, manage one-third of the bank resources of the country and earn half the profits.

With Latin America behind him, Receña was looking into a mirror at what he thought was the United States. If in a given Latin American country a small percentage of the people own a large percentage of the land, or a few businessmen conduct most of the nation's commerce, in them lies the fount of political and economic power. In the United States, however, the fact that a small number of banks show a large percentage of total deposits means nothing of the sort. Deposits are liabilities of banks. People who deposit in them are in no way obligated.

If a bank is large in Latin America, it is probably not because of the services it performs. It may be associated with a wealthy family or some small group with political power. The market for banking services is so small that there is no need for many banks, and this fact also limits the size of competitors.

In the United States, however, the large size of a few banks results from the services demanded of them. They are located in New York, Chicago, and Los Angeles, metropolises whose business requires integrated banking services. They maintain telegraph connections all over the country and with foreign nations; they transfer money anywhere in the world within minutes; they have economics departments capable of assessing business conditions everywhere; they keep abreast of developments in many industries, publish reports for their clients, and perform myriad other services. Banks cannot do what these banks do without being big.

Banks in the United States used to be associated with the names of businesses and wealthy families, but not so now. Like other corporations, they are owned by large numbers of stockholders. Profits which seem large in the aggregate become far less so when distributed widely among shareholders. Furthermore, the large banks are supervised by the Board of Governors of the Federal Reserve System, which sets standards for lending, regularly examines their accounting records, and controls the nation's monetary policy.

Receña's article would come as a surprise to North Americans acquainted with the tradition of small banking in our country. (This may seem odd, after the statistics cited above.) In the nineteenth century, we had a pathological fear of powerful banking interests, for those were the days when banks and businesses did go into partnership and did wield the inordinate power that Receña believes they still have today. To thwart the concentration of financial interests, 32 out of 50 states passed "anti-branch" laws, prohibiting banks from expanding outside the narrow geographic area of their home offices, often in a village or a town. There are now 13,482 banks in the United States,[13] most of them small, independent establishments in rural areas. Had it not been for the antibranch laws, the pattern instead would have been one of city banks with branches in towns and villages, like the systems in other countries. Curiously enough, we would have had fewer but larger banks, and Ceceña could not have pointed to such a high percentage of concentration of deposits!

What Ceceña apparently does not know (or surely he would have added it to his misinterpretations) is that the independent country banks maintain deposits in the big city ones, and call on them to transfer money and perform other services that they themselves are not large enough to do. It is like a telephone system. Telephones are no good unless they are connected with each other. Neither are banks.

Economic and political power—a generalization

Let me venture that as a general rule, applicable in any country and at any time, economic power and political power tend to go hand in hand. The argument of the preceding chapter is a case in point. When for reasons there outlined Porfirio Diaz's economic moorings (the landowners) were cut in Mexico, the way was paved for a shift in political power. The same is occurring throughout Latin America now, as urban industrial progress creates new alignments of economic power. Their interests are antithetical to the haciendas, and the tide of political revolution swells stronger.

The correlation of economic and political power is not one of unique cause and effect. Sometimes the economic shift occurs first, sometimes the political, and sometimes they are intertwined. Once Diaz had fallen, it was Madero, Carranza, Obregón, Calles, Cárdenas, and others—leading with political power—who created an economic transformation in Mexico.

Pluralistic polity in the United States

So also have economic and political movements occurred in the United States. The growing shortage of labor brought greater economic power to unions. Corporations were forced to divide their gains as the price of labor and other inputs increased in rough proportion to their profits. This and other currents leading to a more equal distribution of income had their political repercussions, for they created a Congress that was disposed (beginning in 1913) to assess an income tax on individuals and corporations, according to their ability to pay. Corporate taxes are now 52 per cent of income, in addition to various property and excise taxes. The remaining 48 per cent is taxed again as personal income when distributed to stockholders. High inheritance taxes make it difficult for the wealthy

[13] Number of commercial banks on June 30, 1963.

to leave their assets to their sons. The people of the United States pay 80 per cent of the government's revenue in the form of direct taxes (i.e., based primarily on income), which is a higher percentage than in any Latin American country and compares to 42 per cent in Colombia, 35 per cent in Mexico, 34 per cent in Brazil, 32 per cent in Chile, 23 per cent in Argentina and Peru, and 7 per cent in Guatemala.[14] *The willingness to tax oneself in accordance with one's ability to pay testifies to an egalitarian distribution of economic and political power such as is unknown in Latin America today.*

The distribution of economic and political power is not, however, a linear function of income. As the United States has grown more affluent, higher incomes have enjoyed diminishing marginal economic power. Ahead of their counterparts in less developed countries, lower-income groups have become educated in ways to defend their economic interests through collective organizations and other legislative and judicial procedures. Many have argued (and shown statistically) that distributions of income and wealth have not changed greatly, percentagewise, since before World War I. *But the whole scale has moved upward,* and with it the power of wealthy people over political processes has been diluted. Many Latin Americans, seeing a similarity between their own countries today and the United States at the turn of the century, fail to appreciate the new realities of their northern neighbor.

We are led back to the quotation by a Latin American student cited in Chapter 3, but this time we put a different part of it in italics: "The government of the United States has been directed, and continues to be directed, *by men who possess colossal fortunes,* who are owners of large, landed properties, *and stockholders in the large corporations.* Never would they act against their own interests." Yet despite the existence of wealthy people, the wide diffusion of economic resources in the United States has created a far broader base for political power than exists in any Latin American country.

Latin American students have frequently reminded me that the President of the United States is a millionaire. This is so. We have had other presidents who have been less affluent, but we happen to have a millionaire now. However, a millionaire President in the United States is quite a different thing from one in Latin America. Upon his election, one of Mr. Kennedy's first moves was to sell all his stock in business corporations and invest solely in fixed-interest government bonds, so that he could not benefit personally from his behavior as President. In addition, he is giving

[14] Data for 1959. From U Tun Wai, "Taxation Problems and Policies of Underdeveloped Countries," *Staff Papers,* International Monetary Fund, November, 1962, p. 431. At the time of writing, there is a bill before Congress to reduce United States income taxes, but only by a few percentage points.

his entire salary to charity. Obviously, Latin American students will consider these moves "insufficient," because they know that (in their countries) there are other ways of gaining from political office. I submit, however, that those ways are rare in the United States, and when they do occur, they are the subject of thorough investigation, public scandal, and prison sentences.

To understand a presidential election in the United States, one must have a feeling for the pull and swing of political forces. We have already rejected the idea that a small group of Wall Street capitalists dominates Washington. We must further point out that political groups—such as business, labor, and farmers—are by no means homogeneous. Their divisions are something that Latin Americans, whose countries are smaller economically, do not readily comprehend.

One example is the current political struggle between hundreds of small, independent oil companies whose operations are solely domestic and the fewer, larger producers with international interests. The independents are pressuring Washington to limit imports from Venezuela and the Middle East, while the international companies naturally oppose restrictions. (It might be of interest to note that the small independents have so far succeeded in thwarting the large international companies.) Likewise, when quota limitations were introduced on lead and zinc imports in 1958, many Mexicans and Peruvians, whose interests were damaged, blamed "Wall Street capitalists." In fact, the restriction was brought about by pressure from both labor unions and producers of lead and zinc, as well as the suppliers of these groups. It occurred in spite of vigorous opposition by United States industries using lead and zinc, which would by far have preferred a free choice to buy in any market.

In a large economy such as the United States, there is far less solidarity among businessmen than in Latin America. Suppliers and users come in conflict, and what appears to Latin Americans as a decision by homogeneous, lovey-dovey "Wall Street capitalists" is more often the result of pulling and hauling among various industries and labor.

Nor should labor be considered a unit. As has been hinted in earlier parts of this chapter, individual unions frequently find their bread to be buttered on the same side as their industry's (e.g., import restrictions on lead and zinc were as good for the laborers as they were for the capitalists). The result is that labor embodies the same kinds of conflicts that one finds among industrialists.

The same applies to agriculture. Farmers consume each other's products. Those whose crops are not price-supported by Washington, but who consume some that are, naturally oppose the protection that outsiders often think is cherished by all farmers.

In the 1960 election, far more businessmen (the group allegedly favored by the millionaire President) voted against than for him. His strongest support (although far from unanimous) was from labor. Surprisingly enough the farmers were less enthusiastic for Mr. Kennedy than they were for his "business-favored" rival.

In defending the position that capitalists dominate the government of the United States, Latin American students often cite wartime price controls as a means of exploiting producers of raw materials. A Bolivian student wrote the following about tin:

> In August, 1950, the Korean conflict caused the price to go up to $1.05 per pound; in November, to $1.40; in March, 1951, to $1.75; and later as high as $1.83. Naturally, this trend was not convenient for the interests of the American government, which thereupon began to monopolize the trade. Automatically there followed a decrease in price to $1.34 in March, 1951, and later to $1.03. It is in ways like this that the United States fixes the prices of our raw materials at the lowest levels possible.

Whatever one's feelings about war, however "imperialistic" Marxist students believe it is, however idealistic are the vows of those who want to overcome the "evil" of the enemy, there is one point on which we should all agree: in so far as it is humanly possible, *nobody*—whether producer of raw material or producer of munitions—should be allowed to gain from war. Marxist students have long proclaimed that wars are fought for the profits of capitalists. I do not deny that profits have been made. But the Marxist students that I have encountered have not generally known that rigid price controls were enforced in the United States to minimize, to the best extent that we were able, the wartime gains of *everyone*—capitalist, laborer, professional man, farmer, miner, and what have you. The same Marxists have complained that United States price controls have prevented Latin American countries from sharing what they believed to be the "loot" of war. Granted that Bolivia is a poor country and deserving of assistance; granted that economic development would be spurred if the price of tin were higher; but let not high price be the fruit of war!

The four super-blocks—another misinterpretation

It is with no malice toward Sr. Ceceña that I again single out his work for attack. Rather, it is because his article so admirably sums up a series of miscomprehensions about the United States that I have found particularly rampant, not only among Latin American students, but among professional economists and businessmen as well.

In the same article quoted earlier, Ceceña argues that four super-blocs of banks in the United States (Morgan Guaranty, First National City Bank, Du Pont Chemical Bank, and Chase Rockefeller interests) dominate the fifty largest enterprises through control or participation. The domination (one learns from inference, for Ceceña is not articulate on this point) is based on loans, stockholdings, and interlocking directorates.

In a small economy such as Mexico, or the United States seventy years ago, such interconnected financial interests and community of directorship would clearly signal a concentration of control. But this concentration is dependent on two characteristics of the small economy. In the first place, enterprises must rely on banks and similar institutions for a large part of their financing. In the second place, bigness in industry must not be offset by countervailing power. In other words, the cooperating bankers and industrialists must be united by a thoroughgoing community of interests, and not simply a desire to maintain efficient banking services.

In the United States, the firms that Neceña characterized as "dominated" by banks have in fact other sources of financing that far outshadow bank loans and investments. Between two-thirds and three-quarters of gross private domestic investment in the United States is regularly financed through business saving (reinvested earnings and depreciation allowances). Large amounts are also financed through corporate stock issues subscribed to by the general public. Dependence on bank financing is reduced to a minimum, consisting principally of loans for working capital. In less developed countries, by contrast, banks and related institutions (such as the *financieras* in Mexico) play a far greater role in financing new and growing enterprises.

Interlocking directorships provide analogous opportunity for misinterpretation. If two industrialists appear on the board of a private bank in a less developed country, it is natural to impute a close community of interest between them. In the United States, however, their first community of interest may be their reliance on banking services and banking knowledge (for transfers of funds, research in financial matters, and a multitude of other activities besides loans). In fact, their mutual interests may lie *solely* in maintaining these services. Beyond that, they may be bitter business competitors, or at least on opposite sides in the system of countervailing power.

Once again Ceceña has mirrored Mexico in his interpretation of the United States. When I assigned his article to my graduate students in the United States, they were quick to realize that factually he was probably right. They concluded generally, however, that his sinister interpretations were out of context with the realities of the North American economic and political scene.

THE ANTITRUST LAWS

The North American people do not put all their faith in countervailing power. Indeed, the economy of the United States was not always large enough to accommodate harmoniously all the groupings that now offset each other. In an earlier age, as the first of these blocs was forming, monopolies became a burning political issue. The general decline in prices, intensity of competition, and growing use of the corporation as a form of business organization led to more and more combinations and "gentlemen's agreements" among businesses after the Civil War (1865). Railroads that had earlier cut each other's throats agreed to pool their business, keep rates up, and divide their profits. There arose the Vanderbilt group, the Morgan group, the Harriman group, the Gould group, and others. Petroleum and railroads joined forces under the aegis of John D. Rockefeller, and a Scottish immigrant named Andrew Carnegie came to dominate the steel industry.

Protests against monopolies began to appear in newspapers, in meetings of farmers and labor, and in political conversations throughout the country. A cartoon from one of the newspapers of the day showed an ugly, fat man, his eyes full of greed, called "King Monopoly," holding a sack of dollars in one hand and stretching the other out to a line of ragged people, bending under their burdens, and carrying sacks labeled "Tribute from the laborer," "Tribute from the mechanic," "Tribute from the farmer," and many more.

Two historic pieces of legislation toward the end of the nineteenth century marked a new chapter in the history of North American business. The first (1887) was the Act to Regulate Interstate Commerce, in which Congress established a commission with power to approve or disapprove rate schedules proposed by the railroads. It may also approve or disapprove railroad mergers. The second (1890) was the Sherman Antitrust Law, which permitted the United States government to divide monopolies into smaller competitive enterprises or otherwise to rule so as to preserve competition in industry.

This is not the place to analyze the antitrust laws in detail. Latin American students who proclaim themselves the undying foes of North American monopolies do have an obligation to their profession to understand these laws, and I refer them to the many history books of the United States, or else to a report of the attorney general summarizing the interpretation and application of these laws.[15]

Briefly, the Sherman law (and supplementary legislation) declares that all combinations and conspiracies in restraint of trade (i.e., monopolies) are illegal, and that the United States government is empowered to proceed against them in the courts, if necessary ordering them to be dissolved and divided into smaller units. From 1890 to the present day over 1,700 cases have been instituted against monopolies, the most famous of which divided Rockefeller's Standard Oil Company into several competing entities in 1911.

I have discussed the antitrust laws with many monopoly-hating Latin

[15] Report of the Attorney General's National Committee to Study the Antitrust Laws, Mar. 31, 1955.

American students (most of whom were hearing of them for the first time). Their immediate reaction was universal disbelief. It was not that they doubted I was telling the truth, but they could not accept that any such legislation, no matter how well conceived or how well adjudicated, could succeed in the herculean task it had set for itself. Naturally, they cited the continued existence of "monopolies" as proof of its failure.

One of them wrote:

> Before hearing your lectures I was convinced that the United States was the seat and center of the great monopolies. You have given the lie to this with some compelling reasons. Even so, I think that large monopolies exist in the United States. If there are laws against these enterprises, there are ways of mocking them despite the sanctions imposed by the government. Even if small companies exist in the statistics, we must bear in mind that most of them are controlled by a small group of persons through a series of contracts known as cartels, trusts, and holding companies. These organizations ostensibly satisfy the conditions of the Sherman Act, but actually they get around it.

The great dilemma of the antitrust laws—which has been much discussed in the United States—is that their purpose is to control monopoly without returning to the days of Adam Smith. We have already recognized that there are advantages of scale. It is not the purpose of the laws to destroy efficiency, to create myriad small companies operating at higher unit cost than one large one. Still, efficiency and abusable power sometimes come in the same package.

The courts have taken account of this dilemma. They distinguish between monopolies resulting solely from policies designed to suppress competition and those arising from economies of scale, ability, research, and similar efficiency-making factors. In *United States v. United Shoe Machinery Corporation,* the judge declared as follows: [16]

> The defendant may escape statutory liability if it bears the burden of proving that it owes its monopoly solely to superior skill, superior products, natural advantages (including accessibility to raw materials or markets), economic or technological efficiency (including scientific research), low margins of profit maintained permanently and without discrimination, or licenses conferred by, and used within, the limits of law (including patents on one's own inventions, or franchises granted directly to the enterprise by a public authority).

The decision in this case, however, was against the company, as explained in the following quotation: [17]

[16] 110 F. Supp. 295, 342 (D. Mass. 1953), aff'd *per curiam* 347 U.S. 521 (1954). Cited in Report of the Attorney General's National Committee to Study the Antitrust Laws, Mar. 31, 1955, p. 57.

[17] *Ibid.*, p. 28.

> [The practices of the company] represent more than the use of accessible resources, the process of invention and innovation, and the employment of those techniques of employment, financing, production, and distribution, which a competitive society must foster. They are contracts, arrangements, and policies which, instead of encouraging competition based on pure merit, further the dominance of a particular firm. In this sense, they are unnatural barriers, they unnecessarily exclude actual and potential competition; they restrict a free market.

Human discretion is required to distinguish between "efficient large enterprises" and "perverse monopoly." Once apprised that the laws are not applied with automatic severity, but depend on the judgment of individuals, the Latin American students that I have taught have immediately concluded that herein lies the escape. All you need to do is to persuade the authorities that you have a "pretty" monopoly and not an "ugly" one.

"I should now like to express a few words over the anti-monopoly laws," one of them wrote, "particularly the part that justifies the employment of large amounts of capital where needed to maintain high productivity. This escape clause has in fact legalized monopoly."

Whether or not the exemption for efficiency is indeed an escape clause depends on the integrity of the competent authorities and judges, and whether one accepts that efficient enterprise is to be promoted as a matter of national policy (with reliance on other checks and balances). Many "unjustified" monopolies have in fact been demolished by the laws. A case of interest to Latin Americans is that of the United Fruit Company —already decided and in process of implementation—to which we now turn.

THE UNITED FRUIT COMPANY CASE

The antitrust laws of the United States are not designed to protect foreigners. Their jurisdiction over United States nationals abroad is limited to policing illegal activities whose effects are felt *within the United States.* If a business owned by United States nationals is incorporated in Latin America and transacts business solely within Latin America, it is beyond the laws of the United States.

Even if a United States-owned business does sell goods to the United States, the antitrust laws affect it only in so far as those imports (their prices and marketing policies) are directly concerned. The court's limited jurisdiction abroad was first ruled on in *American Banana Company v. United Fruit Company* [18] in 1909. In this case the plaintiff, which was competing with United, charged that the latter had conspired with the

[18] 213 U.S. 347. See also Report of the Attorney General's National Committee to Study the Antitrust Laws, Mar. 31, 1955, pp. 66–67.

Costa Rican government to seize its properties, including its plantation, supplies, and railroad to the coast. The United States Supreme Court ruled that actions by the government of Costa Rica were within its rights as a sovereign power, and it was not up to the United States to interfere.

The United Fruit Company was treated more harshly in 1958, however, in a case instituted by the Attorney General of the United States. Here the United States government charged that: [19]

> For many years past and continuing up to and including the date of the filing of this complaint, United has agreed, contracted, combined and conspired with other persons, while it has been engaged in importing bananas from foreign nations in the American tropics into the United States, with the intention of restraining free competition in the above described trade and commerce among the several states and with foreign nations in bananas and increasing the market price in parts of the United States of said bananas. . . .

The U.S. Department of Justice charged that United Fruit's monopoly resulted from the size of its plantations (150,663 acres) compared to those of its only competitor of consequence (Standard Fruit and Steamship Corporation, with 17,455 acres) and from the fact that it owned, leased, or controlled 85 per cent of the land in the American tropics suitable for banana cultivation. It also charged that:

> Almost from its inception, United has exercised a policy of ownership or control of all or a major portion of the railroad facilities in the banana producing countries of Central and South America except Ecuador. As a consequence, other importers have been denied, or hampered in obtaining, access to these facilities and consequently to the market in the United States, and thus the operations of competing banana shippers in these areas have been greatly curtailed or eliminated.

The Justice Department further stated that in 1946 United Fruit owned or chartered 73 per cent of all banana-carrying ships and that from 1943 to 1946 it consistently imported more than 50 per cent (by stems) of all bananas brought into the United States. "In each of the seven principal banana-producing countries," the complaint continued, "namely, Honduras, Costa Rica, Panama, Guatemala, Colombia, Dominican Republic and Ecuador, United presently controls between 16% and 92% of all the banana business, and it is from these seven countries that United obtains over 99% of the bananas which it imports into the United States." Except for Standard Fruit Company (which operates principally in Honduras),

[19] Complaint in Civil Action 4560, filed July 6, 1954, in United States District Court, Eastern District of Louisiana, *United States v. United Fruit Company*, consent decree entered and reported 1958, CCH Trade Cases, par. 68,941, Feb. 4, 1958.

". . . all other importers derive almost all of their bananas from Ecuador, Haiti, Colombia, Mexico, Nicaragua, and Cuba."

In the final judgment (1958), the court ordered United Fruit to divest itself of all capital stock and any other proprietary interest in its railroad subsidiaries. In addition, it is required to organize and transfer to a new company all assets, including working capital, plantations, ships, and others, sufficient to import into the United States 9 million stems of bananas per year, and to release to this company such managerial and other personnel as are necessary to carry on that volume of business. The plan by which this transfer will be implemented must be submitted to the court by June 30, 1966, and must be carried out within four years of its final approval. The new company must be entirely separated from United Fruit, with no interlocking directorate and no common officers or employees.

What will be the impact of the decision on the banana-producing companies? Will the new company be truly competitive, or—because it will be staffed by personnel whose experience and former loyalty are with United Fruit—will it *act* as just another branch of the old company? Quite apart from this relationship, will an oligopoly of three companies be any more competitive than an oligopoly of two? Only the future can answer these questions, but a few observations can now be made.

If the judgment is successful in restoring competition, the effect can only be to lower the price of bananas in the United States. Profits of all producing companies will probably be reduced, and the basis on which Central American countries can collect taxes correspondingly contracted. Offsetting this disadvantage to Central America would be a strengthening of the governments' control over their national territories by the weakening of a monopoly.

In a similar case—the division of the Standard Oil Company in 1911—historians have pointed out that several years elapsed before loyalties to the old company were attenuated but that ultimately the several new companies were competing fiercely with each other.

UNITED STATES DIRECT INVESTMENT[20] IN LATIN AMERICA

In 1959, the direct investment of United States enterprises in Latin America amounted to $8,218 million, of which $2,808 million (primarily petroleum) was in Venezuela, $955 million in Cuba, $839 million in Brazil, $759 million in Mexico, $729 million in Chile, and $427 million in Peru.

[20] Direct investment consists of that in which the owner exercises control, as in parent-subsidiary and home-office–branch relationships. It is distinguished from portfolio investment, which consists of securities purchased for all other reasons (e.g., government bonds, loans, and minority interests in stocks).

In each other country, United States direct investments were less than $400 million.[21]

The very existence of this investment has long been a bone of contention. North Americans are fond of pointing out that their companies not only supply needed capital but also provide technology, skills, high-level organization and management, and training. They bring business to local suppliers, pay taxes, and replenish the nation's foreign exchange. While agreeing that these benefits are desirable, Latin Americans have frequently decried the personnel practices of these companies (e.g., where they have not paid the same salaries for similar work by Latin Americans and North Americans). The charges that these enterprises have dominated governments and bribed their way into economic favors have been aired in earlier chapters.

In the last decade or so, Latin American governments have been seriously reappraising the role of foreign enterprise. There has been no sudden shift of direction but an intensification of the belief that these companies should owe their primary allegiance to Latin America. Particularly in export industries (such as bananas in Central America, petroleum in Venezuela, and copper in Chile) they are expected to cease acting like foreign enclaves and identify themselves with the nation.

One way of accomplishing this is to increase their financial contribution to the government (as taxes) and to local labor (as wages). The high rates of taxes paid by oil companies in Venezuela and copper companies in Chile have already been cited. In Venezuela more than Chile, these monies have been put to work financing a wide scope of development projects. Union pressure has also forced wages up, besides bringing about an increase in social services. More liberal personnel policies are being adopted, with greater opportunities and equal pay for Latin American employees. Not all companies are equally enlightened in these policies, but the trend is established.

Additional monetary contributions, however, are not enough. Nor is it felt that the transfer of technology and skill can sufficiently be gained from the experience of nationals working in foreign enterprises. Several governments have concluded that the controlling interests in the companies themselves must be owned by nationals.

In 1961 the Creole Petroleum Company (Venezuelan subsidiary of Standard Oil of New Jersey) established the Creole Investment Corporation, with $10 million of capital, whose purpose is to buy *minority* interests in *new,* non-oil-related enterprises. The hope is to stimulate domestic entrepreneurs, with majority ownership, to start companies that would take advantage of management skills and efficient business methods pro-

[21] *U.S. Business Investments in Foreign Countries,* U.S. Department of Commerce, 1960, p. 90.

vided by Creole. Acceptable projects must be expected to increase Venezuelan gross national product and employment, must either save or create foreign exchange, and must be in activities basic to economic development —e.g., agriculture, dairy, cattle, and manufacturing, but not consumption goods or services. Some of the early investments have been in yucca, cotton yarn, and fiberboard.

The Creole Investment Corporation responds to current trends of Venezuelan nationalism. Some may accuse Creole of contributing $10 million solely in the hope of cutting its losses, i.e., to avoid nationalization of other properties of greater concern. Even the most casual observer must recognize that Creole did not invest in yucca, cotton, and fiberboard primarily for their financial profitability (although this was a requirement) but to improve its image before the Venezuelan people. Nevertheless, there is a contribution to economic development, with majority interest owned by Venezuelans.

The campaign for "Mexicanization" of industry is a longer step toward national control. Mexico now requires 51 per cent ownership by its own nationals of all investment in certain activities, such as automobiles, air and sea transportation, aerial photography, broadcasting, television, reforestation, colonization of national lands, and several others. When the law was first passed, Mexicans hailed it as an act of liberation, while many foreigners warned of a decrease in the inflow of investment.

The latter prediction has not proved correct. Although direct investment declined in 1960 (as Mexico was in cyclic recession), it continued its upward trend thereafter. Foreign investors are coming to discover an advantage in joint ownership. Mexican businessmen are well trained in the principles of scientific management and are acquainted with local markets, laws, labor conditions, and the psychology of the Mexican people in a way that can be of great advantage to any enterprise operating there.

Latin American countries are showing themselves more and more receptive to investment from the United States *provided it enters on their terms* and submits to the jurisdiction of local laws. They further distinguish by quality. Investment is more welcome if it contributes to diversification of local manufacture and the growth of ancillary domestic activity than if it simply exploits raw materials for export.

Sears, Roebuck is a case in point. When Sears opened its store in Mexico in 1947, virtually all its merchandise was imported from the United States. Six years later, in 1953, it bought 80 per cent of its goods from 1,295 Mexican suppliers.[22] In all countries where Sears has operated, it has not only put new suppliers into business but has encouraged them to develop

[22] Richardson Wood and Virginia Keyser, *Sears, Roebuck de Mexico,* S.A., National Planning Association, Washington, D.C., 1953, p. 1.

the exacting standards and quality improvements that were necessary so that it could substitute their product for imports.[23]

One often hears in Latin America the charge that foreign investment no longer contributes foreign exchange to the national economies, and that it may even have become a drain. Especially has this been so, many believe, in the late fifties and early sixties when the inflow of investment has shown some tendency to decline. As years go on and investment builds up, the interest and dividends it pays to foreign owners also increase, and finally (in some countries) one balances the other. In Mexico in 1961, for example, the net inflow of long-term capital was $252 million, but (some would argue) more than half of this was offset by the payment of interest and dividends of $139 million.[24]

Those who argue in this way, however, do not comprehend the full impact of foreign investment on the balance of payments. They are aware only of the credits for capital inflow and debits for interest and dividends. But a third item is the merchandise account itself, exports and imports. The goods and services produced by foreign investment (even extractive investment) either contribute to the nation's exports or substitute for its imports. Much import substitution has occurred in Mexico owing to foreign investment in automobiles, refrigerators, television sets, and other items of consumer goods. Had it not been for this investment, either Mexican incomes would have been insufficient to buy these goods at all, or else the goods would have been largely imported, with a consequent drain on foreign exchange. Those who argue that foreign investment worsens the balance of payments are (one suspects) seeking intellectual bulk to justify an aversion that is really based on deeper, more historic, foundations.

Three stages characterize the history of foreign investment in Latin America. The first—which most of us would like to forget, but cannot—is the era of personalism and government by power. Foreign investors could write their own tickets, provided they contributed adequately to the welfare of the local ruler.

In the second stage—of relatively recent origin—foreign corporations have been required to contribute financially to the nation's economic development. Taxes have been increased in countries such as Brazil, Venezuela, Mexico, and Chile. Union pressure brought higher wages. But these changes alone have not effectively integrated foreign corporations into the national economy. Their financial contributions to economic de-

[23] Case studies of Sears' suppliers in Peru are found in William R. Fritsch, *Progress and Profits*, Action Committee for International Development, Washington, D.C., 1962, pp. 45–54.

[24] Banco de México, *Informe Anual*, 1961, p. 69.

velopment have seemed to them like payments to the local ruler (except that the bite is more severe).

Only one or two countries have entered the third stage, that of identification with the aspirations of local economies. It is characterized by increased participation of Latin Americans in the ownership, management, and direction of corporations, by full equality in employment practices, and by increased willingness of foreigners to invest in those activities that promote national development.

The third stage cannot be legislated or enacted by decree. The responsibilities it imposes on North American investors have already been outlined, and there is evidence that—at least in Mexico—some of them are ready to comply. But there are also responsibilities for Latin Americans. One of these, which accounts in large part for the Mexican success, is political stability.

The correlation between political stability and foreign investment has an unfortunate history. In the past, it has been correctly interpreted as meaning than the current dictator should stay in power. But once the dictator is overthrown and progressive government established, not only foreign investment but economic development as well depend on stability. There will be little incentive for residents to save or foreigners to invest if the economic integrity of investment is not respected. New projects will not be undertaken if economic forecasts are likely to be upset by revolution.

Industries have been nationalized in Mexico, and this is right and proper. But the Mexicans have clearly delineated between the field of government enterprise (public utilities, transportation, infrastructure, and those activities of national importance where private initiative has been inadequate) and the area reserved for private capital. Within this distinction, and within clear-cut definitions of behavior and responsibility, private investors know they will be protected by the laws of Mexico.

FOCUS, OR BALANCE, OF POWER?

The danger of economic development lies in the power that accompanies it. Primitive societies have been stable for many years with uneven distributions of wealth and power. But the balance may be upset as new wealth is created through growth. A struggle is unleashed to control this wealth and the power it entails.

As the era of change in Latin America becomes more intense, thinking persons propose ways of offsetting power concentrations. It is inevitable that the former blocs—military leaders, landowners, and foreign investors—shall ultimately lose prestige, for it is against them that the wrath of the underprivileged is directed. They can never regain their role of a bygone age. If they are to command respect, they must adapt themselves to new ways, to new distributions of income, and to new dimensions of power.

It is widely accepted in Latin America that whatever set of checks and balances evolves from the economic progress of the sixties must lie somewhere on the continuum between extremes represented by the United States and the Soviet Union. It is also accepted that income must be much more evenly distributed than it has been in the past—both for social and moral reasons (because this is the way men should live) and for economic considerations (because development depends on mass markets).

A further reason, transcending the other two, is that an egalitarian distribution of income carries with it a similar distribution of power. This does not imply that all should share equally in the fruits of economic endeavor regardless of contribution. Nor does it mean that identical opportunities are a *sine qua non*. Rather, economic development demands the use of virtually all the talents that a nation can supply and the generation of more. Unless *reasonable* opportunities for material satisfaction, and freedom from undue domination, are available to *most* people, these talents will not be put to use.

In the United States, a distribution of income and power that Galbraith has termed "tolerable" and most North Americans consider desirable has grown out of many economic and political blocs that both cooperate with and tug against each other. This interplay of power has created the highest per capita income in the world and molded a society so satisfactory that many North Americans naïvely cannot understand why the rest of the world does not jump at the opportunity of imitating us.

For various reasons, Latin Americans have been largely omitted from the power blocs of the Western Hemisphere. Tariffs and import restrictions, relative immobility of capital, immigration laws, the small size of markets in Latin America, and sheer ignorance have been some of the barriers to a spread of technology, greater reception to Latin products in United States markets, and more enlightened investment policies. The Latin Americans themselves bear a large share of the blame. Governments that topple from year to year, that are subject to *coups d'état*, and whose policies are volatile hinder the growth of income and the fostering of countervailing power.

Differences in culture, tradition, habits, and ethnology will inevitably drive Latin Americans to seek a positioning of power groups that is unique. Whatever the reason for it, the very fact that their peoples cry loudly for nationalization of certain infrastructure, public utilities, and transportation will mean that the proper share of power allocable to government will be more than the proportion allotted in the United States.

There are, however, some in Latin America who are deluded into thinking that the government itself is not one of these power blocs. "Granted that the people must sacrifice to accumulate capital for economic development," one of my students once said to me, "but when this is done, should not the capital then belong *to the people?*"

Of course it should. But whether popular ownership is more closely approximated in a capitalist or socialist society is a question that is not sufficiently examined and whose answer is too often assumed. Just as socialism has grown from the fear of private power, so also has capitalism, at another stage of history, grown out of the fear of powerful government. The nature of man and his capacity to wield power and harm his neighbor are such that no solution that vests complete power in any one group, whether it be government, private enterprise, farmers, laborers, or any other, is a "final" solution, and we should not yield to the songs of the sirens who would lull us into thinking it is. The problem will be with us forever, and our hopes of controlling it lie in achieving and maintaining reasonable balance.

5 Primary Products

He who has no skills, no trade, and cannot read or write is a poor man. He lives by his "broad and sinewy hands" and his strong back. He splits rails, and society pays him verbal homage for his humble beginnings. When rail fences are supplanted by wire (which he cannot make), he digs ditches. When giant excavators can do his day's work in a few seconds, he polishes boots. When depression comes, people do not have their shoes shined, and even with prosperity they never wear more than one pair at a time. For years he alternates between the breadline and a meager livelihood, for —unlike other people—none of his occupations provides him with skills to cope with an ever more complex society. One day he wakes up to find that continuous charity alone will keep him alive.

THE ABOVE is not quoted from anywhere, but it is a widely held image of countries producing primary products. Minerals and raw foodstuffs are cherished, not for what they themselves are, but for the ever more wondrous products that men of genius can make of them.

Name a country in Latin America, and a primary product comes to mind. Venezuela is oil, Cuba is sugar, Brazil is coffee, Ecuador is bananas, Argentina is meat. Coffee is the major export of six countries, and one of the two top exports for ten—half of all in Latin America. More than 90 per cent of all Latin America's exports are primary products. Contrast this with the United States, where machinery and vehicles constitute over one-third of exports and where no one product dominates.

IMPORTANCE OF LEADING COMMODITIES IN THE EXPORT TRADE OF LATIN AMERICAN COUNTRIES

(*Percentages based on trade in 1958*)

Country	Leading commodities as per cent of total exports		Leading two commodities as per cent of total exports	
	Commodity	Per cent	Commodities	Per cent
Argentina	Meat	30	Meat, wheat	43
Bolivia	Tin	58	Tin, lead	67
Brazil	Coffee	55*	Coffee, cocoa	62
Chile	Copper	67	Copper, nitrates	77*
Colombia	Coffee	78	Coffee, petroleum	92
Costa Rica	Coffee	52	Coffee, bananas	85
Cuba	Sugar	83	Sugar, tobacco	90
Dominican Republic	Sugar	44	Sugar, cocoa	65
Ecuador	Bananas	56	Bananas, coffee	75
El Salvador	Coffee	73	Coffee, cotton	90*
Guatemala	Coffee	72	Coffee, bananas	85*
Haiti	Coffee	74	Coffee, sisal	87
Honduras	Bananas	56	Bananas, coffee	71
Mexico	Cotton	26	Cotton, coffee	36
Nicaragua	Cotton	39	Cotton, coffee	77
Panama	Bananas	68	Bananas, cacao	76†
Paraguay	Timber	29	Timber, cotton	40
Peru	Cotton‡	27	Cotton, sugar	39
Uruguay	Wool	58	Wool, wheat	70
Venezuela	Petroleum	91	Petroleum, iron ore	95

* Based on 1957 figures.
† 1955–57 average.
‡ Since 1958, copper has replaced cotton as Peru's principal export.
SOURCE: *United States–Latin American Relations*, 86th Cong., 2d Sess., S. Doc. 125, 1960, p. 93.

Not all agree that the level of income correlates positively with the degree of manufacturing, but examples of the countries in which it does not—such as Denmark and New Zealand—are scarce enough to be tolerated in the standard deviation. Those who do agree with the correlation argue cause and effect. Does Latin America specialize in primary output because it is underdeveloped, or is it underdeveloped because it so specializes? Some suspect that both are true, and the vicious spiral has been whirlpooling for years.

The predicament of primary producers is threefold. First of all, the

UNITED STATES EXPORTS OF MERCHANDISE BY COMMODITY GROUPS, 1960
(*Millions of dollars*)

Animals and animal products	668
Vegetable and food products	3,721
Textile fibers and manufactures	1,699
Wood and paper	612
Nonmetallic minerals	1,158
Metals and manufactures, except machinery and vehicles	2,060
Machinery and vehicles	7,131
Chemicals and related products	1,680
Miscellaneous	1,571
Total	20,300

SOURCE: *Statistical Abstract of the United States,* U.S. Department of Commerce, 1961, pp. 881–882.

prices of raw materials and foodstuffs seesaw violently, yet the general level of employment depends on them. When they reach their dizzy heights, the high income of exporters puts demands on the economy that strain it to the seams. When they plunge to the depths, mobs descend on the main plaza and governments fall. Taxes depend on the people's income, and how can a government plan for development if it does not know—from one year to the next—what its revenues will be?

In the second place, the long-run outlook is bleak. Over the years the demand for primary products has not been rising proportionately with that for manufactured goods, and Latin America has seen her export prices gradually sink in relation to what she must pay for imports. During the fifties the losses from price movements alone in some countries have exceeded what they have received in foreign aid.

As if two thorns were not enough, primary products have still a third. They neither demand nor supply those ancillary activities on which other types of economic growth depend. Manufacturing calls for skilled labor, repairs and maintenance, supplies and parts, electricity and other services in far greater proportion than does primary output. Once these are available, new factories go where old ones already are. But oil wells and tin mines have little power to attract other activity that might enhance the nation's growth.

These three problems constitute the setting for the present chapter, which is essentially theoretical. In the following chapter we shall turn to specific commodities and countries.

PRICE FLUCTUATIONS IN PRIMARY OUTPUT

In a single year (1950–1951) Brazil's exports increased by $410 million, or 29.4 per cent of her average exports from 1948 to 1959 inclusive. The next year they dropped by $348 million, or 25 per cent of the average. Of course, I have picked the most abrupt fluctuations of the decade, but others were not mean—such as the increase of $258 million from 1949 to 1950, the decrease of $139 million from 1954 to 1955, and the decrease of $149 million from 1957 to 1958.[1]

Other countries do the same. Export earnings of Argentina plunged by $481 million from 1951 to 1952, or all of 47 per cent of average exports from 1950 to 1958, only to rise again by $437 million the following year.[2]

In the United States, where exports are less than 5 per cent of the national income, such fluctuations would cause far less pain. But in Latin America, where exports of many countries are 20 per cent of national income or more, the impact on the domestic economy can be serious.

Price fluctuations and the business cycle

The reasons for more severe price fluctuations in primary products than industrial goods are so well known that a brief summary will suffice here. The supply and demand of primary products are relatively inelastic in the short run—that is, less responsive to price changes than is the case with industrial goods. But they are also unstable, or subject to capricious or cyclic change. Where unstable demand meets inelastic supply or unstable supply meets inelastic demand, prices are subject to violent fluctuations.

The combination of unstable supply and inelastic demand occurs in most agricultural commodities, where output is subject to the vagaries of weather. If consumers will buy substantially the same amounts regardless of price, then a freeze-out will bring very high prices and a bumper crop very low. The other combination—unstable demand and inelastic supply—often results from political vicissitudes, such as wars and United States stockpiling, or from fluctuations in the business cycle. As the demand for minerals and coffee falls cyclically, the mines do not undig themselves and the trees do not ungrow. Supply is not readily contracted. Prices in Latin America and all the incomes that depend on them will fall to greater depths than in the United States.

Many Latin Americans ask whether the United States is *responsible* for the business cycle and, if so, whether we do not owe them some sort of reparation for damages wrought.

Responsibility for the business cycle

When an earthquake devastated a large area of Southern Chile in 1960 and the city of Valdivia was threatened with extinction, a massive airlift

[1] *International Financial Statistics*, International Monetary Fund, November, 1962, and Supplement to 1962 and 1963 issues.

[2] *United States–Latin American Relations*, 86th Cong., 2d Sess., S. Doc. 125, August, 1960, p. 105.

from the United States carried food, medicines, and other supplies to the stricken Chileans. A feeling of warmth and friendship spontaneously arose, and the United States was loudly and widely eulogized. Even the Communists recognized that the Yankees had not caused the earthquake but had supplied life-giving assistance.

An economic crisis shook Bolivia in 1958. The price of tin slumped by 1 per cent from the preceding year and by 6½ per cent from the year before. Lead dropped by 20 per cent, zinc by 17 per cent, and tungsten by as much as 63 per cent. Export value fell from $95.2 million in 1957 to $63.2 million in 1958,[3] and the government faced a sizeable budgetary deficit. There were strikes and rioting as unions demanded higher wages, even though increased money would not buy more if there was no more to buy. The United States came to the rescue with a sizeable cash grant to alleviate the budget and gifts of food to ease the shortage. Somehow the feeling of warmth that the Chileans were subsequently to experience was strangely absent in Bolivia. The Communists continued to heckle the Yankees, and the government received the aid almost as routine.

To North Americans, both earthquakes and the business cycle are acts of God, and rescue from each has a similar quality. The baffling differences in response are attributed either to the mysteries of human behavior or to the fact that cash grants to Bolivia are continuous while earthquakes don't occur every year in Chile (for which we may be thankful). To Latin Americans, however, the two events are a world apart. The Yankees are responsible for the business cycle[4] but can hardly be blamed for an earthquake. If the United States helps its neighbors in a recession, the aid is like German reparations to France after the war. Not all Latin Americans feel this way, but a good many do.

The relationship of capitalism to the business cycle is worth examining. Employment and incomes arise out of the production of both capital and consumption goods, and a slump in the demand for either may lead to recession. Marx thought that a decline in demand would inevitably follow from maldistributions of income. As the few earned more and the many proportionately less, the wealthy would not be able to spend enough on consumption to sustain full employment. Great surpluses would accumulate with no one to buy them.

Every once in a while (according to the Marxists) capitalists resort to war or other means to use up their surplus capacity, and prosperity returns. The cycle is thus viewed as an inevitable tendency downward,

[3] *International Financial Statistics.*

[4] Gross national product in the United States declined from $444 billion in the third quarter of 1957 (at annual rate) to $413.6 billion in the first quarter of 1958, and imports of merchandise from $13,291 million in 1957 to $12,951 million in 1958 (data from *Survey of Current Business*, U.S. Department of Commerce). The Bolivian troubles, however, were attributable not only to the United States recession but more importantly to supply problems in the nationalized mining company.

punctuated by periodic conflicts, government deficits, high tariffs, import restrictions, and dumping abroad (as through foreign-aid programs). In particular, new colonial markets must constantly be found, so that the pressure of surpluses will be released in exports. One Latin American student pictured the reprieves as follows:

> We Latin Americans want to develop our economies so as to weaken the impact of the business cycle, which is chronic and incurable in the capitalist economy, because it is part of its innermost fabric. The prices of our raw materials rise and fall together with cyclic fluctuations in the capitalist centers. But to this must be added the fact that the capitalist centers have certain anticyclic mechanisms for an internal attenuation of their crises, by discharging the greater part of the impact on our weak economies through the medium of foreign "aid," lower prices, decreases in imports, inflation, and the drainage of our foreign-exchange reserves. While the center diminishes its internal cycle, the periphery is all the worse off, forsaken, and exposed to its bitterest consequences.

Another student wrote that ". . . the purchasing power within the Metropole is very low, and hence the national market is insufficient to absorb the increasing production." This Marxist view of the cycle, although not held by all Latin Americans, has wide currency not only among students but among their economics professors as well.

By contrast, the fact that it is held by very few of my colleagues in the United States and is virtually ignored (and often not understood) by our students indicates one of two things: either the theory itself is incorrect, or else we North Americans have been so successful in shifting the onus of the cycle to foreigners and so intellectually ignorant of what we are doing that professional economists and students have grossly misjudged current history right in our own country. A more likely explanation is that the Latin American students and professors—who either have never visited the United States or know it only superficially—have misread into North American history a meaning for the concentration of wealth amid poverty that they have seen in their own lands. Obviously, also, communication between academic circles in Latin America and the United States is woefully inadequate.

In the preceding chapter we have already seen that purchasing power in the United States is not concentrated. In fact, the twentieth century has witnessed an unprecedented diffusion of income and political participation. In 1961 (a typical year) net interest and profits (the return to capitalists) were only $93.2 billion [5] out of gross national income of $518.7

[5] Sum of proprietors' income ($47.8 billion), rental income of persons ($12.3 billion), and net interest ($20.0 billion), minus 12.7 per cent of the above, which is the percentage of personal income paid in taxes. To this is added $24.3 billion of corporate profits after tax. Data from *Survey of Current Business*, U.S. Department of Commerce.

billion (or 18 per cent). The other 82 per cent was mostly wages and salaries but consisted also of taxes and some miscellaneous charges (such as depreciation).

Those who care to study statistics further will discover that less than 5 per cent of United States national product is sold for exports; yet this is the prop that Marxists say temporarily supports the collapsing structure. Marxist students in Latin America have told me that the United States climbed out of the Depression on the strength of sales to the European war machine. But from 1933 to 1939 the increase in exports—*all* exports, not just military—was only $1.9 billion compared to increase in domestic consumption and investment of $29.7 billion.

Yet—the errors of Marx notwithstanding—the business cycle is associated with capitalism. More than that, it is related to economic growth. As technological improvements occur and new capital is formed, the nation learns to produce ever more and more. But when people are accustomed to save a large part of their income, there is no guarantee that even with an egalitarian distribution they will *want* to buy the nation's entire potential output, day by day and week by week. Furthermore, inventions do not come in a smooth, continuous curve but (as Schumpeter pointed out) more often in waves.

The demand for consumption and investment in the United States sometimes exceeds the capacity to produce, and inflation follows. Sometimes it falls short, and there is recession. But the long-run trend of consumption is upward, in direct contradiction of the lengthy morass predicted by Marx.

Socialism, democracy, and the business cycle

The business cycle would readily be extinguished if the State would regulate consumption and investment so that their sum would always equal the national capacity to produce. If the means to avoid it are thus at hand and the United States wittingly does not avail itself of them, is this not—as many Latin Americans believe—good reason to assign it responsibility for the cycle?

The biggest question of communism, socialism, and capitalism is whether it is possible to regulate investment and consumption without concentrating an inordinate amount of power in the government. To those who feel that the government is "the people," such concentration is acceptable. But let us remember that the odium felt by North Americans for strong government is akin to that felt by Latin American leftists toward foreign "monopolies."

Socialism has, of course, been held to be theoretically consonant with democracy, in which State ownership of all means of production might be entrusted to a freely elected government. But it is *government* control that is abhorrent to North Americans, not whether it is exercised by Republicans or Democrats. To understand the North American sentiment, left-wing Latin American students must consider how *they* would feel if given a choice of voting for the United Fruit Company, the Creole Petroleum Company, or the Anaconda Copper Company to govern their countries.

Another question regarding State control is whether the State through its infinite wisdom or the people through their individual choices should determine the ratio between consumption and investment. Theoretically, the State might forecast the demand of the people for consumption and then adjust its investment to the amount necessary to maintain full employment. In practice, the calculations of the Soviet Union are done the other way. The State has investment goals, plus a sizeable military budget, and it reduces consumption to fit those objectives. This process is appealing to many investment-minded Latin Americans, while others (and most North Americans) urge caution on two grounds: that investment is not all there is to economic development and that to be successful the suppression of consumption *must* be carried to an extreme that freedom-minded people would ultimately reject. Collective bargaining by unions, for example, must be sacrificed.

Rather than maintain rigid control over investment and consumption, the policy of the United States—dating from the Employment Act of 1946—is to forecast the amounts of each that the people *want* to undertake, plus how much they can be induced to undertake by appropriate monetary policy. The calculations are made annually and policy recommended to the President by his Council of Economic Advisors. Then the State makes up whatever is lacking, either by its own expenditures or by tax reductions designed to stimulate private spending. Conversely, if the forecasts of demand are higher than national capacity to produce, people will be discouraged from spending by tight monetary policy and high taxes; the government, furthermore, may cut down its own spending. The method is less exact than outright government control over investment, since forecasts are never 100 per cent correct and the tools are crude. Still, the recessions since 1945 have been much less severe than the big Depression of a decade earlier.

The relatively greater popularity of socialism in Latin America than in the United States stems largely from the conviction that it can bring about rapid economic growth. A less obvious but equally cogent reason is that Latin Americans and North Americans assess economic fluctuations differently. In Latin America, where the cycle is more severe than in the United States, there is naturally a more favorable disposition toward the system which is able to eliminate it. In the United States, on the other hand, the cycle is viewed as a cost of free, individual decision (on how much the nation shall consume and how much it shall invest), which is highly esteemed by those who hold to the capitalist ethic.

We have not determined whether the United States is "responsible" for the cycle or not but have only commented on some of the different meanings of responsibility. In the sense that the business cycle originates in capitalist countries where decisions on investment and consumption are left to the people, the United States and other industrial nations are responsible. In the Marxist sense that the business cycle comes from ever-greater inequalities in income distribution, the United States is not responsible, for the facts belie this theory. Whether responsibility constitutes guilt must be left to individual opinions and the judgment of history. Rather than belabor this point, it is more fruitful to study positive steps for attenuating and eventually eliminating the fluctuations of commodity prices.

THE TERMS OF TRADE IN PRIMARY PRODUCING COUNTRIES

Commodity price problems are far more than cyclic. If the only question were that of smoothing out the year-to-year fluctuations, there is hardly a doubt that some international consensus could have been achieved long ago. At least in Latin American eyes, an even weightier question is the general trend and whether over the long run a "fair" or "just" price is paid.

"We Latin Americans claim a just or equitable price for our raw materials," one of my students wrote, "because we believe that our peoples have helped the United States in its economic development through the sale of our products at low prices. Hence the United States has the moral obligation to pay us a higher price." Many Latin Americans have argued that United States aid is simply a form of redress for underpayment by the United States. The Minister of Finance of Venezuela said the following in September, 1960: "The financial contribution that we are today demanding from more fortunate countries is in a certain measure the return of, or compensation for, income lost through the international exchanges. We should clearly not be embarrassed to accept such contributions." [6]

The definition of a fair price is elusive. Whenever I have asked Latin American students how it would be determined, their replies have usually been that the present "unfair" prices are the result of monopolies. The only way to obtain a fair price would be either to destroy the monopolies or else organize a countervailing power within Latin America, such as commodity agreements among producing countries. Despite the offensiveness of monopolies, if they exist on one side, the best *modus vivendi* is to create them on the other and control them by intergovernmental agreements.

[6] Quoted in an editorial in *Ultima Hora*, La Paz, Bolivia, Sept. 8, 1960.

Let us accept that big businesses in the United States buy Latin American primary products. Let us accept that they have some influence over price. To determine what a countervailing force (such as a commodity agreement) can do, one must first set forth its objectives. If it is rational, it will want to maximize *income,* not necessarily price. Income equals price times volume of exports.

If demand is truly inelastic, then an increase in price will increase income, because exports will not decline by much. But if demand is not inelastic (and over the long run it may not be), then it is possible that price increases will be more than offset by an export drop, so that income will fall.

The contrast between Brazil and Colombia in 1953–1954 illustrates the dilemma. Coffee supply was short because of a freeze in Brazil. The price of Brazilian coffee went up 63 per cent in 1954, whereas the Colombian (which is a different grade) rose only 34 per cent. Volume of sales by both countries fell, Brazil by 30 per cent and Colombia by 13 per cent. However, the total value of coffee exports rose in Colombia (from $493 million to $550 million), while in Brazil it fell (from $1,088 million to $948 million).[7]

What are the lessons from this? One is that buyers in the United States were not powerful enough to keep the price low in the face of a supply shortage. Hence the coffee-producing countries, acting in combination, might do what the freeze did—keep down supply and raise prices. But the other lesson is that a higher price will not necessarily yield an increase in income, as it did not in Brazil. With the high price of coffee in 1954, consumption in the United States dropped by 23 per cent.

If this experience can be extended more generally, the lesson may be that producing countries, by combining to restrict output, may within limits increase their income. They must, however, guard against long-run elasticity of demand which might erode markets and leave them worse off than before.

Long-run prospects for commodity prices

Why are the terms of trade (i.e., prices of exports relative to those of imports) turning against less developed countries? One reason may be the growth of concentrated buying power in the manufacturing countries, which we covered in the preceding chapter. But another factor is the long-run market prospects for primary products, which are governed by two opposing forces—one tending to raise prices and the other to lower them.

The first is the increase in world population and income, both of which evoke a higher demand for the products of industry. But raw ma-

[7] *International Financial Statistics.*

terials are fixed in quantity. There is only so much oil in the ground, so much copper, and so on. Many have predicted that prices will rise in the long run because of supply inelasticity.

The second force is the trend toward substitutes (such as rayon, nylon, plastics, and synthetic rubber), as well as economies in the use of primary products (e.g., making a smaller amount of copper do the same work that a larger amount did previously).

There is some indication that the second force is outrunning the first, and this is sad for Latin America. Consumption of raw materials in the United States has not increased in proportion to national income. Schultz finds that from 1904–1913 to 1944–1950, total raw-material consumption fell from 22.6 per cent of national income to 12.5 per cent, even though the value consumed increased by 88 per cent (or from $9.9 billion to $18.6 billion, at 1935–1939 prices).[8]

The concentrated buyer versus long-run trend in demand

If the terms of trade are turning against primary-producing countries, it may not be only—or even primarily—because of the concentration of buyers. These buyers themselves face competition of a broader nature, in which a monopoly of the supply of (say) copper means little as substitutes are perfected and people learn to get along without it. There is virtually no primary product that faces no competition whatsoever, and this is a sobering fact that Latin American governments must face in their decisions on how high a price to demand in international commodity agreements—or indeed, on how much to tax a foreign mining or petroleum company.

Many Latin American students believe the ability to tax a foreign company adequately depends on its relative political and economic strength vis-à-vis the government. One Bolivian student wrote that ". . . unfortunately our government is not in a position to impose a higher percentage of profits tax on foreign enterprises that exploit our subsoil. The United States petroleum companies are not taxed as much as in Venezuela, partly because the government of Bolivia has not identified itself with the defenders of natural wealth and partly because of the pressure by the companies themselves."

It is curious that the revolutionary government of Bolivia—so identified with the interests of labor and progress—should be subject to this charge. It stems obviously from the conviction that for centuries foreigners have been gouging Bolivian natural riches, that they are powerful and wealthy, and that they have much to yield if only the government is

[8] Theodore W. Schultz, "Economic Prospects of Primary Products," in H. S. Ellis and H. C. Wallich (eds.), *Economic Development for Latin America*, St Martin's Press, Inc., New York, 1961, p. 311.

strong enough to take it. But as we shall see in the next chapter, oil is in world surplus, and companies operating in Latin America are in sharp competition with those in the Middle East. Add to this the fact that it is more expensive to produce oil in Bolivia than in Venezuela, and the inability of the Bolivian government to negotiate better terms (than a fifty-fifty split of profits) might have an explanation other than its own weakness.

This is not to deny the political influence and economic power of large companies, nor the contention that commodity agreements and high taxation (both of which I favor) will assist capital formation in Latin America. It is only an appeal for caution and a realistic understanding of how monopolistic (and how competitive) primary products are. We have reached the limits of generalization on this matter, and further discussion must rest until the specific illustrations of the next chapter.

COMMODITY AGREEMENTS

Many times during the first half of the present century it has occurred to primary-producing countries that in union there is strength. This belief has taken concrete form in commodity agreements, or international arrangements to restrict production and exports to increase price. Not only increase it, but stabilize it as well. At present there are international agreements in wheat, sugar, tin, and coffee, although operation of the sugar agreement is in suspense for lack of consensus among member nations on quotas.

Sometimes consumer nations join the agreement. Their purpose is to bargain down the maximum price. Suppose producers agree to restrict output so price will not fall below (say) 50 cents a unit. The consuming countries would say, "All right, we agree to buy x quantity at 50 cents even if the world price goes lower, provided you will supply us with y quantity at 75 cents even if the world price goes higher." The consuming countries may also agree to limit purchases from producing countries who do not adhere to the agreement.

It can hardly be denied that both producing and consuming nations would benefit by softening price fluctuations, provided the general trend is unaffected. The advantages to producers have already been cited—greater stability of government revenue, national income, and employment, and ease of economic planning. Consumers would also benefit from greater predictability of prices and ease in making advance commitments.[9]

[9] The very fact of price stabilization would affect the long-run trend of some commodity prices, but whether the net results would be positive or negative depends on several variables: Excessive fluctuations are costly to those to whom predictability is

Despite the obvious advantage of stable prices to consumers, the United States has long been negative to Latin American proposals for commodity agreements. Only in recent years, with statements at the conferences in Bogotá (1960) and Punta del Este (1961) does there appear to be a significant change, made concrete by the signing of the coffee agreement in 1962. In earlier decades the United States has generally opposed even cyclic controls, and above all any attempt to raise the average price level. What are the reasons for the change in attitude, and is there any indication that it is genuine, and not just a political maneuver stimulated by the exigencies of the times? Let us look at the history.

The United States and commodity agreements

Twentieth century United States policy toward commodity agreements could hardly have been more contradictory. It has justifiably led many Latin Americans to believe that our interest in them correlates with our need for their political support. In the 1945 conference at Chapultepec, in which the United States was consciously cultivating Latin American approval of its peace objectives, the United States representative stated that "we recognize that international commodity agreements may be necessary in exceptional cases of important primary commodities in which burdensome surpluses have developed or threatened to develop." [10] During most of the fifties, however, when Latin American support for United States objectives was not crucial, the United States stood adamant against proposals for buttressing commodity prices.

At the tenth Inter-American Conference (Caracas, 1954), the United States delegate said: "Our own experience leads us to believe that a hemispheric-wide program which would simply shift to this nation a large part of the risk for price fluctuations is not justifiable by the nature of the problem. The cost would exceed our capacities whether the program contemplated direct payments or buffer stocks created to support prices." [11]

A cautious shift in official United States attitude began to be detected in the latter part of the fifties. A series of international commodity-study groups was set up, including groups to study cotton, wool, cocoa, lead, zinc, and coffee. No binding obligation necessarily arose, but at least the

---

an advantage. If producers' costs are reduced by stable prices, they may supply more and cause permanently lower prices. Conversely, if consumers' costs are lowered by stability, they may demand more and cause higher prices. The supply of coffee and other commodities with long gestation periods would probably be reduced with price stability (since output expands in the upswing but does not readily contract in the downswing), and this reduction would lead to a stable price higher than the previous average.

[10] *Department of State Bulletin,* Mar. 4, 1945, p. 338.

[11] *Ibid.,* Nov. 8, 1954, p. 689.

United States was willing to agree that a problem existed and it should be talked about. In a speech before the Organization of American States on November 18, 1958, the Under Secretary of State for Economic Affairs (Douglas Dillon) said the following: [12]

> Because the economies of Latin America are heavily dependent on exports of one or a few primary commodities, they can be placed in serious difficulties by sharp price declines for these commodities in world markets. The United States recognizes the importance of this problem. It understands and sympathizes with the concern expressed by Latin American countries on this subject. We are ready to join in the study of individual commodity problems which are creating difficulties to see whether cooperative solutions can be found. We have already done so in the case of coffee and more recently in the case of lead and zinc. We believe that effective international cooperation to avoid acute and recurring imbalances between supply and demand in these commodities can make an important contribution to our objectives.
>
> This does not mean that we feel that easy solutions can be found. It does not mean that we have altered our view regarding the impracticality of rigid price-stabilization schemes. It does mean that we feel that real gains can be made whenever we sit down together in good faith and discuss our common problems.

Almost three years later, upon his return from the Punta del Este Conference of 1961, the Secretary of the Treasury (the same Douglas Dillon) was asked about the United States position on commodity problems. His reply indicates that the shift was almost complete: [13]

> On the commodity side, I would say there were really two major decisions. One was that we would be willing to join a proper coffee agreement. . . . We will try to help the enforcement of export controls through using controls on countries who are not living up to the agreement. . . . We agreed to study carefully in IA–ECOSOC [Inter-American Economic and Social Council]—and we would join—in this question of compensatory financing which is under study in the U.N.

All but the most blatantly nationalistic of North Americans must agree that the shift in United States policy was largely "horse trading." Washington decided that it needed the support of Latin America in the Alliance for Progress, and the acceptance of commodity agreements became an instrument in the cold war. With this as datum, the question of most concern to practical-minded Latin Americans is whether the shift is a caprice of the moment, subject to reversal when conditions are different, or whether it can be accepted as a long-range modification in policy.

[12] Paul E. Zinner, ed., *Documents on American Foreign Relations, 1958*, New York, Harper and Row, Inc., for the Council on Foreign Relations, 1959, pp. 521–522.

[13] *Department of State Bulletin*, Sept. 11, 1961, p. 444.

To discuss this question intelligently, it is necessary to consider the reasons why the United States has traditionally opposed commodity controls.

Reasons for United States opposition

The students in my classes in Latin America have had a ready answer. It is that the United States is looking for cheap sources of raw materials, and arrangements to support their prices would not be to our best economic advantage. "In many cases," one of them wrote, "the developed nations do not have sufficient resources to satisfy the demands of their industry. Even if they do have them in adequate supply, instead of using their own resources they prefer to acquire them in countries where the standard of living is lower, and where wages are only a miscroscopic portion of what have to be paid in the Metropole."

What this student wrote is true. North American businesses often prefer to buy raw materials from foreign sources, including Latin America, and the lower cost of labor is a factor. Official policy has undoubtedly been influenced by this fact. But this does not explain why academic economists in the United States, who honestly do their utmost to divorce professional opinions from personal interests, have also advised caution in accepting commodity agreements.

The recommendations of professional economists are twofold, one part relating to fluctuations in prices and the other to their average level. Price stabilization is recognized as desirable, but there has been a strong feeling in the United States that its achievement is within the power of the producing countries and furthermore that *they,* and not the United States, "ought" to undertake it. It could be done by the proper use of fiscal policy. Producers of primary products would be taxed when prices are high, and the funds placed in reserve in the Treasury as a bulwark against hard times to come. They could then be spent either as subsidies to the same producers when prices are low or for projects of economic development which would both offset low, recession incomes and be of advantage to the country.

This position, typically North American, is the product of two traditions we have already discussed. One is the belief that the business cycle is not caused by improper behavior in the United States and therefore there is no North American responsibility to overcome it (apart from what we feel toward our own people). The other is the capitalist ethic, which accepts as virtue that local initiative should solve local problems. The Latin Americans are not "doing their duty" when they expect others (North Americans) to straighten their affairs.

Latin Americans find this approach maddening. The business cycle *is* a responsibility of the United States, according to their ethic, and for

North Americans to evade it is not only dereliction of duty but infliction of positive damage. Latin Americans have also argued that their governments are too weak and unfrugal to accept the discipline of holding funds in reserve. The crying need for economic development, and the political exigency to promote projects while funds are ready, make it extremely unlikely that they would be held over for some uncertain recession. Therefore, it falls upon the United States, which is financially strong, to assume the role of protector.

Let us now turn to the general level of commodity prices, apart from the question of stabilization. Here differences of opinion relate to different degrees of acceptance of the marketplace as an arbiter of price. Convinced that the United States is a nation of monopolies and that the so-called "free market" is a subterfuge for both charging high prices and driving down the cost of raw materials, Latin Americans tend to lose faith in their bargaining ability against their more powerful neighbor. Equally convinced that large buying units bring prosperity and progress, North Americans tend to see nothing wrong with the market as they have known it.

I have stated my own position on this in the preceding chapter. There *are* powerful blocs within the United States. They are not so monopolistic as my students in Latin America have believed, and they *do* have their problems in marketing goods at prices that consumers will pay. They must also withstand the competition of alternative products (and, in the case of raw materials, alternative processes) and foreign producers (such as Europeans). Despite all this, they do present a substantial bargaining front when facing competitive producers of bananas in Ecuador, ranchers in Argentina and Uruguay, and even the centrally regulated coffee markets of Brazil and Colombia. I believe Latin Americans will do well to form units of their own, as a countervailing force vis-à-vis these buyers.

But this is not the whole question. North Americans, *to whom efficiency* (as part of the capitalist ethic) *is almost a fetish,* have constantly asked themselves whether powerful producing combinations in Latin America will be as efficient as large corporations in the United States. The general feeling is that they will not, and that commodity agreements and other combinations will force North Americans to pay higher prices that subsidize inefficiency. The "sin" of so doing may well hurt more than the financial burden!

Among Latin Americans with whom I have discussed this problem, I have found little disagreement on the need to enhance industrial efficiency. *How* it should be done is another question. North Americans often argue that competition is essential to imbue in management the urgency of low-cost techniques. If the threat of losing business to a competitor is not present, they say, businessmen will not feel the pinch that impels them to be efficient. One Latin American student's answer to this thesis is summarized in the quotation below:

> In order to increase our capital or, better yet, to form it, we Latin Americans demand higher prices for our raw materials, which form the basis of our foreign exchange. The reply is that prices must fluctuate freely so that the international pricing mechanism can function efficiently. We are told that competition is the best way to force enterprises to use modern methods, to reduce costs, and to increase productivity. And finally it is said that a higher price will destroy the incentive to employ more efficient means of production. We maintain that the international price mechanism already does not function freely, because the organization of the capitalist economy is monopolistic and also because the United States subsidizes its domestic agricultural output. We maintain that competition is not the best instrument for increasing productivity, for if this were so, the output of the United States would be growing more rapidly than that of the Soviet Union. Finally, it is not low prices that permit more efficient methods of production; rather, those methods are possible only with an increase in capital, which can enable the working force to assimilate new techniques.

I do not count myself among those North Americans who argue that competition is the *only* way to maximize efficiency. Other incentives are possible, such as bonuses to management and wage increases proportionate to productivity. Even threats can be used. Without the benefit of competition, the Soviet Union has created one of the most efficient crude-steel industries in the world. With competition—often intense, and among big businesses—the United States has assembled one of the most efficient economies in the world. But I do ask my Latin American friends to recognize that, within the context of United States experience, competition has brought efficiency *and efficiency in turn has caused capital formation.* I also ask them to recognize that, whether or not the United States experience can be applied generally (i.e., whether or not North Americans are mistaken), nevertheless their *belief* that competition brings efficiency is among their reasons for historically opposing commodity agreements. Thus self-gain has not been the only impulse to United States opposition.

There is one point further that I will ask of my Latin American friends. That is to examine their own industries (such as railroads) that have attained monopoly through government license or other privilege, and ask themselves whether *they* (their own industries and not the Soviet steel industry) are operating at lowest possible unit cost commensurate with *current* capital availabilities. The North American opinion of whether Latin America will achieve efficiency through monopoly is, after all, based on observation of Latin America, and not of the Soviet Union.

In summary, the desire to buy at lower prices is one reason, but only one, why the United States has traditionally opposed commodity agreements. It has been fortified by the conviction that the problems of primary producers are *their* problems and *they* ought to be the ones to solve them. Furthermore, there is a strong belief that monopoly organizations in Latin America (and elsewhere among primary producers) will lack incentive to reduce costs. This conviction is strengthened by observation of enterprises such as the nationalized mining corporation in Bolivia and the railroads in many Latin American countries. People in the United States do sympathize with the Latin American need to capitalize but are skeptical of whether this can be done through high prices of primary products, whose demand may be elastic in the long run. Capital can also be obtained through operation of national enterprises at maximum efficiency, and Latin America has a poor record in this respect.

The melting of United States opposition

Why, then, has the opposition of the United States waned in recent years? Why has the United States been willing to join commodity-study groups, and why did she sign the coffee agreement? Is there a political strategy? Has the United States discovered that she needs Latin American support in the cold war, and is she prostituting her economic convictions to gain a momentary perch in world opinion?

The answer is "yes." Only those too naïve to face political reality would reason otherwise. But this is not all. If politics were the entire answer, the United States would have capitulated years ago, for the political exigencies of today are no greater than those of the thirties or the forties (although they may seem so to those whose memories are dim). The political fire alone has not melted the opposition; another one has been burning.

That fire has two flames. One is the development of our own attitude toward the business cycle and the necessity to attenuate it. The other is a growing national consciousness of the problems of primary producers within our own boundaries.

A short thirty-five years ago professional economists were convinced that the best way to cure a depression was to leave it alone. They subscribed to Say's law of markets, the thesis of which was that a lapse from full employment was a temporary maladjustment that would soon correct itself. All you needed to do was to wait, and prosperity would be automatically restored. The great discovery of Keynes—whose story has been told many times—was that this isn't necessarily so.

The same short thirty-five years ago professional economists in the United States thought that any agricultural problem we might face would be both temporary and self-correcting. If the technology of farming should so advance that farmers were willing and able to supply more food than the nation could consume, then prices of foodstuffs would fall, the farming community would be discouraged, and people would leave to go into industry where (there naturally being full employment) opportunities would be abundant. Bitter experience has taught us that this too isn't necessarily so. At least, the shift is not easy. Men who have known no other way of life cannot readily adapt to new jobs and new locations just because classical economists a hundred years ago said they should, nor do they relish abandoning homes in which they have invested their life's savings and their life's dreams.

It is a natural response of human beings that the perception of a general affliction first evokes compassion toward friends and relatives and that only later is sympathy turned beyond one's own doorstep. This is true even though the suffering may be greater abroad than at home. We have already observed that the Alliance for Progress, bringing a United States response to the crying social needs of Latin America, came some thirty years after a sweeping expurgation of social ills at home. So also has public policy evolved toward business cycles and primary producers. From Keynes to the Alliance for Progress a quarter century passed in which the United States felt its duty to attenuate the cycle at home and protect its own farmers from the shock of progress. But it remained adamant in its feeling that it had no obligations abroad—or that if it did, they were discharged by what it was doing at home.

When primary producers in the United States—not only farmers, but miners of lead and zinc and drillers for oil—complained that prices were not high enough for them, they were showered with quotas, price supports, loans, and all other arrangements that the ingenuity of Washington could conceive. When Latin Americans argued for support of their primary output, however, the United States cried "Monopoly!" and "Interference with free markets!" When the price of coffee rose with the crest of the cycle, Congress demanded an investigation to determine whether Brazilians were conspiring in restraint of trade.

The gross inconsistency between domestic and foreign policy could hardly withstand the political currents battering the latter. Thirty years ago, when domestic policy toward the business cycle and our own farmers had not evolved, a magician would have been required to persuade the administration to pay heed to the cyclic and production problems of foreigners. In the sixties no magician is needed. Public opinion, whose support is so necessary in a democracy, has already been educated by what has happened at home.

I cannot predict whether the changeover will be long lived. Its political basis is clear, and it may last simply because the cold war will last. Recent history in the United States stands in its favor. But much will depend on whether efficient production is in fact enhanced in commodities subject to support.

COMPENSATORY FINANCING

A major criticism of commodity stabilization schemes is that they perpetuate the problem. Despite the criticism of free markets that is fashionable in Latin America, market prices *do* serve a function. For example, quite apart from cyclic fluctuations, the world is producing too much coffee. The expanded African output, added to all the Latin American capacity, is simply more than the world can consume. One way of persuading farmers to grow less coffee and to transfer their labors to more needed occupations is to pay them less for it. The decline in price can be graduated so as to minimize the hardship of change. (This technique has been used in United States agricultural price supports, so that farmers will be encouraged to go to the city but not dealt inhuman economic blows.) But if the price of coffee is "stabilized" at too high a level, producers will continue to grow too much.

Compensatory financing has been suggested as a means of avoiding this problem. In a study on commodity trade and economic development in 1953,[14] the United Nations proposed automatic compensation schemes, in which an international fund would lend or donate foreign exchange to governments in years when exports fell below levels previously defined as "normal." The governments would, of course, sell the exchange to their residents for local currency, and these counterpart funds might be used to subsidize producers—if to do so seemed expedient—but they might also be applied to development projects. Or there might be some combination, in which producer prices were allowed to fluctuate but fluctuations were attenuated. The spending on projects would prevent a decline in national income while also stimulating economic growth.

Compensatory financing has been widely discussed since 1953, and a more elaborate report was prepared by the United Nations in 1961.[15] Here the International Monetary Fund is proposed as the appropriate agency for carrying out an insurance plan in which more and less developed countries alike would participate. All would "insure" themselves against the risk of price fluctuations by contributing both a lump sum and annual premiums to a fund from which claims would be paid to governments suffering from export fluctuations exceeding predetermined percentages. The more developed countries would pay their premiums regularly but would not make claims (despite the theoretical possibility). The proposal is ". . . premised on a willingness on the part of the ad-

[14] *Commodity Trade and Economic Development,* United Nations, E/2519, Nov. 25, 1953, chap. 7.

[15] *International Compensation for Fluctuations in Commodity Trade,* United Nations, E/3447, E/CN.13/40, New York, 1961.

vanced economies to contribute on the understanding that their direct benefits would not equal their contributions. Their participation would become a form of multilateral assistance."[16]

To avoid interference with the long-range adjustment of commodities in world surplus, two alternatives are offered: either the claims would not fully offset the losses (and therefore the country would share the burden with the insurance fund), or else they might be made as loans, with repayment required when exports increased.

At the time of writing, compensatory financing is under serious discussion in the United Nations and the International Monetary Fund. In 1963, the Fund authorized the drawing of 25 per cent of the quotas of member countries suffering from decline in raw material prices. This action is a step in the direction of compensatory financing, but it falls considerably short of proposals supported by primary-producing countries.

PRIMARY PRODUCTS AND EXTERNAL ECONOMIES

The third major problem of primary products is that of external economies. These are conditions outside the walls of a producing enterprise that lower its costs in one location rather than another—the availability of power, skilled labor, repair and maintenance services, a steady source of supplies, easy transportation, and the like. Manufacturing both requires and provides external economies, and factories tend to locate where factories already are—not where mines and oil wells are.

Is there a "vicious circle of poverty," as Gunnar Myrdal, Ragnar Nurkse, and others have suggested? Somehow, for historical reasons not necessarily relevant to the current discussion, one group of nations got a head start over others in economic development. These nations now have external economies and attract new industry. Does it follow—as some firmly believe—that short of violent revolution or vigorous state action, all other nations are forever condemned to be purveyors of raw materials to the initially fortunate and never to rise above this humble state?

It is now time for our fairy story.

> Once upon a time, many years ago, explorers from far away discovered two lands, which they named Northlandia and Southlandia according to their geographic positions. Both had rich mineral resources and large rivers that made transportation possible. Both had vast plains and mountains, long seacoasts, and a few good harbors. Both were populated by people called "Indians," whom the white man conquered. The explorers became rulers of all they could see, and they set about establishing "economic order" wherever they went.

[16] *Ibid.*, pp. 35–36.

After many years the settlers became aware of a most remarkable difference between the two lands. The soil of Southlandia was very fertile and well adapted to many crops, whereas Northlandia was colder and unsuited to tropical farming. The Southlandians, who were very industrious people, eagerly exploited their natural advantage. They established large sugar plantations. Not only were the soil and rainfall ideally adapted to sugar, but transportation to the coast was easy, and sugar markets were growing in Europe because of the industrial revolution. All who had eyes could see, in those days, that Southlandia would wax prosperous and become the land of the wealthy and powerful.

And so it came to pass for many years. The more energetic became owners of land. Not just a few hectares here and there, but vast quantities, since with machinery sugar could be produced efficiently on large tracts. Land was cheap because it was abundant. All that was necessary was to conquer a few Indians, cut down some trees, and plant the sugar.

But the white men soon found, to their dismay, that all the Indians had retreated or died and there was no one to harvest the sugar. The job was too demeaning, too demanding, and too copious for them to do themselves. So they went to other lands where people were poor and ignorant and brought them to Southlandia to be serfs on the plantations. The serfs were paid enough to stay alive and to work, because this was all that the white men demanded of them.

There were no need to educate the serfs. One does not have to be literate to slash sugar. The wealthy landowners built private schools for their own children, and when they were ready for the university they went to Harvard, or Oxford, or the Sorbonne. Nor was industry essential to Southlandia. Wherever there was land, it could earn more money in sugar (or sometimes tobacco) than if it had a factory on it. Besides, there was no one to sell manufactured goods to. The serfs did not have money, and the landowners (who by now had become very aristocratic) could import whatever they wanted from Europe and Northlandia.

Sugar was carried to the coast in wagons, and the wagons had to return to the plantation, full or empty. So they might just as easily carry imports, and this was all the more reason why Southlandia did not need factories. All roads went to the coast, and very few connected inland parts.

In the meantime, the people of Northlandia were not idle. They could not grow sugar, because the land and climate were not suitable. So they turned to other tasks. They farmed and founded small factories. At first the factories were not very pretentious, producing glass, textiles, shoes and boots, and other things that people needed. They sold mainly to each other but also to the aristocrats of Southlandia.

Where one factory was, soon came another. When there were five, an electric-power plant would serve them all. People from Europe who knew how to repair machinery came to live in Northlandia. Roads were built from one producing center to another; they didn't all go to the coast. Thus industry began in Northlandia partly for the negative reason that the soil wasn't very good, but it continued for the positive reason that production costs were low.

Another remarkable contrast grew between the two lands. Northlandians realized the value of universal, free education. Whereas one doesn't have to be literate to slash sugar cane, one does have to read and write to learn to operate a machine. The industrialists decided that even their workers' children should go to school. So the Northlandians spent much more money in building a good public school system than did the aristocrats of Southlandia.

The list of contrasts continued to grow. Northlandians did not use serfs in their businesses because they did not (at first) need so many workers in the same place, and also because they wanted literate people who might have been trained by another employer. Factories bid workers away from each other, and wages rose. Unlike the serfs in Southlandia, Northlandian laborers had money, and when they demanded manufactured goods, more and more factories appeared. Banking and insurance companies thrived in Northlandia, for their services were needed by the growing industry.

Finally and inevitably, economic growth brought political power. For many years Southlandians had been living in the dream of earlier days that theirs was the wealthy land. It was only when Northlandia became politically strong that the rude awakening occurred. Northlandian bankers and insurance men began to infiltrate the commercial world of Southlandia. Laws were passed in the capital of Northlandia that discriminated against Southlandians, such as those regulating shipping and transportation. Northlandians protected their manufactured goods with tariffs, and so they were all the more costly for Southlandians to buy. Southlandians began to call Northlandians "Yankees" and "imperialists."

The fever of discontent was fanned into revolution. Southlandians were determined to rid themselves of the hegemony of the North and declare their economic independence. War started with the firing on Fort Sumter in 1861, and a bearded patriot named Abraham Lincoln led the "Yankee imperialists" to a crushing victory over the South.

The crop was really cotton, not sugar, but only in this respect has history been stretched. Today the focus of cotton has moved to the West, and Southlandia is growing into one of the strongest industrial centers in the nation. The status of the erstwhile serf is still in dispute—and we shall say more about the Negro below—but aside from that, they all lived happily ever after.[17]

One hundred years have elapsed between the Civil War and the present modern, industrialized United States South. Where stood a cotton field in 1870 now stands the city of Birmingham, Alabama, with 939 mills, mines, and factories producing over 31,130 different products whose annual value

[17] For a more scholarly version of the same story, see Douglass C. North, *The Economic Growth of the United States, 1790–1860*, Prentice-Hall, Inc., Englewood Cliffs, N.J., 1961, especially Chaps. 1, 7, and 10.

is \$750 million.[18] Low wage rates did help attract industry to the South, and once it was there, wages began to rise. Systems of public education expanded, new highways connected inland points, incomes became more egalitarian, and markets grew.

Memories are short, and North Americans who did not know the South one hundred years ago do not understand the problems of Latin America as readily as they would if they studied their own history more. Latin Americans too, who argue that their problems are "unique"—never before known and therefore not susceptible to anything that history (particularly North American) has to offer them—should also read a page from the story of Southlandia.

Some will say that Southlandia differed from Latin America in that it had free access to the markets of the rest of the United States. This is so. But those who know economics and history well are aware that more powerful forces were necessary to overcome the tremendous comparative disadvantage of the South in manufacturing and transportation. Not only did low wages attract industry to the South, but in addition the North was growing and demanding new products at a far greater rate than it alone could supply. It began to trade with the South according to a new, changing list of comparative advantages.

But one hundred years is a long time, and Latin Americans cannot wait. There are ways of speeding the process, and we shall talk of them when we reach the chapters on economic integration and planning for development. But the important point to note is that we are not fighting history; we are accelerating it. Once this is understood, the job becomes easier.

RACE RELATIONS IN THE UNITED STATES

Let us digress to say something of the Negro. Latin American students ask much about him, and some sneer at the United States for the way we have treated him. Up to this point in the book, I have tried to talk to Latin American students just as I would to North Americans, to be just as blunt and to say the same things. But now I shall depart from this practice. When I discuss race relations with people in the United States, I dwell on how much is yet to be done, because we need to urge ourselves on. When I talk to Latin Americans, however, I tell how much has been accomplished, because usually that is what they do not know.

The North American Negro has long lived in the vicious circle of poverty. Illiterate after the Civil War, accustomed to living in slave shacks no better than the hovels that surround Caracas, Cali, and Rio de Janeiro today, he was not readily accepted in white society. Many viewed him as "the animal closest to man"—just as some Peruvians look upon the

[18] *Encyclopaedia Britannica*, Encyclopaedia Britannica, Inc., Chicago.

Indian of the cordillera. It is not easy for white people accustomed to know the Negro in these terms to accept him as a social and economic equal.

Still, the Negro has been progressing both economically and socially. The number of Negroes in professional service has more than tripled since 1900. Educational opportunities for Negroes, including schools and universities, have continuously expanded. An organization called the National Association for the Advancement of Colored People has become a political force, bringing cases of civil rights to the courts and forcing desegregation and equal rights in the application of city ordinances. In the 1960 elections the Northern urban Negro was for the first time a major voting force, energetically courted by both parties.

Legal segregation of Negroes from whites has progressively broken down in recent decades. Twenty years ago they were required to sit in the rear sections of buses and trains in the South, a practice now outlawed in interstate transportation and in the local buses of some Southern cities. The most momentous event was the Supreme Court decision of 1954 outlawing segregation in public schools. On orders from the Court, many Southern schools have been desegregated (i.e., Negroes and whites placed in the same instead of separate schools), and the process is continuing.

The struggle for social justice is often conceived in its political and social terms, like that of agrarian reform and the rights of *campesinos* and miners in Latin America. Yet as in Latin America, social justice in the United States has its economic dimension. Much of its impulse arises from Southern businessmen, to whom integration is personally distasteful. Yet they realize that if there is no social peace in their cities, if their schools are closed, and if there is dissention between Negro and white workers, new industries will not come there to settle, and their growth will lag. Quietly and in ways not usually reported in Latin American newspapers, these businessmen are working toward the acceptance of social equality in their communities.

North American Negroes are likewise dedicated to the resolution of their problems by nonviolence. Champions of social justice (like Martin Luther King) are convinced that history is on their side and peaceful persuasion is possible. Time and again they have urged their followers to eschew bloodshed, proclaiming that it is possible to win their aims by constitutional means.

The problem is far from solved, since prejudices do not die easily. Many, many white people with social consciences belong to the National Association for the Advancement of Colored People and other organizations (like the Civil Liberties Union and the Council on Human Relations) that have grown up to promote racial equality. There is much opposition by those whose minds are not adapted to the relentlessness of history. They are the ones who burn the crosses, wail loudly, and have their pictures in Latin American newspapers. But they are fighting a losing battle.

A North American student in Ghana was once derisively asked what was the difference between the United States and the Union of South Africa, in the way they treated Negroes. "The difference," he replied, "is that my government is doing something about it." It is not generally considered good etiquette to ridicule a person because he has a problem, and it is in particularly bad taste when he is honestly trying to solve it. Let us hope that Latin Americans will learn the progress of race relations in the United States and see them in perspective rather than in isolated occurrence.

SUMMARY

Problems of primary producers are threefold. In the first place, their prices fluctuate violently, because both demand and supply (at least in the short run) are inelastic. In the second place, the world demand for primary output, while rising absolutely, has fallen in proportion to national income. Although measurements are subject to interpretation and difference of opinion, it is probable that the long-run terms of trade are moving against less developed countries. In the third place, primary output neither provides nor requires external economies in the same measure as manufacturing.

To solve the first two problems, primary-producing countries have long proposed commodity agreements or other forms of compensatory finance. In general, the United States has opposed these arrangements, and any concessions on its part, including the present one, have historically coincided with its political interests vis-à-vis Latin America. Latin American patience has been justifiably short.

There has been a trend of history within the United States that *may* signal a long-run policy change. The Depression of the thirties brought home the necessity of anticyclic measures, and the problems of domestic primary producers—mainly farmers, but also miners—have generated awareness of a need to which the United States was earlier officially blind. One usually does not appreciate the problems of neighbors until he has suffered from them himself.

But there are other factors militating against a permanent policy shift. One is that the recent United States participation in commodity-study groups and the coffee agreement have occurred in the context of the cold war and are suspect for this alone. Another is the North American feeling toward business efficiency (or lack of it) in Latin America. Whether justified or not, there is a strong impression that commodity supports will tend to raise prices and destroy the initiative to lower costs. This impression is fortified by observation of certain nationalized industries in Latin America, such as tin in Bolivia and railroads in Argentina and Brazil.

Latin Americans have argued that efficiency will come only with an increase in capital, and this in turn depends on higher prices. Still, capital can also be obtained by lowering costs (thus increasing business saving), and it is not certain that this is being done in monopolistic enterprises in Latin America. There is a strong sentiment in the United States that measures taken here to increase capital in Latin America should wait until the Latin Americans have done all they can to contribute investment through enhancing efficiency with current capital availabilities.

As an aside, I cannot help commenting that here is a curious problem with roots that lie, according to Latin Americans and North Americans respectively, in the monopolies of the other!

The third problem of primary producers stems from their shortage of external economies, or linkages with other industries. Factories tend to locate where factories are, and whichever nations—by hook, crook, or hazard—are the first to industrialize are at great advantage. Some economists, such as Gunnar Myrdal, have argued that the disequilibrating forces of history are so strong that, short of very positive effort (involving controls and planning), they cannot be reversed.

There is nothing wrong with Myrdal's concept of the vicious circle, except that he is too pessimistic in its application. There are ways of breaking the circle, and North Americans (with their capitalist ethic) tend to feel that he who allows himself to fall beneath it—rather than accept adversity as a challenge—is following a "surrender" policy. The history of the United States South in the nineteenth century, which so strongly resembles that of Cuba in the twentieth (except in its outcome), is testimony that history may ultimately be kind to the newly developing countries.

But these countries want to speed up history, and for persons who will not be here one hundred years hence this is an admirable and understandable goal. Commodity agreements and compensatory finance, if judiciously employed with due respect for efficiency, long-run elasticities, and competition, will enhance stability and progress. So also will careful economic planning and economic integration in Latin America. But we will come to these in future chapters.

6 Four Commodity Experiences—Copper, Sugar, Oil, and Coffee

PRICE INELASTICITY and terms of trade are not just theory. They are tools in understanding the agonizing vicissitudes of Latin American exports. Still, commodity trade itself is the meat of the problem, and specific examples the salt to bring out its flavor. The present chapter is not a catalogue of experiences, and its purpose is not to include every country or every commodity. Rather, it draws on the current history of four commodities to illustrate the economic and political haggling of the marketplace and its revelance to Latin American–United States relations.

The political side of commodity trade is as material as the economic. Those who interpreted my earlier arguments on diffused political power in the United States as meaning that nobody has any will be disabused of this opinion. There are copper interests, sugar interests, oil interests, and coffee interests. There are other interests not discussed in this chapter. They are not all the same people, and they have conflicts with manufacturers, consumers, laborers, foreigners, and other groups. These conflicts are translated into politics.

To those who believe that man should live in State-dominated harmony, the Western Hemisphere story of these four commodities will make sordid reading. Copper is a giant, deadlocked in a political struggle that may topple both it and the government of Chile. The battle of sugar initially shaped up between beet and cane growers, but now it has emerged in a broader front and become enmeshed in the wider concerns of United States foreign policy. Oil is a series of skirmishes between thousands of independent producers in the United States and a few international giants. In coffee the buyers are concentrated but competitive, and the producing countries organized into a countervailing force.

Few are satisfied that the current lineup is either fair or long-lasting. Somehow it will change, and recognition of this inevitability is what constitutes enlightenment. Over the pull and tug of conflicting interests there hovers the shadow of a greater struggle. It is between those who urge that the interests themselves be subordinated to some superpower, defined as "the people" or "the government," and those who believe the need is for fewer rulers and more referees.

COPPER AND CHILE

"The vast expansion plans of the two American-owned copper-mining giants in Chile, hopefully brought forward in 1960, are today just another abandoned mining operation." A $325 million investment program, which would have been both profitable to the companies and a source of badly needed foreign exchange in Chile, dropped quietly into the night. So wrote *The New York Times* on November 25, 1962, describing another scene in the tragedy of capital and natural resources that couldn't agree on how to hold hands.

Chile—so say the Chileans—suffers from two blights. One is copper itself. They remember the tragedy of nitrate, with war-caused scars that still disfigure Peru and Bolivia and which brought Chile a sorrowful treasure soon to be wiped out by technological change. It is too risky, they say, to live perched on a pillar of copper unconnected to other industries—not even to refineries (except a few)—which trembles with violent price fluctuations and which may itself fall some day, as did the nitrate pillar before it.

The other blight is that even the copper is not their own. It is possessed primarily by two North American mining corporations—Anaconda and Kennecott—whose interests are worldwide. The companies, charged Senator Radomiro Tomic in a speech before his fellow legislators in 1961,[1]

> . . . are mere trading conduits of two enormous commercial enterprises of world-wide importance, that produce huge quantities of copper in the United States and other countries, and have or can at any moment have similar and even competing interests in other parts of the world. Their mining, industrial, and commercial interests may well be antagonistic to those of Chile. They possess refineries or participate in foreign refineries dependent on supplies of unrefined copper from Chile, and they own enormous plants for processing and manufacturing copper in the United States or can acquire them at any moment in other parts of the world.

[1] Radomiro Tomic, "El Cobre es Chileno," speech in the Senate of the Republic, July 18, 1961, published in *República de Chile, Diario de Sesiones del Senado.*

The chronology of copper, 1947 to 1960

Copper is the most widely used of nonferrous metals. The United States is the world's dominant producer, and here (in gross tonnage) copper output is exceeded only by iron. Chile ranks second, Northern Rhodesia third, and Canada fourth. In 1958 these countries alone produced 61 per cent of the world's output. Other producers in Latin America are Mexico, Peru, and Cuba, with Peruvian output greatly expanding because of new deposits recently opened in the South.[2]

Unless vast new resources are discovered elsewhere, the copper of the future lies in Chile. The exact quantity of reserves is unknown (and what is known is a closely guarded secret), but Tomic has claimed that ". . . our copper deposits represent almost half of the reserve of this metal in the entire world."[3] In the United States, on the other hand, mines have been progressively depleted. Reporting in 1952, the President's Materials Policy Commission (Paley Commission) was pessimistic about the future of domestic output, since (although the market for scrap is strong) few deposits had been discovered in the United States since 1890.[4] The only serious competitors that Chile may have in newly mined copper are neighboring Peru, Canada, and far-off Africa.

The principal use of copper is in the electrical industry: in wires and transmission lines, generators, motors, switchboards, and the like. Its competition comes mainly from aluminum, plastics, and steel. The United States is the principal consumer as well as producer, using almost 1½ million tons of refined copper in 1959, compared to world smelter production of 4 million tons.[5]

The price of copper fluctuates more than most primary products. During the Depression of the thirties it fell to below 5 cents a pound, and in 1955 it rose to over 45 cents.[6] In postwar years the low (1949) was about 17 cents.

But to the Chilean government, the problem of quantity is far graver than that of price fluctuations. World demand for copper has been rising,

[2] World mine production of copper (in thousands of short tons) was as follows for 1958: United States, 979.3; Chile, 509.5; Northern Rhodesia, 441.1; Canada, 346.8; Japan, 89.1; Australia, 82.3; Mexico, 71.6; Peru, 54.9; Union of South Africa, 54.6; Finland, 31.8; Sweden, 21.4; Norway, 16.5; and Cuba, 14.3. The world total was 3,740. Data from *Commodity Yearbook, 1960*, Commodity Research Bureau, Inc., New York, 1960, p. 104.

[3] Radomiro Tomic, *op. cit.*

[4] *Resources for Freedom*, vol. 2, *The Outlook for Key Commodities*, President's Materials Policy Commission, 1952, p. 33.

[5] *Commodity Yearbook, 1960, op. cit.*, pp. 105–106.

[6] Monthly average price for electrolytic copper in New York. *Commodity Yearbook, 1960, op. cit.*, p. 107.

and magnificent opportunities call for the vast Chilean reserves. But to expand output requires capital—not just a little and not a gradual increase but hundreds of millions of dollars in quick succession. The refusal of the companies to commit themselves to a huge investment program underlies all the current difficulties between them and the Chilean government.

The first postwar skirmish occurred in 1949–1950. Consumer demand left over from wartime restrictions had kept production and prices at a stable plateau in the first postwar years, but in 1949 the slump occurred. World demand, world prices, and Chilean exports all fell. The unwillingness of the companies to expand output in the face of falling demand was understandable. What was maddening was that in 1950, when the world picture was reversed, they still contracted.

Not only did world production increase in 1950, but United States output was also on the rise, and the companies were accused of shifting their production to their home territories because they could not get along with the Chileans. In fact, three explanations for reducing Chilean output have been offered, and those outside the inner circles can only conjecture upon which one (or combination) is correct. The first is that strikes held down production. Strikes there were, but strikes have occurred in other years too. Those of 1950 were not so prolonged as to be more than a scapegoat.

The second explanation lies in the exchange rate. Copper and nitrate companies had long been required to sell foreign exchange at a penalty rate to buy pesos for local operating expenses. This rate had been set at 19.37 to the dollar in 1934 and had remained there ever since, even though peso costs were rising rapidly with inflation and the free-market rate reached 300 pesos in 1954. Each year the government would negotiate with the companies as to the number of dollars they were required to sell at the low rate and how many they might offer on the free market. Consequently, the exchange rate became a form of taxation, which to the companies was vicious not only because they considered it heavy but because it had to be renegotiated every year. Without knowing what their taxes would be, they argued that they could not plan the capital investments necessary to increase output.

A third explanation is that proposals were in the wind to correlate taxes inversely with production as incentive to the companies to increase output: taxes would be high percentagewise when output was low and low when it was high. The companies allegedly responded by building up inventories of semifinished product in 1950 (while the old tax regime was in effect), planning to complete them and show higher final product in some subsequent year when the new tax was on.

Low copper sales hit the Chilean economy hard. Manufacturing, which had been rising steadily since 1945, fell 4 per cent in 1950. Agricultural output was off 5 per cent, and the cost of living went up 22 per cent.

Pent-up feeling exploded, and a variety of issues, long simmering, emerged from both sides. The companies complained that the Chileans did not have a realistic understanding of their costs, that taxation was too high and the exchange rate discriminatory and unpredictable. The Chileans argued bad faith in the cutbacks of output, and there was resentment that two large foreign companies could work such havoc to their economy.

The boiling pot was further fired by the Korean conflict and the intrusion of two foreign-policy objectives of the United States. One was to secure adequate copper for the war effort, and the other to keep Chilean copper out of the hands of the Soviet-Chinese bloc. Price control was an added irritant. The maximum quoted in New York was 24.37 cents per pound,[7] which was the highest price copper had attained since World War I. Nevertheless, criticisms similar to the one cited for Bolivian tin in Chapter 4 (see page 85) were widely heard.

All the issues came to a head in May, 1951, with a comprehensive agreement between the governments of Chile and the United States. Chilean copper would receive a premium of 3 cents above all other (domestic and foreign). Not only would the premium increase Chilean government income, but it would encourage the companies to shift production from the United States to Chile. Chile on her part agreed not to sell copper to the Soviet-Chinese bloc and to withhold for her own use not more than 20 per cent of the output of North American companies (selling the rest to the United States and "friendly" countries).

The agreement was a masterpiece of insult to Chilean national pride, and a year later it was canceled. Output did increase in 1952, but thereafter it leveled off, once again in the face of increases everywhere else. As prices rose in the rest of the world, two sores festered all the more painfully. One was price controls in the United States, and the other the stabilization policies of the companies themselves, by which they sold (outside the United States–price-controlled area) at prices less than those quoted on the London market.

To the companies, a policy of relatively stable prices made sense. Customers, they argued, want a guaranteed relationship with a supplier and are accustomed to buy on contract, one year in advance. One of the companies even has some five-year contracts. If customers know they can be supplied by the major companies, they will continue with them even though world prices temporarily drop, just so they will not be scratched off the preferred list and deprived of a steady supply when copper is short. Of course, if the world price becomes too high or too low, then the companies are forced to revise their quotations. But they try to make

[7] Maximum prices were set on an individual basis, each producer not to receive a higher price than his highest between December 19, 1950, and January 21, 1951. A few companies had ceilings in excess of 24.37 cents.

changes less frequently than the volatile London market. The companies also argued that the quotation in London would not have risen so high above their "stable" price if all their output, as well, had been offered at whatever the world would pay for it.[8]

In protest against the price policies of both the United States government and the companies, the Chilean government imposed export controls designed to force the companies to sell on the world market. To its dismay, the world was not ready to accept copper at the price Chile demanded. The reply was to withhold it and build up a stockpile with which Chile might bargain when supplies became short. But unfortunately Chilean copper—important though it is in relation to world supplies—is by no means a monopoly. Chile saw other countries increasing their output and exports while hers were languishing.

The Chilean stockpile did aggravate the supply shortage in the United States, and as a concession to Chile the North American price controls were rescinded on foreign copper in 1953. (Those who believe price controls are economic imperialism should ponder the anomaly of free pricing by foreign producers while domestic concerns were subject to ceilings.) Chile thereupon offered to sell its stocks to the United States at the world market price. The United States government refused, however, urging that Chile should first restore her embargo on sales to the Soviet orbit. It was also hinted that she should end the discriminatory exchange taxation.

No formal agreement was ever signed, but the two countries gradually acceded to each other's conditions. The United States did buy the Chilean copper hoard at world price (30 cents a pound). In October, 1953, the Chileans began to dismantle their cumbersome multiple exchange system for a more simple one,[9] and in December the senate voted to stop sales of copper to countries in the Soviet orbit.

Finally, in May, 1955, Chile took steps to resolve the uncertainties in taxation. The discriminatory exchange rate was abolished, and a new law (Law 11,828) provided for stable taxes, with a schedule varying from 75 per cent of profit for "low-output" mines down to 50 per cent for "high-output" mines. A Copper Department was formed, with representatives of the producing companies as well as the government. The government

[8] About one-third of the world's copper output is traded on the London market, mostly by African producers, of which those in Northern Rhodesia are most important. The African producers frequently attempt to maintain some stability in the market by themselves buying and selling as necessary. Long-term contracts by United States producers are often based on the average price, over a period of time, on the London exchange.

[9] For a description of Chilean exchange-rate history and the 1953 reform, see Earl Hicks and Stanley Christovich, "Exchange Rates in Chile, 1938–1953," *International Financial Statistics*, December, 1953, pp. iv–vii.

members were persuaded that the stable-price policy was in the best interests of the country as well as the companies. It was hoped that a new era had begun in government-company relations, and that the new investment so badly needed to expand output would at last appear.

The time was also economically ripe, for copper in 1955 was enjoying a cyclic upswing. Gross national product in the United States rose steadily from late 1954 to late 1957. The price of copper climbed to new heights (45.87 cents per pound in mid-1956), and Chilean exports increased from $398 million in 1954 to $542 million in 1956.

But the invited guest never arrived. The long-sought increase in foreign investment did not occur. Some blame the absence of massive investment on a new recession, as the rate of manufacturing growth declined in both Europe and the United States in 1957.[10] But the recession was short-lived, with major indices moving upward again in the spring of 1958. The price of copper dropped from 1956 to 1958 but then took to the mend. Copper was expanding everywhere else in the world, and only very slowly in Chile. Law 11,828 had not been enough to patch relations between the companies and the government. Indeed, behind the show of solidarity something very serious was amiss.

The issues of Chilean copper

The copper companies are not very popular in Chile. This is a sad fact that North American officials cannot readily understand. They have provided Chilean workers with far more fringe benefits than their counterparts receive in the United States. Not only are miners the highest paid workers in all Chile, but housing, utilities, and hospital care are provided them free of charge. At the Chuquicamata mine there is a five-story, multimillion dollar hospital. It has piped-in music and looks like a hotel.

No matter how well the workers are paid, no matter how many benefits are bestowed, there is one point the Chileans cannot forget. It is that the mining companies are foreign. Furthermore, they are two of the three large copper producers that dominate the industry in the United States.

Nevertheless, in spite of this fact, they do compete with both Canada and Africa—and even between themselves—as Senator Tomic has admitted. The companies "sell in the same market," he has said, "and sometimes in fierce competition [*encarnizada competencia*], by which they oblige Chilean copper to compete against itself in the same country and before the same consumer, thus deteriorating its prices and conditions of sales." [11] Although often the Chileans cry "Monopoly!" the crucial factor is that the companies are big and they are foreign, and they wield

[10] *Commodity Survey, 1958*, United Nations, New York, p. 6.

[11] Tomic, *op. cit.*

a powerful influence. It is demeaning to have such a large part of one's economy beyond one's control.

The limitation on sales to the Soviet Union is more than an irritant. Chileans say it not only doesn't work but it imposes a burden that others ought to shoulder. In the first place, they argue, the Soviet Union continues to buy copper from African producers. Very little is produced within the Soviet orbit (about ½ million tons to roughly 3½ million in the Western world). Why, argue the Chileans, should they be deprived of a large market potential when other "free world" nations feel no compunction about where they sell? In the second place, to the extent that Communist countries cannot supply their whole needs, they are impelled to seek copper substitutes in their laboratories. If they are successful, they will undercut future markets for copper everywhere. Finally, even if one does agree to suppress sales to the Soviet bloc, the financial burden suffered by Chile ought to be shared by those who are better able to undertake it and who consider themselves more threatened by the Communist "menace." The United States ought to pay Chile an indemnity for losses suffered in carrying out United States policy.

Some of—but not all—the Chilean arguments are readily challenged. In the first place, if African copper is drained off to the Soviet Union, to that extent it does not appear on the remaining world market to compete with the Chilean. In the second place, in so far as the Soviets are forced to seek copper substitutes, it is clear that their consumption is being diminished. If the purpose is to damage the Soviet Union, the policy is successful. However, not all Chileans are equally enthusiastic about damaging the Soviet Union, and they object to *having* to do so because of pressure from the United States. Furthermore, even those who favor the embargo feel that the losses to Chile should be compensated. As far as the policy is successful, it *does* restrict the world copper market, and there *is* a financial loss to Chile. Whether Chile should bear this alone is a question of equity that ought to bother the conscience of the world, including the United States.[12]

Refining is another festering issue. Less than half the tonnage mined in Chile is refined locally. In 1947, mine output was 470,200 short tons, compared to 282,000 short tons of refined copper. In 1960, the figures were 509,500 and 225,500 tons, respectively. In other words, not only did the percentage refined locally decrease, but the absolute amount as well. The peak year was 1951 when (influenced by the Korean conflict and

[12] Some may point out that the United States is a larger producer than Chile and therefore suffers equally from the restriction. However, since World War II the United States has become a net importer, consuming more than it produces. What it loses as producer, it more than gains as consumer. Chile is the world's principal *exporter* of copper.

lack of shipping space) the Chileans mined 419,600 short tons and refined 318,800 short tons. The experience proves to Chileans that refining can be done at home.

The economics of refining depend on the type of ore, the final product desired, quantities to be processed, availability of fuel, and transportation costs. Copper that has been concentrated or refined can obviously be transported cheaper than ore just out of the mines; hence the earlier processes (concentration and smelting) are done at the scene of the mine.

The ore at Kennecott's Braden mine (at El Teniente, Chile) is one of the purest in the world, and its refining is relatively simple. Copper matte is smelted in furnaces on the scene, producing blister, which can be refined either by fire or electrolytically. Fire refining costs about ¼ cent per pound, and the resultant product sells for only ¼ cent less than electrolytic copper, the refining of which costs about 2 cents. Hence there is a 1½-cent advantage in fire refining, and as much of this is done on the spot as is demanded. Fire-refined copper is utilized for brass. Blister is also useful for some crude purposes and sells for only about ⅜ cent under the price of electrolytic copper. The Braden mine sells about 70 per cent of its output in the first two forms and ships the remaining 30 per cent to Maryland, where it is refined electrolytically.

Copper-company executives will argue that the amount of copper refined in the United States is determined by economics. It is cheaper to build one large refinery than two small ones. Since the markets are primarily in the United States, and production is higher there than in Chile, it makes sense—so they say—that the bulk of the refining should be done there.

It is hard for a general economist to argue against the technical experts. Yet I sense—from talking to both Chileans and copper-company executives—that this is not the whole reason. With the reserves of the United States steadily closer to depletion, with higher proved reserves in Chile than anywhere else in the world (the Chuquicamata mine has the largest concentration of ore known in any one place) and new ones being developed in neighboring Southern Peru, with fuel available and easy transportation to the coast, and given the fact that refined copper weighs less for shipping than ore or concentrates, it would seem to us generalists that the emphasis in refining ought to be shifting steadily to the Southern Hemisphere. That it is not—I believe—is evidence of the mistrust between Chileans and the companies.

More copper will be refined in Chile only if more is produced there, in relation to the United States. So we are immediately led to the most sensitive wound. From 1947 to 1958 world copper production increased by 52 per cent (from 2,464,000 to 3,740,000 tons), whereas Chilean output went up by only 8 per cent (from 470,200 to 509,500 tons). That this slim advance should occur in the country where reserves are highest in the world is considered an indignity. In the same period, Northern Rhodesian production increased 103 per cent (from 217,400 to 441,100 tons), and Chileans suspect that sales to the Soviet orbit may have something to do with this.

The companies, in their turn, argue that the slow rate of growth is double-stemmed. In the first place, costs are high in Chile. Unions have demanded high wages and social benefits, and they strike easily. Uncertainty adds to the burden. Law 11,828—they say—did not resolve the tax question. Instead of negotiating different exchange requirements each year, the government threatens to add supplementary taxes. Already the effective rate is in the neighborhood of 70 per cent of income (and over 80 per cent on one mine).

The second reason looms almost as large. Chileans have been talking more and more of building their own industry, and the word "nationalization" is used with increasing frequency. Those Chileans who feel the capital of the companies has been stolen from their soil may have little respect for the "rights" of owners. But to company executives, this capital represents the savings, not only of wealthy men but of white-collar workers and small earners in the United States who have taken from their weekly wages to buy stocks. To them it is a sacred trust, which they cannot lightly risk in the face of "irresponsible" statements by Chileans who (they think) do not know what the hardships of saving are.

I once asked a copper executive why African output was increasing so much more than Chilean, and whether his company was not sensitive to the immense economic benefits to Chile and profitability to its own stockholders that lay untapped in the Andes. His answer ran along these lines:

> African output has built up because of new properties and new capital. For years we have been reluctant to bring capital into Chile because of the general business climate—primarily the question of taxes, and only secondarily that of expropriation. A change in government—even if Mr. Allende were elected—would not necessarily mean expropriation, and we would be willing to risk that anyway. We would also risk the uncertainties of growth in the copper market. But one thing we cannot risk is uncertain costs. Already our taxes are as high as can be squeezed out of us. We are sharing some 70 to 80 per cent of our profits before tax with the government. All we ask is that the same percentages be continued, with a twenty-year guarantee against increase. But they won't make that promise. They want to compel us to invest rather than induce us. And we don't play that way.

The government has argued that it will offer the tax guarantee on new investment but not on what is already there. The companies point out, quite correctly, that unless the guarantee is on all investment, it is not airtight. The government would be able to tax the new investment indirectly by levying higher percentages on the old, on the theory that the companies were better able to pay because of profits being earned from the new. Once the investment has been made, a "judicious" tax policy might even force the companies to operate at a loss, covering out-of-pocket costs but not depreciation.

One of the abandoned projects was overhaul of the Braden mine. Braden has been known as the "upside-down" mine. It is perched on a hill, and the shafts run downward to the valley. Because of geological conditions and heavy rainfall, it is impossible to expand physical facilities on the site. There is no more room on the mountain, and the surrounding ground shifts in the rainy season. No buildings can stand on it. But new capital is needed for expansion and improvement of workers' houses. The plan had been to move the entire town down to the more stable central valley, and then dig a new shaft upward into the mountain. The valley would have offered ample space for expanded facilities and more comfortable living.

Faith and culture

To any observer who can detach himself from the intense emotions of copper and Chile, it is painfully obvious that the trouble lies in mistrust, and that mistrust in turn stems from failure of both sides to breach cultural barriers.

To the North Americans, copper is a business venture established in the best traditions of private enterprise and individual initiative. The profits are not exorbitant, and in the face of world markets the companies are not monopolistic. The Braden mine has paid some $350 million in dividends over fifty years, or an average return of only 5 to 6 per cent on investment. The companies are contributing much to Chile. They are building up a middle class—a far greater percentage of employees' children go to college than is true in local enterprise. The companies provide impulse to local industry, such as refractories, powder, foundry materials, castings, and railroad equipment. They have introduced management instruction and a safety movement. But above all, they have brought the innovating ability and the determination to do the job. Need I comment—to anyone who has read Chapter 2—on how much these convictions stem from the capitalist ethic?

The companies seriously doubt that the Chileans would have done it, for (they think) Chileans "obviously" have little cost consciousness, little understanding of market forecasts and budgeting, little concept of customer relations, and little management ability. All this has been surmised from the small respect the government has had toward cost stability and price policies. Chilean decisions—so the North Americans believe—are based on politics and emotion, and you "can't succeed in business that way." The reluctance to sell refineries to Chileans stems from a fear of passing over the final product, and thus of entrusting to them the delicate task of customer relations.

To all but a few Chileans the companies are robber barons and interlopers who have stolen and exported the riches of their soil. If Chileans are not competent in managing a copper enterprise, it is because the companies have not trained them to be so (as is their "obvious" duty). They have not hired Chileans in top management positions, relying on the slim excuse that all Chileans capable of the job were already working for the government. The Yankees have maintained a strict aloofness and shown themselves to feel "superior" on account of their greater wealth. They have made their decisions in New York and "communicated" them to the Chilean government, as if to deprive it of the dignity that rightfully belongs to one who owns the soil and all that lies thereunder. The Yankee interests are too far afield, too unrelated to Chilean aspirations, to provide any basis for understanding and trust.

In short, the Chileans and the North Americans do not have faith in each other. The obligations they accept toward society are culturally distinct, and they have differing concepts of the demands society permits to be made upon itself. Each, seeing the other in his own image, cries lack of faith. Here, in a slim land along the Pacific coast of South America, lies a capsule of the tragedy of the Western Hemisphere. We intensely want to be good neighbors, yet we do not know each other.

SUGAR AND CUBA

> The trouble with the economy was sugar.
>
> A warning of the danger of monoculture, of the trend toward a one-crop economy, had been given as far back as 1883 by the greatest of Cuba's heroes. In that year José Martí, revolutionist, orator, poet, philosopher, sounded the alarm: "A people commits suicide the day on which it bases its existence on a single crop."
>
> The warning was justified—death to the economic welfare of the country, death to its national aspirations, were certain to follow if the trend toward monoculture continued.
>
> But in Cuba's case it wasn't suicide. It was murder. In 1883 Cuba was on the road to the top of the cliff, but it was the United States that pushed it over the top.[13]

So wrote two scholars of a rare breed—North American socialists—in their epilogue to the Cuban Revolution. For the economic history of

[13] Leo Huberman and Paul M. Sweezy, *Cuba: Anatomy of a Revolution*, Monthly Review Press, New York, 1961, p. 10.

Cuba and sugar is much like that of the Southern United States and cotton. Some day historians will look back on the Civil War and find some startling similarities between it and the Cuban Revolution.

There are incidental differences. One is that the sides were lined up awry. In the Civil War the "Yankee imperialists" were fighting the Southern "aristocrats," and the slaves were political pawns whose freedom was important because it became the rallying cry of the North. But the exact lineup is a hazard of history, whereas the fact of conflict stems from its fundamental currents. Of greater relevance is that freedom was the rallying cry of each movement and the path to freedom was led by intellectuals. Under what other circumstances could two intellectuals from the United States accuse their country of murder?

Except that migrant laborers and local illiterates substituted for black slaves, the one-crop Cuban economy was a close image of United States cotton plantations more than a century before. Sugar cutting depended on unskilled labor. There was no need for widespread public education. The economy was oriented toward the coast, with plantations selling their crops in nearby ports and acquiring consumer goods (for the wealthy) through imports. The statistics show that Cuba had one of the highest per capita incomes in Latin America, but these data do not reveal the lopsided distribution. There was little manufacturing, for land that was good for sugar was so good for sugar that no one would think of using it for anything else, except to hold in cattle until the market for sugar expanded. There were a few other crops, tobacco being another good earner. But the truck farming that grew the food people could eat occurred mainly close to Havana. Why? Because Havana is where the people lived who could afford to eat.

There were a few other primary products in Cuba. It became a principal source of nickel during wartime. And then there were the oil refineries. They were built because the companies thought political conditions in Venezuela were too unstable. They had to drill the wells there, because that is where the oil was found. But the refineries could be in Curaçao, Aruba, and Cuba. For nothing short of the United States itself could be safer.

Sugar and Cuban–United States relations

Sugar, believed to be native to the South Pacific or monsoon Asia, was known to the ancient world. As late as the fourteenth century it was a luxury reserved for kings, queens, and nobility. In 1532 the Portuguese introduced it to Northeastern Brazil, and later on in the same century they popularized its consumption in Europe, assuring themselves a booming market and prosperity such as that part of Brazil has not seen since. When the Dutch captured the city of Salvador in 1624, they learned the technique of the cultivation of sugar. Upon their subsequent expulsion, they carried the cane back to the smaller Caribbean islands, which were ideally suited to it, partly because of soil and climate and partly because their fields were always close to ocean transportation. With the twentieth century and the economies of mechanized sugar, the comparative advantage shifted to lands where larger plantations were possible. It was then that Cuba became the king of sugar cane. Brazil remained the queen, while Mexico, Argentina, Puerto Rico, the Dominican Republic, and Peru constitute the princedom of the Western Hemisphere.

Sugar is more widely grown than most people are aware. In the mid-nineteenth century production by beet was popularized, and climates unsuitable to cane began to yield sugar. Every country in the Western Hemisphere now produces it in commercial quantities, and of these Canada and Chile are the only ones with no cane at all. The United States produces over 2 million tons of beet sugar every year, or one-third to one-half of the quantity that Cuba produces from cane. Europe grows in the neighborhood of 20 million tons a year, almost exclusively from beet, compared to a roughly equal amount, mostly from cane, in the Western Hemisphere.

Two years before the independence of Cuba, North Americans owned only 10 per cent of its sugar land. But the twentieth century brought changes. They bought land while it was inexpensive, installed modern machinery, assembled some 9,000 miles of railroads (while the Cuban government built close to 5,000 more), and then—for the cheap labor needed on plantations—they drew on other Caribbean islands, particularly Haiti and Jamaica. They even went as far as China.

In World War I they broke the bank. They had invested when sugar was bobbing about at 2½ to 3 cents a pound. But European sources were cut off, and a world shortage set in. The price rose steadily—4, 5, 6, 7 cents. When the war ended European sugar fields were in ruins, and the price climbed dizzily on—15, 18, 20 cents, until its zenith of 22½ cents in May, 1920.[14] Caribbean labor was poorly housed and poorly fed, but it was abundant—no need to pay the cutters more than the price of 3 pounds of sugar a day. More and more lands were bought, more and more money borrowed, more and more mortgages signed, and more and more the profits swelled.

The ensuing orgy has been dubbed the "dance of the millions." Money danced into the casinos, into houses of prostitution, and into luxurious mansions in Havana and exclusive country clubs on the beaches. Those who wonder how Latin American Marxists ever got the notion that the motor of capitalism is fed by war and that war entails profits, wealth,

[14] *Ibid.*, p. 21.

landowning, and power need only look at Cuba on New Year's Eve, December, 1919.

But then the bubble burst. Europe was being reconstructed, and beets grow quickly. From May, 1920, until just before Christmas the price went steadily back the way it had come, and finally it shivered at 3¾ cents. Property values collapsed, loans were defaulted, and mortgages foreclosed. With the lands and mills of its erstwhile debtors, the National City Bank of New York organized the General Sugars Company. The twenties was not an era of contraction by any means, despite the fact that until 1934 the sugar price fell yearly (except 1925). Rather, they were a decade of consolidation in the hands of large companies, of modernization, reorganization, and expansion.[15]

The 10 per cent of Cuban mills in the hands of North Americans just before independence grew to 35 per cent in 1914 and up to 63 per cent in 1926. With the Depression of the thirties, North Americans again found it necessary to consolidate and this time to contract. They sold many mills to Cubans, so that by 1955 only 39 out of 161 mills were owned by North Americans, and 118 by Cubans. These 39 mills, however, were the large ones, producing 40 per cent of Cuban output.[16]

One who is prone to reflect and moralize cannot help observing that the "dance of the millions" had its counterparts in North American domestic history. The money that was made in Cuban sugar in World War I was not unlike the profits accumulated in oil, steel, and land speculation some decades earlier in the United States. Yet the impact in the United States was not a Marxist revolution but a succession of antitrust laws, regulation of utilities, encouragement of unions, and government controls to reduce business cycles and limit price rises in wartime. Is there anything in the North American experience that would indicate that the excesses of capitalism, with their patent injustices, can be peaceably resolved?

There are mountain-sized differences between the experiences of the United States and Cuba. When Rockefeller was accumulating his fortune in oil, Harriman and Gould in railroads, and Carnegie in steel, the victims—farmers and consumers—were not distinguished by nationality from the aggressors. All were citizens of the United States. Not only were they equal according to the laws, but they had been exposed to popular education. They knew how to read and write, and to take their cases to the courts and legislative assemblies. Furthermore, the rapidity with which economic growth was occurring brought labor shortage, higher real wages, and the diffusion of political power already mentioned in an earlier chapter.

[15] *Ibid.*
[16] *Ibid.*

But there is something else, of greater causality in the differing histories. To grasp it, let us return to a sentence a few paragraphs back (on page 140): "They bought land while it was inexpensive, installed modern machinery, assembled some 9,000 miles of railroads (while the Cuban government built close to 5,000 more), and then—for the cheap labor needed on plantations—they drew on other Caribbean islands, particularly Haiti and Jamaica."

The Marxist student—and many non-Marxist Latin Americans as well—will find these actions reprehensible. They constitute invasion by a foreign power. The land was bought when it was cheap, and speculative profits, *which should have belonged to Cubans,* derived from its subsequent appreciation. The railroads were a violation of the virginity of Cuba, for they cut across her land to connect it to the ever-growing "colossus." The dignity of the laborer was infringed. He was taken from his home, placed in a cruel shack, and paid only a fraction of what his employer would have had to pay a worker of his own nationality.

Most North Americans (laborers as well as capitalists) reading the same sentence would find the actions exemplary. To them land does not belong to nations but to those who use it rationally. It was cheap because Cubans did not farm it properly, and they cruelly wasted its potential. It became expensive because of what visionary North Americans did to it. The railroads were built for sugar, but Cubans also benefited from transportation. Unlike their ancestors (whose slavery they would not approve) the North Americans did not import anyone forcibly. "Obviously" the worker should not be advanced to the status *earned* by his counterpart in the United States. Still, the move must have been economically and socially attractive, or he wouldn't have come. Within his means (which were greater than before), it was the duty of the laborer to look after his own housing.

Divergent values incite different reactions in the two groups witnessing the "dance of the millions." To Marxists the cycle is part of the "innermost fabric" of capitalism, and war and excesses are the escape valve by which the system gasps on to its dying breath. North Americans are equally disgusted by the performance but look upon it as a flaw in a system whose better face they have known in the Western farms and labor unions of their country. They do not tear down the house when only one room is structurally weak.

Commercial patterns for sugar

World production of, and demand for, sugar are on the rise. Just before World War II total output was in the neighborhood of 35 million tons. It slumped in the war and immediate postwar years, but by 1950 it was back to the prewar range. And then it began to shoot upward. By 1958, the world was growing over 55 million tons. The increases were gradual in Asia and Oceania, moderate in Europe and North and Central America, and heavy in South America and Africa.[17]

An interesting feature of World War II was that the shortage created no "dance of the millions." The same control system that prevented the prices of copper and tin from rising also curtailed the profits of sugar producers in Cuba, whether North American or anyone else. The quotation in New York remained at a steady 3¾ cents from January, 1942, until January, 1946.[18]

As world production expanded by 70 per cent from 1948 to 1959, however, world exports of sugar climbed by only 19 per cent, reflecting an increasing tendency on the part of countries to consume their own product. Guerra points out that in the Northern countries of Europe (e.g., the United Kingdom, Denmark, and Sweden) consumption increased only in proportion to population, even though income was rising. But in the Southern countries (e.g., Italy, Turkey, and Portugal) per capita consumption increased along with incomes.[19] From this he concludes that income elasticity of demand is high in low-income countries but low in high-income countries. In Mexico and South America increases in consumption paralleled production, but in Cuba, the Dominican Republic, and the British West Indies the new output was largely for export.

Sugar is perhaps the least freely traded of the commodities. Geographically, it is divided into various preferential markets, of which the United States and the British Commonwealth loom largest. Roughly two-thirds of the world's exports and imports are traded in such arrangements, and the "free market" absorbs the rest under quotas established by the international sugar agreement.[20]

The United States consumes more sugar than any other country (about 8½ million tons in 1960). Its preferential area grew out of an economic and political struggle between its own beet sugar producers and cane growers in Cuba. Beets are grown in significant quantities in eight different states, whose senators and representatives have always fought for protection against Cuban cane. But much of the latter was also grown by United States interests. During the twenties the battle lines were drawn primarily over the tariff, the beet interests urging 2 cents or more per pound and the cane producers trying to keep it down to 1 cent, with a discount for Cuba.

In 1934 the two interests reached a compromise, resulting in the pref-

[17] *Commodity Yearbook, 1960, op. cit.*, p. 318.

[18] *Ibid.*, p. 398.

[19] José A. Guerra, "El convenio internacional del azúcar," *El Trimestre Económico,* April–June, 1957, pp. 111–142.

[20] In suspension at the time of writing.

erential area. The tariff would continue, but it was lower and became a secondary weapon. Imports were to be limited, and quotas assigned to domestic beet producers and foreign countries accustomed to supplying the United States. The quantity restrictions would maintain a price approximately 2 cents higher than that in the free market. Beet producers, whose unit costs are higher, would be able to survive while cane growers could hardly complain of an arrangement that awarded them such a price advantage. While sugar fluctuated around 3½ cents a pound in the world market in 1958, quotations in New York varied in the neighborhood of 5½ to 6 cents.

Upon hearing Latin Americans complain of the low prices paid by the United States for primary products, North Americans sometimes wonder how the high price of sugar can fail to be appreciated. The answer is that (before the Cuban Revolution) it was paid primarily to United States producers. While the Cuban quota was higher than any other, one must remember that (in 1955) about 40 per cent of Cuban sugar was grown by United States interests. Mainland United States producers (both beet and cane) have jointly had quotas almost as high as the Cuban, and the rest has been assigned almost entirely to Hawaii and Puerto Rico (politically associated with the United States; Hawaii is now a state), and the Republic of the Philippines, whose ties with the United States have been close. Below are the charges against the sugar quota by area of origin in 1958. "All others," with a meager 287,000 tons, includes all Latin America except Cuba and Puerto Rico.

SUGAR-QUOTA CHARGES IN THE UNITED STATES BY AREA OF ORIGIN, 1958
(*Thousands of tons, raw value*)

United States mainland:	
Beet	2,240
Cane	681
Hawaii	630
Puerto Rico	823
Cuba	3,441
Republic of the Philippines	980
All others	287
Total	9,082

SOURCE: *Commodity Yearbook, 1960,* Commodity Research Bureau, Inc., New York, 1960, p. 321.

With the loss of North American properties in Cuba and suspension of the Cuban quota in 1960, the United States began to reassess its preferential price system. In the first place, it has long been criticized for paying its benefits to individual growers and not to the national Treasury in producing countries. In the second place, the division of the Cuban quota among other countries—mainly in Latin America—opened the way for high-level political sparring. The government of Brazil ran an advertisement in *The New York Times* pleading its case for an increased quota, and other countries as well hired lawyers to argue their cause before individual congressmen.

At the time of writing various proposals have been advanced to abolish the country-by-country quota system, substituting a world quota in which foreign producers would compete for a share of the bonus market. It has also been suggested that the excess price should not be paid to growers but contributed to the national treasuries of producing countries as economic assistance under the Alliance for Progress. The details of these proposals have not been formulated, or at least not made public to date, but sentiment in favor of them is growing.

Outside the preferential areas, sugar is traded on the free market. Even here, the prices and quantities are not free, for they are more or less regulated by international agreement. First negotiated in 1931, the sugar agreement was renegotiated in 1937 and allowed to lapse with the war. It was revived in 1953, was revised in 1958, and again lapsed in 1961 because its exporting members could not agree on quotas.

Under the agreement of 1953, annual export quotas were assigned to producing nations, in order to contain prices within the range of 3¼ to 4¼ cents per pound. Importing countries, which participated in the negotiations, would agree not to buy from nonmember countries.[21] The price would be allowed to fluctuate freely within the extremes, but as it approached either one, quotas would be revised: reduced if the price fell, and expanded if it rose. An International Sugar Council was established to administer the agreement, with representatives of both exporting and importing countries.

The history of the agreement is one of difficult negotiations mixed with acrimony. Differences of opinion over quotas and price limits threatened several times to scuttle the agreement before they finally did so in 1961. The range was lowered to 3.15 to 4 cents in 1956, and then a series of bad crops shortened supplies in 1957, causing the price to rocket to well over 5 cents. Quotas were suspended, but the Council could not keep the price down. The final blow came in 1961 when members were unable to settle on a quota for Cuba. The others were willing to grant her an increase equal to what she had lost in the United States preferential market, but Cuba insisted on more, and agreement could not be reached.

[21] The United States participated as an importer, but its contribution was of minimal importance, because virtually all its sugar was bought under its preferential system.

Summary

Economically speaking, sugar leaves a bitter taste in the mouth. The major preferential arrangements—of the United States and the British Commonwealth—have not fully succeeded in stabilizing prices, although they have helped. To the extent that they have controlled supply and demand within their bailiwicks, they have rendered all the more violent the marginal fluctuations in the free market. The history of the sugar agreement has not been an easy one. It is perhaps too much to ask the representatives of member countries to cope with a problem so inflamed by the events in Cuba.

The behavior of the United States in its quota system shows the scars of domestic political battle between beet growers and cane producers with Cuban interests. Beet sugar is more costly than cane, and its protection constitutes a violation of the free-trade philosophy to which the United States has been turning in recent years.

United States growers of sugar beets are small farmers. They are not Wall Street capitalists of the type that Marxists believe control the United States government. Their political influence lies in the fact that they are dispersed over many states, and all the more legislators will therefore represent them. The cane producers in the United States also have high costs, because they are largely bit plantations and frequently face the possibility of a freeze. Consequently they are glad of the same protection accorded to beet farmers.

Before the Cuban Revolution, the political battle for sugar was waged primarily between beet farmers and United States nationals growing cane in Cuba. Although many Latin Americans feel the political strength of the latter was strong, the fact is that they had no formal representation in Congress (as did the beet growers). Herein lies a principal reason why the beet quota is so high.

Recent proposals for change in United States legislation are promising. If put into effect, they will divert the bonus price of sugar away from the purse of the grower and into national treasuries of Latin American countries, for use in programs of economic development. The United States might have enhanced its reputation by putting this plan into effect *before* its own nationals had lost their sugar properties in Cuba. In failing to do so, it lost one opportunity to demonstrate that enlightened foreign policy *can* be molded at the cost of economic interests in the United States.

OIL AND VENEZUELA

Oil has heated more passion than it has furnaces. Well over one-third of all United States investment in Latin America ($3,312 million out of

$8,990 million in 1959)[22] is in oil. Venezuela lives on it, for every year oil is more than 90 per cent of her exports. (In 1961 it was 92 per cent.[23] Ten years ago, before the development of iron as a second export, it was closer to 98 per cent.) Over 60 per cent of government revenue is contributed by oil companies. (In 1958–1959 it was 3,381 billion bolivars out of 5,090 billion.)[24] If oil is in surplus, Venezuela is in trouble.

If man learns to live with oil, it can be a rich blessing. It has been the major source of finance in a vast program of developing basic industries, transportation, iron and steel, and interior parts of Venezuela. Those who cite the primacy of capital in economic development point to Venezuela as the example of what a Latin American country can do when it has sufficient capital. But the going is not easy. In the mid-fifties substantial surpluses built up the government's reserves (deposits in the central bank), but of late these have been drawn down by deficits. Either Venezuela's current needs for capital are more than her availabilities, or else the other essentials of development have been inadequate to stabilize the capital she now has.

Three issues haunt Venezuela in her struggle to live with oil. One is that oil is in world surplus. Long-range prospects are good, but the near future lies heavy. The "oil giants" are facing more world competition than they like to think. The second is the national policy of the United States. A domestic battle—analogous to that between United States beet growers and cane interests in Cuba—has shaped up between small, independent oilmen and the major international companies with foreign interests. The Venezuelan government is not unaffected. The third issue lies within Venezuela itself. It is the relations between the government and the oil companies and how to maximize the contribution of oil to what Venezuela (like the rest of Latin America) most needs—economic development.

Oil in the world economy

The major threat facing the Venezuelan oil industry is the Middle East. Middle East output of crude oil (from Iran, Iraq, Kuwait, Qatar, and Saudi Arabia) increased by 445 per cent from 1947 to 1960, compared to 132 per cent in Venezuela and 38 per cent in the United States. Whereas in 1947 the production of crude in the Middle East was about two-thirds that of Venezuela (297 million barrels compared to 435 million), by 1960 it was producing 60 per cent more (1,619 million barrels compared to 1,010 million).[25]

[22] *U.S. Business Investments in Foreign Countries,* U.S. Department of Commerce, 1960, p. 93.

[23] *International Financial Statistics.*

[24] International Bank of Reconstruction and Development, *The Economic Development of Venezuela,* The Johns Hopkins Press, Baltimore, 1961, p. 414.

[25] *Commodity Yearbook,* 1960, *op. cit.,* p. 249.

The Middle East holds the largest known reserves of oil in the world—some 70 per cent of the total outside the Soviet bloc.[26] Yet it is a Johnny-come-lately in the market. The early growth of the oil industry occurred in the Western Hemisphere, and later on the Middle East cut its teeth on exports to Europe. Although Europe remains its principal market, in the last fifteen years it has been supplying the United States more and more. In 1946, it sent only 2 million barrels across the Atlantic, or ½ per cent of United States oil imports. By 1956 it was shipping 105 million barrels, or 20 per cent.[27]

Competition between Venezuela and the Middle East is fierce, for both investment and production. A curious aspect of this competition is that it is to some extent between companies and to some extent within them. There are over thirty-five major international oil companies, but seven of them produce approximately 90 per cent of the oil of *both* Venezuela and the Middle East. Each of these companies more or less specializes in one or another of the three major producing areas (Venezuela, Middle East, and North America). Standard Oil of New Jersey and Royal Dutch/Shell, for example, are associated primarily with Venezuela, while Gulf is mainly in the Middle East. British Petroleum is entirely in the Middle East (except for a tiny output in North America). Texaco, Standard Oil of California, and Standard Oil of New York are about evenly split between North America and the Middle East, with only minor operations in Venezuela.[27a] To the extent of this regional specialization, competition between Venezuela and the Middle East means real competition between

[26] Percy W. Bidwell, *Raw Materials,* Council on Foreign Relations, Harper & Row, Publishers, Incorporated, New York, 1958, p. 301.

[27] *Ibid.,* p. 301.

[27a] The percentage output of the seven major companies from the three major areas is shown below for 1957:

Company	North America	Middle East	Venezuela	Other
Standard Oil of New Jersey	27	20	50	3
Royal Dutch/Shell	18	26	45	11
British Petroleum	1	99		
Gulf	31	53	15	1
Texaco	42	37	14	7
Standard Oil of California	42	40	10	8
Standard Oil of New York	40	38	16	6
All companies	27	37	29	7

SOURCE: *The Economic Development of Venezuela,* International Bank for Reconstruction and Development, The Johns Hopkins Press, Baltimore, 1961, p. 133.

these groups of companies, and those who refer loosely to North American "oil monopolies" should know this.

Nevertheless, each of the seven companies (except British Petroleum) has interests in all three areas, and to some extent the interarea competition is within the companies themselves. Each company must decide how much it will invest and how much it will produce in each region. The fact that this decision is made outside Venezuela and that Venezuela is subordinated to international companies moved by allurements other than the good of their country is a sore to Venezuelans just as the copper situation infects the wounds of Chile.

During the fifties the Middle East began to capitalize on certain advantages over Venezuela. In the first place, her exploration costs are lower, mainly because of such natural factors as terrain, e.g., whether the oil is under Lake Maracaibo or not. In the second place, there is a far greater flow of oil in the Middle East, where each well produces an average of 5,000 barrels per day. This compares with 220 in Venezuela and 13 in the United States. In the third place, wages are higher in Venezuela, where workers earn as much as their counterparts in the United States. The total cost of producing a barrel of oil is somewhat less than 40 cents in the Middle East and slightly more than 90 cents in Venezuela.[28] In the fourth place, taxes are higher in Venezuela, taking 60 to 70 per cent of profits compared to 50 to 60 per cent in the Middle East.

Back in 1950, the natural advantages of the Middle East were not only less well articulated than now, but Venezuela also enjoyed lower cost of transportation to East Coast refineries in the United States. But technological improvements in tanker freight have brought a sharp decline in rates and shaved the differential. In December, 1959, the price of crude oil delivered in New York was the same, on long-term charter rate, from Kuwait and Punta Cardón, at $2.86. At the single-voyage spot rate, Kuwait had a $2.13 to $2.65 advantage over Punta Cardón.[29]

World output of oil increased every year from 1942 through 1959, but Venezuelan production reached a zenith in 1957 and thereafter leveled off (and even declined in 1958). The net inflow of foreign oil investment in Venezuela also tumbled after 1957. From $385 million in 1956 and $803 million in 1957, it crashed to $69 million in 1958 and $108 million in 1959. Instead of a new inflow in 1960, there was a net outflow of $90 million.[30]

Besides increasing costs in Venezuela in relation to the Middle East, two other reasons account for the drop in foreign investment. Preponder-

[28] *The Economic Development of Venezuela, op. cit.*, pp. 127–131.

[29] *Ibid.*, p. 129.

[30] *Balance of Payments Yearbook*, International Monetary Fund, June, 1962, vol. 13.

ant is the world surplus of oil. From World War II on through most of the fifties, everyone was madly seeking oil. In a turnabout tale that will surprise many Latin Americans, there are over eighteen thousand independent companies searching for oil in the United States, clamoring for (and receiving) government protection against the "giants" in Venezuela! The Suez crisis further stimulated exploration. Competition has also taken on a nationalist tinge, as governments all over the world want to secure their own supplies by encouraging their companies both at home and abroad.

Long-range prognostications for oil have been generally good—a U.S. Department of Commerce spokesman predicted that demand will remain high until the year 2000 [31]—so surpluses are considered temporary. But possession is permanent (or so it is thought), and both companies and countries have felt the incentive to find and capture as much as possible now. Only in the late fifties did they begin to think they had discovered enough. And then, of course, high-cost regions such as Venezuela (and the United States) felt the first reverberations.

The second reason is the nationalization of oil refineries and other United States–owned businesses in Cuba, and the ensuing political instability in Venezuela. Oil companies fear for the future and are not willing to bring investment into places where it is likely to be expropriated. Not only that, but Venezuelans themselves have increased their flow of funds to foreign banks.

The decline in output after 1957 was not compounded by the price weaknesses characteristic of much commodity trade. The value of petroleum exports from 1958 to 1960 remained higher than in 1956, although less than 1957. Oil can be stored or left in the ground and thus has a supply elasticity such that its prices are not so volatile as other commodities. From 1936 to 1941 the average price of crude petroleum at the Oklahoma-Kansas wells fluctuated only from 96 cents to $1.16 per barrel. During the war it was controlled at $1.11, but in the postwar years it moved to a higher level. From 1948 to 1960 its high was $3.07 (in 1957) and its low $2.57 (controlled price, 1948–1953).

Venezuelan oil is gripped in sharp-edged scissors. One blade is the Middle East competition we have just discussed. The other is a strong political bloc within the United States, its principal consuming market, to be discussed in the section that follows. It would be possible to dull both at once through an alliance with Middle East governments, and this is precisely what Venezuela has tried to do.

Late in 1960, Venezuela joined the Middle East in forming the Organization of Petroleum Exporting Countries (OPEC), whose objective is

[31] Paul W. McGann, "The Long-term Outlook for Petroleum," in *Commodity Yearbook, 1960, op. cit.*, pp. 33–38.

to "stabilize" prices at as high a level as feasible. (Libya and Indonesia joined later.) Through it, she has tried to persuade those governments to increase their royalty schedules and withdraw the privilege of deducting royalties in the calculation of income taxes.[32]

The future of Venezuela hinges on what happens not only in the Middle East but in oildom everywhere. In the long run, it will depend on economic development in Latin America and its integration movement. If the principal consuming nations have a "monopoly" over oil, the best way to break it is to develop other consuming nations. In the immediate future, events in the United States will have a telling influence on Venezuela's markets. It is to these events that we now turn.

Oil and politics in the United States

One of my students—this time a North American—wrote the following about oil and politics in the United States:

> [We do not have] a rational, well-calculated, overall program designed in the national interest. It is a series of responses to a variety of domestic pressure groups which have exerted themselves on the supine Eisenhower and scarcely more interested Kennedy administrations as circumstances have affected them. In all deliberations about this program, the domestic consumer and the foreign nations dependent on exports of oil to the United States have received scant, if any, attention.

To understand the oil policy of the United States, it is necessary to know something of the industry structure. There are some thirty-five large companies, producing about 58 per cent of the world's output outside the Soviet bloc and refining about 65 per cent.[33] Of these, fifteen are defined as "integrated"—that is, they include all activities from exploration to refining.[34] Five of them (Standard of New Jersey, Standard of New York, Standard of California, The Texas Company, and Gulf Oil) are dominant, although competition among these has been promoted by the antitrust laws. Even the casual motorist in the United States is aware of the competition from price wars that occur whenever oil is in surplus. However, these companies are linked with the two major foreign producers—Royal Dutch/Shell and British Petroleum, with which they jointly hold subsidiaries (such as the Iraqi Petroleum Company), agree on purchases and sales, and share patents.

Side by side with the major companies are the 18,000 independent producers already mentioned. These are small companies with little capital, who get their financing partly from the majors, who explore ex-

[32] *The New York Times*, Sept. 2, 1962.

[33] Bidwell, *op. cit.*, p. 303.

[34] Sebastian Raciti, *The Oil Import Problem*, Fordham University Press, New York, 1958, p. 16.

tensively, and who drill about 85 per cent of the nation's wells.[35] They take risks, and there is a rapid turnover. In general, they do not sell oil to the consumer but market it through the major companies.

The existence of a few majors and many independents sets the stage for what might seem to the uninitiated to be monopoly exploitation. Because the independents sell to the majors and have no other marketing channels, are they not crushed by overwhelming power?

While the independents do run a minor battle with the majors concerning prices and terms of transportation, their principal sensitivity lies in the amount of oil the majors are importing.

There is a long history of contention over imports, particularly as the United States has shifted from being a net exporter to a net importer of oil. In the early and middle twenties, while the automobile industry was growing, there was no problem. But new oil discoveries and improvements in techniques were the harbingers of oversupply, and in 1929 the Independent Petroleum Association of America was formed to be the political voice of the independents. The discovery of promising new fields in eastern Texas in the early thirties, coupled with depression, placed the problem in focus. Since that time there have been bitter internal struggles, partly over unregulated drilling versus conservation but mainly about import policy.

If competition from the Middle East has brought a pox to Venezuela, it produced a scourge for the independent producers in the United States. Their cost of production is higher than in Venezuela because of lower average output per well. The majors, whose concessions extend to both Venezuela and the Middle East, are pressing for unlimited imports, while the independents want to clamp down.

The independents would like tighter restrictions more against the Middle East than Venezuela. Competition between Texas and Venezuela is less strong, because Texas oil is light, more suitable to gasoline, while Venezuelan is heavier and used more for residual fuel. On the other hand, the coal interests in the United States have joined the battle for import restrictions against Venezuelan oils, because they see competition in the market for heating homes and other buildings.

To date, the independent producers and coal miners have succeeded, to the detriment of both Venezuela and the majors. The Trade Agreement Extension Act of 1955 permits the President, upon investigation, to restrict the entry of any article that he has reason to believe ". . . is being imported into the United States in such quantities as to impair the national security." Through their association, the thousands of independent producers have urged that, to supply the United States adequately in time

[35] Bidwell, *op. cit.*, p. 305.

of war, there must be experienced explorers and drillers, and their activities are discouraged by cheap imports.

The controversy has burned a hot, emotion-blown flame. Many believe it is obvious that national security has nothing to do with the matter, that the independents want protection, and that they are numerous enough—and scattered over enough states—to demand it in Congress and through the President. In 1957, President Eisenhower asked for a "voluntary" reduction of imports, in the hope that the importing companies—spurred by a sense of patriotism—would see the need for reinforcing national security. But the companies saw no such need, for they did not believe security was at stake. Some reluctantly complied and others refused. In 1959, therefore, mandatory quotas were imposed, limiting imports of crude oil and many other products to 9 per cent of national sales. President Kennedy further tightened these quotas in November, 1962.

The phenomenon of 18,000 independent producers able to stand before five giants and blow them down ought to be emotionally appealing to many Latin Americans, despite the fact that their economic interests lie on the other side. How is it possible? An obvious answer is that they are politically organized, and they vote for representatives in Washington. But there is another factor, not so readily recognized. It is that the United States is a growing economy, and there are many opportunities for employment and investment of capital. If an independent producer is not satisfied with the terms by which he deals with the giants, his mobility makes him free.

Company and government relations in Venezuela

Like the copper companies of Chile, the foreign oil companies in Venezuela have never been popular. Ever since dictator Gómez allowed them to draft the petroleum legislation in 1918, they have been accused of stealing the nation's wealth. There was the question not only of how much tax the companies should pay but of whether the government was spending the proceeds properly. In other words, the companies were accused of collusion with dictators to steal the oil and divide the loot.

There have also been disputes over refining, just as in Chile with copper. Before 1943 virtually all oil was refined outside the country, mostly at Curaçao and Aruba. Since then, however, the government has insisted on the refining of 10 to 15 per cent of crude within the country. In the late forties, there was an inflow of investment to build refineries on the Paranaguá Peninsula.

The tax legislation introduced since the October, 1945, revolution has now made history. A fifty-fifty split of profits between the government and companies had already been instituted under Medina in 1943, but the schedule was not flexible enough to preserve the government's relative share as sales increased. In December, 1945, the new government declared an extraordinary tax of $27 million and then rewrote the law to provide a fifty-fifty split regardless of the output. It also launched plans to build a national refinery and eventually to go into the oil business itself. In 1946 the Venezuelan Development Corporation was organized, with oil revenue to stimulate agriculture and industry.

Further reforms were thwarted by the counterrevolution of November, 1948, and the decade of military government associated with Pérez Jiménez. Pérez Jiménez continued to tax the companies, but instead of devoting the proceeds to genuine development projects, he made a showplace of Caracas with luxury apartment and office buildings, and a cable car and hotel enshrouded in cold mists atop a mountain.

The oil prosperity of the early fifties supplied the Pérez Jiménez regime with plenty of capital. Foreign exchange reserves reached their height in 1957, and government deposits at the central bank rose until 1958 and then began to fall. Deficits had started by the time the dictator was ousted, and the downswing was on. But Venezuela was by no means bankrupt.

Nevertheless, the incoming government felt the need of added revenues. In December, 1958, it suddenly increased oil taxes to yield a sixty-forty split instead of the old fifty-fifty formula. After Betancourt had returned to the Presidency in 1959, a new labor agreement was negotiated calling for increased wages, more fringe benefits, and a shorter workweek.

It is one of the unfortunate coincidences of history that the oil cycle peak coincided with the overthrow of Pérez Jiménez. The succeeding government has had to cope with compounded financial pressures. Oil investment had fallen off for both political and economic reasons. The government has felt obliged to pressure the companies for higher taxes, and they in turn have complained that competitive pressures in the Middle East limit their ability to pay. There is some evidence that Betancourt has been influenced by the competitive outlook, and he is reported to have made a personal appeal to congressmen not to increase oil taxes further. Such a move does not endear him to the ultraleft.

The companies, for their part, are uneasy. When I questioned an oil executive concerning Betancourt and Pérez Jiménez, he did not reply immediately. "Let me put it this way," he said. "Pérez Jiménez was a dictator, and the worst of them, but at least we knew what was going to happen next. The Acción Democrática makes impulsive decisions, such as the overnight increase in taxes on December 20, 1958. They didn't even consult us on this, although we would have been willing to talk to them."

Not all Venezuelans see any need to consult the oil companies on the level of their taxes. They believe they were consulted too much before 1958, and this is one reason they are so powerful. Yet the company executive's response is typical of his capitalist-ethic background. Businessmen run so many "legitimate" risks, he would say, that they should not be compounded by political uncertainty.

The government of Venezuela is going into the oil business. It has announced that no new concessions will be granted to private companies but will belong—along with some fields of proved reserves—to the new Venezuelan Petroleum Corporation, established in April, 1960. This is, of course, another factor that has limited the influx of foreign investment and added to the nation's foreign exchange problem. The World Bank—whose concerns are economic and not political—has suggested as tactfully as possible that the new corporation should assume operations only slowly.[36]

> The mission is aware of the reasons why the Venezuelan Government wishes to embark on this new field of endeavor. However, we consider it prudent to suggest that the activities of the company be, in fact, of a very limited nature in the next few years. Any attempt to create a comprehensive operating business would require a very large capital investment. This would impose a heavy demand on the relatively limited investment funds available from the budget at a time when they are urgently needed for other purposes for which alternative sources of funds are scarce—education, health, housing and agricultural reform.

The capitalist ethic helped shape the World Bank's approach. One of its tenets is that decisions are made on rational economic grounds, not motivated by nationalism. The difference between foreign and domestic capital is not readily appreciated by those of this ethic. If foreign private capital is available for investment in oil but not in social development, what could be more logical than to reserve the public investment for sectors where the private will not tread? Even President Frondizi urged the same for oil in Argentina. But Sr. Frondizi isn't President any more.

COFFEE AND HALF OF LATIN AMERICA

From 1947 to 1959, the difference between the lowest quotation for coffee and the highest was 64.6 cents (U.S.) per pound.[37] If the price of

[36] *The Economic Development of Venezuela*, *op. cit.*, p. 25.

[37] Average spot price per month of Santos No. 4 in New York. The high was 88.3 cents and the low 23.7 cents. Commodity Research Bureau, Inc., *op. cit.*, p. 98.

coffee drops by *1 cent,* Brazil's loss runs to $23,809,680, or 4 per cent of her gold and foreign-exchange reserves.[38] Colombia would lose $6,205,-300, or 4 per cent of her reserves. Costa Rica would lose $6 million, or 2 per cent of her reserves. Multiplied by Brazil's quota in the international coffee agreement, a price differential of 64.6 cents (U.S.) is equal to $1.5 billion, or about 20 per cent of her national income.

Coffee ranks as one of the first two exports of half the Latin American countries. In 1957 it was second only to petroleum in Latin American exports everywhere and was first in those to the United States.[39] The United States is not only the largest buyer of coffee but imports more than all the rest of the world combined.

In sum, coffee is the most valuable commodity to Latin America. Its price is among the most volatile. Raging prosperity has come in on its waves, and depression and unemployment are the jetsam of its ebb. As the largest buyer, the United States is often held responsible for the ups and downs of the coffee cycle. Bitter charges have been hurled at the large roasters for whatever price control may be attributable to them. Equally acrid tempers have been loosed in the United States Congress at Brazilian speculators thought to be controlling the market.

The trouble with coffee is that it is easy to grow, yet takes so long to mature. If the price is high, it is no trick to plant new trees. But they will not bear in commercial quantities for about five years. Another problem is that few know what the others are doing. Coffee statistics are inadequate, and even if they were the most accurate in the world, the backlands farmer in Uganda, or even Brazil, would probably not read them. Everyone plants when prices are high, and five years later the world has too much coffee. Price drops, growers are discouraged, and few plant. Seven to ten years later the old trees have reached their commercial peak, and again there is shortage. Over- and undersupply also result from political events, the business cycle, and freezing weather.

The chronology of coffee, 1947 to 1960

With World War II Latin America lost a sizable market in Europe. Its only sales were to the United States, which controlled prices and set country quotas on imports. Plantations were abandoned, and production fell to new lows. In 1941–1942 it was 23.8 million bags, compared to 30.8

[38] Provided it exports its quota in the International Coffee Agreement. Reserves are taken as of December 31, 1961, and include the gold and exchange assets of the monetary authorities. *International Financial Statistics.* Quotas in the ICA: Brazil, 18,000,000 bags of 60 kilograms each; Colombia, 6,011,280 bags; Costa Rica, 950,000 bags.

[39] *United States–Latin American Relations, Commodity Problems in Latin America,* 86th Cong., 1st Sess., S. Doc. 125, p. 8.

million for 1938–1939. After the war the European market was partly regained, and output picked up just enough to meet current demand. Prices rose from the war-controlled 13.6 cents a pound to over 27 cents in 1948, and planting was encouraged.

As demand increased in the postwar years, supply did not at first keep pace. World exportable production remained virtually constant from 1948 to 1951 (at 29 million to 30 million bags), while price rose from 26.6 cents to 55.5 cents per pound. But plantings were being made, and by 1952 the new supplies made a dent in the market. Exportable production increased from 29.8 million bags in 1951 to 33.3 million in 1952.

In July, 1953, the great frost struck the coffee plantations of Paraná in Brazil. In its purely physical impact, it hardly deserves the adjective "great," for Brazilian exportable production fell by only about 6 per cent from 1952 to 1953, and world production even increased. But it touched off a massive speculation, with blast-off prices and consumer resistance in the United States. It led Congress to order the Federal Trade Commission to make a full-scale investigation of coffee, of who sells and who buys, and of how monopolistic is the industry. This study furnishes a valuable insight into the operations of a commodity market.[40]

Much of the responsibility for the speculative activity was attributable to inadequate crop reporting. So decided the Federal Trade Commission. Growers in Paraná, aware that the frost had occurred but not really conscious of how extensive it was, began to speculate in coffee futures, bidding up prices on the New York exchange. As brokers and roasters saw the price of futures rise, they began to lay in heavy inventories, pushing the spot price from 61.3 cents in December, 1953, to 88.3 cents in July, 1954.

As the price of packaged coffee in the grocery stores rose to over $1, the consumer rebelled. His widespread resentment shook the sacred belief that the demand for coffee is forever inelastic. So it may be at around 50 to 80 cents (consumer price), but above $1 it clearly was not. Consumption in the United States tumbled from 19.1 million bags in 1953–1954 to 14.8 million in 1954–1955.

Producers had bought heavily in anticipation of higher prices and were overstocked. Imports, which had increased in 1953, dropped about 19 per cent in 1954, and the spot price to 68½ cents by December.

It would have declined steadily from that point on, since the increased plantings of the late forties were now in bearing. But further frosts in the next years delayed the day of reckoning until 1957. At that time production expanded from 34.6 million bags (world output of exportable coffee in 1956) to 46.2 million bags. And it continued on up to 51.3 million bags

[40] *Economic Report of the Investigation of Coffee Prices,* Federal Trade Commission, 1954.

in 1958 and 58.6 million in 1959. Prices, of course, plunged, to about 36 cents by the end of 1959.

The structure of the United States coffee industry

The study by the Federal Trade Commisison shed much light on the nature of the coffee industry in the United States and how competitive or monopolistic it is. Coffee is imported by both jobbers and roasters, and the jobbers obviously sell to roasters (usually through brokers as intermediaries). The FTC collected information on imports individually by companies, but did not have data on purchases by roasters from jobbers and brokers. The five leading roasters were General Foods, the Great Atlantic and Pacific Tea Company, J. A. Folger Company, Standard Brands, and Hills Brothers. A total of 19.9 million bags was imported in 1953, as follows (in millions of bags):

5 leading roasters	5.0
Next 20 leading roasters	1.6
10 leading jobbers	5.9
Next 46 leading jobbers	5.0
All others	2.4
Total imports	19.9 *

* *Economic Report of the Investigation of Coffee Prices,* Federal Trade Commission, 1954, pp. 138–139.

In assessing whether the coffee industry consists of monopoly buyers exploiting Latin American producers, one must bear in mind several factors. In the first place, roasting and sales to consumers are concentrated in a few large companies. However, in the second place, these companies are not able to keep the purchase price down in the face of supply shortage. They were obviously bidding against each other in the scramble to obtain inventories in 1954. In fact, the higher prices of Latin American coffee from 1950 through 1957 generally would indicate that the buyers were not an organized monopoly. In the third place, the companies have not been able to keep consumer prices high in the surplus years when they themselves were paying less. The price in the grocery store correlates closely with the spot price in New York, indicating that the companies compete actively against each other for sales.

The fact that North American roasters are competitive, however, is no reason for coffee growers to refrain from conspiring against them. In the first place, the volatility of coffee prices is a serious disrupter of economies and their development, and the need for stabilization is patent. In the second place, a coffee agreement that will organize growing countries into a monopoly, restricting their output and raising their prices, is a laudable endeavor. Will not the North American consumer contribute more cheerfully to their economic development as he drinks a cup of coffee than he will when he makes out his income tax return?

Controls of coffee output

The only question is whether it can be done. Price stabilization schemes are not new, and history reveals them to have been successful only when their purpose was not to keep prices indefinitely high. Latin Americans believe the United States should pay a "just price" for coffee—meaning by this some price (not clearly defined) higher than the average level now paid. What they do not realize is that the United States government cannot *make* the consumer drink coffee.

Brazil's early valorization plans were successful because they were limited to buying coffee in surplus years and selling it later when the price was high. In the disastrous drop of 1901–1902 (when price hit the all-time low of 3.55 cents) the government of São Paulo bought almost eleven million bags. But it sold them beginning in 1911 and liquidated the loan in 1914 at considerable profit. Similar interventions were undertaken toward the end of World War I and in the early twenties.[41]

Since those days Brazil has tried every trick in the bag to curtail output and increase prices. She has created government organizations, bought crops, controlled them, licensed them, destroyed them, regulated their transportation and the quantities allowed in ports, loaned money to producers, and enforced price floors. Current policy is carried out by the Brazilian Coffee Institute, which fixes quotas by port or producer and supervises the shipment of coffee within the country. It also buys stocks and fixes prices of foreign sales.

Other countries have analogous arrangements. In Colombia, where output is entirely on small farms (of which four-fifths are owner-cultivated), there is a free market, but the Federación Cafetera Colombiana undertakes to buy unlimited quantities at a minimum price. By divorcing its grower price from that of the world market and incurring losses in some years and profits in others, the Federación promotes price stability within the country.[42] The Banco Cafetero provides seasonal financing. So that the grower will not depress prices by selling at the peak of production, the bank lends him the wherewithal to hold his crop for sale in the off-season.

But the greatest attention of producer countries is on an international coffee agreement. Although the largest producer, Brazil far from domi-

[41] Winfield C. King, *Brazil's Coffee Industry,* U.S. Department of Agriculture, FAS-M-131, March, 1962, pp. 5–6. (Pamphlet.)

[42] *Colombia Is Moving Ahead,* National Federation of Coffee Growers of Colombia, New York, 1961. (Pamphlet.)

nates the market. The restraint of a single country, or even a group of countries not representing the entire industry, can only inflict losses at home while allowing others to benefit from higher prices. An inter-american coffee agreement, with export quotas, was signed by the United States and fourteen Latin American countries during World War II, but it was allowed to lapse in September, 1948.

In 1957 Brazil and six other countries (the "Mexico Club") agreed on export quotas and production restrictions. A year later they were joined by nine more. But it was painfully obvious that no coffee agreement of Latin American countries alone would be successful, since production was increasing in Africa. Whereas in 1937–1938 Africa produced 6 per cent of the world's output, by 1959 it was producing 14 per cent. In that year the principal African producers (except Ethiopia) joined the agreement, which thus became worldwide.

The producing countries have long felt that their agreement would be successful only with the support of consumers, particularly the United States. For not all producing countries have been eager to join. All are aware that the grower who stays out will enjoy higher prices all the more for not having to mess with the restraints that brought them about. Only if importing nations refuse to buy from such renegades—or at least limit purchases with reference to some base year—would they be deprived of their illicit fruits.

In 1958 the U.S. Department of State joined informal talks with major producing countries, creating a Coffee Study Group of thirty-two producing and consuming members. These talks yielded the International Coffee Agreement of 1962, with the most pervasive set of controls ever undertaken.

The agreement establishes an International Coffee Organization, whose duties are performed through an International Coffee Council. Quotas are assigned to all producing members. Each year the Council estimates the world demand and adjusts quotas by whatever percentage is necessary exactly to meet it. Although the agreement does not so state, nevertheless the maintenance of a certain price is implicit in the estimate of demand. Demand is not entirely inelastic but does depend on price.

Exports to a list of countries defined as "new markets" (where coffee is not yet popular) are exempt from quota. Producers are encouraged to advertise and expand sales in these countries.

So long as the members of the organization represent 95 per cent or more of world exports, the obligations of importing members are only nominal. But if at any time nonmember output exceeds 5 per cent, each member shall restrict its purchases from those countries to the amount imported in three years prior to the agreement.

The ideological commitments of the United States are not happy bedfellows with commodity controls, and it did not join the coffee agreement lightly. Latin Americans tend to believe that earlier United States opposition was based solely on desire to buy at a lower price and any acquiescence (as in World War II and after the Cuban Revolution) is politically motivated. They are right in the latter but not in the former.

The United States government does not care whether consumers pay another 5 cents or so for a pound of coffee. If the price approaches $1, as it did in 1954, Congress may investigate. But between 40 and 60 cents it doesn't matter much. Tempers won't flare, and the government doesn't fall easily. Coffee consumers are not a political group, and they have more important issues on which to base their votes. If they find the price too high, their answer is not to vote for a different President but to drink less coffee. Since coffee is not grown in the United States, the roasters are not organized in the same sense as sugar-beet farmers or independent oil companies. If anything, they fear antitrust prosecution and try to steer clear of any suggestion of collusion.

The opinion—so often heard in Latin America—that the United States government *wants* cheap coffee for its people does not coincide with political reality. Latin Americans who argue this point with North Americans merely reveal their ignorance of what is, and what is not, politically important in the United States. There are other issues—more real and more vital—to influence the decision of the State Department.

Foremost along these is that the Department does not cherish the role of international policeman for coffee producers. If (say) Ethiopia is reluctant to participate, the United States does not want to say, "You *must* join the agreement, or we, with our immense political and economic power, will punish you." The United States (believe it or not) is sensitive to the charge of imperialism so often hurled at it.

The role of policeman becomes less attractive because he believes the coffee agreement *really* won't work. Demand is *not* inelastic in the long run. If the price is kept high, people *will* begin to drink other beverages. This won't happen tomorrow, or even next year, but it may be noticeable ten years from now. Furthermore, supply is also *not* inelastic in the long run. It is easy to plant a coffee tree. In Uganda virtually all coffee is grown by peasant farmers on small plots. In Kenya and Tanganyika there are state farms, but peasants still come into, and go out of, production easily. Price can be very low—possibly as low as 10 cents a pound—and these peasants will still have incentive to produce, since their alternative economic opportunities are so limited. If prices are kept higher than the level dictated by supply and demand, the pressure will be continuous for both increased output and decreased consumption. The policeman's lot is not a happy one.

Why, then, did the United States join the coffee agreement? There are two reasons. The first is plainly political. There is a cold war, and inter-American solidarity is considered essential. The State Department is not so puritan as to hold steadfast to its economic convictions in the face of political urgency in the opposite direction.

The other reason is more salutary, more pleasing to one's esthetic sense. It is recognition that the problem is of crucial and immediate urgency, and that it cannot be solved by being ignored. Coffee is in world surplus, and far too much is being grown. Economics moves fast these days, and the quick application of long-run forces can bring suffering. We discovered this in the case of our own farmers. There is surplus output of wheat, peanuts, and cotton in the United States which the government is easing by purchase of excess stocks, with prices gradually declining. The fact that United States farmers are moving into other employments and that their per capita income is not advancing as rapidly as that of the rest of the nation indicates that the long-run solution is on the way. It is hoped that the same—not easy, but less rough—adjustment can be made by coffee producers.

It will happen only if output is consciously reduced. Fortunately, governments of the producing countries are aware of this. Members of the Agreement are obligated to reduce production to the amount needed for domestic consumption and quota-restricted exports, and they must report the measures they are taking.

Even so, in the long run all controls will fail unless enforced by either military oppression or economic incentive. The farmers in Uganda will not grow coffee at 10 cents a pound if there are guns to prevent them from doing so. But they also will not grow it if other, better opportunities are offered. As in so many problems, the long-run solution to coffee prices lies in the growth of other economic sectors.

CONCLUSION

The ancient concept of general equilibrium, cherished by classical economists, has taken on a political flavor. To future theorists, it will belong to the social sciences as a whole, and disquisitions confined to economics will recognize that partial equilibrium is the highest level they can attain. The markets for Latin American commodities in the United States are an example. The rub, push, and pull of a profusion of economic forces and political blocs could well be the subject of an integrated theory that once again merits the name "political economy."

He who believes that the government of the United States is dominated by a small group of homogeneous wealthy landowners and corporate stockholders, that Washington revolves around how to secure raw materials cheaply and sell manufactured goods dearly, is not awake to the subtleties by which our politicoeconomic system functions. The proliferation of countervailing forces—a collection of small beet-sugar farmers, 18,000 independent oil producers, three giant copper companies, five large coffee roasters, uncounted importers, jobbers, brokers, and many more—all have found their niche in our society and have overflowed into others where mores are different.

To some of them (such as the beet farmers) security is momentarily political. So long as their representatives in Congress can maintain sugar at 2 cents above its "normal" price, they will survive. But the economic element may some day rub the political, when artificial sweetners supersede sugar generally, as they are now doing for some purposes. Another political facet may pull against the first, as the output of foreign cane growers increases and the United States finds its long-range international interests are more weighty than those of a few beet farmers. If foreign aid is given through high sugar prices, beet growers may live on the strength of a weightier force. But if not, they may some day be pushed into the background. Their future is comparable to that of Latin American coffee growers.

To others—such as the copper companies—equilibrium is a delicate balance between command within their industry and assault from substitute products, with the watchful eye of Uncle Sam ready to signal for an antitrust action at any moment. A new political factor is the increasing talk of nationalization in Chile and the inability of the companies to reach an understanding with the government on promotion of their mutual interests. This force alone may rupture the equilibrium of the past, setting up new patterns of politicoeconomic forces both repelling and attracting each other.

Politics is counterpoised against economics in the petroleum industry. The economic reality of competition in the Middle East and genuine inability of the oil companies to yield more revenue to the Venezuelan treasury are confronted by the political reality of forces that feel the companies should never have achieved their foothold in the first place. Still, it is impossible to sow petroleum in the fields of development if installations are blown up in Lake Maracaibo. Across the Caribbean in the Washington arena, the Independent Petroleum Association of America is the toreador to challenge the rampaging majors, and the Venezuelan government finds itself in the uncomfortable position of cheering for the bull.

Inter-American commodity problems are further confounded by cultural clashes. There are honest, genuine differences between peoples in what are fundamentals normally accepted as the minimum of decency and morality. One of these lies in the nationality of land. To Latin Americans, the land belongs to him who lives upon it or to him within whose national boundaries it lies. Oil beneath the surface of Venezuela or

Mexico is Venezuelan or Mexican, and there is nothing to discuss. If the Venezuelans or Mexicans choose to leave it there or use it for their own development, or even burn it and waste it, that is their choice and privilege.

To North Americans, natural resources are God-given for the benefit of mankind. Not all mankind, necessarily, but they belong to him who has the determination and ingenuity to find them, to save and acquire the capital to dig for them, and to take them from the ground and sell them to others. In a formal sense, North Americans recognize the sovereignty of nations, but sovereign nations may sell the rights to their soil, and once the bargain is struck, it is sacred. If in an earlier age North Americans showed greater pluck in locating oil and copper, and in developing sugar fields, and if others who were closer to the land failed to appreciate or recognize its value, then the die of history is cast in favor of the venturesome.

It is not for us here to determine the code of ethics by which primary products should initially have been secured and marketed, or indeed whether such should ever have occurred. Nor should we now rule on whether bribery of a tyrant was adequate compensation or whether heed should have been paid to the "rights" of those whose only claim—a weak one in North American eyes—is that they happened to have been born there. To be pragmatic (as I myself must, for my background lies in the capitalistic ethic) let us be concerned more with the morality of today than the evils of yesterday.

Morality is a function of economic growth. One can shoulder one's way about in a growing space without infringing upon one's neighbors, but restless people are a menace in cramped quarters. So long as his own real income is rising, the United States consumer doesn't object if the beet grower, or even the Latin American coffee grower, asks a few cents more a pound. Of course, he may reply by spending his money on something else, but the decision is made amicably. The protection of vested interests in a society where virtually everyone has one and where they offset each other in a spectrum of politicoeconomic equilibrium is not a dangerous sin. But to intrude them into another nationalism, at a different stage of economic growth, invites cultural clash over what is moral and what is not.

7 Inflation

NOT ONLY IN Latin America but in many parts of the less developed world inflation is a way of life. The cost of living in Indonesia has increased over sevenfold in the last decade, in Korea it is more than 5 times the 1952 level, in Chile over 16 times, and in Bolivia more than 750 times! In another group of countries, inflation runs a milder course. Mexican living costs are a bit less than twice what they were ten years ago, while those in India and Pakistan are only 20 per cent higher. In a few countries, such as El Salvador, the rise in the cost of living has been smaller than in the United States. Economists in both the more and less developed world have come to speculate on whether there is a cause-and-effect relationship, one way or the other, between inflation and development.

Almost anything can be "proved" empirically. "Look at Brazil," the proponents of inflation will argue, for here is a country whose rapid growth has belied the dire predictions of those who say inflation leads to disaster. "Look at Chile," the opponents will say, for a country in which prolonged inflation has been accompanied by relative stagnation. The Argentine stabilization program of 1958 brought about a resumption of real economic growth that lasted at least until the chinks in monetary stability reappeared. But then again, Bolivia's stabilization program, still in effect after only one major retreat in seven years, is far from a paragon of economic advancement.

Inflation is such a hot-tempered issue that its proponents are ready to credit it with anything good that may occur in an inflationary country, while its opponents are equally prepared to charge it with anything bad.

The opinions of economists may be divided into four groups, some of which contradict each other while others overlap. Each group has its favorite countries to support its position:

1. "Inflation is good." Inflation is a means of stimulating saving where all others fail. It can redirect resources into channels of growth, in both the private and public sectors, and has contributed substantially to the development of such nations as Mexico and the United States.

2. "Inflation is bad." Inflation is a way of distorting and eventually stopping economic development. If indeed it does promote saving, it directs funds into the wrong channels, encouraging industries that either are not competitive or do not contribute to growth. Eventually, it destroys the incentive to save. It has, in fact, been disastrous in Korea, Vietnam, Indonesia, Argentina, and Greece.

3. "Inflation is inevitable." Like it or not, inflation is an inevitable consequence of economic development. Countries that do not inflate, stagnate. Although it may bring some evils with it, the greatest of them all is to suppress the inflation, which is also to suppress economic growth. Did not the Chilean stabilization program cause manufacturing output to level off during 1960 and 1961?

4. "Seek the good; control the bad." Inflation presents both dangers and opportunities. If properly supervised, it can promote saving and investment. Careful vigilance must be undertaken, however, to prevent disruptions. Some say this can be accomplished through price and exchange controls, but others argue it is only a matter of keeping the inflation mild. Has not Brazil been able to extract the "good" from inflation while controlling the "bad?"

DEFINITION OF INFLATION

While some say inflation is merely a rising price level, I shall adopt a more sophisticated definition. Inflation is a condition in which the exercise of financial resources (e.g., money) to buy goods and services is greater than the value, at current market prices, of real resources available for purchase out of the nation's production or other domestic trading.

This more precise statement of the traditional definition ("too much money chasing too few goods") implies two possible outlets for inflation: The excess of financial resources may lead to price increases in the real resources bought. But it may also lead to an influx of imports, as foreign goods supply the lack in national resources. Thus an inflationary condition gives rise *either* to an increase in prices *or* to a deficit in the balance of payments, and usually to both. In Chile, for example, the increase in prices of recent years was mitigated by an import surplus.

By following particular policies rather than others, nations can direct the impact of inflation into either the foreign or domestic theaters. For example, exchange control and currency depreciation tend to restrain the inflationary push from the foreign markets. What cannot be spent on imports will attack domestic prices all the more ferociously. By not devaluing its currency and by making foreign exchange available (as long as reserves last), a country can minimize the effect on domestic prices and channel the inflation all the more strongly into the balance of payments.

In the long run, however, the balance of payments is a limited channel for inflationary pressures, because a nation's exchange reserves are finite. While measures of year-to-year inflation would be inaccurate if they did not include the balance of payments component, the cost-of-living index alone is a reasonably good indicator for longer periods. The table on page 168 divides Latin American countries into three groups: (1) those experiencing heavy inflation in the last decade, (2) those with mild inflation, and (3) those with relative stability. The measure might be refined slightly if the table took account of decreases in foreign-exchange reserves, plus foreign grants and loans for balance of payments purposes. To avoid arbitrary definition of what is balance of payments assistance and what is for other purposes, these elements have not been included.

This definition of inflation does not imply any causal relation between price rises and the balance of payments, or whether the monetary authorities are active or passive. Inflation may come because the authorities promote loans and encourage the use of newly made money. Or it may occur because the government, through its economic development board, imports capital equipment for investment projects, causing foreign-exchange losses, depreciation, higher domestic prices, and the printing of more money to support the new price level. Either of these possibilities—to which we will refer again in the sections following—fits the definition already postulated.

"INFLATION IS GOOD"

Those who call inflation good say it is a "means of taxing where other taxes can't be collected." Economic development requires capital (among other things). The real resources (buildings, factories, highways, ports, etc.) must come from people producing more than they consume, an action which economists define technically as saving. Under stable conditions, this saving is either voluntary (financial resources being released from people's incomes for private or public investment) or taxed (with the government exacting financial resources from the people to use either for public development projects or for loans to investors in the private sector). In either case consumption is limited to less than what is produced and the surplus resources added to the nation's patrimony.

INFLATION IN LATIN AMERICA, 1953–1961
Cost-of-living indices, 1958 = 100

Country	1953	1956	1959	1960	1961
Heavy inflation (cost-of-living increase 500% or more):					
Bolivia	4	45	120	134	144
Chile	13	63	139	155	167
Argentina	46	61	214	272	309
Brazil	42	73	137	185	258
Mild inflation (cost-of-living increase 50 to 500%):					
Uruguay	57	74	140	194	237
Paraguay	45	81	108	120	152
Colombia	66	76	107	111	121
Peru	74	86	113	122	128
Mexico	66	84	102	108	109
Relative stability (cost-of-living increase less than 20%):					
Costa Rica	89	96	100	101	103
Nicaragua	83	99	97	95	95
Honduras	90	99	101	99	101
Venezuela	97	98	105	109	106
Ecuador	98	98	100	102	106
El Salvador	90	99	99	99	97
Haiti	89	98	95	91	94
Guatemala	95	100	100	98	98
Dominican Republic	98	97	100	96	93
Panama	101	100	100		

SOURCE: *International Financial Statistics.*

Here is an example of voluntary saving: Suppose the people produce $100 a day of gross domestic product, of which $80 is consumer goods and $20 capital goods. Each day incomes of $100 are paid to the factors of production. If they in turn decide (voluntarily) to spend only $80 on consumption and lend $20 to those who want to finance capital investment, then conditions are stable, for the same set of transactions will recur day after day. If the economy is growing so that product (and income) increase beyond $100, price stability is maintained if income recipients decide *voluntarily* to save the same amounts that the community as a whole (either the private or government sector, or both) decides to invest.

Stable conditions can also be maintained even if people do not voluntarily save the $20, provided taxes make up the difference. Suppose, under the same conditions (product of $100, with consumption $80 and investment $20), people are willing to save only $15 and want to spend the other $85 on consumption. If the government taxes $5, and if the people as a result reduce their consumption (to $80) and not their saving (which would remain $15), then there would be stability. The government might either invest the $5 itself or loan it to the private sector to invest. In either case, production of capital goods could continue at $20, and there would be no rise in prices.

It is where people are unwilling (or presumably unable) to forgo consumption that a conscious policy of inflation plays its role. Incomes are very low in less developed countries, and it is hard to persuade people to save voluntarily or to pay taxes. There is some argument as to whether they do not save because their incomes are low or whether it is because they are not culturally oriented toward saving. Nurkse argues it is because incomes are low: "On the supply side of the problem of capital formation the vicious circle of poverty runs from (*a*) the low income level to (*b*) the small capacity to save, hence to (*c*) a lack of capital, leading to (*d*) low productivity and so back to a low real income per head." [1] Some contend that even low-income people have the capacity to save but are not oriented toward capital investment. Lewis calls the peasant class one of "thrifty temperament." ("Peasants learn to be thrifty because they know how close they live to the brink of disaster.") [2] However, he argues, they do not use their saving productively but think of it as something with which to buy cattle (for prestige rather than commercial purposes) and land. Others say the peasant spends too much of his money on drink and fiestas. The Andean Indian may exhaust several months' earnings on a single occasion. "Money is a transient thing to his mind," wrote Ford of the Peruvian *campesino*, "—welcome, but of limited utility. A new hat, a shirt, some coca and *chicha*, and the month's wages are gone." [3]

Improper use of the savings of wealthy people is another plague to less developed countries. Their compounded shame is that income disparities are great and those who have resources do not readily invest them. Rather, there is the tendency toward conspicuous consumption (of cattle and buildings) and purchase of securities and bank deposits abroad. In more advanced Latin American countries—such as Brazil, Mexico, Peru, and Colombia—these tendencies are being offset by the growth of an

[1] Ragnar Nurkse, *Problems of Capital Formation in Underdeveloped Countries*, Oxford University Press, Fair Lawn, N.J., 1953, p. 57.

[2] W. Arthur Lewis, *The Theory of Economic Growth*, Richard D. Irwin, Inc., Homewood, Ill., 1955, p. 227.

[3] Thomas R. Ford, *Man and Land in Peru*, University of Florida Press, Gainesville, Fla., 1962, p. 91.

entrepreneurial class, but in those where capital is needed most, they are as strong as ever.

The obvious questions of tax reform—so that the wealthy will shoulder their share—and of inducements for private domestic investment are pertinent here. But the problem is more immediate. Given the inelasticities of saving and the tax structure, as they are today, and given the fact that development does hinge (in large part) on capital investment, which cannot be delayed pending tax reform or a new culture of saving, is there not a place for forcing investment through inflation?

It is easy to finance investment through inflation. The central bank simply prints the new money, lends it to the government (or to private business), which then spends it on capital goods. Consumption is bound to diminish (at least temporarily), because if resources are devoted increasingly to investment, less will be available for consumption. The hope is that the increase in national capacity will some day restore consumption.

Before using a model to illustrate inflation, I should like to mention (what economists already know) that there are *two* ways of creating new money. One is by lending it—the banks create it and lend it to the government or to private business. This is known as *money of internal origin*. The other way is through the foreign-exchange market. If an exporter sells merchandise abroad and receives foreign exchange (such as dollars), which he sells at his bank for local currency, the latter is newly created money. This is known as *money of external origin*. Conversely, money is extinguished through imports. An importer pays local currency into the bank (hence a decrease in money), receiving foreign exchange which he pays to the exporter abroad.

A model for inflation

Let us suppose the people of a given country produce $100 of domestic product each day, of which $20 is capital goods, $25 goods for export, and $55 goods for domestic consumption. But we shall suppose that foreign exchange earned from exports is paid out for imports of consumption goods. Therefore the people consume a total of $80, of which $55 is produced at home and $25 imported.

The gross domestic product is summarized as follows:

Consumption goods produced at home	$ 55
Goods produced for export	25
Goods produced for investment	20
Total (gross domestic product)	$100

The factors of production responsible for this output receive income of $100, which they allocate as follows:

Consumption:		
Goods produced at home	$55	
Imports	25	
Total consumption		$ 80
Saving		20
Total (gross domestic income)		$100

Economists would write the statement for gross domestic product as follows:

Consumption	$ 80
Investment	20
Exports	25
Subtract (−): Imports	−25
Gross domestic product	$100

In other words, consumption is entered at its full value ($80), even though $25 of it was imported. To adjust for this, imports of $25 are subtracted, and gross domestic product is reported at $100.

The only difference between this and the earlier model is that, instead of producing all their consumption goods at home, the people produce for export and buy consumption goods from abroad with the proceeds. This model more closely approximates the conditions of Latin American countries dependent on exports of primary products.

Let us now carry out an inflationary model. The authorities would like to increase investment from $20 to $30 by building a power plant whose capital cost is $10 a day (for an indefinite period). They expect gross domestic product to increase when the power plant is built, but in the interim (the period in which we are interested) we shall postulate no change. If more is to be produced for investment, less must be produced for consumption and export. The authorities would prefer not to reduce exports; they therefore endeavor to reduce consumption by $10 a day.

If the authorities are able to divert $10 of daily output from consumption into investment, we shall label the inflation successful. If the people resist, and find ways to keep their consumption high (thus precluding the increase in investment), the inflation is not successful. We shall work out various possibilities.

Suppose the central bank agrees to print new money and lend it to the Corporación de Fomento, which is responsible for building the power plant. Part of the new money will be spent abroad (i.e., used to buy foreign exchange) for machinery, while the rest will defray local expenses such as labor. To clarify the exposition, however, we will first assume that all is spent abroad and none locally. Then we will start over again, assuming all is spent locally and none abroad. Then we will concede that in real life some of each would occur.

First assumption: all spent abroad. Each day $10 of new money is created (internally) through the loan to the Corporación. Each day the Corporación takes the same money back to the bank, extinguishing it (externally) by buying foreign exchange. On balance there is no new money. So long as the foreign exchange doesn't run short and there is no depreciation, the domestic economy will feel no pain. It will not know there is any inflation, for the same incomes will be earned, the same consumption occur, and prices will not change. Gross domestic product is as follows:

Consumption	$ 80
Investment	30
Exports	25
Subtract (−): Imports	−35
Gross domestic product	$100

In the earlier statement, consumption alone had an import component (of $25). Now domestic investment does also, for only $20 of the $30 is produced at home; the other $10 comes from abroad. The total for domestic product ($100) is reached by subtracting both import components together ($35).

The inflation has been translated entirely into a balance of payments deficit, for imports ($35) now exceed exports ($25). If the exchange deficit is made up by foreign assistance (loans or grants), it can go on forever, and there will be no need to reduce consumption. Ultimately the power plant will be completed and will contribute to an increase in domestic output. But if it is not financed from abroad, then foreign-exchange reserves will run short, and it will be necessary to depreciate the currency or restrict imports through exchange controls. When either of these happens, the inflation will enter the local scene.

Suppose the exchange is depreciated, to encourage exports and restrict imports. Since investment imports are wanted (for economic development) and consumption imports are not, the planning objective would be to reduce consumption to $70 a day (in constant-value terms). If $10 of capital goods is to be bought daily from abroad at a depreciated exchange rate, the central bank will have to lend more local currency than before to the Corporación de Fomento. Suppose this is done, and exports—encouraged by lower prices quoted in foreign exchange—increase by $2 (in constant-value terms) while consumption imports—discouraged by higher prices in local currency—decrease by $8. Total consumption drops by $10, because $2 of domestic product (which would have been consumed) has been diverted to abroad. The new statement of gross domestic product appears as follows:

Consumption	$ 70
Investment	30
Exports	27
Subtract (−): Imports	−27
Gross domestic product	$100

Despite the apparent stability of the above accounts (since imports and exports are balanced), in the absence of restrictions consumption will remain depressed only if more and more money is poured into the economy. Because people really *want* to consume $80 (and are consuming $70 only because $70 in consumption goods is all there is), they will persistently offer their local currency for imports, and the demand for foreign exchange will always be greater than the supply. To maintain balance of payments equilibrium, the authorities must depreciate the currency daily. Each day, in order to buy $10 of foreign exchange for the power plant, the authorities will have to borrow more and more from the banks. Each day they will pay it back to the banks for foreign exchange, and the banks will immediately pay it out to exporters. The exporters will distribute it in wages, profits, and other factor payments, and thus it is released into the economy to support the higher level of prices caused by the shortage of consumer goods.

Gross domestic product is stated (above) in constant-value terms. At current prices, all the amounts will increase together (unless other events alter the proportions). As gross domestic product rises to $150, consumption will be $105, investment $45, and exports and imports balanced at $40.50. They will all go on up higher, and higher, and higher. But in real terms consumption can theoretically be depressed, and investment increased, forever. If theory is translated into practice, the inflation is successful.

Second assumption: all spent locally. The effect will be similar if the entire $10 is spent locally. Assume again that it is not possible to increase gross domestic product (at least until the plant is completed). Hence if investment is increased to $30 a day, consumption must decline to $70, since $100 daily is the maximum the nation is capable of producing. Factors of production will be bid away from consumer goods into capital goods. Household income will remain $100, and people will *want* to consume $80 but will be unable to do so, since only $70 of consumer goods is produced.

All costs and prices will rise. Every day the authorities will have to spend more than $10 (in current value of local currency) in order to buy

$10 (in constant value) of new investment. Each day they will create larger amounts of new money. Each day it will be paid once for investment, and then the same money (which goes to workers and other factors of production) is free to be spent for the diminished quantity of consumer goods. As exporters' costs rise, they will have to increase their local-currency prices, and foreigners will not buy unless the currency is depreciated. Furthermore, the demand for imports will go up (because prices are rising at home, but not abroad), and a balance of payments deficit can be avoided only if depreciation increases the price of imports (expressed in local currency). Theoretically, the spiral can continue forever, provided new funds are continuously created and the exchange continuously depreciated. Every once in a while the currency will be abandoned and new units issued, with millions changed to thousands and thousands to units. But so long as consumption is reduced and investment increased, the inflation is successful.

"INFLATION IS BAD"

Thosc who argue that "inflation is bad" have no quarrel with the sequence of events outlined above, except that it is incomplete. The Corporación de Fomento may very well have increased its investment by $10 a day and soon have a new power plant to show for it. But the rise in prices, particularly of consumer goods, may cause others—who would have invested in capital—to redirect their resources into producing more profitable consumption items or into capital flight. While public investment goes up from zero to $10, private investment may decline from $20 to $10. The basic values in the statement of gross domestic product would be unchanged.

Not only will inflation (ultimately) not increase the nation's investment, but it will distort it as well. As prices continue to climb, producers tend to invest in assets with values that traditionally rise in proportion to the general price level. Luxury apartment houses and office buildings are considered a better speculative venture than cement plants and textile mills, although the latter might contribute more to the orderly development of the econmy. In La Paz, Bolivia, one finds many uncompleted structures, started during the heyday of the inflation but unprofitable after the stabilization of 1956.

There are other abnormalities. Persons with funds buy foreign securities instead of investing at home, thus depriving the domestic economy of their savings and using up valuable foreign exchange all at one blow. Credit for normal agriculture and trading dries up, and the farmer and merchant may cease their usual activities. Possibly the greatest distortion is that of people, for those with entrepreneurial genius tend to become traders rather than promoters of new enterprise.

Real resources can be diverted from consumption into investment only if those who invest have greater financial resources (proportionate to their "normal" share of gross domestic product) than those who consume. In our model, consumers (before the inflation) devoted $80 of financial resources daily to consumption and supplied investors with $20. The inflation began when one day the investment sector was provided with $10 more, thus increasing the ratio on that day from 20:80 to 30:80. Thereafter, the investment sector passed the financial resources on to the consuming sector (by paying wages, dividends, etc.). To preserve the 30:80 daily ratio between the two sectors, ever more money had to be supplied to investors.

The success of inflation depends on the deception of consumers. They are receiving more money but buying less. Since consumers are money-oriented, in the early stages of inflation they will believe this condition is to their advantage. If the inflation is of minor degree and slow in developing, they may be so deceived for many years. But if it builds up (as in Argentina, Chile, Bolivia, and Brazil), ultimately they become disenchanted. An "inflation-wise" citizenry is the greatest obstacle to "taxing" the people via inflation.

The wisdom of consumers is most manifest in bargaining for wages. In the early stages of inflation, workers are satisfied with wage hikes proportionate to the rise in cost of living. Soon they "discover" that living costs go up between pay days and their adjustment is therefore lagged. In more severe inflations they inevitably demand increases higher than what is "justified" by the cost of living, on the ground that prices will rise again before the next adjustment.

What workers—let us take them as representative of all consumers—are really asking is that employers restore the $^{80}/_{100}$ consumption share that the government has diluted to $^{80}/_{110}$. The employers cannot do this out of ordinary revenue. So long as the government, with its money-making power, bids resources away from them, their costs will go up faster than their revenues. Often, for political reasons the government backs the demands of the workers, and to satisfy them employers must either borrow or draw down their capital. In practice, they do both. If they were accustomed to keep one-fifth of their total assets in cash, they may squeeze this to one-tenth. They liquidate other assets. But this is never enough, and their working capital is drawn down to where it can be decreased no more. Employers have no other resort than to turn to the banking system.

Political pressure thus mounts to make money-creating loans not only to the Corporación de Fomento but to employers in general, whose purpose is not to invest but to pay the higher wages demanded. In the normal world, employers would prefer to go out of business rather than borrow to cover losses. In the world of inflation, they prefer to borrow, for they know the real value they must repay will be only a fraction of what they receive.

Enterprises that were sound before the inflation and that incurred losses as their costs went up once again become profitable when the doors of the bank are opened to them. So also does *any* business, granted the power to borrow, become profitable. The ordinary laws of the market, for whatever they were worth in distinguishing sound from unsound ventures, are held in suspense. There is no way for the private sector to determine which businesses contribute most to the nation's development.

Loans to employers are not primarily for investment but for the consumption of their workers. At this point the investment-consumption ratio, earlier raised from 20:80 to 30:80, begins to swing back the other way. A rip-roaring inflation may be in progress, but if the new money is loaned to investors and consumers in the same proportion as their "normal" share of gross domestic product (20:80 in the model), *there will be no diversion whatsoever from consumption into investment.* The inflation will have failed to "tax" the people. Yet the nation will be plagued with all the dilution and distortion of investment (that which remains), the agonies of which were outlined above.

"INFLATION IS INEVITABLE"—THE STRUCTURALIST SCHOOL

A third school of thought proposes that inflation is inevitable if Latin America is to grow economically. Proponents of this school have been dubbed the "structuralists," because they argue that inflation is inherent in the structure of the economy. It is caused by the clash of economic development against inelasticities of supply, particularly in agriculture and export industries. As incomes rise with the growth of urban manufacturing, there is more demand for foodstuffs and imports. Unresponsive to monetary incentives, the hacienda system cannot supply more food. Even if the *hacendado* genuinely wanted to increase his output, he could not do so without changing the entire social order that is so dear to him. He would have to offer the peon higher pay for more work, he would have to compete against his fellow *hacendados,* and there would be some mobility of labor among them. All this is anathema to his way of thinking.

Furthermore, development plans call for imports of capital goods, which can be satisfied only if there is more foreign exchange. But exchange is gained from exports, and demand for the primary exports of Latin America is inelastic. Exchange depreciation will cause less income rather than more, because losses through lower price (in foreign exchange) will more than offset gains through increased sales.

To explain the structuralist position, we must again change the conditions of the model. Here we shall assume that the economy *has* the physical capacity (capital and labor) to increase output from $100 to $110 but (because of rigidities) does not have the capacity to withstand the multiplier effects on demand for foodstuffs and imports. Suppose investment can be increased from $20 to $30 daily, thus changing the composition of gross domestic product as follows:

	Before	After
Consumption	$ 80	$ 80
Investment	20	30
Exports	25	25
Subtract (−): Imports	−25	−25
Gross domestic product	$100	$110

The increased investment will still have to be financed by new money, just as in the earlier model. The difference between the two models is that we now assume the capacity to increase output by $10, whereas earlier we had to decrease consumption by $10.

Unfortunately, the increased income will have multiplier effects. Workers on the power plant will want to buy more to eat and import more. But agricultural capacity is not elastic, nor are supply curves in the export industries. As they spend money on foodstuffs, the *hacendados*, with higher profits, also increase consumption, much of it from abroad. If they save, they tend to do so in foreign securities, constituting a demand for scarce foreign exchange just as if for imports. I have already referred to the conflict between the growing industrial classes in the city and the *hacendados*, which will ultimately destroy the hacienda system. But its end will not occur soon enough to stop inflation.

Higher prices of foodstuffs will lead to higher wages, and the cost of the power plant will be increased. More will have to be borrowed to cover it. Likewise the demand for imports causes exchange depreciation. Since exports are supply-inelastic, the bulk of foreign exchange must be saved through reduction of imports as their prices increase in local currency. The *hacendados* and others who have money will spend it locally instead of abroad, and import-substitute industries will be encouraged. Workers will be bid away from the power plant into the new industries, and it will be necessary to bid them back with higher wages. More must be borrowed, and the inflation continues on and on.

The inflation could be stopped, argue the structuralists, by not lending the money to the Corporación de Fomento in the first place. This would be a shame, however, when the nation has the physical capacity to build the power plant. It is more of a shame, they insist, because ultimately it will come into production and further increase the nation's capacity, thus supplying the flow of goods and services to end the inflation.

The position that inflation is inevitable—and that to stop it stops growth—runs directly counter to the orthodox monetary policies urged by more developed countries and insisted upon by the International Monetary Fund. The division between proponents and antagonists is not entirely on national lines, but the literature does evidence a preponderance of Latin Americans in the structuralist camp and of North Americans in the orthodox camp.

I am compelled to stand with my compatriots. My persuasion is based as much on the environment from which I come as it is on sheer logic. The structuralists—I believe—think economic development is easier than it is. Clearly they have not overestimated the inelasticities in Latin American economies, which are painfully there. They recognize the "inflation-is-bad" arguments and agree that a prolonged and serious inflation can harm the economy. But they are overoptimistic in their faith that the structural defects can be cured before inflation has taken its heavy toll. In other words, I believe the inelasticities are far more serious and far more pervasive than they do, that economic growth is far more difficult and complex, and that the ill effects of inflation are more immediate and more distressing than they think.

The inflation will continue until the amount of voluntary saving equals the investment. So long as the capital costs of the power plant ($10 a day, and subsequently more in local currency) are financed by new issues of money, there will be inflation. If incomes rise enough so that people will *voluntarily* save $10 a day, investing it in the power plant (which now becomes symbolic of the nation's continued investment plan), then the inflation will end. If people are accustomed to save 20 per cent of their income (a high estimate for Latin America), incomes must rise by $50 (in constant value terms) a day before voluntary saving will increase by $10 (or 20 per cent of $50).

The rise in incomes can occur in two ways. One is that supply rigidities will be removed, and real output will increase. Zealous government intervention is necessary. Land reform must occur, and the new structure of property holding must provide the incentives for higher output. Both import-substitute and export industries must be protected, to make the supply of foreign exchange more elastic. All this requires time—years and years and years of it. Even a revolution will not achieve it overnight. It was some twenty-five years after the Mexican Revolution that agricultural output was just being restored to its previous levels. The Bolivian and Cuban revolutions show little promise to be better.

The other way would be for the power plant to be completed and for its increase in output to provide the flow of goods necessary to counter the flow of money. This argument has great currency, although I confess I have heard it more often verbally than I have seen it in the literature. A simple model will show how unreal it is.

Let us suppose a capital-output ratio of 3 to 1 (i.e., that every $3 of capital invested will increase the annual flow of income by $1), and a marginal propensity to save of 20 per cent of income. Both are optimistic assumptions for Latin America (i.e., are as favorable to its success as could conceivably be postulated). Assume an increase in capital investment (inflation financed) of $10 a year, the effect of which is to increase income by $3.33 a year. The saving from the increased income is expected ultimately to finance the investment, thus causing a gradual decline in the amount of new money needed. Assume a time lag of one year before the new income starts, but when the first $3.33 rolls in, 20 per cent (or 67 cents) will be saved, so that only $9.33 of new inflationary financing is needed the following year. In the succeeding year, with a second $3.33 added to income (for a total of $6.67) $1.33 is available from genuine saving, and only $8.67 must be financed from the bank. And so on.

Even under these favorable conditions, inflationary financing must continue for fifteen years before capital stock will be augmented by $150, the amount necessary to yield an annual income increment of $50, which in turn is necessary to generate annual saving of $10. If there is a further time lag between investment and income yield, the fifteen years will be lengthened by that much. Thus even under the very favorable conditions postulated, the span of inflation would be sufficient to wreak much havoc.

Other assumptions, which may be more realistic, would increase that span. A capital-output ratio of 4 to 1 and marginal propensity to save of 10 per cent (which are not unreasonable suppositions) would lengthen the inflation from fifteen years to forty! The income increment would have to reach $100 to yield saving of $10, and capital of $400 would be required to yield the income of $100. Forty years is a long time to control an inflation.

But am I not far too pessimistic? Have I not, in effect, said that a nation possessing the factors of production to create a power plant should not do so? Perhaps. But I have not said it could not use those resources profitably. If it can increase gross domestic product by $10 a day, it should devote $2 of this to the power plant, and the other $8 to consumption goods to satisfy the multiplier effect. Money creation of $2 a day for this purpose would not be inflationary.

But do not the inelasticities lie in the field of consumption? Perhaps, but not all bottlenecks are equally rigid. Out of all the possibilities for increased agriculture, increased exports, or increased import-substitutes, search must be made for those that can be done. And foreign exchange will be earned or saved. One can grant that inelasticities are fierce and at the same time be skeptical that a nation capable of producing a new power plant is somehow incapable of increasing production anywhere else.

In summary, my disagreement with the structuralists is twofold: (1) The inelasticities and bottlenecks they mention are more serious than even they believe. It will not be possible to overhaul the nation's economic structure before the inflationary virus has damaged the tissue. But (2) there are possibilities of increasing the output of consumption goods (to save and earn foreign exchange) that they gloss over. Any nation that can increase its investment can also increase its output for consumption, if it has a mind to.

In the final analysis, it appears that Latin America is seeking a means of devoting to investment—and not to consumption—whatever increase in real output is possible. If the capacity exists to produce a $10-a-day power plant, then why not control the people's consumption so that they do not eat up $8 of each day's capital possibilities?

This is a laudable endeavor, but it cannot be achieved by inflation. Admittedly it is hard to persuade people voluntarily to save, but it is also impossible to compel them, by inflation, to do so continuously over a long period. Consumers are too intelligent, too able to defend themselves. Ways to promote voluntary saving are neither easy nor swiftly applicable. Until they can be accomplished, nations unwilling to reduce consumption forcibly through despotic governments have no choice but to devote a portion of their growing resources to the output of consumer goods.

But what about Brazil? Does not the very fact of Brazil rudely deny this contention? On the surface it may seem so. In fact, however, there are solid reasons for Brazil to grow, based on its geography, history, culture, and economics, and it is these—not the inflation—that are compelling. The sorrow of Brazil is that, beneath the surface of a booming national product, there are serious misallocations of resources that have made her production costs far too high. The real tragedy of inflation is that it is cancerous. It can grow in a healthy body for a long time, and only when it is too late does the realization dawn that something was amiss. I shall return to Brazil later in the chapter.

"SEEK THE GOOD; CONTROL THE BAD"

Many economists argue that inflation is both good and bad—good in small quantities and bad in large. While the inflations of Bolivia, Chile, and Argentina clearly have gone beyond acceptable grounds, they say, still those of Colombia, Peru, and Mexico may have contributed noticeably to economic growth. There are, however, differences of opinion on how the inflation shall be kept mild—whether through direct controls (such as exchange restrictions and price ceilings) or through orthodox monetary policies. Let us consider these two positions separately.

Direct controls to minimize inflation

One school of thought proposes that the positive effects of inflation—diversion of resources from consumption into investment—can be enjoyed if only the bad effects can be controlled. Domestic price increases can be suppressed by ceilings and rationing, while the balance of payments deficit will be held within bounds by exchange restrictions.

If demand for imports is more abundant than the availability of exchange, this school argues that importing should be done selectively. Luxury goods should be suppressed either by the denial of exchange licenses or by high tariffs. Certain basic exports may be encouraged by favorable exchange rates, while the full impact of an overvalued currency falls on other, less favored exports and in the encouragement of import-substitutes. Multiple exchange practices, coupled with restrictions, have been implemented by several Latin American countries, notably Argentina, Brazil, and Chile.

If exchange losses become excessive despite controls, the nation may always devalue its currency, thus reversing the deficit by making exports cheaper to the foreigner and imports more expensive to residents. This cleans the slate. However, the inflation will presumably continue, starting the balance of payments cycle all over again with the hope that this time controls may keep it in hand.

As exchange controls and successive devaluations presumably keep the balance of payments deficit within bounds, so also are price controls intended to avoid internal disruptions. Certain necessities, such as food, rent, and clothing will be subject to rigorous ceilings, while the price effect is expected to spill out on goods of the luxury type. In other words, consumption will be limited, but let the consumer have enough to eat, and he can do without an automobile. Mobs have been known to shout, "We want bread!" but if they have enough bread, they will not march across the main plaza crying, "We want automobiles!"

The trouble with controls, both domestic and balance of payments, is that they do not work. So long as people have money, either they will find ingenious ways of doing what is not permitted, or else their use of money in authorized channels will indirectly negate the effects of controls. Either rent controls will be clandestinely avoided, or the construction of dwellings will cease. If bread is subject to a price ceiling while other prices rise, the farmer is put in a squeeze; his costs are increasing but his revenue is not. Such is the case of Chile, whose agricultural lands are shrinking in both size and output as the nation, with great natural advantages in farming, has changed from net exporter to net importer of agricultural products.

Often a control in one theater (domestic or balance of payments) merely shifts the problem to the other. A favorable exchange rate for imported foodstuffs (so the people will have enough to eat) worsens the domestic farmer's position by subjecting him to "unfair" competition from abroad, and his output declines. If exchange controls in general succeed in decreasing imports, they only divert the people's spending into the internal markets, thus enhancing the price pressure. Controls on the import of luxuries encourage their production at home, coopting resources that might be better used in other types of output. Argentina, with heavy import duties, has twenty-three automotive producers, when two or three would easily be enough. Price controls at home will discourage output in controlled industries, and with limited quantities available consumers will tend to buy abroad, thus shifting the pressure on to the balance of payments.

In addition to all other reasons for their inefficiency, controls imply human management, and this leads to graft. Control bodies must select favored importers over others and are called upon to make "necessary" exceptions to regulations. Exchange control in Bolivia in the early fifties enabled favored importers to pay only 190 bolivianos for a dollar, which to others cost up to 7,500 bolivianos. It was like buying a dollar for 2½ cents. Those who could buy dollars cheaply did so without much reference to the quality of their imports, and sometimes their purchases were not brought to Bolivia at all. For example, they might buy a dollar's worth of foreign goods for 190 bolivianos, sell them in Peru for 19 soles, and exchange the soles in Bolivia for 7,500 bolivianos.

One Bolivian businessman told me of an importer who said to him, "I have a permit to buy dollars for capital goods. What shall I buy?" My friend said he had replied, "How about some soft-drink bottling machines? I know where you can outfit a small plant with these for $3,000." "It won't do," the other replied. "My permit is for $5,000."

In an empirical study of trade and exchange controls in developing economies, Margaret de Vries observes that restrictions designed to suppress luxury imports end up by curtailing capital-goods imports instead. Rising money incomes create so much pressure for consumption goods—both produced at home and imported—that some way or other is inevitably found to vitiate the controls. Nor do countries want to restrict imports of fuel and semifinished goods, for fear of limiting employment opportunities at home. When the restrictive machinery is applied, it is found that capital goods are the easiest, politically, to limit. Mrs. de Vries's study cites a number of countries in Latin America as well as elsewhere in which this is observed.[4]

The economy endeavoring to limit inflation by exchange controls and price ceilings is like a man inside a balloon trying to keep it from exploding while someone else pumps it up. He patches up one weak spot only to discover that another has developed on the other side. He blows the air in one direction so it will not flow in another, but its circuitous currents work their way around him. Every once in a while he is persuaded (usually from the outside) to seal off the intake, but then people complain that the structure has ceased to grow. His big dilemma is whether he can better strengthen the walls while the air is rushing in or during a breathing spell in which the pump is turned off.

Controls through orthodox monetary policy

Will a small inflation—perhaps with price increases of 4 to 6 per cent a year—contribute to capital formation if it is not allowed to expand further? Economists who rigidly toe the orthodox line would outlaw even this. But it is on this point that anti-inflationists (including myself) tend to break down. I believe there *are* conditions in which a slow-developing inflation can contribute to economic growth. I believe it has done so in Mexico.

The success of inflation depends on perpetuation of the monetary illusion. People must *think* that more money in their pockets is preferable to more bread on the table or a car in the garage. There are two conditions under which this illusion can be prolonged. One is that the inflation shall not be pronounced. The other is that national product shall be increasing for reasons other than the inflationary financing of investment. That is, there must be ingenuity, entrepreneurial ability, education and skills, genuine saving, and all the other requisites of economic development. *If the nation has these already,* then—and only then—will inflation supply an additional nudge.

Under these conditions consumers may *never* be aware they are being disadvantaged by inflation. If income and consumption are capable of rising by (say) 5 per cent a year, they may not consider an increase in consumption of only 4 per cent objectionable. They see more bread on the table, and maybe they have begun to build the garage. To be sure, prices are climbing, but money incomes are climbing faster.

Such was the case in Mexico. Mexican economic growth has been occurring for a long, long time. It was noticeable before the turn of the century, with transportation growth and the inception of new, small industries.

[4] Margaret G. de Vries, *Trade and Payments Policies and Developing Economies: Lessons of the Postwar Period,* Chap. 4. (In preparation.)

It was interrupted from 1910 to 1920 but took up again as if the eclipse had not occurred. The revolutionary government supplied better education, technical assistance to agriculture, new credit facilities in the twenties, and a more salutary distribution of land and income in the thirties.

Although statistics cannot measure its responsibility, there is no doubt (in my mind) that the inflation of the forties and fifties spelled a different mix in Mexico's domestic product and resources were diverted from consumption into investment. In large part this was made possible by the simultaneous occurrence of voluntary saving. Unfortunately, the national income accounts do not label saving as voluntary or forced. One can often distinguish, however, by the instruments in which it is invested. Mexicans were not only building up their shareholdings in industry but were not afraid to invest in savings deposits and obligations of the Nacional Financiera. At the end of 1961 savings deposits and other quasimoney were equal to fully 30 per cent of the amount of currency and (nonsavings) deposits,[5] a high ratio not found in countries where the only saving is forced.

The Mexican monetary accounts for 1957 reveal that an overwhelming proportion of new bank credit (2,285 million pesos) was supplied by private sector deposits or other purchases of bank obligations, and only a small portion (801 million pesos) through the creation of new money, as follows (in millions of pesos):

Supply of credit from the banking system:	
To government	646
To the private sector	2,183
Unclassified	464
Total	3,293
Less, supplied by the private sector to banks	2,285
Difference	1,008
Extinction of money through balance of payments deficit	207
Net new money created	801

SOURCE: Annual report of the Bank of Mexico, cited in *International Financial Statistics,* July, 1959, p. 180. Also cited in John P. Powelson, *National Income and Flow-of-Funds Analysis,* McGraw-Hill Book Company, Inc., New York, 1960, p. 288.

Brazil is another case where inflation has diverted output from consumption into investment. Like Mexico, Brazil has been growing for many years. Much capital was accumulated through her successive sugar, gold, and coffee booms. The abolition of slavery in 1888 caused the state of São Paulo to launch an immigration drive, in which Europeans—largely from Italy—came to work on the coffee plantations. With the coffee col-

[5] *International Financial Statistics.*

lapse of the thirties, these people were released to go into more profitable trades—and they did. Some say they were more culturally oriented to entrepreneurship than most Latin Americans, but I shall not judge on that. The transportation routes constructed for gold and coffee served the new industry well. Another factor in Brazil's favor is its long tradition of peaceful succession of government. Still another is the size of its country and the large common market it affords. Finally, one should not forget the favorable climate and rich agricultural lands in the Southern states. In all these prosaic factors—far more so than in the inflation—lies the explanation of Brazil's growth.

There is no doubt that inflation has supplied Brazil with real capital. The city of Brasília is an example. The petroleum industry is another, and much of the private sector—such as the automobile industry—has gained financial capital from the banks. But most of this would not have been possible if national income had not been rising as a prior condition, for otherwise the workers would not have tolerated the loss of consumption that this investment implied.

But Brazil has gone too far and made too much of a good thing. Amid all the exuberance over phenomenal increases in her output, cracks in the structure can be found by those who look closely.

In 1962 the inflation began to run rampant. Wage adjustments were made more and more frequently. Businesses that value their assets in foreign currency began to report losses not noticed by those who keep accounts in cruzeiros. (The cruzeiro cost of output produced in June could be less than the sales value in July, but the reverse would be true if both were quoted in dollars.) Government enterprises, such as the railroads, were incurring heavy losses. New issues of currency were more and more spent to cover losses and less and less to promote new capital investment. Many industries had large excess capacity, for they had built themselves up to a size far greater than their market could support. Unit costs were high, and they depended on heavy inflation and protection for their existence. For years the impact of Brazil's inflation had been shunted into the balance of payments through the tolerance of her creditors abroad. More and more there is evidence that their indulgence is strained, and that credit will be granted no more unless sincere corrective measures are applied. With 1958 as base year, the cost-of-living index had increased to only 185 by the end of 1960. In 1961 alone it jumped to 285, and by May, 1963, it stood at 610.

In summary, the authorities in both Mexico and Brazil have used inflation to divert resources from consumption into investment. They could do this because real national income was independently rising. Noninflationary finance has been available in both countries. In Mexico (as shown in the financial statement cited) much of it came through the banking system and *financieras*. Very little noninflationary finance has recently been channeled through the banking system in Brazil, but it has been forthcoming in other forms (such as corporate stock issues and from abroad).

The difference between the two countries is that Mexico knew where to stop. Its inflation has been slow and jumpy. Every once in a while it would hold the line for a breathing spell and when it relaxed the line, did not let go. The gains from inflation have probably been preserved in Mexico, and the increase in gross domestic product may now be sustaining a higher national income than would have been possible otherwise.

The excesses in Brazil, on the other hand, have taken their toll. Its citizens are inflation-wise, and laborers are not apt to allow the money-printing machine to reduce their consumption much longer. They know how to protect themselves. Businesses cannot incur heavy losses forever—even government businesses—nor are foreign suppliers likely to keep up the flow of imports without being paid. The 7 per cent annual increase in Brazilian national income [6]—and some say the statistics are optimistically defective—is heavily weighted in industries selected by inflationary criteria. Their high excess capacity and heavy unit costs can only impair their ability to compete in the stable economy that is inevitable when the burden of inflation becomes too heavy for the country to bear.

THE INTERNATIONAL MONETARY FUND

The International Monetary Fund was not created to deal with inflation. Stabilization programs were not on the agenda of the Bretton Woods Conference, where the Fund's Articles of Agreement were hammered out in 1944. In its early years, the Fund was tolerant of budgetary deficits, exchange restrictions, and even multiple rates. How, then, does it happen that this organization has become the bogeyman of inflation in Latin America? What business is it of the Fund if a Latin American government decides to finance development by printing new money?

Neither Latin America nor inflation were principally on the minds of the conferees who molded the initial character of the Fund. Here was an organization to oversee an international monetary system, supplying resources to countries in balance of payments difficulties. Some even wanted it to be a world central bank, able to create international reserves. It was also to be a policeman, requiring that no country should export its depression through currency devaluation, as big nations had done to the detriment of primary-producing countries in the thirties.

At the outset there was much discussion of whether the Fund would be

[6] If the production of surplus coffee is included, it amounts to about 9 per cent.

a real central bank, *creating* new monetary reserves, or whether it might only lend to some member countries the reserves supplied by others. An organization that could create new reserves had the power (by lending them) to transfer to the borrower the real resources of a country in which they would be spent—at that time principally the United States. But the United States did not approve of a world central bank, for if it were to lend economic assistance to other countries, it wanted to decide itself how much this should be and to whom it should go.

What had not been clear at the outset soon became evident in practice—that there was another reason for favoring this kind of Fund. The fact that it could lend only the reserves supplied by its member governments put a certain restraint upon it. If it could create new reserves freely, it might lend them to countries with "irresponsible" monetary policies, who would borrow to finance continuing balance of payments deficits. The new reserves would flow into surplus countries, and they also would face inflation.

The controversy over the world central bank has never died; it is as much in the limelight today as it was in 1944. Nor have its polemicists fully resolved the reason for debate. Is such a bank unacceptable because the more prosperous nations do not want it to have a determining voice in how they share their income and how much of it is to be shared? Or is it unacceptable because more conservative nations believe it would be a vehicle for inflation, the initiation of which would be beyond their control but the effects of which would invade their shores? Since the more prosperous and more conservative nations are generally the same ones, is it perhaps not a little of each?

In more than fifteen years of experience with balance of payments problems in growing countries, the Fund has become convinced that growth without monetary stability in the long run is no growth at all. It is not necessary to repeat the arguments, for they are essentially the ones I have outlined above. Contrary to most beliefs, the Fund *is* tolerant of a little inflation. It would never say so officially, for any such pronouncement could readily be misinterpreted. Its tolerance can only be judged from the fact that minor price rises do occur in nations with stabilization programs. Ceilings have been breached from time to time for special reasons, and the Fund has continued to lend support. But there is a limit to this tolerance, and when it is exceeded the Fund will withdraw.

Among students in Latin America there is an opinion (whose currency I believe is limited) that inflation can redistribute income from the wealthy to the poor. I have heard this from students who believe that the road to economic development, which in Latin America is "not in the interest of the rich," is paved with inflation. One wrote the following:

> Two roles of inflation must be distinguished according to the structure of the economy affected. In a free economy, it is a calamity that leads to collapse, for interdependence with foreign countries determines the equilibrium of supply and demand. In a revolutionary economy, however, in which there is no saving or investment for economic development, inflation is a necessity of life or death. It achieves the following objectives:
>
> 1. It is a means of redistributing income from more favored to less favored sectors.
> 2. It is an instrument of destruction for the old structure, paving the way for creation of a new, dynamic one, as in the case of the Mexican Revolution, and later the Russian one.
> 3. Controlled or regulated inflation is a lever for economic development, as in the case of Brazil. It provides a counterweight against foreign investment, since the internal resources come from the saving of domestic public and private sectors.
> 4. Inflation is a way of seeking the two *sine qua nons* of economic development: (*a*) generation of domestic saving and investment without foreign aid and (*b*) as a means of obtaining national capital for economic development.

The writer of this quotation is apparently unaware that inflation redistributes income from the poor to the wealthy more often than vice versa, although in theory it may do either. There is also strong evidence that the prewar inflation of the Soviet Union was an undesired one, and the Soviets did their utmost to suppress it. Planned wage increases were always less than the projected increase in productivity, but price increases played havoc with the prewar Five-Year Plans.[7] With the monetary reform of 1947, which repressed wage funds available to state enterprises and rigidly controlled their credit, the inflation was stopped, and prices have been declining since. Like the International Monetary Fund, the Soviet Union is convinced that inflation and economic growth are incompatible.

To some in Latin America, the Fund—"lackey of the imperialists"—intervenes in domestic economies to suppress inflation because it wants to suppress growth. Fortunately, this critique is confined largely to the ultra-left. There are many more—such as the structuralists—who recognize an honest difference of opinion between themselves and the Fund but who object to the Fund's activities, which (they believe) hold back growth even though this is not the intent.

It is hard to say what constitutes intervention and what does not. In a sense, no international organization can exist without intervening in the domestic affairs of its members. To the Fund, the matter of its intervention is simple. It comes only upon invitation. Any nation not wanting its assistance need only say so, and the Fund will withdraw.

[7] Franklyn D. Holzman, "Soviet Inflationary Pressures, 1928–1957: Causes and Cures," *Quarterly Journal of Economics*, vol. 74, no. 2, pp. 167–188, May, 1960.

Whenever the Fund does proffer its reserves, it does not just tender paper money or bookkeeping credits. They are the real resources of other member countries. It is the Fund's feeling that these reserves should be used wisely. Nay, more, if they are not closely husbanded, if the Fund itself were to wither away because reserves had been spent and not paid back, no more would be forthcoming. The Fund cannot exist if it lends to nations whose balance of payments problems are of an indefinite character, never to be terminated.

The stabilization programs proposed by the International Monetary Fund consist of a solemn pledge on the part of the government not to incur a deficit either in its general budget or in the budgets of state enterprises such as railroads and oil companies. An exchange depreciation is usually necessary to restablish a realistic relationship to foreign prices. High reserve requirements are set for commercial banks and a ceiling on loans from the central bank, so that monetary creation is stringently truncated. Many projects must be stopped at once, and buildings left incomplete. A pall comes over the nation, and many fear that economic growth has been stopped in its tracks.

Stabilization is politically unacceptable to much of the nation. Its victims are those of all social and economic classes who have a vested interest in inflation. The type of industry growing up under stable conditions is different from that fostered by inflation. If stability is suddenly restored, there are workers and industrialists, poor people and rich, government officials and messengers, who will be jolted. Many will lose their jobs. Furthermore, it is much easier to tear down a distorted structure than it is to build a sound one. Consequently, the destruction will take place before new growth begins, and in the interim there will be people without work and a major job of feeding the hungry.

To those of the capitalist ethic, stabilization is akin to the years of suffering necessary for genuine achievement. The Minister of Finance or Economy (like Alsogaray of Argentina) who can face the slings and arrows of those who assail him is admired, for—according to this ethic—nothing real was ever built without hardship. Economic growth based on the determination to conquer obstacles and to build a structure *of quality* is more solid, more secure, more longlasting, than the patchwork of inflation.

The stabilization program in Argentina (1958–1959) was doubly damned in public opinion. Damned once because the rosy glow of prior inflation had glossed over the growing weaknesses in the economy; the old days were remembered with nostalgia. Damned again because growth during stabilization was equally invisible, until it was too late because it had been abandoned.

Although the cost of living in Argentina increased sevenfold from 1948 to 1958, the workers' basic needs were supplied (at least until 1955). Caught in a price squeeze, farmers decreased their output. But bread (which could be seen) was kept on the table, while exports (which could not be seen) were curtailed. Exports of wheat fell from $200.6 million in 1951 to $126.1 million in 1958, while those of wool dropped from $176.4 million to $99.1 million. Meat was served in homes (where it could be seen), and even exports were increased, but the public did not observe the slaughter of prize herds and stud bulls whose maintenance cost was too high. The cost to transport food was kept relatively low by controlled railroad rates, but the people did not notice that roadbeds and rolling stock were deteriorating. The people saw the imports available for consumption, but they did not observe the outflow of foreign-exchange reserves, which fell from $704 million in 1948 to $129 million in 1958. The workers remember the inflation era as one of high employment and plentiful food. Maybe they would have been disillusioned if the chief protagonist of inflation had not been removed from office in 1955 but had stayed to face the day when wheat was grown no more, when there were no more herds of cattle, when foreign exchange was exhausted, and when the railroad engines ceased to puff. But history was kinder to him.

Instead, the proponents of stabilization had to cope with the havoc already wrought. Less meat was on the table in 1959, but the people did not see the herds of livestock being replenished. The chance circumstance of bad weather damaged crops in the first year of stabilization. People saw imports curtailed as exchange depreciation raised prices, but they did not observe that reserves jumped in 1959 by $147 million in addition to the $73 million drawn from the Fund. Consumption was also restricted as exports increased in face of the urgent need for reserves. The economic hardships of stabilization brought on prolonged strikes, and the index of industrial production dropped from 100 in 1958 to 89 in 1959. But thereafter it increased, reaching 93 in 1960, 102 in 1961, and 104 in 1962.

Economic growth had resumed in Argentina by 1960. This boom was not due entirely to stabilization, for Argentina (like Brazil and Mexico) had sound historic reasons for growth. Unfortunately, the Argentine people were unable to accept, politically, that damage had been done to their economy. Instead of recognizing that inflation had depleted their reserves, weakened their agriculture, distorted the structure of their industry, and worn out their railroads, they pictured their plight as having been brought on by the Monetary Fund and stabilization. The elections of 1961 would not sustain the program. The central bank began to expand its loans to the government, and commercial banks followed. Foreign exchange gushed outward, with reserves falling from $705 million on March 31, 1961, to $181 million on March 31, 1963, and the cost of living rose from 282 to 469 in the same period (1958 = 100). At the time of writing, the chute is on again, and the outlook is bleak.[8]

CONCLUSION

The theoretical capacity of inflation to divert a nation's resources from consumption into investment is limited in practice. By printing new currency and spending it on capital projects (either the government directly or through loans to the private sector), the authorities can obviously create capital where none was before. It can be seen. It is tangible and can readily be associated in the minds of the people with the nation's economic growth.

But the practice can continue only so long as consumers are subject to the monetary illusion—that is, are deceived into thinking that more money is preferable to more consumption. If the inflation is small and if economic growth is occurring independently, this illusion can be nourished for many years. But if the inflation is large or is applied in a country whose growth has not already started apart from the inflation, the monetary illusion is not apt to persist for long.

Inflation fails to distinguish between types of investment: good or bad, competitive or noncompetitive. A distorted production pattern is generated, in which enterprises are undertaken which would never be competitive under stable conditions. The corrective stabilization measures require retraction of the bad and initiation of the good. Since it is always easier to destroy than to create, the former usually takes place first, and the latter may or may not follow. Stabilization alone will not propel development (as Bolivians are painfully aware).

Even when the nation has the capacity to increase real output, it is a mistake to assume that the entire increment can be devoted to investment. For investment has a multiplier effect on consumption. If the nation has the factors of production to increase gross domestic product by (say) $10 a day and if the marginal propensity to consume is 80 per cent, investment cannot be increased by $10 without generating $40 of daily new demand for consumption. All that could be achieved, consonant with stability, would be an increase in investment by $2 a day (with newly created money). Consumption would increase by $8, and the nation would be living within its resources.

Although opinions do not divide entirely on national lines, nevertheless the Latin American literature evidences a far greater tolerance of inflation—nay, more, the belief that it is an essential to growth—than is found in the writings of North Americans and Europeans.

[8] All data in this paragraph and the preceding two paragraphs are from *International Financial Statistics.*

Among North Americans, the belief is rife that Latin Americans addicted to inflation either underestimate the hardships of growth or are psychologically not prepared to undertake them. The structuralists are eloquent in elaborating the nature of bottlenecks but somehow imagine their resolution will occur before inflation has committed its ravages. Vigorous government action, or the product of inflationary investment, will appear as the savior. They are singularly immune to the historical lesson that bottlenecks are not easily removed (even by revolution), or else they believe current history will be more rapid than past. Yet the slow unfolding of development plans in Latin America, and the small number of projects undertaken to date—which will be discussed in Chapter 10—can hardly make one optimistic on the latter score. The structuralists are also not impressed by the impossibly high ratio of output to capital, and high marginal propensity to save, necessary to evoke sufficient voluntary saving to finance the new level of investment within the short period of grace that inflation allows.

Latin Americans often insist that their structural rigidities are something new in history. They argue that we in the United States either never experienced bottlenecks or when we did, we were able to resolve them by means not now open to Latin Americans (such as foreign trade unimpeded by exchange shortage). Unfortunately, the economic development of the United States seems all too easy now that it has been accomplished. Yet the fact is that we too, in our earlier days, relied on primary exports to accumulate our capital, we too had structural inelasticities in our agriculture (with the plantation system in the South and the slow and painful opening of the West), we too had monopolies and all their rigidities, and we too experienced competition from an already industrialized Europe as we tried to establish our infant industries. But this was 150 years ago, and the similarities between our histories are shrouded by the starkness of the contrast today.

That inflation can cure the illness of underdevelopment appears to those of the capitalist ethic as a chimera, all the more hideous because it obscures the real requirements. It assumes that capital alone is the focal point of growth and glosses over the necessity for institutions—such as an educational system, capital markets, and development banks—and a spirit to save and to innovate. It not only conceals the need for rationalism and political stability but puts a premium on irrationalism and even political instability.

Some Latin Americans—of more leftist persuasion—believe that the International Monetary Fund was established by "imperialists" to suppress growth, which is not to their interest. Yet the relationship between inflation and economic development is not a point on which left and right are ideologically split. Planners in the Soviet Union have restricted the spending of incomes, so as to avoid inflationary pressures, in manners far more stringent, and with far less liberty, than anything the Monetary Fund has ever proposed.

There is, perhaps, one escape yet open to those nations whose industrial structure has already been distorted by inflation. It lies in the move toward economic integration. Not many in Latin America have proposed integration as a means of overcoming the damage already wrought. Yet it seems that plants with excess capacity, or whose products are not attuned to the needs of domestic populations under stable conditions, might find markets in neighboring countries. Some unsound ventures, made profitable by inflation but rendered sterile by stabilization, might again become solvent as their size conforms to a bigger space. It is not easy to integrate a continent like Latin America, but in integration may lie hope. We turn to this subject in the next chapter.

8 Economic Integration

> Free trade (like other systems) has made its historical appearance with differences in character and even objectives. Still, whatever be its form, it has the following common denominator in capitalist economies: *it has been implanted upon countries which, after achieving great economic power, have sought free trade as a means of expansion,* such as the conquest of markets that can absorb their production surpluses. Conversely, protectionist tendencies have corresponded to the early period in the national economic ascent. Or better yet, they have belonged to less developed countries in their fight against political vassalage to the great powers. (Iván Anaya O., *Breve intento de análisis económico de Bolivia,* Imprenta Universitaria, Cochabamba, Bolivia, 1958, p. 23.)

COMPARATIVE ADVANTAGE, PROTECTION, AND ECONOMIC DEVELOPMENT

Classical economics has long cherished the doctrine of free trade. It is based on Ricardo's law of comparative advantage, the burden of which is that nations will maximize their real incomes by specializing in those goods and services the costs of which are lowest, in relation to their other production possibilities, and for which there is demand either at home or abroad.

The phrase "relative to their other production possibilities" is important. Paraguay's comparative advantage in timber may not lie so much in her natural endowments as in the scarcity of alternative occupations. Economics professors often explain comparative advantage in terms of the lawyer who could type faster than his secretary. Yet because of his productive capacity as a lawyer, he could use his time more fruitfully practicing his profession than typing. The arrangement was also advantageous to his secretary, whose only other gainful possibility (say, hoeing her garden) would have yielded her a lesser return.

In the quotation at the beginning of this chapter, Iván Anaya contends (in effect) that comparative advantage is not a universal law, applicable at all stages of history, and may in fact have some sinister political implications. In the same work he correctly points out that England was protectionist before it devised the theories of free trade and that the United States also had a long history of protective tariff before emerging as the champion of economic liberalism in the twentieth century. Could it be, as Anaya hints, that protection *is* compatible with the early stages of development and that the "advantage" of comparative advantage is more limited than Ricardo would have made us think?

No less an economist than John Maynard Keynes has argued that when for a long period of time economic thought and political practice are at variance, there is reason to believe that the insights of the practitioner are keener than those of the theorist, even though he has not found it within his literary vocabulary to explain why. "For we, the faculty of economists," wrote Keynes of protectionism, "prove to have been guilty of presumptuous error in treating as a puerile obsession what for centuries has been a prime object of practical statecraft." [1]

In his criticism of free trade, Keynes was preoccupied not so much with economic development as with employment and what amount of money (dependent in part on the balance of payments) was sufficient to maintain low interest rates conducive to investment. Yet the comment on practical statecraft is equally applicable to those nations trying to achieve a higher per capita income and an improved standard of living. The statesman in Latin America has become aware that a century of relatively free trade has not contributed to economic development in any measure comparable to that of the United States.

To those of Marxist persuasion, the reason is easily found. The nation that has already gained the advantage and is more advanced in the stages of capitalism needs outlets for its surplus production. Only if it can persuade others to lower their barriers and accept its bounties will it succeed in postponing the inevitable demise of the system. The same nation may offer to lower its duties in reciprocity, but this is also to its advantage, because it needs cheap raw materials for its factories.

[1] J. M. Keynes, *The General Theory of Employment, Interest, and Money*, Harcourt, Brace and Company, Inc., New York, 1936, p. 339.

To those who subscribe to this doctrine, the preachment of comparative advantage is a sham, bordering on intellectual dishonesty. It attempts to wrap into an attractive theory a set of propositions designed to make the less developed nations believe they are maximizing their income when in fact they are being manipulated as the tools of imperialism.

In preceding chapters I have rejected the Marxist contention of industrial surpluses, but I am not therefore excused from confronting the problem of comparative advantage and economic development. Like the Marxists—but for different reasons—I agree that for a nation simply to produce those goods and services in which it has a comparative advantage is not necessarily the road to economic development. The corollary to this view is that protection may (within bounds) be necessary.

The classical economists wrote of comparative advantage primarily in terms of natural endowments. Differences in climate, resource availabilities, geographic location, and the like determined what a country was best fitted to produce. England was a shipping nation because she was an island, France produced wines because her soil was good for vineyards, and Spain and Italy grew fruits because the climate was propitious. They did not deny, but likewise did not stress, that the source of comparative advantage might also lie in technical competence, skills, and capital accumulation.

As years of economic development have passed, the relative role of natural endowments has receded, and man-made factors are more and more recognized as determinants of comparative advantage. Climate and availability of raw materials do not explain the present predominance of the United States in Western Hemisphere industry, although they may have helped its beginning. Rather, it is the accumulation of capital, the educational system, the skills, the political stability, and above all a certain mentality toward innovation and the development process. Without these, the United States economy would be nothing.

The more one concedes that man-made factors determine comparative advantage, the stronger becomes the argument for protection. In its role as maximizer of income, comparative advantage is static doctrine. Professor Harberger has estimated that Chile could increase its real national income by up to 2½ per cent if it would liberalize its trade, shifting factors of production from the output of domestic consumption goods into exports.[2] If Harberger is right, the percentage of damage by protection is small. Furthermore, we have already questioned whether the exports in

[2] Arnold C. Harberger, "The Fundamentals of Economic Progress in Underdeveloped Countries: Using the Resources at Hand More Effectively," *American Economic Review*, May, 1959, p. 135.

which Chile—or any Latin American country—has comparative advantage are conducive to developing the skills and external economies essential to growth.

A word of caution must be interjected. The above is not a blanket endorsement of tariffs as a prime mover in economic development. The mere fact of protection will provide no impulse whatsoever unless other forces are present—innovators seizing upon it, economic plans judiciously wrought and aggressively implemented, political and economic institutions being molded, skills being created, and responsible government machinery (that does not make radical policy changes upon impulse) being constructed.

Even the existence of these is not enough. Protection must not be applied indiscriminately. Hardest of all, it must not be assigned for political reasons. It should be accorded only to those industries in which adequate engineering and economic studies have shown that a comparative advantage can be developed. Finally, it should be supplied in moderate doses. Fifty per cent should be the outside limit, and even that is a bit high.

That an outer limit must curb the protective impulse of developing nations is attested to by three fundamental economic principles. In the first place, the search for industries in which comparative advantage may be developed requires the skill of the engineer, the brain of the economist, and the audacity of the entrepreneur. Properly chosen projects will not need tariffs above a certain limit, and those that do usually turn out to be haphazard choices not based on scientific analysis.

In the second place, the developing nation must look to its future as an exporter. After it has developed its internal market, after all imports have been substituted for that can be, after the economy has been diversified away from ultradependence on primary products, then the future of its balance of payments must lie in the growing export of manufactured goods. It must begin to talk over with other countries the terms on which its exports will be accepted. Is not this point a long way off for Latin America? Not so. Mexico has reached it already.

Finally, after all is said and done, there should be sober realization that comparative advantage *do* diminish their current real income. Since in-their production away from those goods and services in which they have comparative advantage *do* diminish their current real income. Since investment depends on income, they may also reduce their capital formation. In its enthusiasm for protection, Latin American literature on economic development has not always accorded due respect to this fact. It is proper to violate the law of comparative advantage; the crime lies in doing so without a full understanding of the immediate consequences and a reasoned appraisal of the possible long-run gains.

THE THEORY OF ECONOMIC INTEGRATION

Latin America is committed to protection. The very existence of two regional groupings—the Latin American Free Trade Area and the Central American Common Market—implies a differentiation between commercial policy within the respective areas and that to be accorded to outsiders. Most Latin Americans relate their protectionism to economic growth. They are convinced that it is possible to develop, within their regions, comparative advantages in long lists of manufactured goods. To do so it is necessary, at least initially, to protect the growing industries from the outside competition of more developed nations.

The creation of regional groupings is based on another premise, that Latin American countries are too small, economically, to provide separate markets for industry of the scale necessary to compete successfully with that of the United States or Europe. The United States, after all, is a common market of fifty states, and Europe is rapidly integrating its national economies in order to assure a broader base for industrial expansion.

Both premises are sound—that protection will contribute to development and that its capacity to do so will be enhanced by its implementation on a regional basis. Still, the rosy glow of the distant future should not obscure problems of the present. If Argentina is to buy heavily protected machinery from Brazil and pay a price to cover high unit costs when it could buy the same more cheaply from the United States, the real national income of Argentina will decline. There is a cost to integration.

Whether on balance integration will reduce or raise real costs (thus raising or reducing real national income, respectively) depends, according to economic theory, on whether it is trade-creating or trade-diverting. The difference is illustrated as follows:

Suppose country A, which can produce a given amount of electric wire for $1, is considering integration with country B, which can produce the same product for 90 cents. Another country, C, outside the area, can produce it for 80 cents. For the sake of simplicity, we shall assume no transportation costs. If there is no tariff, users of electric wire in country A will buy it in country C, where it is cheapest.

We shall assume that electric wire is used all over the world, and the amount bought in A is so small that importers cannot affect world price. Hence no matter what tariff A imposes on wire, the real cost (to the nation as a whole) will always be $1 if it is bought in A, 90 cents if in B, and 80 cents if in C. A tariff would tax the importer, but his added cost would be offset by the gain to the government, thus yielding no change in net national cost.

Suppose before integration the tariff in A is 15 cents. Importers will still buy from C, since the price to them is 95 cents, and they cannot buy more cheaply either at home or in B. The cost to the nation is 80 cents, since the importers' cost of 95 cents is partly offset by the government's gain of 15 cents. After integration with B (and assuming the same tariff), importers in A—paying no duty on imports within the region—will buy in B, since *their* cost is reduced to 90 cents. The cost to the nation as a whole, however, is increased from 80 cents to 90 cents. A's trade has been *diverted* from C to B. Such diversion inevitably increases the cost to the nation.

Alternatively, let us assume that the duty is 25 cents but all other conditions are the same. Before integration, users of wire in A would buy it at home, for the domestic price of $1 is for them the cheapest. The duty is so high that neither B nor C can compete within the market of country A. After integration with B, however, they would buy in B. International trade is thus *created*, and the cost to both the buyer and the nation is reduced to 90 cents. Trade creation inevitably decreases the cost to the nation.

The lesson for Latin America is clear. If economic integration causes (say) Argentinians to buy in Brazil rather than in Argentina, there is trade creation, and the cost to Argentina is reduced. If, on the other hand, it causes them to buy in Brazil rather than the United States, there is trade diversion, and the cost to Argentina is increased.

Both the Latin American Free Trade Area and the Central American Common Market contemplate (initially) more trade diversion than trade creation. One reason is that the former is less painful than the latter. For Argentina to buy in Brazil rather than the United States (trade diversion) constitutes no visible harm to any Argentine industry. Although the cost to the nation is higher, even the importer feels no pain, for his purchase in a higher-cost market is compensated by the fact that he pays no duty. If, however, Argentina buys in Brazil rather than Argentina (trade creation), a loss in market is suffered by the high-cost Argentine producer whose product is supplanted by the lower-cost output of Brazil. The nation may score a gain in real national income, but the individual damage suffered by one sector becomes both a political and a social problem.

Recognizing this fact, the framers of the Latin American Free Trade Area have provided (Article 23 of the Montevideo Treaty) that:

> The Contracting Parties may, as a provisional measure and providing that the customary level of consumption in the importer country is not thereby lowered, authorize a Contracting Party to impose non-discriminatory restrictions upon imports of products included in the liberalization program which originate in the Area, if the products are imported in such quantities or under such conditions that they have, or are liable to have,

serious repercussions on specific productive activities of vital importance to the national economy.

In other words, there is an escape clause against trade creation that may *unduly* damage the domestic economy of any country. The extent of damage that is "undue" will be revealed only as the exception is applied in practice, for no definition of "serious repercussions" is provided in the treaty.

Latin Americans will argue that theories concerning trade creation and trade diversion have only limited relevance to their economic integration. Although admittedly influenced by the European Economic Community and other historical experiences with customs unions and free trade areas, nevertheless both Latin American integration movements have a character of their own. Europe already had more of a vested interest in industry than Latin America. Both Germany and France, for example, are already industrial countries. It is a weighty question to them whether increased purchases by Germany in France shall supplant prior purchases in the United States (trade diversion) or in Germany herself (trade creation).

Criteria in Latin America are different. All countries are committed to planning for economic development, and they contemplate (if they are successful) ever-rising incomes. Many envision integration as a movement which will not much affect present channels of production and trade but the purpose of which is to mold the growth channels of the future. If (for example) X is produced in Argentina at higher cost than in Brazil, LAFTA should not interfere with the present productive capacity and employment in Argentina, which might apply temporary restrictions under Article 23. However, all expansion in industry X would be expected to occur in Brazil, and Argentina's purchases over and above her present output would be made there. Furthermore, since Article 23 protection is provisional, the Argentine producer would have ample notice that he might gradually withdraw his capital as it depreciates and invest it in another industry with a more promising future.

Economic expansion constitutes trade creation in a broad sense, but it is neither creation nor diversion in the meaning of the theory just described. Argentina's additional purchases in Brazil supplant nothing (either in the United States or in Argentina) but constitute a new channel of expected growth.

Once again we are at a point where Latin Americans believe that traditional theory and the experience of others have limited applicability to their continent. They challenge the skeptics who have argued that Latin America's imports and exports are primarily with third countries and not with each other and that therefore integration will be diversionary and costly to their economies. A few go so far as to charge that such theories are a sham to cover up the interests of those third countries (the "imperialists") in Latin American markets. Still others believe that application of the trade-diversion theory is an honest error on the part of economists, mainly foreigners, who are influenced by their own history of slower economic growth and who have little appreciation for Latin American potential.

A Latin American who reasons this way is both right and wrong. He is right in that his continent has the potential for growth, that comparative advantage is mainly a matter of technology and only in lesser degree of natural endowment, and that comparative advantage can be created. To the extent that this is done, economic integration will broaden markets and make the new technology effective and economic.

But he is wrong who supposes that these delicious events will occur simply because of integration and the development plans currently adopted or in process. With one or two exceptions, such as the study of chemicals by the Economic Commission for Latin America (ECLA) in 1962,[3] the industrial studies necessary to determine exactly what industries can be promoted, what are the advantages of location, and what is the extent of the market—studies that are essential if tariff negotiation is to be scientific and not just political haggling—have either not been done or are abysmally inadequate. We shall return to this thought in the following section.

THE LATIN AMERICAN FREE TRADE AREA

The Latin American Free Trade Area (LAFTA) is a brainchild of the Economic Commission for Latin America.[4] As far back as 1948 an ECLA resolution referred to a "Latin American customs union," but its interest was not translated into action until the formation of a Trade Committee in 1956. Although its principal objective was to study Latin American payments problems, the committee incidentally promoted plans for a free trade area. The proposals were gradually shaped in a series of meetings in the latter fifties, culminating in the Montevideo Conference and signing of the treaty in 1960 by the governments of Argentina, Brazil, Chile, Mexico, Peru, and Uruguay. Since that time Paraguay, Ecuador, and Colombia have also joined.

Trade liberalization is the keystone of the Montevideo Treaty. The Contracting Parties have committed themselves to the elimination, within twelve years, of all duties on goods currently traded among them. There are two ways of doing this. In the first place, negotiating conferences

[3] *La Industria química en América Latina,* United Nations Document E/CN 628.

[4] For a history of LAFTA and the Central American Common Market, see Victor L. Urquidi, *Free Trade and Economic Integration in Latin America,* University of California Press, Berkeley, Calif., 1962, especially part 2.

will take place annually (or oftener), in which nations will bargain with each other bilaterally and multilaterally for the reciprocal reduction of duties, with the prior commitment by each that such concessions will total at least 8 per cent a year of the weighted-average duties applicable to third countries, based on trade within the zone during the preceding three years. Duties so reduced are listed on *national schedules.*

In the second place—to make up for omissions that might otherwise occur in the national schedules—a *common schedule* is established consisting of products ". . . which, in terms of the aggregate value of trade among the Contracting Parties, shall constitute not less than . . . twenty-five per cent during the first three-year period; fifty per cent during the second three-year period; seventy-five per cent during the third three-year period; (and) substantially all of such trade during the fourth three-year period" (Article 7). Duties on goods listed in the common schedules shall be eliminated.

The "products not now traded" controversy

Protocol 1 of the Montevideo Treaty makes it clear that reduction of duties is obligatory only on those goods currently being traded between members of LAFTA. The countries are therefore not *required* to reduce duties on any other goods (i.e., those that are imported entirely from third countries), but may do so as a result of negotiations. The relevant provision (Protocol 1, Title I, Section 6) follows:

> In calculating the weighted averages for each of the Contracting Parties, the following shall be taken into account:
>
> Products originating in the territory of the other Contracting Parties and imported from the Area during the preceding three-year period and further products included in the National Schedule concerned as a result of negotiations.

In connection with this protocol an academic tiff has occurred between Raymond Mikesell (of the University of Oregon) and Victor Urquidi (of the Bank of Mexico) [5] over the objectives and aspirations of LAFTA. Mikesell notes that LAFTA does not, like the European Economic Community, contain any automatic provisions for the complete elimination of duties.[6]

> Trade in manufactures constitute less than 5 per cent of intra-LAFTA member trade, and about a third of this trade is represented by semi-processed copper manufactures. Most of the trade in non-agricultural primary commodities, which constitutes less than 5 per cent of total intra-

[5] See Albert O. Hirschman, *Latin American Issues,* Twentieth Century Fund, New York, 1961, pp. 125–160; also Urquidi, *op. cit.,* p. 123.

[6] Hirschman, *op. cit.,* p. 137.

LAFTA trade, is not likely to be affected significantly by a reduction in tariffs. Hence, it is clear that most, if not all, members of LAFTA could reduce their average tariffs on imports from the other members by 90 to 95 per cent in accordance with the formula established by the Treaty—which presumably would represent substantial compliance—without reducing restrictions on manufactures or on other commodities which might involve competition with domestic producers.

In counterattack, Urquidi hints that Mikesell has not given due weight to LAFTA's position as part of a broader movement toward economic development, in which capacity it *ought* to be different from the European Economic Community. Urquidi points out further that the opportunity is provided to negotiate on duties for products not currently traded within the region. As economic plans develop and as the goods in which each country will specialize become more clearly defined, the opportunity—even necessity—to negotiate on such duties will inevitably arise.

The disagreement smacks of cultural difference. We North Americans (and Europeans) have a penchant for prior commitment to a well-defined set of goals. Such commitment is not easily come by (as negotiations for the European Economic Community testify), and may involve major sacrifices on the part of some national interests. In Europe the concessions were so great that—in its early stages—businessmen and governments showed only mild enthusiasm for a common market. Once the community was inevitable, however, and industries were retooling to broaden their horizons, there was a growing clamor for acceleration, and impatience with political problems that restrained the starting gun. When once a factory is expanded and new capital installed, a commitment has been made. Those who so commit demand that others—such as governments—commit as well, so that the market will be assured when the plants are ready to produce. North Americans and Europeans tend to look upon commitments as the crucial point. To our way of thinking, nothing has happened until they are made.

Urquidi is probably wrong in supposing that Mikesell is not concerned with economic development.[7] Rather, the Urquidi-Mikesell dispute is one of many instances—more of which will unfold when we treat of national economic planning—in which differences in willingness to commit become magnified into issues of international import. Mikesell is obviously wary of the Latin American intention *really* to create a common market as an instrument in its economic development. (If they are purposeful, why don't they commit themselves in advance?) Urquidi is equally convinced

[7] In Hirschman, *op. cit.*, p. 152, Urquidi states that ". . . he [Professor Mikesell] says little—perhaps understandably, since he is confined by his immediate subject matter—about the basic economic development problems."

that prior commitment is not a necessary ingredient, that those who think otherwise are "pessimists" who make a "too literal interpretation" of the treaty, that the opportunity to negotiate on other duties is a sufficient condition and that ". . . the idea that the treaty is restricted to the liberation of existing trade is entirely unfounded." [8]

In his overall assumption, Urquidi is probably right, but not necessarily in the sense that he intends to be. A prior commitment is not a sufficient condition for gauging the future unless it conforms to the reality of the present. The Contracting Parties of LAFTA are *not* prepared—psychologically or economically—to make commitments on what duties they will reduce at which dates, or even whether they will reduce them at all, until they have a better idea of how the complementarity provisions (to be discussed below) will operate, which industries will constitute the integrated market, and where they will be located.

There is (I sense) an even deeper dimension to the matter, reflecting a different relationship between government and industry in Europe and Latin America. Europeans trust the government's word but not its wisdom. Like Latin Americans, they look forward to trade expansion in their economic community, but they are more willing to trust competition and market forces to bring it about. In these they have experience and can gauge risks of whatever magnitude. But the government must show its hand first. Once this is done, businessmen trust it to keep its word, and all play the game according to established rules.

Latin Americans, on the other hand, trust the government's wisdom but not its word. They have more reason than Europeans to distrust the latter. The French and German governments are not likely to fall by *coup d'état,* and a successor government is not apt to void the agreements of its predecessor on the ground that the latter was illegally constituted. Latin Americans must feel their way more than Europeans, and the ability of governments to commit themselves in advance to economic moves is correspondingly more limited. It is an honest gesture on their part to erect no more than the bargaining table, and their ability to do this should not be deprecated.

Complementarity

Tragically, the Latin American faith in government astuteness comes more by default than reason. Competition has failed them, for they have not developed the proper comparative advantages for growth. Their businessmen have tended to be monopolists, operating on license and privilege in preference to innovation and risk. Foreign governments have supported foreign interests, which were not necessarily congruent to

[8] Urquidi, *op. cit.,* pp. 123–124.

their own. But their own governments are on their side (most of them, anyway). However weak they may be as supporters, at least they are cheering for the right team.

The most credible reason for the Latin unwillingness to be committed on goods not currently traded is thus the desire to negotiate between governments on economic development plans. Uruguay will promote such and such an industry, Argentina another, Chile another, and so on down the line. Each will bargain for lower duties for its own, and through the most-favored-nation clause [9] will be assured of no higher duties than its competitors in any country within the area. Economic complementarity is provided by Article 16:

> With a view to expediting the process of integration and complementarity referred to in article 15, the Contracting Parties:
>
> (*a*) shall endeavor to promote progressively closer co-ordination of the corresponding industrialization policies, and shall sponsor for this purpose agreements among representatives of the economic sectors concerned; and
>
> (*b*) may negotiate mutual agreements on complementarity by industrial sectors.

The very concept of complementarity is the subject of inter-American debates. To Latin Americans, it is a means of avoiding, within their continent, the disparities of growth that have characterized their countries vis-à-vis the United States, or the South versus the North within the United States, or the Northeast of Brazil versus Minas Gerais, Guanabara, São Paulo, and Paraná. The rapidly growing nations must show some *responsibility* for the others. Whether this responsibility is defined as "carrying the others along" or as "restrictions on the ability of more powerful nations to infringe upon the rights of others" is a contentious matter in which North Americans and Latin Americans are not apt to take the same side. (It must be added that the stronger Latin nations did not agree to this concept without a certain show of reluctance.)

The overt side of the debate centers on whether the backward nations will be a drag on the forward. Will the industrial growth of Brazil be retarded or that of Paraguay advanced by some sort of requirement that they should proceed at equal pace? Or, alternatively, will Brazil's slice of the complement be bigger than Paraguay's? Beneath the surface, a question of morality is involved. To those of the capitalist ethic, it is

[9] Most-favored-nation treatment is provided by Article 18: "Any advantage, benefit, franchise, immunity, or privilege applied by a Contracting Party in respect of a product originating in or intended for consignment to any other country shall be immediately and unconditionally extended to the similar product originating in or intended for consignment to the territory of the other Contracting Parties."

reasonable for a wealthy man to contribute to a sick brother, but it is unthinkable (and not in the interest of the brother) that he should be so devoted as to neglect his own advancement. Many Brazilians feel this way too, and I suspect that in practice the strong nations will not allow the complementarity provision to hold them back.

In addition to the general protection of the complementarity provision, less developed countries within the region have special temporary concessions. The Contracting Parties may authorize such countries to reduce duties at a slower pace than is required in the general agreement, to receive concessions without extension of most-favored-nation treatment to third countries within the region, and to take other nondiscriminatory measures to protect domestic output. Special attention may be paid to the industrialization programs of these countries, and technical assistance in their favor is encouraged.

An urgent task for LAFTA

In the preceding chapter we observed that inflation has left Brazil, Chile, and Argentina with high-cost industries, many of them with surplus capacity. Misallocation of resources is common to other Latin American countries as well. Even Mexico, where growth has been high and inflation moderate, boasts some industry with excess capacity.

In an unpublished study of LAFTA,[10] John Delaplaine demonstrates that Latin American chemical plants have high production costs and prices, stemming from small markets and uneconomic size of plants, high input costs, incorrect selection of raw materials, improper design of plant, inferior administrative capacities, high transport costs, and monopoly positions with high profit margins. Each of the seven largest Latin American countries already has a chemical industry, and some output would definitely be harmed by competition from other countries within the area. The industry covers thousands of products (although there are substantial gaps). If there were adequate markets to take advantage of scale economies, Delaplaine argues, most countries could produce the important synthetic chemicals (such as fertilizers, insecticides, detergents, plastics, and fibers) at competitive costs. Not only would there be import substitution (and saving of foreign exchange) but encouragement to consumers of chemicals, such as farmers whose fertilizer costs are now excessively high.

It is obvious that many studies need to be made. Delaplaine (himself a strong advocate of LAFTA) nevertheless complains that current activity concentrates on the wrong track. The first two negotiating conferences have brought about some liberalization of agricultural products, in many

[10] John W. Delaplaine, *Toward a More Effective LAFTA*, December, 1962. (Unpublished.)

of which duties were already low or there was little competition, so that patterns of trade are not much changed. Instead of devoting its prime attention to agreements that *appear* to have spectacular results,[11] Delaplaine argues that LAFTA should be more concerned with studying excess-capacity industries and how unit costs and prices can be brought down through market extension. The Secretariat itself might make these studies, or ECLA, or some other responsible organization. Whoever makes them should then influence the Contracting Parties to organize their bargaining around planned expansion of industries where costs might thus be reduced, or around the creation of new ones that show promise. Surely this is an urgent task.

THE CENTRAL AMERICAN COMMON MARKET

Unlike LAFTA, the countries composing the Central American Common Market have committed themselves to complete free trade in their area, to be accomplished within five years of ratification of the agreement (1960). Beneath this action, which appears on its surface more purposeful and positive than LAFTA, the same fears were voiced concerning equal development in all countries, and a set of reservations—not fully resolved—concerning integrated industries was established.

The Central American Common Market was first proposed at the ECLA session of July, 1950, and was gradually molded in a ten-year period replete with studies, suggestions, and tentative agreements. In proportion to the size of the market, a far greater amount of research and thinking has gone into the Central American union than into LAFTA. Studies have covered such items as industrial integration, training in public administration, research in industrial technology, finance and development banking, the integration of transportation and electric power, uniform tariffs, and resources.[12]

The four nations comprising the agreement of 1960 (Guatemala, El Salvador, Honduras, and Nicaragua) decided to eliminate immediately all tariffs on goods originating within the region except those appearing on a specified list (goods on which suppression of duties would have harmed national producers). Even those on the list, however, will gradually be eliminated over the five years.

Two outstanding features of the Central American Common Market are the stress on integrated industries and the establishment of a Central American Bank for Economic Integration. Although provisions for inte-

[11] Duties were lowered on 2,900 commodities, covering well over the 8 per cent required for the first year.

[12] Joseph Pincus, *The Central American Common Market*, U.S. Department of State, Agency for International Development, September, 1962.

grated industries were considerably watered down in the final version from what had been contemplated earlier, nevertheless the objective of the treaty is to promote new enterprises that will serve the region as a whole and not individual countries. The Bank (with capital of $16 million called or callable) is especially charged with seeking long-term projects in industries of a regional nature. In addition to its own capital, it is expected to apply loan capital from the United States government and Inter-American Bank. It also has loans from the Bank of Mexico and the Bank of America (a private commercial bank in the United States).

North Americans tend to admire the Central American Common Market for its ability to do "what LAFTA ought to be doing"—positive studies of integration and specific commitments for reduction and elimination of duties. Central America, however, presents certain features not found in LAFTA. Foremost among these is its history of unity amid dissension. In colonial times the Central American states were united under the Captaincy General of Guatemala, and after independence they were a single country for fourteen years (1824–1838). Despite regional jealousies, several attempts have been made since then to promote political or economic union; consequently a common market is not so radical a proposition as in the rest of Latin America. In the second place, the area is smaller and more homogeneous than LAFTA. The capacities of other countries are more or less known, and suspicion more easily allayed. In the third place, the weaker countries (El Salvador, Nicaragua, and Honduras) have always been the ones where unionist tendencies were strongest, whereas in LAFTA the weaker countries have been more apprehensive in their approaches to the stronger. Finally, one should not ignore the real difficulties encountered in organization—those that led El Salvador, Guatemala, and Honduras to jump the gun with a smaller agreement of their own and those that kept Costa Rica from being one of the original signatories (although it has subsequently joined).

THE UNITED STATES AND INTEGRATION

Had United States opposition to commodity agreements not been so vigorously expressed in the early fifties, one could argue that we also disapproved of economic integration. By comparison, however, our silence on Latin American union almost constitutes tacit assent. Before the Buenos Aires conference of 1957, there was virtually no indication from Washington as to whether it planned to offer support or contest.

There is real evidence that the United States did not much care one way or the other. We supported the Organization for European Economic Cooperation and the European Payments Union because we considered Europe strategically important. Considerations were far more political than economic. Latin America was not believed to be a bulwark against imperialism from the Soviet Union and was therefore not important. Our State Department erred in its assessment, but this is the course that history ran.

Politics was not the only explanation of United States support for a European customs union and silence vis-à-vis Latin America, for economic arguments had currency also. Here (alas!) it is not always possible to distinguish between those reasons which are economically valid per se, and those in which United States interests are involved (particularly when one tries to fathom the collective mind of the State Department). The European countries are competitive, buying their common supplies from outside sources. A customs union therefore tends more to create trade than to divert it, particularly if the United Kingdom were to be a member. As we have seen before, trade creation lowers costs and is therefore to the advantage of the countries concerned.

So long as there is trade creation and not diversion, the economic interests of the United States would not suffer. In an analysis of specific United States exports to Europe, Emile Benoit has concluded that ". . . only a small number of items will actually be pushed out of EEC trade by tariff changes, and the net loss of exports arising from EEC trade diversion is, therefore, likely to be small and to constitute only a minute share of U.S. total production." [13] Others are not entirely in agreement with Benoit, and the problem of agricultural exports to the European Economic Community is unsettled and unsettling. Still, the State Department has not felt that the economic burden to the United States would be unbearable. On the contrary, if European prices were lowered through trade creation, the terms of trade might even change in our favor.

Such is not the case with Latin America, where the prospects of trade diversion are more pronounced. Marxists, of course, argue that the United States would object to being deprived of markets for dumping capitalist surpluses. Even if this point is made in milder form, the development of manufacturing in Latin America will probably impinge on exports from the United States. Has the silence of the State Department and skepticism of academic economists been more because trade diversion brings higher costs to Latin America or because the diversion would be from the United States?

Those close enough to Washington to feel the pulse must conclude that the political considerations are paramount and—contrary to the beliefs of Latin American Marxists—economic considerations not a motive. Exports to Latin America are only about 17 per cent of total United States

[13] Emile Benoit, *Europe at Sixes and Sevens*, Columbia University Press, New York, 1961, p. 173.

exports, and this total in turn is less than 5 per cent of national product. Many would not be immediately affected anyway, because of limited Latin American capacity to compete. Besides, United States exporters to Latin America are not an organized political group. When their interests are on the balance with overall political objectives, the latter weight the scale.

The first indication of official thinking in the United States—at the Buenos Aires economic conference in 1957—was favorable to economic integration in Latin America. In reporting on this conference, Mr. Rubottom (Assistant Secretary of State for Inter-American Affairs) said: [14]

> No concrete proposals for common-market arrangements were before the conference for consideration. It was agreed, however, that such arrangements, properly devised, could be beneficial. The United States supported the conference resolution on this subject, which declared it to be desirable to establish gradually and progressively a regional Latin American market, in a multilateral and competitive form, and recommended the continuation of studies designed to provide for the development of information essential to the establishment of such a market.

To understand the import of this statement one must know what else was occurring at the conference. Forty-one resolutions were presented, of which forty were adopted unanimously. The remaining one, in support of commodity agreements, was marred by the dissenting vote of the United States. From 1955 on the decline in commodity prices had been especially severe, and for the United States to persist in its opposition was a body blow that stung the Latin delegates. The United States delegation must have sensed this, and it is not unrealistic to suppose that our initial support for integration was (unfortunately) no more than a booby prize to offset the slap we had just dealt on what was then a more crucial concern.

Still, from 1957 on the interest of the United States became more positive. A mission sent to study the Central American proposals helped negotiate the charter of the Central American Bank for Economic Integration, and technical assistance was provided to El Salvador, Guatemala, and Honduras in their "jump-the-gun" Central American union. In 1959 the United States sent an observer to the working group of economists (under ECLA) studying the Latin American Free Trade Area. Far from opposing LAFTA, the United States observer (Professor Mikesell) suggested that it was not going far enough toward a union, in that it contemplated elimination of duties only on goods currently traded.

[14] Roy R. Rubottom, Jr., "Developments in Latin America," *Department of State Bulletin*, Oct. 28, 1957, p. 675.

In a speech in 1960, Secretary Rubottom indicated that the United States position in favor of integration was by then complete: [15]

> The United States looks with favor on all of these projects (for economic integration) as long as their goal is a higher standard of living for the people of the countries involved by means of greater productivity, increased competition, and gradual reduction of trade restrictions. . . . We know that there must be a considerable increase in intra-Latin American trade if living standards in Latin America are to rise, and hence we regard this movement with keen and sympathetic interest.

In summary, the silence of the State Department during the late forties and early fifties was a combination of "wait-and-see" mingled with skepticism, plus the feeling that the most crucial political problem was to put Europe on its feet and so fortify the world economy. The economic arguments, whether for or against integration, had little political foundation and hence were not pertinent. The United States entered the discussions in 1957, supporting integration as a sop to her negative attitude on commodity agreements. The interests of Washington became more positive the more it became aware of the political importance of Latin America and as the Alliance for Progress began to unfold. Verbal support has been fortified by technical and financial assistance in the case of Central America.

It is worth noting, however, that both citations from Rubottom expressed the hope that economic integration would be conducive to increased competition. Many North Americans have wondered whether the State Department was not indulging in wishful thinking in the face of an organization dedicated to complementarity (and monopoly?).[16]

A PAYMENTS UNION FOR LATIN AMERICA?

Economic integration—as first conceived by ECLA—was to be a two-pronged spear: customs union and payments union. Like Europe after the war, Latin America suffered from incomplete currency convertibility and restrictive bilateral payments and trade agreements. What could be more logical than for her to follow Europe's example—with increased economic cooperation *and* a regional payments mechanism? To be sure, the European Payments Union had been a temporary arrangement, but would not that of Latin America be the same? If ECLA had had its way, surely one would have been created.

[15] Roy R. Rubottom, Jr., "Progress through Cooperation in Latin America," *Department of State Bulletin*, Feb. 22, 1960, p. 289.

[16] Mikesell even commented that ". . . the concept of competition is certainly not a respected one in Latin America." See Hirschman, *op. cit.*, p. 141.

In 1949 ECLA asked the International Monetary Fund to study the possibilities of a payments mechanism that would multilateralize the bilateral balances between Latin American countries. Although the Fund did not take a formal position itself, it assigned members of its technical staff to do an unofficial study. This group reported that "the effort involved would almost certainly be out of proportion to the benefits received." [17]

Why should the staff of the Monetary Fund oppose a Latin American payments union while at the same time sanctioning one in Europe? Those who feel the Fund is a "lackey of the imperialists" will say the reasoning was political and comparable to the greater interest shown by the United States in European economic integration than in Latin American. It is, however, obviously not proper to take this position without at least reading the Fund's report and considering some of the economic factors.

The economics of a payments arrangement depends on whether it is solely for clearing or intended for lending as well. To determine its usefulness in both these areas, the Fund staff distinguished three types of intraregional exports and imports:

1. Those that can be balanced bilaterally (e.g., Argentina exports to Bolivia, and Bolivia exports the same value to Argentina)

2. Those that can be balanced multilaterally within the region (e.g., Argentina exports to the rest of Latin America and imports the same value from Latin America, while running surpluses and deficits with individual countries)

3. Those that cannot be balanced multilaterally within the region (e.g., Argentina has a net surplus or deficit with the region as a whole)

A clearing arrangement, in which no credit is extended, is useful (the Fund staff argued) only if trade in the second group is a large proportion of the total. Trade that would be balanced bilaterally anyway (first group) would not be helped. Furthermore, no simple clearing arrangement can help a country's balance of payments surplus or deficit (third group) unless creditor countries are willing and able to extend credit to debtors. The Fund staff concluded that Latin American trade in the second group—unlike that of European countries—was very small indeed. Less than 10 per cent of imports and exports are with other Latin American countries, and of these a large portion is balanced bilaterally anyway. Also, Latin American countries were not (in 1949) in any position to grant large amounts of credit to each other to satisfy intraregional surpluses and deficits.

[17] *Multilateral Compensation of International Payments in Latin America,* United Nations Economic and Social Council, E/CN.12/87, May 27, 1949. Report of a working group of the International Monetary Fund.

> In these circumstances multilateral clearing by itself is likely to contribute to an expansion of trade only as part of a regional payments scheme in which members are prepared to extend special credits to each other, or can call on an outside source of foreign exchange if it is needed to help countries that are net creditors within the group to convert their surpluses for use elsewhere. When considering the possibilities of special arrangements for regional convertibility in any particular case it may be wise to ask whether the proposed members can command sufficient foreign exchange resources which they would be willing to pool, the strong for the benefit of the weak.[18]

In contrast to Latin America, the case for a payments union in Europe was strengthened by an analysis made by Ragnar Frisch in 1947,[19] in which he argued for combinations of countries to discriminate against a scarce currency (the dollar). By using matrix models, Frisch demonstrated that a given group of countries which jointly have a balance of payments deficit with an outside country can maximize their international trade by discriminating against that country alone while carrying on normal trade with each other (perhaps through a payments union). Such a procedure would be far better, Frisch argues, than for each country to balance its payments individually. Suppose, for example, that all the European countries jointly have a balance of payments deficit with the United States but France has an equal deficit with the United States and Germany. Left to her own devices in a multilateral world, France would reduce her imports from both countries. But the reduction from Germany would cause a new balance of payments problem there, and Germany would have to reduce her imports from (say) Belgium which in turn might have to reduce imports from France, thus completing the circuit and leaving France again in deficit. But if France initially balanced her payments by applying controls only against the United States (even to the extent of running a dollar surplus to offset her deficit with Germany), she would minimize the repercussions in Europe and at the same time supply dollars for Germany.[20] The obvious conclusion is that a clearing union within Europe is justified and that all member countries

[18] *Ibid.*, p. 5.

[19] Ragnar Frisch, "On the Need for Forecasting a Multilateral Balance of Payments," *American Economic Review*, September, 1947. See also Charles P. Kindleberger, *International Economics*, Richard D. Irwin, Inc., Homewood, Ill., 1958, pp. 296–300.

[20] Polak has observed that this logic depends on the United States *not* reducing its imports in the face of exchange restrictions in the same proportion that Germany would, a condition which he considered likely *at the time*. See J. J. Polak, "The Trade Matrix: Balancing International Trade—a Comment on Professor Frisch's Paper," *American Economic Review*, March, 1948, pp. 139–144.

should apply exchange controls against the United States. Such was the case in Europe in the late forties.

The Fund staff decided differently in the case of Latin America, however. It was not so much that the theory was different, or the Frisch principles necessarily inapplicable, as a combination of the small gain to be achieved from limited inter-area trade and the technical difficulties in organizing the union. They cited, for example, the use of multiple exchange rates, the problem of disposing of the foreign-exchange proceeds of foreign-owned export companies, and the fact that central banks in Latin America do not have a tradition of close cooperation with each other. In short, the Fund staff said that for such limited benefits, it wasn't worth the trouble.

Echoing the sentiments of the Fund, Professor Kindleberger wrote as follows: [21]

> The European Payments Union was a spectacular success in permitting the emergence from a contracting deflationary spiral of intra-European trade. When dollars were in short supply, it paid for any one country to discriminate against European imports to acquire dollars. When all countries tried it, however, it could only eliminate intra-European trade, without expanding the European dollar supply, so long as the resources engaged in European trade could not be diverted to working for dollar markets. In these circumstances, a concerted effort to eliminate discrimination against European exports was highly desirable.
>
> The system worked, however, primarily because the countries of Europe conducted a large amount of trade among one another. In Asia and Latin America, similar payments arrangements have little utility. . . . For the most part, the Asian and the Latin American countries have only limited trade among themselves, trading mainly with the countries of Europe or with the United States. Their trade structure, therefore, does not lend itself to an automatic payments arrangement.

The Fund reasoning was hardly acceptable to Latin Americans, who envisaged a payments union (or at best a clearing mechanism) as a means of encouraging further intra-area trade, in connection with expanding output. "A payments system must be established," wrote José Epstein of Bolivia, "not so much to allow Argentina to import more Brazilian coffee, but to import Brazilian steel, and to sell automobiles to Chile more than to sell it more wheat." [22]

At a meeting of the central banks of Latin American countries in Montevideo in September, 1959, the Fund was again asked to state its

[21] Kindleberger, *op. cit.*, pp. 569–570.

[22] José D. Epstein, "A System of Multilateral Settlements for the Latin American Free Trade Association," November, 1962. (Unpublished.)

position on a payments union. Again the Fund was negative, but its opposition had a slightly altered basis from that of 1949. Monetary conservatives would now argue as follows:

In the first place, the world payments situation has greatly changed. There has been a pronounced trend toward convertibility, and interchangeability of all the major currencies is now virtually free in international trade. The European Payments Union was abolished for this reason. Why impose a new system in Latin America when the old is working so well? Is it not easy to finance intra-area trade in dollars or other convertible currencies, just as it has always occurred? Since trade channels are already established and banks *know* what they are, is there not some risk that a new, unknown system will slow up the process of exchange? Cannot trade expansion under LAFTA occur just as well in dollars as in some mythical currency unit (the "alalc"—composed from the initials of the Spanish name for LAFTA—has been suggested)?

In the second place, if the payments union is to extend credit (as some have proposed), the strong countries (e.g., Mexico, Colombia, Peru) will have to lend to the weak (e.g., Bolivia, Paraguay). Which one of these is *so* strong that it can undertake to transfer real resources to others without running the risk of inflation itself?

There is nothing in the Articles of Agreement of the International Monetary Fund to prevent any group of member countries from establishing a clearing union. The Central American states have done it. There is, furthermore, nothing within the articles to prevent member nations from extending credit to each other, either long-term or of a commercial nature. There is, however, an interdiction on discrimination against any currency, and—outside the Articles of Agreement but within the arrangements made for advances and standby credits from the Fund—there is a limitation on currency expansion that might limit trade-surplus countries in the amount of credit they might extend to those with deficits.

One may *surmise* (and I do not have inside information) that the Fund is not opposed to the institution as such but is wary of how it will conduct itself. Surely it would make no difference to the Fund if Latin Americans should denominate their trade surpluses and deficits in alalcs, provided the alalc itself is convertible. Nor (I suppose) can the Fund see why this would make any difference to the Latin Americans unless *they* intended to loosen their monetary policies so that the alalc would not be convertible. In other words, can one not *suspect* that a Latin American payments union would in fact be a device for spreading inflation?

Take the following fictitious sequence: Suppose inflationary Brazil runs a deficit with the rest of the area, financed by a credit from the payments union. Mexico, let us say, is the surplus country required to lend to the union. It can do so either out of its saving (which is costly because of interest) or by creating new money (which is free and more tempting). If it selects the latter, the net effect will be the same as if Brazil had the right to print Mexican money (with the approval of the payments union). Whether inflation is exported will thus depend entirely on the rules of the union and how they are applied.

If the rules are so applied that inflation will spread, will there not be pressure for the alalc itself to be devalued, or at least subject to exchange restrictions? Will not the whole ignominious history of multiple currencies and successive devaluations be repeated but this time spread throughout Latin America, instead of confined to the watertight compartments of individual countries?

The sequence *need* not occur. Perhaps, on the other hand, nations that have not individually shouldered the responsibility for sound money may be forced to do so collectively. Why (let us ask ourselves) has the United States been so concerned with stabilization in Latin America? Only in part because of an intellectual acceptance that the road to economic development is paved with stability. A more cogent reason is that historically the United States is called on to supply reserves when Latin nations fall short. What will happen when Mexico, Peru, and Colombia (for example) find themselves in the shoes of the United States?

In terms of the above illustration, the question is how long Mexico would allow itself to be buffeted by the excesses of Brazil. Will not the time arrive when creditor nations within Latin America will begin to sound like the Monetary Fund? I suspect so, and that only then will monetary stabilization become respectable in that part of the world. No one can be sure, but it is worth a try.

Dreams of a continent-wide inflation should not, therefore, inhibit formation of a Latin American payments system based on convertible reserves. Several proposals have been made, principally those of Professors Triffin and Mikesell.[23] The following arguments are advanced in favor of such a system:

In the first place, trade implies credit. One of the reasons more advanced countries are more advanced is that sellers extend credit. Capital is not all factories, power plants, highways, and harbors. Goods in process, goods in transit, and goods on the retailer's shelf are all part of the nation's capital. They must be financed by saving. The saving is done by people, but it is channeled through institutions. The institutions are no good if the people do not save, but conversely the savings will not be used properly if the institutions are not capable of handling them. The creation

[23] Presented at the seventh operative meeting of the Latin American Monetary Studies Center (CEMLA) in Mexico City, September, 1962. See CEMLA documents DT/I-III/8 (Mikesell) and DIE/III/1 (Triffin).

of a dynamic banking system, able to manage international reserves and extend short-term credit for exports, is as much needed in Latin America as are power plants and highways.

In the second place, banks must be developed in other ways. Those unfamiliar with export-import procedures are often unaware of the extensive role of banks. By their credit arrangements they gain insight into money markets and economic activity in other countries, and they become a clearinghouse for information as well as funds. New York banks not only publish reports on trade conditions abroad but (as was mentioned in Chapter 4) even study particular industries (such as petroleum and steel) where their clients buy and sell. Latin American banks have little *expertise* in this sort of activity. The former vice-president of a commercial bank in Bolivia reports that he has always found it easier to obtain trade data from banks in New York than in La Paz.[24] Yet apart from their superior development, New York banks are not in a position to service Latin American clients as well as banks close to the scene of action, who know local conditions and can be consulted readily. Latin American banks ought to educate themselves to this function but will have incentive to do so only if international finance is channeled through them.

In the third place, expanded Latin American trade will require additional international reserves. If each country must build up its reserves separately, the total requirements for Latin America will be greater than if all did so in concert. If the payments union is based on convertibility, its reserves must be convertible, and convertible currencies can be obtained only from two sources: saving or borrowing abroad. If the Latin American countries save, they in effect export more than they import, and they consign the excess gold and dollars to their average holdings of reserves. Thus they transfer real resources abroad, which could alternatively be used in capital-hungry countries at home. Or they can acquire reserves by borrowing from outside the area. In either case their sources are limited, and any economy is welcome.

On balance, some sort of payments mechanism in Latin America appears to be desirable. The reasons are different from those for the European Payments Union, for they are based more on institution building as a factor in economic development. One must always be careful that institutions are neither too far ahead nor too far behind the conditions calling for them. Some fear that a Latin American clearing or payments organization is an intellectual concept, engineered by fanciful economists who would establish it long before economic events cry for it. Such would be tragedy, for it would fall into disuse and stand as an ugly precedent deterring its rebirth when its day finally came. Others say the events are upon us now and failure to have the channels dusted off and open would

[24] Epstein, *op. cit.*

be to delay economic growth. The side one takes is a measure of one's optimism for the Latin American free trade area, and for economic growth in general.

SUMMARY

Moderate protection is conducive to economic growth. It can assist young nations to develop comparative advantages in manufacturing, commerce, and other activities that promote cost reduction through large-scale output and external economies. But protection by itself does not stimulate growth; it must be correlated with those other measures—such as rational economic planning and fostering skills, entrepreneurial capacities, and political stability—that are part of the development syndrome.

To advocate tariffs is not to reject the law of comparative advantage. Governments must recognize that there is a cost to protection, for until new comparative advantages are developed there will be losses in real income. These losses must be rationalized and plotted against the discounted value of real gains expected in the more distant future. Above all, protection must not be accorded on a political basis but only with realistic studies of industries to be promoted. While Latin American countries have been making overall development plans (discussed in Chapter 10), adequate studies of particular industries and their role in a future pattern of comparative advantage are sadly lacking.

Protection on an individual-country basis will not lead to rational comparative advantages, for most Latin American countries do not have large markets. Because they cannot compete with stronger countries in world exports, they must develop larger-scale manufacturing within their region. Herein lies the theoretical justification for the Latin American Free Trade Area and the Central American Common Market.

The United States has not opposed economic integration in Latin America, although some have interpreted her long silence (before 1957) as tacit disapproval. Any economic interest of the United States has been subordinated to the political and to the United States objective to see Latin America strong as a bulwark against imperialism from another part of the world.

Academic economists in the United States have shown some skepticism toward integration in Latin America. One school points out that it will be more trade-diversionary than creative and therefore will increase costs. The most effective Latin American answer to this criticism is to recognize its truth but to stress the long-run advantages of scale and external economies. The position one takes then depends on one's relative optimism for the success of Latin American development plans.

Another school points out that LAFTA not only is not a common market but does not really commit itself to being a free trade area. The Contracting Parties are obliged to reduce or eliminate duties only on those products currently traded among them. Economic development, however, requires that they eliminate intra-area protection on goods not now traded, so that new industries may grow within the region. Latin Americans do not feel ready to do this yet, for they argue that development plans are still fluid and they need to bargain with each other on complementary industries. North Americans tend to criticize LAFTA for its indefiniteness, but Latin Americans—who have different cultural interpretations of when commitment should occur—look upon these critics as pessimists who read the document too literally.

Many Latin Americans would like to form a payments union as one of the instruments of integration. Conservative economists argue that one is not necessary, in view of the small amount of trade now carried on among Latin American countries. Probably they also fear such a union would spread inflation. But on the other hand, it may foster in the more rapidly growing countries an appreciation of the need for monetary stability to maintain orderly trading relations with their neighbors. In addition, a payments union would educate banks on how better to serve intraregional trade.

9 Foreign Aid *

For we are launching a Decade of Development, on which will depend, substantially, the kind of world in which we and our children shall live. (From President Kennedy's Special Message on Foreign Aid, Mar. 22, 1961.)

FROM LATIN AMERICAN students I have heard much about foreign aid that would not have occurred to me had I never left my own country. Many of their views have been critical, but some have not. An example of the latter is the following:

> North Americans deserve the admiration and affection of all the peoples of Latin America. I understand perfectly the good faith implied in their efforts to assist the economic growth of underdeveloped countries. Clearly this is one of the most noble gestures that a more developed country can make toward its less advantaged neighbors. Whether North American or Latin American, together we constitute one single Fatherland and Nation, the young and vigorous America of the future.

But the reaction to United States assistance is not all of this ilk. Far from it. Most students I have encountered have been highly skeptical of foreign aid and have argued (with differing degrees of fervor and emphasis) that it serves four sinister purposes:

* Certain portions of this chapter were first presented in a paper on "Education and U.S. Foreign Policy" at the Duke University Commonwealth Studies Center in 1963. They are used here by permission.

In the first place, they say foreign aid is a palliative. Its objective is to suppress social unrest so that Latin Americans will not rise up in revolution against the semicolonial conditions imposed upon them. In addition, it salves the consciences of those North Americans who realize that prices for primary commodities are too low. Latins should accept it as something rightfully theirs, in lieu of adequate compensation for exports. There is no reason to express gratitude for it or to offer friendship in return. These views have already been quoted from a speech by the Foreign Minister of Venezuela (see page 107).

In the second place, Latin American students have told me that foreign assistance is one of the means by which the United States dumps its capitalist surpluses abroad. These arise—as predicted by Marx almost one hundred years ago—out of the very nature of our productive system, and they must be disposed of or the mechanism will break down. Some (as already cited on page 104) have called aid a means of discharging the impact of the capitalist-generated business cycle abroad, as a shock-absorber for the domestic economy.

In the third place, some students have said that foreign aid is a means of disrupting Latin economies, so as to prevent their growth, which is not in the interests of the United States. Latin American economic development would cause the United States to lose an important market for consumer goods. One student wrote as follows:

> The fear of this vacuum causes the country to the north to look askance at our development. Only machinery and capital goods would be exported to Latin America, and fewer consumer goods—this would represent a loss for the United States. This explains why the North American government emphasizes consumer goods in its aid to underdeveloped peoples, and small quantities of money insufficient to push their growth. If American aid were given in capital goods, it would be much more effective and would meet the desires of our peoples. In consumer goods, however, it serves only to kill off national industries.

Another wrote the following (but not in one of my classes): [1]

> The intimate dependence of the economy of our country on that of the cyclic center is revealed in these relations of interchange. It is a dependence taking on political and cultural aspects as well, influencing in decisive form the backwardness of Bolivia. It is expressed not only through the imposition of prices by the United States but also in the "American aid," which destroys incentive to produce within Bolivian territory and serves to dump excess North American production in Bolivia.

Finally, and what is perhaps the most serious, students point out that

[1] Iván Anaya O., *Breve intento de análisis económico de Bolivia,* Imprenta Universitaria, Cochabamba, 1958, p. 80.

United States aid has not really filtered down to the people but has paid off politicians who are no more than vassals of the North American government. For example, thousands of dollars of *free* United States commodities were *sold* by the government of Bolivia to the general public, with the intention that the proceeds (in bolivianos) should be put to work on development projects. For years neither the Bolivian nor the North American government made much attempt to force the buyers—suspected to be favorites of the politicians—to pay their bills.

Before commenting on these positions, let us consider the history and nature of foreign aid.

HISTORY OF UNITED STATES FOREIGN AID

The Export-Import Bank

Latin American students who relate United States foreign aid to our domestic economic ills are not entirely wrong. Far from it. Foreign aid has been so intermingled with internal problems, including escape from depression and the morass of agriculture, that it is hard to identify its emergence as an entity or what is now the demarcation line between foreign and domestic affairs.

Two points are certain: that foreign aid began before the Marshall Plan and that it began in Latin America. Yet the Export-Import Bank, founded by Congress in 1934, was not at first a foreign-aid agency. Its avowed purpose was to finance the international trade of the United States with intermediate-term credits. In practice, this has meant United States exports, not imports. Its origin has subjected it to the onslaughts of Latin American students who dwell on the excesses of capitalist dumping and the business cycle. Still, the "Eximbank" has served some positive purposes that belie the contention that United States assistance lies mainly in the field of consumer goods.

A prime example is the Volta Redonda steel mill. By invitation of the Brazilian government in 1939, the United States Steel Products Company studied the feasibility of a mill and accompanying industrialization in a country that was then essentially agricultural. Vast supplies of iron ore in Minas Gerais, plus easy access by highway and railroad to growing markets in Rio de Janeiro and São Paulo, made Volta Redonda a logical spot for a steel mill despite the inadequacy of coal, which is mostly imported.

The mill was constructed between 1941 and 1946, financed by a $45 million loan from Eximbank to buy capital goods in the United States. Its initial rated capacity was 1,000 tons a day, but by 1950 it was producing at better than 100 per cent capacity, with an output of some

366,000 tons of ingots and 324,000 tons of finished steel. Eximbank made a further loan of $25 million for expansion in 1950, followed by a third loan of $35 million for the same purpose in 1956.[2] By 1959 Volta Redonda was producing 635,000 tons of pig iron and 872,000 tons of steel ingots per year. Mainly because of this rapid growth of domestic output, Brazilian imports of steel products dropped from 427,000 tons in 1946 to 341,000 tons in 1955. Self-sufficiency in steel is now a goal to be measured in years rather than decades.

Like any steel mill, Volta Redonda is the progenitor of other types of economic activity. It not only provides steel products for subsequent stages of manufacturing, but it also requires electric power and other inputs that promote industrial growth generally. The surrounding region has become one of the most highly industrialized in Brazil. By-products of coal distillation provide a plentiful supply of benzol, sulfate of ammonium, tar, and other derivatives useful to the chemical industry. Growing industrialization eagerly consumes virtually all of Volta Redonda's products (only 0.2 per cent was exported in 1959).

During World War II and immediate postwar years most of Eximbank's loans to Latin America were for general balance of payments assistance. Still, Volta Redonda was not the only capital project. As early as 1938 a $5 million credit was awarded to Haiti for the construction of public works, and $17 million was loaned to the Chilean Corporación de Fomento de la Producción for agricultural and industrial development in 1939 and 1940. Other loans to Latin American countries during the forties were devoted to highway construction, heavy transportation equipment, and other capital goods. From its inception in 1934 until June 30, 1961, Eximbank authorized credits of $3,461,170,000 to nineteen out of the twenty Latin American republics (all except the Dominican Republic), of which $2,362,169,000 had been disbursed.[3] These compare with Latin American commitments of the regular foreign-aid program (Agency for International Development and its predecessor agencies) of $990,795,000 and expenditures of $664,365,000 from its inception on April 3, 1948, to December 31, 1961.[4]

The Institute of Inter-American Affairs

Quite independently of Eximbank, another—albeit smaller—program of aid to Latin America was shaping up in the latter thirties. For many years Latin American governments had been requesting technical assistance from the United States in such fields as public health, education, and

[2] Annual *Report to Congress*, Export-Import Bank, 1956.

[3] Details of loans can be found in the annual *Report to Congress*, Export-Import Bank.

[4] *Operations Reports*, Agency for International Development.

agriculture. The State Department forwarded these requests to the appropriate government agencies, such as the Department of Agriculture.

By the latter thirties they were becoming so numerous that more formal organization was required. The Inter-Departmental Committee on Scientific and Cultural Cooperation was formed in 1939 to receive and channel requests, but in 1940—as war clouds darkened—President Roosevelt elevated this function to the new Office of Coordinator of Inter-American Affairs. His purpose was to relate technical and economic cooperation in the Americas to hemispheric defense.

In 1942, the Office of the Coordinator ceased to be a mere channel and began to cooperate directly with Latin American governments in joint economic programs. The Institute of Inter-American Affairs was established under the Coordinator to concentrate on three problems: public health, education, and food supply. These activities were supplemented in 1944 by the Inter-American Educational Foundation, organized to provide assistance in preuniversity education.

From its inception in 1942 until June 30, 1951, the Institute of Inter-American Affairs spent only $88 million in technical assistance to Latin America. Among its accomplishments, however, were the establishment of health centers, safe water supply and sewage systems, the control of malaria and other diseases, and soil and water conservation in various countries. Together with the Inter-American Educational Foundation, it provided for the training of medical, nursing, and teaching personnel, and for vocational, technical, and other education.[5]

The European Recovery Program (Marshall Plan)

The foreign-aid program was thus well under way in Latin America before the Marshall Plan began. With the close of the war, however, the focus of assistance moved across the Atlantic. Europe's industries had been devastated by the conflagration just passed, and in 1947–1948 the United States launched a massive program to restore them. A new United States government agency, called the Economic Cooperation Administration, was established to handle the aid, and the recipient countries in their turn formed the Organization for European Economic Cooperation to administer its distribution among countries and uses. From April 3, 1948, (the beginning of the Marshall Plan) until May 31, 1954, $22,241.4 million had been spent on European aid.

The plan was a success. European recovery was astounding and rapid. Despite gloomy forecasts that reconstruction would require decades, cities that had been leveled were again flourishing, with hardly a trace of rubble, by the beginning of the fifties.

[5] *Foreign Aid by the United States Government, 1940–1951,* U.S. Department of Commerce, 1952, pp. 24–25.

Military assistance and Point Four

The recovery of Europe did not bring about the end of foreign aid, which soon became merged with overall United States foreign policy. Two events occurred before the end of the forties to bring this about. One was that the wartime alliance between the Soviet Union and the United States was already strained and the United States government was fearful of the advance of the Communist countries. The other was that the needs of underdeveloped countries were more and more intruding themselves on the consciousness of the North American people and official Washington.

Military assistance became part of United States strategy in 1949, with the enactment of the Mutual Defense Assistance Program. At first it was designed solely to reconstitute European armed forces, but with the onset of the Korean conflict in 1950 it was extended to the Far East and soon became part and parcel of the foreign-assistance program in all parts of the world.

Point Four, or the technical-assistance program, introduced the problem of underdevelopment to United States foreign policy. In his inaugural address of 1949, President Truman announced four points of departure in United States policies. Few can name the first three, which have long been forgotten. But his fourth point was that ". . . we must embark on a bold, new program for making the benefits of our scientific advances and industrial progress available for the improvement and growth of underdeveloped areas. . . . For the first time in history, humanity possesses the knowledge and skill to relieve the suffering of these people."

It is unfortunate that the Korean conflict coincided with the implementation of Point Four, for the result was a military-mindedness on the part of the United States Congress which eclipsed technical assistance for its own sake. There followed a four-year period in which all aid programs were identified with the Communist military threat. In 1951 all foreign aid was gathered under a single heading by the Mutual Security Act, which implied that both economic and military assistance would be allocated with a view to the security of the United States and recipient countries from Communist aggression.

Point Four in Latin America

As the Marshall Plan came to a successful conclusion in Europe and foreign aid became indefinitely embedded in United States policy, the countries of Latin America began more and more to complain that they had been forgotten. Europe had received billions in capital grants and loans, while only a dribble of technical assistance was being accorded to

Latin America. A United States Senator received the following message in a letter from a Latin American friend: [6]

> We admire and feel pride in the immense role played by our American friend in maintaining by himself half of the whole world; the USSR is doing likewise to the other half. But even when we know perfectly well that the USA has no obligation to help us or anybody else, nevertheless under the circumstances the proportion of the help received by us is shameful; the loans and gifts to Europe, including the enemies, during the Marshall Plan were annually over 5,000 million dollars—while for Latin America it was only a matter of a few hundred! What we felt, you can put in a far-western way. Imagine a cowboy who enters a cantina and shouts loudly: "Wine for everybody, except for this fellow—for whom a glass of water will do!"

It was true. In November, 1951, the Institute of Inter-American Affairs was transferred to the recently organized Technical Cooperation Administration, which became the agency for carrying out Point Four within the Mutual Security Program. It provided no development loans to Latin America during this period—just technical assistance, amounting to $17.4 million in fiscal year 1952, $18.5 million in 1953, and $26.8 million in 1954.[7]

The generally accepted explanation for our neglect of Latin America is that Congress and the people of the United States were so preoccupied with the needs of defense and the danger of Communist aggression in the Far East that we paid little heed to crying necessities within our own hemisphere. We looked at social inequities in Latin America but did not see them; we heard the commotion of restive peoples but did not understand it; we had the occasion to speak but were dumb. Only when our Vice President was pelted with rotten tomatoes and spat upon and only when Fidel Castro marched over Cuba did we awaken to the enormity of our neighbor's distress.

All this is true. But history is not unblended, as we have seen so many times. One of the great successes of the Marshall Plan was that it provided capital where capital alone was lacking. Europe already had the skills, the trained manpower, the executive capacity, the political traditions and stable government, the spirit of entrepreneurship and willingness to accept change, the ability of labor and management to cooperate within contrasting interests, the institutions of finance, the propensity to save, and all the other ingredients for high productivity and output. If

[6] William Benton, *The Voice of Latin America,* Harper & Row, Publishers, Incorporated, New York, 1961, p. 144.

[7] *Operations Reports,* Foreign Operations Administration and International Cooperation Administration. The fiscal year of the U.S. Treasury ends June 30 (i.e., fiscal year 1952 is from July 1, 1951, to June 30, 1952).

we provided wine to Europe and water to Latin America, it was partly because we thought one could hold his liquor better than the other.

It was here that United States official thinking caught up with our cultural (Schumpeterian) tradition that economic growth depends as much on genius and organization as it does on capital, if not more. Our capitalist ethic also told us that the greater problems should be met by Latin Americans themselves and that without their resolution capital would be meaningless. Under the circumstances, technical assistance—which was not very expensive—was the best we could provide. Within a decade the United States had come to a different conclusion, but this is the way we were thinking in 1950.

With the inauguration of the Truman administration there was, in fact, a revulsion against the emphasis on capital and a gross exaggeration of what technical assistance alone could accomplish. Congress was assured that economic development would occur in a short time and with little cost. A few better seeds, the introduction of fertilizer, communication of new methods of business management, and the job would be done. It was in this era also that the United Nations embarked on its technical-assistance program.

Technical assistance is not education in its formal sense. Nevertheless, it implies the transmission of knowledge and embraces the assumption that showing people how better to perform their job will somehow cause them to do it better. Since United States technical assistance has had a longer history in Latin America than elsewhere, it was here that its initial implements were fashioned. Among these was the *servicio,* decline and fall of which are indicative of the changing United States attitudes toward technical assistance.

The *servicio* is an organization designed for both training and implementation of programs. It is sponsored jointly by the United States and a Latin American government, operating in such fields as health, highways, education, and agriculture. Education *servicios* have built schools and provided teachers, but their essential object is to show developing countries how to build schools and structure their educational system. Their purpose is to be innovators. Once the schools are established, they are turned over to the Ministry of Education for routine administration.

The *servicio* as a means of training has been widely proclaimed and widely condemned by foreign-aid officers. Its proponents argue that North Americans working side by side with their national counterparts constitute the most effective means of communicating skills. The *servicio* is also touted as an instrument of accomplishment in governments noted for ineffectualness. Its opponents have argued that in practice it has turned out to be an extragovernment device, bypassing and failing to develop usual channels like the ministries of education, public works, and agriculture. They say their purpose has been more one of getting things done than of educating national counterparts.[8]

The opponents have won. Instead of being expanded to Asia and Africa (as was once contemplated), the *servicio* is being quietly dropped in Latin America. But the decision stems not only from the superiority of its opponents' logic but also from the growing conviction that technical assistance is not the magic wand it was earlier thought to be. Neither capital nor technical assistance alone, or even both together, is capable of achieving steady economic growth without some additional factors.

The names of United States government agencies responsible for foreign aid reflect the changing characteristics of the program. In 1951 the Institute of Inter-American Affairs was subsumed under the Technical Cooperation Administration, part of the State Department. In 1953 TCA was abolished and supplanted by the Foreign Operations Administration, a semiautonomous agency. The name of FOA implied an operational program no longer limited to technical assistance. The idea of a joint effort with other governments was recognized in 1955, when FOA was superseded by the International Cooperation Administration. Only in 1961 was the connection between aid and economic growth implied in the agency name. In that year ICA gave way to the Agency for International Development, whose Latin American Regional Bureau is the official link between the United States government and the Alliance for Progress.

The human being in economic development

Whether the direction taken by foreign aid in the late fifties and early sixties is attributable to Fidel Castro, to anti–United States demonstrations, or simply to the maturing of ideas that had been growing for years is a matter of dispute for future historians. Whatever the cause, by 1961 the human being had been discovered as a factor of production and critical link in the development process. Criticizing the undue stress on capital and external resources, Galbraith called for a "positive approach to aid," with emphasis on education, social justice, reliable public administration, and ". . . a clear and purposeful view of what development involves." [9] At approximately the same time Schultz was proclaiming that investment in human capital is as important as (perhaps more important than?) investment in physical capital. He proposed that the principal

[8] Richard H. Wood, "The Servicio and other Joint Methods of Administering U.S. Technical Assistance," *Economic Development and Cultural Change*, January, 1962, p. 201.

[9] John Kenneth Galbraith, "A Positive Approach to Foreign Aid," *Foreign Affairs*, April, 1961, p. 444.

reason for changes in the capital-output ratio over time was its failure to include investments in human capabilities as part of the national capital.[10]

The writings of at least three other scholars have reflected and influenced the trend of the times. Albert Hirschman calls for a "binding agent," or the ability to mobilize existing resources and latent abilities.[11] Everett Hagen refers to the "creative personality"[12] and David McClelland to the "need for achievement" as essentials to the development process.[13] Could it be that the Alliance for Progress, with its stress on individual liberty and social advancement, has been affected by thoughts such as these? The Alliance was already in effect before the Hagen and McClelland books were published, but these men were forming their ideas long before Nixon visited Venezuela and Colombia and while Fidel Castro was still mustering support in the Camagüey.

Hagen distinguishes between authoritarian and creative personalities. The former is one with little scope for curiosity and investigation. Children are taught to obey their parents unquestioningly and are discouraged from experimenting outside a given set of norms. Authority stems from position, not from achievement, and position is inherited. When a child assumes paternal status (not necessarily when he becomes a father, but more likely when his father dies), the mantle of authority is passed to him. Since his instructions are unquestioned, they need not be reasoned or rational. The father also has his place in society, in which he in turn obeys and never questions the authority of those above him, such as the *hacendado,* the labor leader, the military leader to whom he is subject, or the President of the Republic. Societies composed of authoritarian individuals, Hagen contends, are not susceptible to economic growth.

Hagen's thesis may well be a description of the revolutionary movement in Latin America. According to him, the shift from an authoritarian to a creative society requires time, maybe two or three generations. It starts with the displacement of one group (through discrimination against religious or racial minorities, or because some are disadvantaged by historical or economic circumstances). The first generation, Hagen argues, will be too dazed and depressed to do more than stand the shock of the

[10] Theodore Schultz, "Investment in Human Capital," *American Economic Review,* March, 1961, p. 1.

[11] Albert O. Hirschman, *The Strategy of Economic Development,* Yale University Press, New Haven, Conn., 1959, pp. 6–7.

[12] Everett E. Hagen, *On the Theory of Social Change,* Dorsey Press, Homewood, Ill., 1962.

[13] David McClelland, *The Achieving Society,* D. Van Nostrand Company, Inc., Princeton, N.J., 1961.

new condition. (Was this perhaps the case in Mexico, 1910 to 1920?) Sons and grandsons, however, will cease to respect the authority of fathers and grandfathers (does this describe Fidel Castro?) and seek ways to prove their individual worth. In so doing, they become creative personalities.

Hagen's thesis is hardly operational in the sense of suggesting positive action. It is useless to tell officials in Latin American countries that their greatest need is for disadvantaged grandfathers. They already have them. Still, he provides a theory of revolution. Latin Americans should be particularly motivated to read the chapter on Colombia and his version of economic progress in the Valley of Antioquia.[14] In contrast to Hagen, McClelland proposes stimuli to growth. He argues that the need for achievement can be encouraged. Society must be so organized that achievement brings material rewards and even prestige. Competitive instincts must be awakened.

As the Alliance for Progress was enunciated, the United States was ready—politically, economically, culturally, and intellectually—for a shift in its attitude toward Latin America. It is not hard to understand the numerous pieces that fit together peg into niche. What is regrettable is that it is often explained as monolithic.

UNITED STATES MOTIVES FOR AID

"As an illustration of the proper attitude, an American senator in judging an aid program proposed by his government should not ask whether it is in the interest of the United States, but whether it is an example of how a country should behave if we want to make this world a proper environment for a thoughtful and broadminded international regime." [15]

To judge by this quotation, Professor Tinbergen (of the Netherlands) believes the people of the United States will vote for a senator whose perspective is worldwide and not confined to the interests of the United States. Another way of putting it—which may be more realistic—is that the United States is no longer isolationist but has interests that conform with those of other countries.

To discover the political basis for United States foreign aid requires some deep probing. The United States is a pluralistic society, and a senator addressing himself to foreign policy must bear in mind that his constituency has diversified opinions and (if he is to be reelected) he must respect a delicate balance.

[14] *Ibid.*, chap. 15.

[15] Jan Tinbergen, *Shaping the World Economy,* Twentieth Century Fund, New York, 1962, p. 107.

There is no single way in which the United States looks at the foreign-aid program, for North Americans range from those who are totally ignorant of occurrences outside their backyards to those so extremely sensitive to disease and starvation abroad that they willingly expose themselves in efforts to overcome them.

Social consciousness

Long before the Peace Corps was established, university students were spending summer vacations (and sometimes taking an academic year off) in underdeveloped countries, where they would build water systems and sanitation facilities in remote villages, thus helping in some small way the process of development. In Latin America these activities were virtually confined to Mexico, because of its proximity to the United States. The Peace Corps, which gave governmental recognition to a movement already under way through voluntary organizations, has spread the effort to include countries in the rest of Latin America, and Asia and Africa as well. Peace Corpsmen are paid only enough to live by the standards of their counterparts in host countries, and their objective is to teach, bring technical assistance to agriculture, and perform other social and economic functions. Most are students just graduated from the university. I have participated in their preservice training programs and can report firsthand that they are highly motivated and oriented far more toward worldwide interests than those of the United States.

Insensitivity

But the senator in Washington must also respond to constituents who are not at all sensitive to the feelings and aspirations of those who live outside their boundaries. Such people are found in every country, and the United States is no exception. Much of their insensitiveness arises because they have not traveled or been exposed to different cultures. Their own limited horizons have closed from them the possibility of understanding their mutual interests with people abroad. It is our problem, belonging to those North Americans who consider ourselves more international-minded, to educate the less sensitive to their responsibilities and interests in the less developed world. We cannot force them to contribute or to vote for senators who will favor foreign aid, since force is contrary to our way of governing. Rather, we must persuade them. Sometimes, in the process of democratic persuasion we must make concessions which, if taken in isolated fashion by those who believe our government is monolithic, would give the appearance that *all* North Americans are insensitive. These concessions include, for example, the import quotas on lead, zinc, and oil, and other unfortunate elements of our trade policy.

Mutuality of economic interests

In between the extremes of dedicated and insensitive citizenry are North Americans who consider that it is to our mutual economic advantage that less developed countries should grow. Businessmen and labor unions have both recognized that manufacturing countries, with high incomes and high standards of living, are the best customers and best suppliers of each other. If incomes in Latin America are high, Latin Americans will buy more goods and services from the United States than if they are low. Even if economic development implies the growth of consumer industries which compete with those of the United States, the resulting higher incomes will cause such a market expansion that United States producers will probably not suffer on balance. This paradox has been borne out in the history of manufacturing economies and is seen in the trade between Europe and the United States, and among European countries. The Latin American student who said (see the quotation on page 222) that United States aid emphasizes consumer goods was wrong not only in his facts but in his reasoning as well.

President Paz Estenssoro of Bolivia recognized this relationship when he said the following in a speech before Bolivian labor unions in 1954: [16]

> Some young comrades of the Party have asked me in good faith whether there is not some trick behind American aid. On the other side, the communists have immediately accused me of delivering us up to imperialism by accepting aid in foodstuffs, as if bread made from the donated wheat were indigestible. But if the problem is analyzed well, the explanation becomes perfectly logical. Since the second half of the past century up until the second World War, industrialized countries felt their interests were counterpoised against those of countries producing foodstuffs and raw materials, and that their advantage lay in maintaining the backward condition of the latter, blocking their industrial development by every means at their disposal. . . .
>
> Since the second World War there has been a radical change. New economic theories, principally those of Keynes, have displaced the center of gravity in the doctrine of international trade, away from prices and toward income. That is, they no longer relate to the international division of labor or to the question of prices, but to the fact that a country's imports depend on its income. Thus a country can buy much more if it has a high income. If the industrialization and economic development of backward countries tend to raise their real income, causing all the people to have more money, then finally they promote the interchange of goods and

[16] Victor Paz Estenssoro, "La Situación económica de Bolivia: la revolución nacional trabaja para el futuro," speech at the inauguration of a course in labor-union training, February, 1954. Reprinted in *El Trimestre Económico*, July–September, 1954, p. 352.

services. These economic theories succeeded in convincing the politicians of the great powers that to raise the standard of living of backward countries was good business from the point of view of their national interests.

President Paz's description of a radical change in theory is perhaps too cleanly cut, and his portrayal of how economic theory affects United States politicians may be overemphasized. Still, he has hit the essential point, that there are many in the United States—within the ranks of both labor and capital—who consider economic development in Latin America (and elsewhere) to be to our mutual interest.

Latin American students have often challenged this position, on the ground that economic growth would raise wages. This in turn would cause higher prices for primary products, which are "obviously" not to the advantage of the United States. Herein lies another of our failures to communicate with each other. North American producers do not think in these terms at all. While naturally they prefer low wages to high, they have for years been oriented toward offsetting increased labor costs by higher productivity. They view Latin American producers as inefficient monopolies, sadly in need of cost-reducing investment and enlightened management, which economic development would supply. It just does not occur to them that Latin American economic growth will impair their terms of trade.

Political goals

But it is not fair to overemphasize the humanitarian and economic interests of the United States in foreign aid. There are political concerns as well, and they may even predominate. The job of the State Department is to conduct foreign policy, and herein lies its stake in the aid program.

There are two ways to approach the political. One is to portray the United States as bribing other countries to follow certain foreign policies, such as their conduct of trade with the Soviet bloc, reimbursement for expropriated industries, how to vote in the United Nations, or whether to maintain diplomatic relations with the revolutionary government of Cuba. There has been all too much of this, and it is an activity on which Latin Americans do not look kindly.

It is regrettable that the United States has ever offered foreign aid for votes in an international conference, from its own point of view as well as that of Latin America. The fact that it has done so has obscured a political objective of foreign aid that many Latin Americans would laud. At the behest of Latin Americans themselves, the economic power of the United States may be brought to bear in the direction of enlightened change.

Two questions dominate the problem of United States political goals in the Alliance for Progress. One was asked at the end of Chapter 3: do Latin Americans really want their reforms to be undertaken by pressure from Washington and in exchange for Alliance funds, or do these levers become undesirable intervention in internal affairs? Since I cannot answer this one, I turn to the second. From the point of view of the United States, how effective a weapon is the Alliance for Progress in bringing about the desired political and economic changes in Latin America?

Once again the Alliance may be compared with the Marshall Plan. The chief objective of the United States in the latter was a strong and undivided Europe, to act as both trading partner and bulwark in maintaining worldwide political balance. The Europeans' objective was the same, and the bargain was easily struck. We supplied the funds, and they did virtually all the rest. The Organization for European Economic Cooperation, organized and directed by Europeans, had far more voice in the disposition of Marshall Plan funds than the United States has ever conceded to Latin American countries in the Alliance for Progress.

To the United States, the Marshall Plan was a more solid organization for carrying out political objectives than is the Alliance for Progress, for two reasons. The first is the one cited earlier, that unlike Latin America, Europe was equipped with all the requisites for recovery except capital. The second is more delicate. The United States felt greater confidence in the commitments of European governments than in those of Latin America.

The United States has kept full control of the purse strings in the Alliance for Progress. In the first two years, no formal Latin American organization comparable to the OEEC existed, although the nine "wise men" (most of them Latin Americans) screened development plans and offered their opinions. Only in the latter part of 1963, at the behest of two ex-Presidents of Latin America—Lleras of Colombia and Kubitschek of Brazil—did the United States show itself willing to join an Inter-American Development Committee, which at the time of writing has not been established.

The reluctance of the United States to trust the Latin American governments is another instance—I believe—of the different weight put on commitments in our two halves of the hemisphere. There is constant pressure in Congress to withhold aid from Latin America until definite commitments are made concerning agrarian reform, stabilization, development plans and the like, and to suspend aid at any point where it is apparent that these commitments are not being carried out.

But agrarian reform laws, stabilization programs, and even development plans are fraught with so many uncertainties that Latin Americans (so it seems to me) do not look on them as commitments in the same sense as North Americans. Rather, they are statements of intent, to be carried out more loosely and flexibly (and maybe abandoned) as unforeseen circumstances may require. This does not in any way imply a lack of sincerity on the part of Latin Americans in undertaking them (as is so often suspected in the United States), but only a recognition of what *to them* is reality.

The Inter-American Development Committee would assume the political burden of policing the Alliance for Progress. It would formulate priorities and recommend slowing the aid to laggard nations. This is an unpleasant task that the United States would be glad to pass on to the Latin Americans. The very creation of the Committee would be a step toward mutuality in political goals of the Alliance. But the fact that Washington would not entrust funds to the discretion of the Committee is an indication that the interchange of faith is not yet complete.

Summary

In summary of this and the preceding section, United States foreign aid has a varied history and discrete evolution. It began before World War II, stemming in part from depression and the desire to promote exports and in part as a response to demands from Latin America for technical aid. After the war it concentrated on the capital requirements of Europe, partly for the political reason that Europe was a vacuum which we would fill rather than allow the Communists to do so. But another reason was that capital was the only ingredient lacking for rapid growth. We did not believe this to be so for Latin America.

After the success of the Marshall Plan, the swing took two directions. One was toward military aid, in response to Communist moves in Greece, Korea, and Southeast Asia and to threats in Turkey. The other was toward technical assistance, in the mistaken belief that it alone could do what we were convinced capital alone could not do. As the fifties moved on and Communist threats were contained, the direction was again unified, and the center of gravity shifted. Once more the motives were a blend of social conscience with the economic and political.

It is impossible to desegregate the blend. Even in the Peace Corps, where social consciousness predominates, the volunteers are concerned with improving the image of their country. They not only have a deep concern for the development of other nations, but they want it to be known abroad that they do. Social scientists have reasoned that economic growth is not just a matter of capital or technical assistance or even education but is the child of a political, social, and cultural environment. Provide all the capital possible, all the schooling needed, plus hordes of agricultural experts, and the peon on the hacienda will reject them all if he does not have his own land and the incentive to maximize its yield. Economic aid cannot be given without impinging on the political structure. Richard Nixon and Fidel Castro helped teach us this, but they were not the only impulses. North American scholars like Hirschman, McClelland, and Hagen were molding our thoughts as well. Yet the blend of economic and political makes difficult—yea, grave—the resolution of what constitutes intervention in the sovereign rights of another nation and what does not. The Alliance for Progress is indeed a delicate keg of powder.

OPPOSITION TO FOREIGN AID

In 1957 a North American named Eugene Castle wrote a book called *The Great Giveaway*. In it he argues that the foreign-aid program has been ruinous to United States taxpayers, has sapped the nation of vital resources that might better have been used at home, has failed to obtain political advantage for the United States, and has detracted from—rather than added to—the economic development of other nations.

> It is soberly proposed that we continue pouring out our billions in a give-away program which our chief policy-makers would project ten years ahead. Such a program simply does not make sense. Even a moderate downturn in our national economic well-being could precipitate an overnight situation of acute distress to most Americans. And it must be remembered that tens of millions of us who can least afford it would be the most severely hurt. The time to lighten the load of such a ruinous program is right now, before our nation has been permanently harmed.[17]

The book is not an isolated cry of distress in an overwhelming wave of enthusiasm for foreign aid. Alas, it is a more and more popular position. North Americans are sensitive about the way in which their tax money is spent, and if they do not consider it to be used wisely, they will instruct their Congressmen to curtail the aid program severely, if not abolish it.

The growing unpopularity of foreign aid is manifest by the tight controls that Congress has placed on its administration. Funds cannot be committed for more than one year in advance. In 1961 the President requested a law that would permit five-year commitments, and Congress refused.[18] Each year Congressmen examine the expenditures of the past with an increasingly critical eye. Each year they pare down the President's request for money. In projecting the program for fiscal year 1963, the President asked Congress to appropriate $3,310.8 million for economic

[17] Eugene Castle, *The Great Giveaway,* Henry Regnery Company, Chicago, 1957, p. 37.

[18] Congress decided that the foreign-aid agency might project its activities over a five-year period, but funds would be provided only on a yearly basis.

assistance. Congress replied by voting for only $2,603.9 million.[19] In other words, the President asked for 27 per cent more funds than Congress was willing to commit.

The size and quantity of the foreign-aid program came under national scrutiny in 1963 when a committee, appointed by the President to study United States government foreign operations in the economic and military fields (the Clay committee) issued a report containing the following views: [20]

> We believe that we are indeed attempting too much for too many and that a higher quality and reduced quantity of our diffuse aid effort in certain countries could accomplish more. We cannot believe that our national interest is served by indefinitely continuing commitments at the present rate to the 95 countries and territories which are now receiving our economic and/or military assistance.

While the Clay committee supported foreign aid in principle, it was sharply critical of the quantities involved and the manner in which funds were being expended. The President immediately responded with a substantial cut in his request to Congress for the foreign-aid budget for fiscal year 1964.

The most cogent contention of opponents to foreign aid is that it retards more than promotes the development of other countries. We have seen that Latin American students have argued in similar vein. Castle differs from them, however, in attributing the negative results to the ineptness and naïveté of United States officials, rather than to calculated design. For example, the United States has contributed general budgetary support in Latin America to Guatemala, Haiti, and Bolivia.[21] The *theory* is that this support will buy time, during which governments will put their financial houses in order, revising tax systems and trimming expenditures to what is covered by revenues. In *practice*, the politicians may feel that so long as Yankee dollars are available, financial pressures do not coerce them into reforms.[22]

> Although the aid program prides itself upon the services it has rendered to foreigners, the program, after its first crisis beginnings, all too often has not aided the foreigner but has actually harmed him. This is true because foreign aid has all the inescapable weaknesses of a hot-house operation. It saps the will to self-help by offering the foreigner easy exits

[19] Agency for International Development, Budget Division, Office of the Controller.

[20] *The Scope and Distribution of United States Military and Economic Assistance Programs,* Department of State, Report to the President of the United States from the Committee to Strengthen the Security of the Free World, Mar. 20, 1963, p. 4.

[21] At the time of writing it is continued only for Bolivia.

[22] Castle, *op. cit.*, p. 34.

from his political and economic dilemmas. It supplies artificial props and supports to the foreigner's economy which keep it in a perpetual state of false expectation and dislocation.

Castle is unquestionably correct that some types of aid have subsidized inefficiency rather than promoted reform. Still, his remark that "It saps the will to self-help . . ." smacks of the capitalist ethic and the belief that nations will succeed better if left to sink or swim than if they are "coddled along." This conviction is widespread among North Americans and may spell trouble for the aid program in years to come.

ECONOMIC AID AND SURPLUSES

> The entire meaning of the economic problem has been changed, nay inverted. In past ages the problem to be solved was: how can the requirements of consumers be satisfied by production? To-day, on the contrary, it is: how can the immense quantity of commodities, which are easily produced, be rendered accessible to the consumers, so as to be effectively consumed? [23]

At the end of 1961, the Commodity Credit Corporation, an agency of the United States government, owned 1,261,300 bushels of corn, 1,242,518 bushels of wheat, 307,018 pounds of dried milk, 392,311 hundredweight of sorghum, and various other grains, foodstuffs, and primary products that had cost it $5,563 million. In addition, it had outstanding loans of $1,523 million disbursed to farmers on condition they would put their own crops into storage.[24] Furthermore, the United States Government was actively dissuading farmers (sometimes through subsidy payments) from growing foodstuffs of which they were capable. Besides all this, many surplus agricultural products had been given to other countries and were still being given, as part of the foreign-aid program.

Almost one hundred years ago a political philosopher named Karl Marx predicted that all this would happen. His thesis was that capital begets capital in a cumulative upward spiral, causing a small part of the population to become more and more wealthy, while the counterpart to wealth lies in masses of people who do not have enough to eat. Recurrent crises would stem from the inadequacy of markets, but the inevitable collapse might be postponed for many years by wars that would consume the surplus wealth or the opening of new territories where it might be dumped. Is this the role of foreign aid?

[23] Julian Borchardt, "The Theory of Crises," in Karl Marx, *Capital*, Vintage Books, Random House, Inc., New York, 1959, p. 313. Borchardt's essay is in explanation of chap. 24 of Marx.

[24] *Statistical Abstract of the United States*, U.S. Department of Commerce, 1962, p. 634.

The North American government has a completely different explanation of agricultural surpluses. From its point of view, any exploitation has been confined to the poor hen, who was laying an average of 181 eggs a year in 1953, as opposed to 112 in 1925, and producing 37.5 kilograms of broiler meat for every 100 kilograms of grain in 1952, as opposed to 28.8 kilograms in 1925. In a short two decades (from 1930–1933 to 1950–1953) the output of wheat, per unit of input, increased to 169 per cent of its earlier amount, cotton to 149 per cent, hog raising to 132 per cent, and so on. In 1955 farm-labor productivity in general was 250 per cent of what it had been in 1925.[25]

All this was strictly in accordance with Marx, who expected to see output per worker rise as more capital was applied. Where, then, does the North American experience differ from what Marx predicted? In the first place, it differs in the way the wealth has been distributed. Let us recall (from Chapter 3) that United States agriculture is done on family farms, with an average of less than one employee per farm. In other words, the farm owner and his sons constitute the primary labor force. Already we have violated Marx's strict distinction between capitalist and laborer. Furthermore, farm wages have been rising as laborers have had alternative opportunities in the cities.

The second point of difference is more compelling than the first. Marx contended that the concentration of wealth would be reflected in an army of unemployed laborers, starving while craving to consume the surplus output if only they could. Yet this army does not exist in the United States. Wages are high, the laborer is well fed, and unemployment is generally below 5 per cent of the total labor force.[26] Even the unemployed are fed and housed through insurance programs and could not possibly consume the total of surplus output.

A third point of difference is that Marx attributed the accumulation of surplus product to capital. United States agriculture *has* used more capital; the amount of tractors, trucks, automobiles, milking machines, combines, and other devices on farms has increased greatly over the last thirty years. But capital alone has limited potential to improve farm productivity. It may replace horses and mules, or workers who have been attracted to better opportunities in the cities, but (as we pointed out in Chapter 3) it cannot make more cotton plants fit on an acre of land or

[25] Glenn L. Johnson, "Agriculture's Technological Revolution," in The American Assembly, *United States Agriculture: Perspectives and Prospects,* Columbia University Press, New York, 1955, pp. 27–44.

[26] Since 1957 unemployment has crept above 5 per cent, to the increasing concern of the United States Government. It went as high as 7.7 per cent in 1961 but dropped to 5.8 per cent in 1963.

extend the number of growing days in a year.[27] Far more importantly, the increase in agricultural productivity has been due to better methods of production: the introduction of hybrid corn, experimentation for higher-yielding seeds, improved methods of breeding cattle and poultry, better types of fertilizer, and the like. To employ new methods exploits no one, but it yields spectacular increases in output.

It has been beyond the capacity of the United States to consume the increase. Our stomachs have only a certain size, and there is a limited number of cotton shirts we can wear each year. According to classical economics and the law of markets, farmers should have decreased their output as prices fell in response to declining demand. Had the agricultural revolution not been rapid, this is surely what would have happened. But three decades are only one generation, and this is too short a time to expect thousands of farmers to abandon their homes, change their lives, and move to the cities. I have explained all this in Chapter 3. Here indeed was a problem of human suffering and governmental compassion that contributed to the erosion of individualism in the United States. As I have suggested before, the Alliance for Progress and United States adherence to the coffee agreement are in no small way due to the change in popular thinking within the United States that stems from the farm problem.

A further discrepancy with Karl Marx is that according to him the surpluses would be universal and not confined to the farm. But the United States does not have surplus industrial products. The government does not have vast programs for buying surplus steel billets, or refrigerators, or automobiles, or television sets. It must seem odd to Marxists, if they stop to think about it, that North American surpluses have not accumulated in the giant industries and rolling mills, in the large capital-intensive corporations where thousands of laborers are employed, but instead on the family farm, where more often than not the laborer and capitalist are the same man.

Commodity assistance

Surplus agricultural commodities, however, are not the only ones that the United States includes in its foreign-assistance program. In fiscal year 1962, $518 million of commodities were purchased in the United States to be supplied under loans and grants to less developed countries, including $129.9 million of machinery and equipment, $90.1 million of iron and

[27] Capital can improve productivity if it is employed in irrigation. Even here, however, its possibilities are far more limited than most persons believe. Irrigation in the United States is virtually confined to eighteen Western states and Louisiana, and only 1.5 per cent of total farm lands are subject to it. From 1949 to 1959 the increase in irrigated farm lands was 0.002 per cent of total farm acreage in 1959.

steel mill products, $40.8 million of chemicals, $36.3 million of motor vehicles, $33.4 million of fertilizers, and $29.1 million of railroad transportation equipment. Does this fact contradict the preceding paragraph, in which it was said that only agricultural products are in surplus?

Not so. Until late in 1961 dollars provided by the United States for commodity purchases were spent anywhere in the world. In the fiscal year ended June 30, 1961, for example, 57 per cent of the commodities provided by the United States under its foreign-aid programs were bought in third countries. Nor did these dollars necessarily find their way back to the United States by a devious route, for supplying countries often used them to build up their own exchange reserves. Only when the United States balance of payments worsened in late 1960 did President Eisenhower introduce the "buy America" policy, requiring that more aid commodities be purchased within the United States. As a result, only 40 per cent of aid commodities was purchased in third countries in fiscal year 1962.[28] It must be stressed, however, that this shift occurred in response to balance of payments pressures, and not because the aid program had been designed (over a decade earlier) to aborb surplus commodities.

Disposal of surplus agricultural commodities

The problem of agricultural surpluses has not been an easy one for the United States, and least of all for rival producing countries. Price supports had to be bolstered by import restrictions, for otherwise foreign products would be sold for consumption within the United States while the domestic crop would be bought by the government for storage. Export subsidies were introduced to maintain a foreign market that would otherwise be lost because farmers preferred to sell to the government at higher prices. Obviously neither import controls nor export subsidies was popular with foreign producers, who complained of competition and dumping.

The Agricultural Trade Development and Assistance Act of 1954 (Public Law 480) firmly linked farm surpluses to the foreign-aid program. Under this act surplus agricultural products are sold abroad for payment in local currency to be deposited in United States accounts. This currency may not be converted into dollars but may be used to defray certain expenses of the United States abroad or be loaned or granted to government or private enterprises for development projects within the recipient country. With the permission of the government of that country, part of it may be loaned to third countries for their development. By far

[28] James P. Lockard, "The Impact of the 'Buy American' Procurement Policy on the Alliance for Progress," unpublished paper presented at the Institute for International Development, Johns Hopkins University, October, 1962.

the largest portion is used for development projects—in 1962, $668.5 million out of total withdrawals of $672.8 million.[29]

In 1959 the agricultural surplus sales program was renamed "Food for Peace," in an effort to emphasize the development projects springing from local currency collected. These expenditures have not been small. In fiscal year 1962 five million pesos of food-generated money was spent on the development of industry and mining in Colombia, 6.3 million sucres on agricultural improvement in Ecuador, 585 thousand pesos on industry and mining in Mexico, 140 million guaranis on transportation in Paraguay, and nearly 7 million pesos on transportation in Uruguay.[30]

Despite the benefits of projects thus financed, Public Law 480 imposes certain burdens on agricultural-exporting countries whose products compete with those of the United States. If wheat is sold for local currencies in Latin America, are not inroads cut into the export markets of Uruguay and Argentina? And does not surplus United States cotton compete against the crops of Mexico, Peru, Brazil, and several other Latin American countries? And what about the "normal" exports of farmers within the United States?

To take account of these dangers, the President is directed, under Public Law 480, to "take reasonable precaution to safeguard usual marketings of the United States and to assure that sales under this Act will not unduly disrupt world prices of agricultural commodities or normal patterns of commercial trade with friendly countries."[31] This loosely defined directive is intended to be carried out through projects designed to increase the consumption of foodstuffs, so that Public Law 480 exports will move into new channels not currently occupied by world trade. An example would be a school luncheon program, in which children are fed who would not otherwise eat luncheon at all. Another would be colonization projects, in which food would be used as part payment to laborers building roads.

In practice, it is impossible to distinguish between "normal channels" and "increased consumption," as many Latin American complainants have pointed out.[32] Possibly the greatest dilemma of the foreign-aid program lies in the fact that surplus agricultural products of the United States *can* provide capital to less developed countries (by feeding workers who are producing capital goods) but *cannot* do so without running into compe-

[29] *Counterpart Funds and A.I.D. Foreign Currency Accounts,* AID, Sept. 30, 1962, p. 13.

[30] *Ibid.,* pp. 57–62.

[31] The words "or normal patterns of commercial trade with friendly countries" were added in an amendment to Public Law 480, under Public Law 85-931.

[32] See, for example, Miguel S. Wionczek, "Los excedentes mundiales y la política agrícola exterior de los Estados Unidos," *El Trimestre Económico,* September–December, 1954, pp. 481–505.

tition with "normal" farm suppliers. A secondary dilemma arises from the fact that agriculture is one of the bottlenecks holding back economic development in Latin America. As the "structuralists" have amply pointed out in the inflation debate, high food costs have been an obstacle to the construction of capital goods in the cities. The United States has the means to overcome this rigidity, but to do so with full force will deprive the Latin American farmer of the price stimulus to increase his output.

Surely the solution to these dilemmas is not beyond the capabilities of imaginative men. Surely there must be some way by which the use of surpluses can promote agricultural efficiency rather than hinder it, and improve the markets of traditional suppliers rather than replace them.

One such way might be to tie agricultural surpluses to land reform, as both deterrent and incentive. Large landowners refusing to subject their property to reform might be deprived—through taxes or other restrictions—of their usual privilege of selling in urban markets, with the loss being made up by surpluses. (The unsold products would have to be consumed on the hacienda, thus improving the lot of the peon.) On the other hand, lands subject to reform might be guaranteed against losses in output during the initial period of adjustment, with surplus foodstuffs serving as the insurance fund.

There are other ways in which surpluses might be used as insurance. Farmers are often reluctant to try new techniques because they are already on the verge of starvation, and failure of an unsure method might spell disaster. Surplus foodstuffs could be their insurance, to be paid in the event of crop failure—but only if the new methods are tried.

Surpluses might also promote community development in the nonmarket sector. Remote Indian villages in many Latin American countries do not consume the wheat exports of Argentina or the cotton exports of Mexico; often their people eat only one or two meals a day. With some imagination it should be possible to find capital projects at home—such as road building, schools, better housing, or the upgrading of some local product and its introduction to the market—which could be done by villagers paid with United States farm surpluses.

The difficulties of finding and promoting such projects are enormous, and many who have tried have already failed. All the political obstacles to land reform stand in the way. Capital development is not easy in villages, where labor is unskilled, resources scarce, external economies lacking, and markets remote. No definitive solution is suggested here, but rather the direction in which imagination should be applied. It is one thing to reject the Marxist explanation of abundance in a starving world, and—by implication—to reject the revolutionary means to resolve it. It is quite another thing to adopt the methods and compromises necessary to put resources to use in a rational way.

ECONOMIC AID: UNITED STATES OR SOVIET UNION?

Latin American students have often asked whether their governments should not turn more to the Soviet Union for assistance. The Soviet bloc already has extended aid to several countries in the Middle East, Africa, and Asia and to some in Latin America, such as Argentina (in the age of Perón) and Brazil. Revolutionary Cuba has of course received the greatest commitments.

The acceptance of any assistance—whether from the United States or the Soviet Union—poses the question of what additional relationship, overt or implied, by agreement or *de facto*, is established between the aid-giving and the aid-receiving country. Does aid imply agreement with, or even a predilection toward, the ideology of the lending country? President Sukarno of Indonesia insists on receiving aid in almost equal amounts from the United States and the U.S.S.R., on the ground that only thereby does he show strict neutrality.

Any country extending economic assistance to another establishes its presence in the latter. The United States government is represented not only by its embassies but unofficially by the operating missions of the Agency for International Development, whose officers talk to cabinet members, to the president of the central bank, and to the President of the republic. Each comes to know the other, and they acquire a better understanding of each other's motives and polity. These personal relationships also constitute channels through which matters of inter-American import are discussed. Some argue that the very presence of foreigners is intervention in a nation's internal affairs.

The Soviet Union would also like to establish its presence abroad. It has provided the capital for steel mills in India, and it is building a giant dam in Egypt. Aid such as this is accompanied by Soviet technicians and other "informal ambassadors" who open lines of communication with appropriate persons in the Indian, Egyptian, or other governments.

The presence of one country in another is not good or bad per se but may be either, depending on how it is used. Communication between governments is essential, and it is often smoother through the informal channels of aid missions than over long distances or through protocol-minded embassies. The very fact that the personnel of another country (such as the United States or the Soviet Union) can talk freely to the Minister of Finance or the President of the republic does not mean that an entente has been forged. Depending on their behavior, Soviet or United States officials can either bring closer ties or increased disaffection for the country from which they come. The latter occurs when presence is abused, by its conversion into a vehicle to promote national interests that are not mutual.

Economic assistance offered by the Soviet Union often has the appearance of being less offensive than that of the United States. Rarely (if ever) does the Soviet Union ask why a nation wants aid or what it is going to do with the proceeds. In 1954, for example, the government of Afghanistan allegedly asked the United States to pave the streets of its capital city, Kabul, as part of foreign aid. The United States is said to have refused, contending that the same value of resources could contribute more to Afghan development elsewhere, such as in irrigation. The Soviet government eagerly filled the gap, paving 40 kilometers of Kabul's streets in 1955. They proclaimed it was up to the Afghans themselves to state their priorities, which were no business of either the United States or the Soviet Union.

A similar circumstance occurred in Bolivia in 1960. The Bolivians have long yearned for a tin smelter, which stands second only to a seacoast on their list of national aspirations. Comibol, the nationalized mining company, was hardly in a position to build one, since it lacked capital, engineering ability, and virtually all the other requisites. The United States government would not provide one through foreign aid. The necessary studies had not been made. For years little geological exploration had taken place, and no one knew whether the Bolivian mountains contained enough tin to make a smelter feasible. Quite possibly they did, but no one had found it. There was also the question of whether adequate fuel was available. Besides, the "rational" way to lead toward a smelter (the North Americans would have argued) is to build a concentration plant first, which would separate the ore from the major impurities. Once this is in operation, it is easier to know the economics of a smelter.

Many Bolivians considered the North American answer too slow, too hedging, too "North American." Late in 1960, at a meeting of the United Nations in New York, Premier Khrushchev—without ever having seen Bolivia—announced that the Soviet Union was prepared to lend some $100 million for a smelter. A Soviet mission visited Bolivia shortly thereafter, and the Bolivian Vice President went to Moscow. To date, there is no smelter. Quite aside from lack of accomplishment, it is interesting to conjecture on the reasons why the Soviet Union might have made the offer while the United States would not.

Attitudes toward individual projects reflect the ideologies of both countries. The United States is committed to an orderly, peaceful process of revolution, in which institutions to be preserved must be distinguished from those that must be changed or abandoned. According to the North American philosophy, there is much in the present politicoeconomic order that ought to survive and be strengthened. The market as regulator of economic activity (subject to government intervention where necessary) is one. Democratic government is another. Other institutions, such as the hacienda system, are doomed, not by United States policy but by the inevitable thrust of history. By adhering to the Alliance for Progress, the United States has committed itself to cooperation in their peaceful demise. Doubtless it felt that a tin smelter was not consistent with those institutions—such as democratic government and a market economy—that ought to be preserved.

Bolivians will not like the suggestion that a tin smelter is not consistent with democracy in their country. Yet this may be so. Their government has already constructed a pipeline going across the Andes and descending from Sica Sica to Arica, Chile, to pump out oil that has not yet been discovered. Much valuable foreign exchange was used to build this line, and more was lost by not selling the oil that must be stored in it to preserve it from rust. The Bolivian government is running a budgetary deficit and does not have the resources to maintain such activities that do not support themselves.

The Soviet Union is not so exacting in its distinctions. It is not committed to the market as regulator of economic activity, nor is it devoted to democratic government or virtually any of the institutions created by Western society. It is committed to revolution, which its present leaders *say* will be peaceful (although there is some dispute among Communists as to whether orderly change is possible). Demonstrations by Communist sympathizers often cause property losses, usually directed at "Yankee imperialists," such as explosions in oil wells and burning of warehouses. The waste of resources in an unprofitable smelter would be but another of these.

The very fact that the Soviets would offer a smelter before the necessary studies had been made—something they would never do at home—indicates no commitment to its economic success. Why did it do so? Some cynics have argued that Premier Khrushchev never intended to deliver, but only wanted the propaganda effect of the offer. Others suggest that he wanted to gain a foothold, to establish the Soviet presence in a country where (he considered) United States influence was already too strong. Perhaps the Soviets would themselves subsidize the smelter, considering the cost a small one compared to the political gains.

There is another reason why the United States government insists on rigorous priorities for economic aid, passed on by its own missions abroad. This is that—unlike the Soviet Union—United States aid programs are subject to critical review by Congress and the people of the United States. In a pluralistic society such as ours, one of whose unifying forces is a belief in rationalization of economic activity, it is hard to explain an undertaking the motive for which is entirely political, not economic. Any project that does not yield a return more than equal to its costs will inevitably be censured by congressional and popular opponents of foreign aid, and its failure may jeopardize future appropriations for assistance in general.

It is often felt, both at home and abroad, that a principal objective of foreign aid is to gain the friendship of the recipient countries. I believe this is more the case with the Soviet Union than with the United States. Their philosophy—which may not prove sound in the long run—is to decide which countries they need (or can afford) to befriend and how much it will cost. Then they offer that amount of aid for whatever projects —like the Aswan Dam, paving the roads of Kabul, or a tin smelter in Bolivia—are most demanded by national aspirations.

The United States also covets the friendship of recipient countries, but most foreign-service officers would not rank it top priority. Often they encounter antagonisms for refusing specific loans. They may be pressed to approve projects that they deem poorly planned, or whose marketing and technical feasibility studies are not adequate, or that are motivated by political opportunism (e.g., the minister who wants a highway to his hometown, whether the traffic would justify it or not).

A North American foreign-service officer once reported the following conversation with a government official in an Asian country.[33]

> We came to know each other well, and could talk freely. I asked him what he thought of our aid program, as compared to that of the Soviet Union. He complained bitterly about the U.S. bureaucracy, and the infinite delays in securing project approvals in Washington. He spoke of hopes and frustrations, and disagreements over the adequacy of project analysis or the criteria of a successful proposal. There was no trouble on this score with the Soviet Union, he said. A request would be made, and within a week the goods were delivered.
>
> Then he paused, and finally he looked at me and added: But do you know, after some years we are beginning to understand what makes U.S. officials tick. The mystery of why you are here is gradually being removed, and we discover that your motives are not really so frightening as we thought at first. But we have never understood the Soviet Union. They do not say what they want, they only say they want what *we* want. We are not so naive as to believe that.

I have not proved that the assistance program of the Soviet Union is more motivated by desire for friendship than that of the United States. Rather, the discussion has shifted to a more philosophical plane. Between nations as between individuals, true friendship rarely comes where it is sought for itself alone, and those who never disagree with each other are probably not really friends.

[33] I am indebted to Hans Heymann of The RAND Corporation for this quotation.

In short, if international ties are more tightly drawn by the aid program, this fact comes as a valued byproduct. From a political point of view, the major objective of United States assistance is to demonstrate that economic growth and diversification can occur under a democratic society and that people are capable of taking upon themselves the responsibilities necessary to attain these ends, which need not be forced upon them by autocratic leadership. The United States is committed to peaceful revolution in which essential institutions of the present politicoeconomic order will be preserved and strengthened. It is not necessary to destroy everything to start over again.

10 National Economic Planning

POSTWAR ECONOMIC growth in Latin America has been spectacular. Whether one examines the national-product statistics (as in the accompanying table), or the growth of institutions such as development banks and capital markets, or data on saving and investment, or whether he simply looks about him as he drives from Callao to Lima or through the streets of Monterrey or Caracas, all indicators point in the same direction. "As I stood in downtown São Paulo," an economist from the Inter-American Bank told me, "I could see the gross national product increasing at 7 per cent a year. It was almost like seeing the hands of a clock advance." Rostow characterizes the take-off as a jump in investment from less than 5 per cent of GNP to 10 per cent or more. In these terms, Latin America has taken off.

Although real, the upward movement has been sporadic. It has been punctuated by political crises. In recent years it has lagged because of lower prices for primary products and a glut in the world oil market. Investment has been restrained by pessimistic business psychology arising partly from monetary stabilization and partly from fears of violence. But such setbacks are temporary. Few doubt that the substance for growth is there.

One who examines only the statistics may well ask why there is such a furor over development. Why awaken so suddenly to a need for planning? Why the dissatisfaction with a high rate of growth already achieved? The answer lies in the incompleteness of the pattern. Latin America is a swamp of poverty and stagnation out of which a few peaks are pointing upward. The statistics measure the growth of these peaks, and economists

GROSS NATIONAL PRODUCT OF SELECTED LATIN AMERICAN COUNTRIES
(In millions of monetary units at prices of base year)

Country	Base year	Monetary unit	1950	1954	1955	1956	1957	1958	1959	1960
Argentina	1950	Peso	62,291	65,226	68,292	67,703	70,415	72,350	68,900	71,933
Brazil *	1949	Cruzeiro	100 (1949)	129.6	138.4	141.0	150.7	160.7	172.5	183.4
Chile	1960	Escudo	3,450.9	4,217.4	4,387.5	4,134.9	4,322.2	4,495.4	4,530.6	4,646.0
Colombia	1958	Peso		18,039	18,770	19,500	19,786	20,267	21,791	22,787
Costa Rica †	1958	Colon	1,509.5	2,028.7	2,138.6	2,210.2	2,357.4	2,450.0	2,530.0	2,628.7
Cuba ‡	1953	Peso	2,089	2,225	2,296	2,496	2,864	2,614 †		
Ecuador	1950	Sucre	7,068	8,940	9,164	9,444	9,949	10,249	10,725	11,356
Guatemala	1950	Quetzal	466.5	424.4	496.6	537.9	558.7	588.8	632.0	657.4
Honduras	1948	Lempira	378.2	467.0	475.0	496.6	533.7	538.2		
Mexico ‡	1958	Peso	72,115	84,043	92,296	100,000	103,381	101,800	106,863	111,204
Panama ‡	1958	Balboa	228.1	301.2	322.5	333.4	366.5	375.7	401.9	423.1
Paraguay §	1956	Guarani		15,455	16,704	15,762	16,434	16,921	15,116	15,231
Peru	1954	Sol		25,082	27,051	27,070	26,056	28,815	29,100	
Venezuela	1957	Bolivar		17,749	19,325	21,366	23,848	24,164	26,065	26,433

* Net domestic product at factor cost.
† First two quarters only.
‡ Deflated from current prices (as supplied by UN) by cost-of-living index in *International Financial Statistics.*
§ Gross domestic product.

SOURCE: *Yearbook of National Accounts Statistics,* United Nations, New York.

perch on them in the capital cities. But the folly of both statistics and economists is that they do not probe beneath the surface of the quagmire.

Furthermore, the spectacular growth in GNP is competing against an equally impressive increase in population. In the mid-fifties, Spain, Portugal, France, and Italy were growing by less than 1 per cent per year. Population in the United States was rising by about 1.8 per cent per year. But in Latin America, the average increase was approximately 2.7 per cent, higher than for any other continent. Seven countries were growing by more than 3 per cent, and only four by less than 2 per cent. At 2 per cent a year, a population will double in thirty-five years, and at 3 per cent in only twenty-three years. In 1960 the population of Latin America was approximately 215 million. If present rates of growth continue, it will reach almost 600 million by the end of the century.

Economists tend to set an increase in population against an increase in gross national product. This is right and proper. If population is increasing by 2.7 per cent each year, then GNP must increase at that rate so that incomes per capita do not decline. But other things must happen, as well. A growing population needs capital. A large part of national saving is "lost" in simply providing new people with implements already known and used. Furthermore, the delicate balance in welfare (if indeed it has been balanced) will be upset if income—rising at the same rate as population—tends to be distributed more proportionately to the wealthy. Latin American statistics are not adequate to tell us whether this is happening.

National economic plans hardly need to be defended. Both the United States and Latin America are dedicated to planning in the Alliance for Progress. Yet it may well be questioned whether students in Latin American universities, officials of Latin American governments, *campesinos* in remote villages, congressmen in Washington, and United States ambassadors in Latin American countries, all conjure up the same picture as they pronounce the word "planning."

PLANNING AND THE ALLIANCE FOR PROGRESS

> La Paz, Bolivia, March 14—Two Bolivian cabinet ministers, who attended a meeting in Chile on Latin-American developments under the Alliance for Progress, strongly criticized United States policies and the aid program on their return here yesterday.
>
> Roberto Jordán Pando, Minister of Rural Affairs, and Guillermo Bedregal, Minister President of the Bolivian State Mining Corporation, declared in a statement that Bolivia was one of the few Latin-American countries that had met the reform requirements of the Alliance for Progress.
>
> Yet, they added, Bolivia is receiving little help under the program. Latin

countries without agrarian reform programs or economic development plans, they declared, were receiving considerable assistance.[1]

Latin America has lofty ambitions under the Alliance for Progress. Within ten years (so it is contemplated) national income will be increasing at a rate of 2.5 per cent per capita annually. Economies will be diversified, with less dependence on primary output. There will be agrarian reform, a drastic decrease in illiteracy, low-cost housing, improvements in water supply, medical and sanitary facilities, and significant increases in the productivity of both industry and agriculture. To accomplish this, $100 billion will be invested, of which $80 billion will come from within Latin America itself. Only the remaining $20 billion will be supplied by foreigners.

First and foremost among the "basic requirements for economic and social development," as listed in the Charter of Punta del Este, is: "That comprehensive and well-conceived national programs of economic and social development, aimed at the achievement of self-sustaining growth, be carried out in accordance with democratic principles." Yet despite the assertions of support for planning to achieve the difficult goals of the Alliance, one wonders—when comments occur such as those by the two Bolivian ministers—whether the twenty signatory nations of the Alliance have really verbalized a common position. Can it be that their agreement lies only in the wording of the document and that language is an inadequate indicator of unanimity or lack of it?

One might suppose that a major dissention between the United States and Latin America would lie in the ideology of planning and the extent to which a government-directed economy is called for, rather than one of private enterprise. Yet if any disagreement has occurred here, it has been kept to a minimum. It is generally believed that planning under the Alliance is consistent with a mixed economy of government and private initiative, that it will require much government direction, but that it can be so implemented as to encourage individual choices that promote the national welfare even though motivated by private gain. The Charter of Punta del Este makes this clear in the following paragraph:

"The active participation of the private sector is essential to economic integration and development, and except in those countries in which free enterprise does not exist, development planning by the pertinent national public agencies, far from hindering such participation, can facilitate and guide it, thus opening new perspectives for the benefit of the community."

Such a position toward planning is consistent with the ideologies of both Latin America and the United States. In each case certain productive functions belong to the State, while others are in the private sector.

[1] *The New York Times,* Mar. 15, 1962.

More importantly, both accept that private enterprises are rightly subject to the overall jurisdiction of the State in certain matters. They differ in the specifics of which activities belong in each sector and in what ways the State should regulate, as indeed Latin American countries also differ among themselves. Nations can cooperate in planning without coinciding in their politicoeconomic structures, but it helps to have some common ground in ideology.

Two different sets of forces have led Latin America and the United States to a common ground on planning. To many Latin Americans, planning is a reaction to the free-wheeling liberalism of the nineteenth and early twentieth centuries which they have discovered did not lead very far in the direction of economic growth. Planning is a way of rationalizing the organization of resources. It is intended to encourage investment by specifying the sectors and projects where it is most needed and to coordinate overall economic policies that will sometimes limit or restrict, sometimes induce or even compel. Its further object is to create the institutions and types of behavior most conducive to its stated goals.

The trend toward economic planning in the United States also evolved from recognition that untrammeled individualism has not always led to desired social goals. Unlike Latin America, there has not been general dissatisfaction with the long-run growth rate (although some have evinced even that), but rather with interruptions in its continuity, such as by depression. The need has also been felt to curtail strong, concentrated power (monopoly) that would otherwise unduly limit the economic potential of weaker groups. It is more and more popularly recognized that the Federal government must assist certain geographic or economic areas —such as coal mining and farming—which have been disadvantaged by the rapidity of factor-displacing innovations and for which sudden adjustment within a single generation is humanly difficult.

All these developments have been treated in earlier chapters. It is appropriate here only to mention that they are cardinal forces in a phenomenon that some have marveled at—that the United States, bastion of economic liberalism, should endorse a vast planning structure in Latin America and assist it financially. It couldn't have happened thirty years ago. Current history makes planning inevitable in Latin America, and only those who participate in it can influence it into democratic channels.

Yet all is not sweetness among the planners. Beneath the basic ideological consistency the ranks are rent by a dispute over the stuff of which planning is made. On the one hand, there are those who conceive it in overall terms. Start with some comprehensive goal, such as an annual percentage increase in the gross national product, and plot the sectors (transportation, power, agriculture, various industries) by which it shall be attained. These *macro-planners* are said to start from the top and build downwards, until they arrive at the specific projects and enterprises through which the ultimate goals will be achieved. *Micro-planners,* on the other hand, prefer to look first for projects, or economic activities, which in themselves are feasible on grounds of profitability, social need, foreign-exchange earnings, or other criteria. They will put them all together, iron out inconsistencies, and then calculate (for those who are interested) the percentage increase in gross national product to which they add up.

Virtually no one admits to being only a micro- or only a macro-planner. Everyone who is asked (including the present author) turns out to be both. There is nothing inconsistent between them. One may start at the top and bottom at the same time, for the processes are separate and check one another. If they do not meet in the middle, there is an error in one or both calculations, and they must be tried again. Besides testing each other, they serve in different fields. Macro-planning helps the government determine overall economic policies, such as the incidence of taxation, the value of foreign exchange, and the rate of interest. Micro-planning sets out criteria for analyzing project proposals and arranging them in a list of priorities.

Yet in practice they do conflict. Furthermore, the conflict appears to be along national lines. Despite many exceptions among both theorists and planners, it is fair to generalize that Latin Americans manifest a faith in macro-planning equal only to the skepticism felt in the United States. North Americans, on the other hand, have firmer confidence in micro-planning, whose techniques are (to them) tried and proved.

While the Economic Commission for Latin America has not neglected project analysis, its writings are heavily weighted on the side of macro-planning. All country plans so far presented for review by the nine "wise men" smack heavily of macro techniques. "The principal deficiency in the formulation of the present plan," states the Bolivian document, "is the small number of investment projects, studied in all their details, that it has been possible to include." [2]

The North American predilection was voiced by the Clay committee in its report to the President on foreign-aid policy in 1963: [3]

> Extrapolation of mathematical models based on questionable statistics for debatable base periods seems to have a way of going wrong, even when it is possible to find economists who agree with each other. Furthermore, these long-term projections have been of little or doubtful value and

[2] *Plan nacional de desarrollo económico y social, 1962–1971,* Republic of Bolivia, La Paz, Bolivia, 1961, p. 24.

[3] *The Scope and Distribution of United States Military and Economic Assistance Programs,* Department of State, Report to the President of the United States from the Committee to Strengthen the Security of the Free World, Mar. 20, 1963, p. 16.

frequently have proved harmful by directing attention to the theory of economic development at the expense of its practical implementation.

Of course, this position is extreme even among North Americans. The staff of the Agency for International Development contains men in key posts who are known for their work and writings in support of macro-planning. Yet when it comes to dispensing funds, there is strong reluctance (or refusal) to commit for purposes other than specific projects that have been checked out and analyzed through the techniques of micro-planning.

The Agency for International Development does commit nonproject funds, such as to finance a balance of payments deficit or to support a government budget, but it has been severely censured in the United States for so doing. The belief is strong that these commitments are a grudging concession to the insufficiency of well-analyzed projects available for financing, and the necessity for *some* activity to keep the Alliance going on a minimum basis. If this is so, it does not bode well for the lofty aspirations proclaimed at Punta del Este. Herein may lie one factor in the slowness of the Alliance, as well as the undergirth of criticism voiced by the two ministers from Bolivia.

MACRO-PLANNING

To be generally informed on the role of planning in the Alliance for Progress, one does not have to be a mathematician, accountant, or business forecaster. But it is desirable to have a more than passing acquaintance with the techniques of planning and project analysis. The present section and the following one are intended to fill this need. They are a compromise between the brief definition of macro- and micro-planning given earlier and exhaustive studies found in other books and articles.

Macro-planning includes an examination of the economy as a whole, in which its potential for growth—both overall and in designated sectors—is estimated within maximum and minimum limits. It is based on a network of relationships among various parts of the economy that have been observed empirically and whose behavior has been explained theoretically. Given the amount of income, for example, the nation's consumption can be estimated within limits. Given its capital endowments, rate of investment, level of technology, and the like, the amount of its output can be estimated within limits. Taxes depend on income, income depends on output, output depends (in part) on government expenditure, and government expenditure depends on taxes. A whole set of relationships such as these is postulated. Then the planner manipulates variables in a paper model (e.g., taxes can be increased), following out the expected consequences to government expenditure, output, consumption, saving, and others. The more variables he manipulates, the more complicated the model becomes.

Definitional equations—national product and flow of funds

The variables are set out in two types of equations. The first are definitional equations (or identities), which define the nation's economic structure. The economy is divided into sectors (usually four: producers, households, government, and the rest of the world, or foreigners who carry on business with resident persons and institutions). The transactions of these sectors are then labeled as consumption, investment, taxes, exports, saving, and the like. A set of intra- and intersectoral relationships is established, so that the planner knows the lines of communication by which the activity of one sector is transmitted to others and the range of variables that it might affect.

The major definitional equations are outlined in Chart 1, The National Product Accounts, and Chart 2, The Flow-of-funds Accounts. These charts are illustrative only; not all possible combinations are shown. A few sample equations are explained below, so the reader will have an idea of how the charts are constructed. He may then peruse them to any extent he wishes in order to discover other equations.

The focal point in Chart 1 is gross national product (the total of column 2), which is (by definition) the sum of all the items listed above it. These include personal and government consumption, domestic investment (i.e., real investment, or the construction of factories, machinery, highways, ports, etc.), and exports. Since each of these has an import component (i.e., consists of imports as well as goods and services produced domestically), it is necessary to subtract the nation's imports in order to arrive at gross national product.

Gross national product is (by definition) equal to gross national income. The proceeds of GNP are divided into the items shown in column 1. Some are paid to households as wages, interest, and dividends; some are retained by businesses as depreciation allowances and reinvested earnings; and some are paid in taxes. These three allocations may be traced across to the other sectors, where payments to households and taxes are shown as receipts. Business saving (depreciation and reinvested earnings), which is not paid to anyone, is carried across to a national saving and investment account, where it is listed under the sources of domestic investment.

In the household and government accounts, the income (columns 4 and 6 respectively) is shown to be equal to expenses and saving (in columns 3 and 5 respectively); i.e., saving is defined as the excess of income over expenses. The rest of the world account, which is the current account of the balance of payments, records all receipts by foreigners in column 8

CHART 1. The National Product Accounts

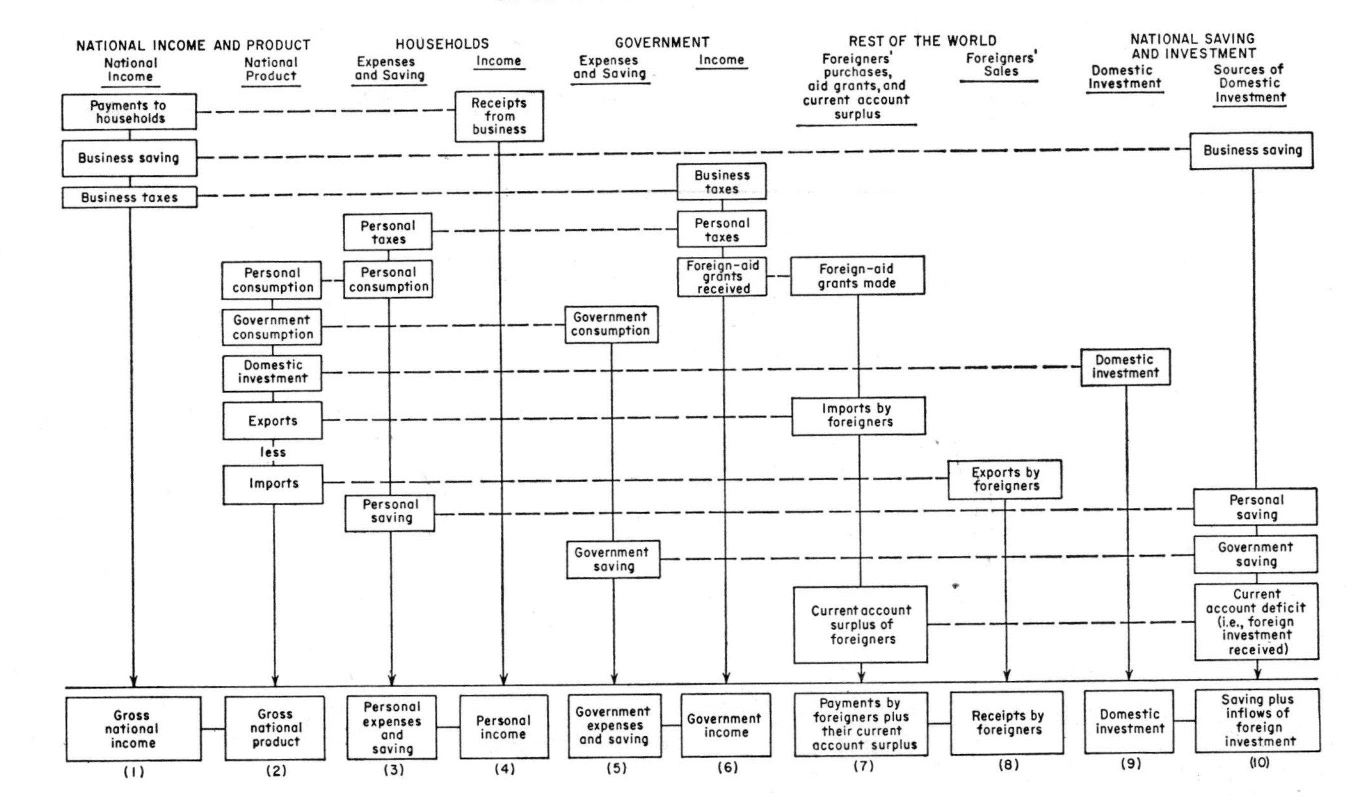

(consisting of *their* exports, equal to *our* imports in column 2). Payments by foreigners (column 7) include aid grants (e.g., by the United Nations or the United States), which are income for the local government (column 6). Other payments by foreigners consist of *their* imports, which are *our* exports (column 2). Finally (assuming that foreigners sell more to us than the sum of their purchases and aid grants), they have a current account surplus shown in column 7. The sums of columns 7 and 8 must be equal (since the current account surplus is defined as the difference between foreigners' receipts and payments).

The final account (national saving and investment) shows the amount of (real) domestic investment in column 9 and its sources in column 10: some is financed by business saving, some by personal saving, some by government saving, and some by the current account surplus of foreigners, which implies an inflow of foreign capital.

Every item above the total line appears *twice* on the chart. If it is income of one sector, it is a payment by another. The residuals in the sectors (investment, saving, and current account balance) are then grouped in the national saving and investment account, which demonstrates the equality (in its totals) between the nation's investment and its sources of financing.

Chart 2 demonstrates intersectoral financial relationships, including the instruments (such as shares, bonds, and loans) by which the saving of three sectors and investment by foreigners is supplied for domestic investment. The first line depicts the equality between domestic investment and its sources, as taken from columns 9 and 10 of Chart 1. Below this is a network of financial assets and liabilities, in which sectors borrow from and lend to each other. The simplest equation is that of households, which demonstrates that personal saving (column 6) is equal to households' acquisition of money, plus their purchase of government bonds, plus their purchase of corporate shares (all in column 5). Each of these assets (including money) is a liability of some other sector (money is issued by the banking system). In columns 1 and 2, it is shown that new issues of money must equal the banking system's increase in foreign exchange holdings (via a balance of payments surplus), plus loans made to government and business.

All these equations are obvious to economists and will readily be seen by those who have studied mathematics, national income, or accounting. The uninitiated reader may have no more than a general feeling that various groups within the economy interact in a complicated grid, and perhaps he understands one or two of the relationships. If so, all well and good. The point to remember is that it is impossible to effect any economic transaction without influencing a whole chain of events in which many people and many institutions are involved.

CHART 2. The Flow-of-funds Accounts

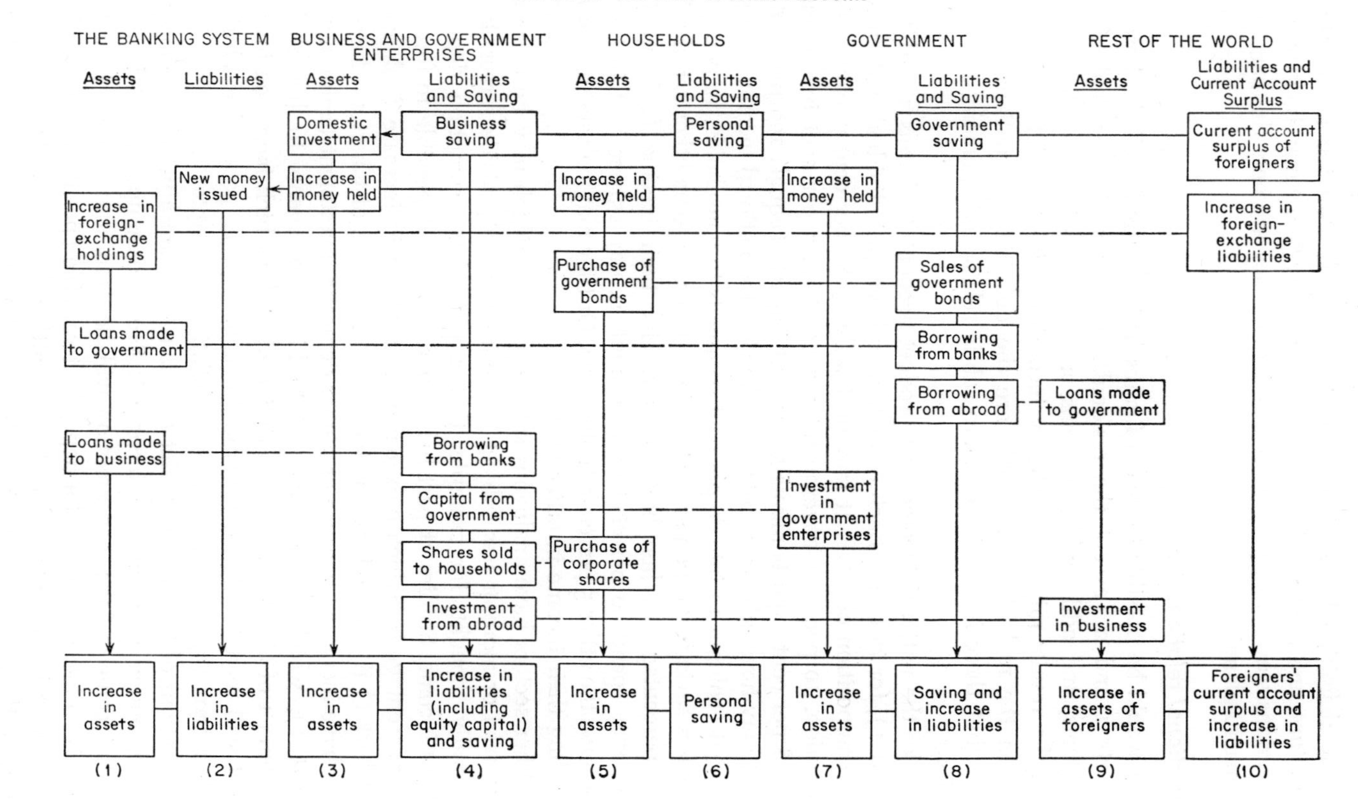

The definitional equations (Charts 1 and 2) describe an *economic structure,* and they are the same for any country. They may be expressed in various ways, with greater or less detail. They are only the beginning of macro-planning.

Functional relationships

It would be possible to invent figures haphazardly for all the boxes in Charts 1 and 2 (except the residuals, such as saving), calculate the residuals, and add up the columns, and all equations would balance. But the results might be patently inconsistent if applied to any country. In the real world, not only are the definitional equations in balance, but there is a series of more subtle relationships among the variables.

Take the national income and product account (columns 1 and 2 of Chart 1), for instance. Each country may have an individual pattern for the composition of GNP. It may ordinarily be 80 per cent personal consumption, 10 per cent government consumption, 5 per cent investment, plus 8 per cent exports minus 3 per cent imports (equals 100 per cent). Or it may have other percentages. Likewise, the national income may be divided (column 1) into 60 per cent payments to households, 10 per cent business saving, and 30 per cent business taxes, or some other set of normal percentages. When households receive their income (column 4), they may spend 80 per cent on consumption, pay 15 per cent in taxes, and save the other 5 per cent (column 3). Or they may be accustomed to dividing their income in other ways.

Other sectors have analogous sets of patterns, which may be more or less fixed or more or less subject to the influence of outside forces. It is generally thought, for example, that a person's consumption depends on his income. Studies of past behavior may make it possible to forecast the percentage by which personal consumption will increase (column 3 of Chart 1) if personal income increases (column 4 of Chart 1). Income may have increased because of higher domestic investment (column 2 of Chart 1), which has in turn led to higher payments to households (column 1 of Chart 1). This multiplier effect, by which increased investment will lead to higher demand for consumption goods, has already been referred to in the discussion of inflation in Chapter 8.

Equations of this nature depict *functional relationships.* They compare two schedules of values (if income is $100, consumption will be $80, but if income is $150, consumption will be $120, and so on). In each, there is an independent and a dependent variable (personal consumption depends on income, government consumption depends on taxes, and the like). If the dependent variable is a constant percentage of the independent (e.g., consumption is presumed to be 80 per cent of income at all levels of the latter), the relationship is linear; if the percentages change, it is nonlinear.

Some variables within the system of Charts 1 and 2 are functions of (i.e., depend on) variables outside the system. For example, exports and imports (column 2 of Chart 1) may depend (in part) on the foreign-exchange rate, which is not found in any column. Likewise, saving and investment may be influenced by the rate of interest. Increases in gross national product may depend not only on the amount of investment but also on the stock of capital, and on population and its rate of increase. Certain variables outside the system are hard to identify, such as the level of a nation's technology and the rate at which new methods are introduced. Nevertheless, technology may be quantified as a growth coefficient in equations depicting the annual increase in GNP.

Techniques of macro-planning

The first task of the macro-planner is to set forth his objectives, such as a given increase in per capita gross national product, employment of so many additional workers, narrowing a balance of payments deficit, or balancing the government budget. His task would be simplified if he had but one goal, but unfortunately he may have to take account of all these. It is furthermore possible that his objectives are not consistent with each other. He will find this out as he goes along and will scale them down accordingly.

To establish policies, the planner must divide his variables into four groups, as follows:

1. Target variables, reflecting policy objectives, e.g., gross national product, exports, domestic investment
2. Instrument variables, or those through which the policy will be carried out, e.g., rate of interest, exchange rate, government consumption, taxes
3. Data, or those variables which are taken as given and which either cannot or will not be changed, e.g., labor supply, capital supply, rate of population increase
4. Irrelevant variables, which may or may not change as the model is tested, but which do not significantly affect either the choice of policy or the targets

The third type of variable—data—consists of those that limit the objectives of the plan, either in terms of overall accomplishments or in consistency of targets. The economy may not contain the requisite labor supply or capital stock to achieve a 5 per cent per capita increase in GNP without running a balance of payments deficit. If equilibrium with the rest of the world is one of the objectives, then the increase in GNP must be scaled down to be within the realm of possibility.

Some variables may belong in more than one group; in particular, instrument and target variables may be the same. For example, an objective may be to increase the amount of domestic investment (target). But part of domestic investment—that by government corporations—is manipulated by the planners (instrument).

On the basis of his knowledge of the economy, the macro-planner will then set forth his equations. Examples of these are as follows:

1. Capital-output ratio. An injection of $4 of capital may be expected to increase GNP by $1 a year. Therefore

$$\Delta GNP = \frac{\Delta I}{4}$$

where ΔGNP is the increment in gross national product and ΔI is the increment of investment.

2. The consumption function. An increase in personal income of $1 will lead to an increase in consumption of 80 cents. Therefore

$$\Delta C_p = 0.8 \Delta Y_p$$

where ΔC_p is the increment in consumption and ΔY_p is the increment in income.

3. The business tax function. An increase in gross national income of $1 will lead to an increase in business taxes of 25 cents. Therefore

$$\Delta T_b = 0.25 \Delta GNI$$

where ΔT_b is the increment of business taxes and ΔGNI the increment in gross national income.

There will be many more equations, of greater or lesser complexity, describing not only the functional relationships but also outlining the definitions in Charts 1 and 2. For example, the definitional equation for gross national product (column 2 of Chart 1) is

$$\text{GNP} = C_p + C_g + I + X - M$$

where C_p = personal consumption
C_g = government consumption
I = domestic investment
X = exports
M = imports

Usually the functional relationships are not known exactly but only estimated within limits. For example, it may be reasonably supposed that personal consumption will increase by, say, between 80 and 90 per cent of the increment of income. In this case the macro-planner may make two models, one using the higher function and the other the lower. Since other functional relationships will also have upper and lower limits, he may find himself with a large number of alternative sets of equations.

Any problem in which the number of unknowns is equal to the number of equations is soluble. In macro-planning, there is almost invariably a larger number of unknowns than equations. The planner will therefore try out his model by assuming certain reasonable values for the instrument variables (hitherto unknowns). He will try out, for example, a rate of interest of 8 per cent, a corporate profits tax rate of 30 per cent, a schedule of personal income taxes from 10 to 80 per cent according to income bracket, a level of government investment of $50 million, and whatever others he chooses. Finally he will have assigned enough values so that the remaining unknowns are equal in number to the equations. Then he will solve for his target variables, to see if he has met his objectives.

If he has not, he will try again, changing the values of his instrument variables, but always within an achievable range. It may be that he cannot meet any of his objectives, in which case they must be scaled down to more modest proportions. It may be that he can meet some only at the expense of others, in which case he must decide whether to sacrifice the latter or whether to start over again with more modest assigned values.

Finally, he may discover that there are alternative routes to the same set of objectives, in which case he must select one that appears superior on such bases as ideology, political factors, and welfare considerations. He may decide, for example, that a loose monetary policy (low interest rates) is better than a government budgetary deficit, or on ideological grounds he may prefer to impose a higher personal income tax rather than set wage ceilings.

The task of the macro-planner may end at this point. He has established a set of policies involving such instrument variables as the level of taxes, rate of interest, foreign-exchange value, imposition of exchange controls, minimum bank reserve ratio, subsidies to business, and so on, whose purpose is to facilitate a change in the target variables within a specified range (maximum and minimum), such as increase in GNP and employment. He may also have outlined the capacity of the economy or the range of target increases possible (within their absolute limit) under alternative policies from which the political leaders will choose. The projected results will not automatically follow from the application of recommended policies. Much else needs to be done, including the selection of specific investment projects, as will be discussed later in this chapter. But at least there is a set of overall policies that do not conflict with each other and that are consistent with the desired range of objectives.

Input-output tables

Often, however, the macro-planner will go further, as he has done in the Latin American plans presented to date. He wants to know not only the extent to which aggregate product will increase but its expected composition. If income increases by 2.5 per cent per capita each year, as is hoped under the Alliance for Progress, what will people want to buy? How much food? Clothing? Furniture? What specific types of capital equipment will be required for their production? What raw materials? What transportation facilities? What electric power? In short, where does one look for the specific projects by which growth will be implemented?

To supply a bird's-eye view of the economy by sectors, macro-planning may thus require forecasts of demand by industries. The marketing analysis frequently requires the same techniques used in micro-planning, to be outlined later in the chapter (pages 272 to 287). For the overall view, however, it is not necessary to know demand for specific products (e.g., cotton shirts) but only for sectoral output (e.g., textiles). Research may be done on how consumption is historically related to income, both in the aggregate and for individual industries. The course of history in a more advanced Latin American country may yield some insight into what may be expected for the future of a newly developing nation.

Once there is a rough indication of how demand for a given industry's output will increase, the macro-planner considers whether other sectors are capable of supplying that industry's needs for inputs or whether recourse must be made to imports. This analysis may require an input-output table, such as shown in Chart 3 with partial data. Suppose a given industry, B, is producing $75 of output for the gross national product, of which $45 is for personal consumption, $15 for government consumption, $10 for domestic investment, and $5 for exports. These data are shown horizontally in the upper right-hand quadrant of the chart. Industry B also produces intermediate products for itself and other industries (e.g., materials and supplies for other firms both within B and in industries A, C, and D). These amount to $25 and are shown horizontally in the upper left-hand quadrant of Chart C. B's total output is therefore $100, of which $25 is interindustry and $75 final.

Normally the input-output table will be filled in for all industries for some current year, based on empirical observation. Chart 3 is completed only for industry B, since it is on this that we wish to focus. The planner observes that industry B requires inputs (shown vertically) of $30 from itself and other industries: it uses $8 of the output of industry A, some firms in industry B sell $6 of their output to others, and it uses $4 and $12 respectively of the outputs of industries C and D. All these are shown in the upper left-hand quadrant.

The lower left-hand quadrant details the extraindustry inputs of B (or those not purchased from other industries). It uses up $2 of its own capital in depreciation, pays taxes of $19 (which are treated as if it were buying the government's services in this amount), buys imports of $11, and pays wages, dividends, interest, etc., of $38 to households. Undis-

CHART 3. Sample Input-Output Matrix with Data for Industry B Only

(In Units of National Currency)

INPUTS		OUTPUTS: Inter-industry outputs: A	B	C	D	Total inter-industry outputs	Outputs of final product: Personal consumption	Government consumption	Domestic investment	Exports	Total final product	Total outputs
Inter-industry inputs	A		8									
	B	3	6	7	9	(25)	45	15	10	5	(75)	100
	C		4									
	D		12									
	Total inter-industry inputs		(30)									
Extra-industry inputs	Use of capital (depreciation)		2									
	Government services (taxes)		19									
	Imports		11									
	Household services (wages, etc.) and undistributed profits		38									
	Total extra-industry inputs		(70)									
	Total inputs		100									

tributed profits are included in this $38, on the theory that industry B is owned by stockholders in the household sector.

Since outputs constitute sales (or income) and inputs include all costs and profits, the sum of the inputs and outputs ($100) must be equal (i.e., profits = income minus cost).

A glance at the upper left-hand quadrant of Chart 3 shows that industry B both provides outputs to other industries A ($3), C ($7), and D ($9) and requires inputs from them ($8, $4, and $12 respectively). Some firms within industry B also provide output of $6 to other firms within the same industry. The interaction among industries has led macro-planners to conclude that it is not possible to forecast the overall demand for output of a single industry without forecasting the demand for them all.

Suppose, for example, the planner has forecast a certain demand for lumber, based on estimated building requirements. What inputs are needed? How much labor, how much transportation, how many axes to cut the trees? He calculates all these, only to discover that the axes require lumber for their handles. Thus lumber requires axes, and axes require lumber. He goes on to discover that steel is needed for both ax handles and transportation, lumber is needed for steel and transportation, and other inputs are interrelated in ever-widening circles. He throws up his hands and declares that he cannot forecast the inputs required for the lumber industry as an isolated entity.

If the input-output table is complete for all industries, however, a mathematical solution becomes possible. Suppose for every $1 of output, the lumber industry requires axes whose handles use 10 cents worth of lumber. Each $1 of lumber in final product therefore *really* requires $1.10 of lumber. By the same token the extra 10 cents of lumber requires another 1 cent to cover the ax handles to cut down the trees to make the ax handles to cut down the original $1 of lumber. The process can obviously be carried *ad absurdum* (if we haven't already done so), for the incremental lumber becomes less and less with each stage and approaches a limit of zero. To produce $1.00 of lumber for final product, not much more than 11 cents of additional lumber is needed for ax handles.

A similar process can be applied to all industries simultaneously, no matter how complex their interrelationships. If the final demand for every industry is forecast, it is possible also to forecast all interindustry inputs and outputs together.

Given the data on Chart 3, which we now pretend is filled out for all squares, the macro-planner wishes to project the impact on the economy of an increase in final demand for B from $75 to (say) $85 or $95, or any other amount. Simultaneously, he wants to solve for increased outputs of A, C, D, and any other industry.

As a first approximation (which may not be true in practice), the planner will assume that the *production function* is linear. The production function is the relationship of inputs to total output, as shown in the vertical column. Linearity presumes that the input proportions do not change with output. Thus if $100 of output requires $12 of input from D (as shown in the chart), then $50 of output requires $6 of input, $1 of output requires 12 cents of input, and so on. On this basis, the inputs required for $1 of output of B are as follows (from the vertical column of Chart 3): $1B = $.08A + $.06B + $.04C + $.12D + $.02 depreciation + $.19 taxes + $.11 imports + $.38 household services.

But the production function is not the final answer. The planner notes that $1 output of B requires an input of 6 cents of B, plus other quantities of B needed for the inputs of industries A, C, and D (just as in the case of the lumber and ax industries). If he knows the production functions of the other industries, he can solve simultaneously for them all. The result is an *inverse matrix*. It will show how much of every other input, *exclusive of B and B content in other industries,* is required for every $1 of B in final product. Simultaneously, it will do the same for other industries.

Still assuming linearity of production function, the inverse matrix permits the planner to prepare an input-output projection for any combination of quantities demanded. Suppose the demand for final product of B increases from $75 to $85. The new input-output table may then show total demand of (say) $115, depending on the increases in demand for products of other industries. Similarly for A, C, and D.

The macro-planner uses input-output projections for several purposes, the validity of each of which has been challenged. The tables are used to estimate labor requirements by industry, which are compared with labor supply in various geographic regions. As a result, the plan may call for some relocation of labor or new housing projects. Import needs are estimated by industries, so that nations with foreign-exchange shortages may allocate available supplies rationally. Demand is forecast by industry, to guard against bottlenecks in supply. Finally, macro-planners use input-output tables to look for specific projects. They see them as the starting point for micro-analysis, for bottleneck industries are expected to reveal the most profitable possibilities for new enterprise.

But input-output tables are the most controversial element in macro-planning, and attacks on them have been numerous. They have three principal faults. The first, and most striking, is the problem of aggregation, and the validity of a production function by industry. The "rubber" industry, the "cement" industry, the "chemical" industry, the "iron and steel" industry are not homogeneous groups of entities all (within an industry) producing the same product at the same costs. An increase in iron and steel output, for example, will not necessarily draw inputs from the chemical industry in the pattern shown by the historic tables. The inputs depend on the individual iron and steel products whose output is increased and often on which enterprises produce them. This implied criticism of input-output techniques would be removed if, instead of data by industry, the tables were constructed on a company-by-company basis. Apart from the obvious unwieldiness of so many enterprises, such an endeavor would not be practical because of inadequacies in data collection.

In the second place, the production functions are criticized for their linearity. To assume that input proportions do not vary as output increases is to assume away economies of scale. Virtually all enterprises distinguish between fixed and variable costs. As output increases within a given plant, the proportion of fixed cost to total will decline. If a larger plant is substituted, fixed costs will probably increase. It is not proper to project a new input-output table by simply multiplying the functions of the old by a given coefficient of expected production increase.

Finally, technological innovation changes production functions. New methods are the marrow of economic development. Not only that, but new goods and services will be produced; new industries not previously known will be called for. Very little of the historic interindustry structure may still be applicable at the conclusion of a plan period.

Supporters of input-output employ three counterarguments. First of all, they say production functions will not be multiplied blindly by some coefficient of increase but will be adjusted by engineering estimates that recognize the individuality of products within an industry, economies of scale, technological improvement, and the introduction of new industries. In the second place, they argue that refined data are not needed. The tables will not be applied without reason or without micro-analysis. They are a crude instrument to draw attention to economic gaps that might not otherwise be noticed. Finally, they will be subject to constant revision as the plan progresses.

Mountain plans and valley plans

The dispute between proponents and detractors of input-output tables and other methods of macro-planning seems, however, not to depend so much on the sum of statistical merits and defects as it does on overall attitudes toward planning. In this arena especially economists appear to be human beings. Each of us has adopted a basic philosophy toward economic development which either does or does not accept the pivotal mission of macro-planning. Depending on his philosophy, the economist will magnify either the virtues or the vices of macro techniques.

Macro-planning is associated with balanced growth and with the belief that the government must keep a watchful eye over the infant economy to see that it does not err into slothful ways, that it does not waste its resources. It does not necessarily imply socialized enterprise, but it does suggest that private initiative must conform to an overall pattern set by the State. Otherwise (many Latin Americans believe) inefficiency and duplication will result. Without macro-planning, the Economic Commission for Latin America has suggested, ". . . the individual entrepreneur is not fully informed of market prospects or of the plans of his fellow entrepreneurs, [and] there is in many cases an inevitable duplication of effort, with the consequent waste of the community's resources."[4]

Proponents of macro-planning argue that the private enterpriser is like the man standing in a valley, seeing only his own terrain and that adjacent to his. He makes his decisions on the basis of what he can see, and his horizon is limited. If he knew that a new steel mill was planned for another property around the bend, he would know that his costs for steel products would decrease, and he would embark on undertakings not profitable in present terms. "The weakness of this type of economic policy," wrote Mayobre, "lies in its failure to visualize the future of the economy as a whole and to recognize how closely the various sectors are related."[5]

The economic development board, say the macro-planners, is like a man standing on top of a mountain. Through a knowledge of the functional and definitional relationships among the various sectors, plus an input-output pattern of growing industries, he is in a better position to direct the vast grid he sees below. He need not be totalitarian but can formulate overall policy using instruments of influence, like the exchange rate, tariff schedule, taxes, subsidies, zoning patterns, and licenses. He will nudge the private investor toward the decisions that the latter would make by himself if he were omniscient.

Some say, however, that the planner on the mountain looks down through a pink cloud. The haze is too great for him to detect the realities of the picture below. His data on GNP have been sketchily compiled and are often sheer guesses. Human limitations confine him as much as the man in the valley. How well can the two cooperate? Micro-planning, as we shall see in the next section, employs many criteria, and the planner

[4] *Analyses and Projections of Economic Development: II. The Economic Development of Brazil,* United Nations (ECLA), E/CN.12/364/Rev.1, April, 1956, p. 27.

[5] José Antonio Mayobre, "Global Programming as an Instrument of Economic Development Policy," in H. S. Ellis and H. C. Wallich (eds.), *Economic Development for Latin America,* St Martin's Press, Inc., New York, 1961, p. 32.

must assign weights among them. How much emphasis he places on each one may well depend on whether he speaks the dialect of the mountain or the valley.

MICRO-PLANNING AND PROJECT ANALYSIS

All the techniques of macro-planning, all the carefully balanced national product and financial accounts, the neat mathematical equations and compact models—all are nothing but a child's game if the plans are not translated into substantive projects. On this there is no disagreement. But there are some philosophical questions to be settled before we can know how to analyze a project for its feasibility in a national plan.

Project selection

Does the critical shortage in development planning lie more in capital itself or in the genius to find new investment opportunities? I have already suggested (in Chapter 2) that Latin Americans tend more to recognize capital as the bottleneck in development, while North Americans stress the shortage of entrepreneurial talents. Often it is felt that the macro-planner is shaping grandiose schemes for using capital but that his vision does not extend to the grubby details paramount in the mind of the entrepreneur.

Economists from the World Bank and Export-Import Bank have told me informally that they stand ready to finance any soundly conceived project from any underdeveloped country so long as it fits the legal and economic criteria set out in their Articles of Agreement or basic legislation. I have also informally heard officers of the Agency for International Development, and even the Inter-American Development Bank, cite the need for more and better projects. There is no shortage of capital, these men suggest. They have all the funds they need for their slim intake of well-analyzed loan proposals.

Is it not curious, therefore, that the aid agencies of the United States government and the international institutions focus almost exclusively on lending capital? And that their technical assistance is designed primarily to help implement projects already selected, or to increase general levels of industrial and agricultural productivity? They expect Latin American countries themselves to provide sound projects and hint that their hands are tied until these projects come forth. Yet one reason an underdeveloped country is underdeveloped is that it lacks entrepreneurial skills.

I propose that a new international organization is needed, one which has no money to lend but which has adequate capital to hire engineers, agricultural technicians, experts specializing in a variety of industries that are likely targets of development plans, selling and advertising men, economists, and the like. They would not simply outline areas where projects are likely to be found and then stop. Rather, they would help the government and private sectors to identify sound projects. Such an organization could do engineering, marketing, and other studies necessary to determine technical and economic feasibility. But more important than that, it would first seek out the projects themselves.

If properly managed, the organization would not simply perform this task but would teach both governments and private industrial groups how to do it themselves. It would open up a permanent office in each country, staffed by engineers and project analysts familiar with the terrain. The office might be associated with a development bank or national planning organization, and the host government might cover its local operating expenses. There would also be an international pool of experts available to visit individual offices as needed.

To some extent the Economic Commission for Latin America is already performing this function. As part of its macro studies, it has done some pointing toward the areas where projects ought to be sought. But it does not have the budget to hire experts nearly to the extent needed, and it has decided that macro-planning carries more claim to its limited funds than detailed project analysis. United States aid missions have also done some work in this field, but they too rely mainly on the host government or private enterprises to initiate the project proposals.

Project selection has many stages. The first, and most ethereal, is to come up with an idea. There is no set of instructions, no preordained series of steps by which an idea will be implanted in the mind of a man. Macro-planners point to input-output tables to show the sectors where projects must first be sought. They, and micro-planners as well, have also suggested other gadgets, such as looking through import data to see what is demanded, investigating local raw materials and skills to see how they may be employed or upgraded, considering how new technology can be applied, examining the opportunities under development plans, studying industry lists, and so on.[6] All these are useful techniques and may result in a plethora of ideas for further exploration and analysis.

Still, there is no sure-fire way of ferreting out a good project. One North American economic consultant, who has little faith in macro methods, referred to market research as ". . . simply grubbing and hoeing, keeping your eyes open, asking the right questions to the right people in the right places, and then sitting down to think."

> When he runs out of statistics, the researcher must go out and talk to people. Not to consumers in Latin America, because they aren't so cul-

[6] Murray D. Bryce, *Industrial Development: A Guide for Accelerating Economic Growth,* New York, McGraw-Hill Book Company, Inc., 1960, pp. 19–20.

turally oriented to public-opinion polls as we are. They suspect ulterior motives, such as taxation or special assessments. Instead, talk to people acquainted with the trade: Chambers of Commerce, businessmen, labor leaders. They can tell much about existing markets, costs, and prices. Talk to them where they are—at their own place of work—and not in some artificial environment. Much may be observed on the premises. By scanning a factory you can discover products being thrown away. Ask what's in those dirty old barrels standing by the door. What the management thinks is waste may turn out to be the potential for a valuable by-product. Animal feeds, for instance. Rice hulls and grain wastes are often thrown out, but they could be processed and sold.

Talk to a great many people, and check their answers against each other. Where does a producer get his raw materials? What does he sell? Compare what he says with his suppliers and customers, to offset errors of prejudice. Wander through stores and street markets, to find out what products are sold. Are they overpriced? If so, this may indicate a supply shortage, or a monopoly that needs to be broken.

Don't say much—just listen. If you give your own opinions, you will prejudice the answers. Polite people often say what they think you want to hear, not what they really believe.

Keep your eyes open for bottlenecks, like the woman whose broiler output was limited by the space she had in three small freezers. Or the producer of avocados that were rotting because he had no cold storage warehouse. Or the excess supplies of grapefruit going to waste because there was no cannery. All these are examples I saw in Latin America. If you have eyes and a sense of proportions, you don't need input-output tables and marginal propensities to consume. In fact, as they call your attention to one direction, they may blind you to the reality that lies in another.[7]

In the words of this quotation, the task sounds easy. But how many people are skilled enough to know the questions to ask, weigh the answers, and look for the proper leads?

Many United States economic consultants believe that when used to seek individual projects, macro techniques are a refuge from reality. They are glass eyes for people who want to appear as if they see when they really don't know how to look. Latin American planners, these economists suggest, will not soil their hands by going into factories (beyond the manager's office) or sleeping in unsanitary hotels in the country, which is the only way to discover where opportunities for development really lie. It is far easier to project the nation's output from a drawing board in the capital city.

If applied to the Economic Commission for Latin America, this charge

[7] Edward Tenenbaum of Continental Allied Company, Inc. Notes from a lecture at the Institute for International Development, Aug. 21, 1962, used by permission.

is grossly unfair. ECLA's researchers scour the fields and industries, and each country study includes an exhaustive description of the economy by sectors which could only have been prepared by a team that knows it intimately. Yet to a pragmatist, the proof lies in the results. Somehow, as the plans of Latin American countries filter in to the financing institutions, there is a dearth of well-analyzed project proposals.

The profitability criterion

Suppose a project has been checked out for all technical and economic considerations. Both the engineering and cost studies have been done. Alternative production methods have been checked, and the most economic selected. The all-important market study—so often the Achilles' heel of new enterprises—has been done and found satisfactory. On the basis of all data gathered, a profit and loss statement is projected for (say) the next five to ten years. From this and the balance sheet, the researchers have forecast a statement of sources and uses of funds, to know that the project will be liquid as well as solvent.

How good is the project? Suppose there are two or more, but only one can be financed. Which one will be selected? What are the criteria?

To many analysts, the profitability of an enterprise is the most important single index of its worth. The entrepreneur and the banker obviously want it to yield a return and pay off its debts. To the project analyst, however, profitability has another meaning. It measures the net contribution the enterprise will make to the nation's resources.

The reason is easy to understand. Income measures the value of the project's output; cost measures the sacrifice. A project that earns $1,000 has produced real value (capital or consumer goods) of that amount. If its costs are $800, it has consumed that much labor, materials, or other inputs that might alternatively have been devoted to something else. The profit of $200 measures net yield in real goods and services. The economy is better off by that amount.

Unlike the businessman or the banker, the project analyst assumes nothing about profit distribution. Profit may be paid to the owner, it may be taxed away, it may be distributed in workers' bonuses or consigned to programs of national welfare. The profitability criterion is equally applicable to nationalized and private enterprises. It is, in fact, used in Communist countries, although the prices on which it is based are not necessarily those of the market.

The compelling logic of the profitability criterion is quickly seen when cast in real terms. Suppose identical output is forecast for each of two projects—say, 10,000 units of some commodity of a certain quality. Project A's costs are 1 hectare of land, ten laborers, and three machines. Project B, by using only two of the same machines, nine laborers, and ½ hectare, can produce the same goods. Project A obviously uses its resources inefficiently. Project B is more profitable because its costs are less; that is, it consumes fewer inputs. The extra machine, extra man, and extra land become available for something else. Alternatively, we might have assumed that project B produced more units than project A with the same inputs. In that case, its income would be greater.

Dependence of the profitability criterion on the price system

Profitability comparisons are possible in real terms only in an illustration such as the above, where identical output is produced with different amounts of identical inputs, or where the same inputs produce more or less units of an identical output. If different products are compared, such as wheat and corn, or the choice is between different inputs, such as labor and machinery, then whether one product is "more" than the other or costs "less" depends on relative values of output and alternative inputs in money terms. These values depend on prices.

If a system of market prices does not command respect, if the price mechanism is not deemed a satisfactory agent of distribution, then it follows that profitability may not be highly reputed as a criterion for project selection. If price is distorted by widespread monopoly, if wealth is concentrated in a few, and if income is imperfectly distributed according to one's present or prior contributions to output, then there is reason for dissatisfaction with the market mechanism.

The most elementary principles of economics reveal that price depends on supply and demand, and demand has two components: utility and *income*. If only the rich are able to buy, Cadillacs will be produced while poor people live in mud huts. This anomaly has called forth a full-fledged branch of theory known as "welfare economics," which is concerned with social justice in distribution as well as with production. Aside from political considerations, the key economic question that comes between communism and capitalism is whether the market is a valid means of selecting economic ventures.

Many North Americans do not appreciate how much their enthusiasm for the market mechanism depends on the determination of their ancestors that monopolies shall not dominate industry, that no economic bloc—labor, capitalist, or other—shall have unbridled power, and that social justice shall be assured by such government intervention as unemployment compensation, social security, regulation of the stock exchange, and aid to agriculture. I suspect that the Latin American inclination toward macro-planning, on the other hand, is in part revulsion against the extreme maldistribution of income, lack of restraint on power, and the market's consequent bias in favor of the wealthy. The profitability criterion has been made unpalatable, and macro methods are more popular by contrast.

Profitability will become a fully accepted criterion of project selection only if market imperfections are compensated. National planning must alter the channels for distributing income to make them more respectable —perhaps more egalitarian, certainly more responsive to a person's output than to his hereditary position. Agrarian and tax reforms are needed. Farm and industrial wage structures must be adjusted and monopoly strangleholds broken.

Shadow prices in profitability analysis

Even if one does accept the profitability criterion, market prices are not sacred. Sometimes a project will yield a revenue to someone other than the entrepreneur, such as the government in taxes, tariffs, and exchange profits, or a cost borne by someone else, perhaps a government development bank whose interest rate is artificially low. In such cases, profitability may be judged by what the project yields to the nation as a whole (social profitability, or social marginal product), not just to the entrepreneur.

To measure social profitability, shadow prices are substituted for market prices.[8] If the exchange rate is artificially low, a project's imports and exports will instead be judged by an estimated market rate that would reflect the "true" cost or yield to the economy as a whole. If public policy demands that a project be taxed at an exceptionally high rate, thus sharing its fruits with the government, its profitability would be determined without charging the tax, so that in effect the government's profit is added to that of the entrepreneur. Projects that are socially profitable but that privately incur a loss (based on market prices) may have to be subsidized.

Sometimes a project has costs but no revenue, such as a road that opens up new farming land. Here, profitability is measured by the income increment of the farmers, minus their incremental costs and those of the road. The same would apply to harbors, bridges, and power plants whose product is sold at less than cost in order to stimulate new industries by making the latter more profitable.

Profitability as the sole criterion?

Suppose, finally, that market prices or shadow prices are deemed consistent with social justice. Suppose an equitable method of distributing profits is found, through a graduated income tax, land taxes, and con-

[8] Compare Jan Tinbergen, *The Design of Development*, The Johns Hopkins Press, Baltimore, pp. 39–41, and Murray D. Bryce, *op. cit.*, chap. 10.

tributions to social security. Suppose also that market prices can be adjusted to approximate social rather than private profitability. Is not the logic of the profitability criterion then compelling—that the net yield of projects measures their net contribution to the economy? Should not profitability become the *sole* criterion for selection, to the exclusion of all others?

Most economists who accept all the above conditions would still argue that other criteria may be overriding. In the first place, the less profitable of two alternative projects may employ a larger number of people, an important consideration if unemployment is a problem. In the second place, as proposed in Chapter 8, an industrial program designed to foster changes in comparative advantages may imply selection of projects not currently the most profitable. Such enterprises will subsequently either demand or supply external economies (power, highways, and the like) that will make them successful when complemented by industries that would also be unprofitable in isolation. In the third place, some suggest that a project's ability to earn or save foreign exchange ought to be assessed apart from its profitability. Finally, some projects such as education, housing, and health and sanitation do not sell their output. In their case profitability is obviously not a logical criterion.

The employment criterion

Unemployment in Latin America is high. In most countries it is not statistically measured. Even if it were, the data would probably not be relevant, for a large portion of the work force is "underemployed," or doing something just to fill an otherwise boring day. They may tramp the fields in halfhearted manner or sell fruit or lottery tickets on the sidewalk. The number of street vendors seen in an area is an index of its unemployment. In Bolivia, for example, one is more conscious of them in La Paz than in Santa Cruz.

Those who are sensitive to social ills cannot but agree that projects designed to employ the idle are worthwhile even if they are not the most profitable. The question then becomes whether the profitability criterion will automatically select the projects that will contribute the most to employment. The answer is unfortunately ambiguous—sometimes it will, and sometimes it won't.

There are at least two fundamental causes of unemployment in Latin America. One is that demand has not kept up with increases in productivity. Science may be so advanced that the cheapest ways to produce do not fully employ the rapidly growing labor force. The other is a tendency for entrepreneurs to select the most modern technology, capital-intensive because it is fashioned in the United States and Europe where labor is scarce and capital cheap. If unemployment occurs because overall productivity has outstripped demand, then the profitability criterion will not lead to the selection of projects that employ the most people. But if it occurs because the wrong technology has been selected, then there is hope of correction. Unfortunately, it is not always easy to make the proper diagnosis.

Productivity increases and the factor-proportions problem. The so-called "factor-proportions" problem arises when the introduction of machinery reduces not only the amount of labor needed but that of capital as well. Suppose, for example, that a woman working alone (without the benefit of machinery) requires one week to spin yarn and weave a certain amount of cloth. Two machines could do the same job in an hour. The textile producer must choose between buying the machines, which are expensive but which require only a few workers, or employing hundreds of laborers with only a bobbin and other hand equipment. The laborers are otherwise unemployed, with no alternative opportunity. They will sell themselves for very low wages, maybe only a bit above zero.

The sad fact is that even if labor worked free, the mill owner might discover that the machine method is cheaper. Each square meter of cloth produced by hand is backed by a week-long assembly line tying up much yarn and half-finished inventories. The faster machine method, however, requires only a short assembly line in which very little work in process keeps the finished output flowing smoothly. In short, the depreciation cost of the machinery may be less than the working-capital cost of the hand method. If the machine method saves more working capital than it costs in fixed capital, it employs not only less labor but less capital, as well. Clearly, the hand method is not the cheaper, and the profitability criterion does not lead to employment of the largest number of workers.[9]

Quite aside from the factor-proportions problem, Hirschman has suggested that poor management capacity and less efficient labor may make capital-using methods more profitable. The machine may follow instructions better than the laborer, or be easier to manage, with less waste of time and materials.[10] In this event also, the profitability criterion does not lead to methods employing the otherwise idle labor.

The use of "overly modern" technology. There are other cases, however, where the profitability criterion would cause labor-using technology to be selected, but—alas!—the capital-intensive method may be employed because the other is not known, or not fashionable, or not shiny enough.

[9] For a technical description of the factor-proportions problem, see Richard S. Eckaus, "The Factor Proportions Problem in Underdeveloped Areas," *American Economic Review*, September, 1955, pp. 539–565.

[10] Albert O. Hirshman, *The Strategy of Economic Development*, Yale University Press, New Haven, Conn., 1959, pp. 150–152.

Tenenbaum tells of a producer of storage batteries in British Guiana who attempted to acquire machinery in the United States.[11] Salesmen urged him to buy a machine that would manufacture over one hundred batteries a day, but he wanted to produce only six. By using hand methods, dipping and inserting plates individually, he found that the combination of cheap labor for himself and high transport costs for his importing competitors enabled him to sell profitably at lower prices than those of batteries manufactured in the United States. Unfortunately, not all entrepreneurs are as astute as this one, and too often it is believed that the machine method is naturally the best and cheapest.

Many production techniques in Latin American factories are carried over from the United States and Europe. Indeed, there is a widespread belief that technology is no problem in economic development, for new ways of producing have already been discovered. The bottleneck (it is thought) lies in obtaining the capital to apply them.

But production techniques in the more advanced countries have been evolved in the face of growing labor shortage and higher wages. Kendrick has shown that in recent decades wage rates in the United States have increased a bit more than the productivity of labor,[12] and entrepreneurs have therefore been pressed to substitute laborsaving machinery. At the same time, high wages have promoted demand for new products, so that the men and machines remain employed.

Technology developed in the United States under these circumstances is not necessarily applicable in Latin America, where capital is expensive and labor abundant. In many cases it is cheaper to use old-fashioned methods, which employ the largest amount of labor. Once again the textile industry is an example (but not with hand methods as an option). Large-scale automatic looms are now used in the United States, but old-fashioned ones may be more feasible in Latin America. They are cheaper, and often good ones can be bought secondhand. Their low price more than offsets the added cost of inventory and labor. Here is a case where the profitability criterion leads to techniques that alleviate unemployment.

The suggestion of old equipment for Latin America and new for the United States sounds heretical, and I am sure to be accused of economic imperialism—attempting to keep Latin America as a second-rate power. Yet paradoxically this technology is precisely what will enable Latin America to compete more effectively with imports from the United States.

[11] Edward Tenenbaum, in a lecture at the Institute for International Development, Washington, D.C., Aug. 1, 1962.

[12] John W. Kendrick, *Productivity Trends in the United States,* National Bureau of Economic Research, Princeton University Press, Princeton, N.J., 1961, pp. 124–130.

The choice of technology. As in so many economic problems, the choice of technology cannot be summarized in a few rules. Sometimes application of the profitability criterion will help the unemployment problem, and sometimes it won't. Economic planners therefore have two possibilities, and the final choice can be a combination. One is to set the profitability criterion aside and select projects primarily on the basis of employment. This extreme will be costly and will reduce the real national product below the capacity of the country.

The other is to stick rigidly to the profitability criterion, which will maximize output. If the public administration is adequate, this choice will provide the greatest resources with which to assist the unemployed, through social welfare programs or to finance special "make-work" activities.

But the public administration, and especially the tax machinery, may not be adequate to carry out programs of this nature. The final choice of projects and their technology is therefore a matter of judgment, in which the profitability criterion is weighed against the social benefits of greater employment. Where the two are consistent, the choice is easy. Where they are not, the wisdom and social conscience of the planner must be relied on for an appropriate selection.

Changing comparative advantage

Nations will produce those goods and services in which they have comparative advantage, so the classical economists tell us, if their entrepreneurs are guided by profit and unimpeded by government. But the sad dilemma is that Latin American comparative advantages historically lie in primary products, so lacking in external economies, incentives for education and self-improvement, and other requisites for growth. We concluded in Chapter 8 that infant-industry and infant-nation tariffs are justified even though they imply, at least temporarily, a reduction in real national income. Does it not follow that projects should be selected by such criteria as the extent to which they demand the services of other industries or an educated citizenry? Will not such selections violate the profitability criterion but improve the composition of the nation's industry?

Some economists have answered in the affirmative. Leibenstein,[13] for example, argues that the profitability criterion (social marginal product)

> . . . does not allow for the following important elements: (1) the indirect effect of the investment allocation on the expansion of the growth factors,

[13] Harvey Leibenstein, *Economic Backwardness and Economic Growth,* John Wiley & Sons, Inc., New York, 1957, pp. 258–259.

that is, on the expansion of entrepreneurship, on the increase in the quality of the labor force, and on the expansion of skills; (2) the effect of the investment allocation on future savings habits and, therefore, on the future rate of investment; (3) the effect of the investment allocation and policy on the future consumption pattern, which, in turn, determines whether the consumption is simply on population maintenance or on the expansion of the growth agents; (4) the indirect effect of the investment allocation on the rate of population growth, which, in turn, is a consideration in determining what happens to per capita output.

Hirschman too implies an attack on the profitability criterion when he suggests that the selection among possible projects ought to be based on their forward and backward linkages. That is, A is selected before B, not because it is more profitable, but because once A is in existence, B will be needed earlier than A would be if B alone existed.[14]

Neither Leibenstein nor Hirschman argues that the profitability criterion should be abandoned. ECLA also agrees that net social profitability should be the most weighty factor. Other criteria supplement it but do not substitute. While the *most* profitable project is not necessarily chosen, nevertheless all selections should earn some profit or at least incur a minimum of loss. Otherwise they would be a drag on the nation's resources, consuming more than they produce, and would unbalance the government budget.

The criteria proposed by Leibenstein and Hirschman therefore presuppose a large number of projects whose selection is limited only by shortage of capital, competent management, skilled labor, or other factors of production. In practice, however, Latin American development plans do not include an abundance of projects that await financing.

Profitable projects are hard to find. Even scarcer are technicians sensitive to the subtleties that spell the difference between profit and loss. With a range of other tests at their disposal, planners may be deceived into approving ventures that have lovely trimmings but no guts. One begins to wonder whether the wealth of selection criteria is indeed a boon to planning or a deceptive quagmire.

The argument that forced-draft change in comparative advantage requires subsidizing unprofitable ventures must not be overdone. To the extent that it is valid, the subsidy can be supplied by tariffs. But it does not follow from Latin America's unfortunate specialization in primary products that suitable industrial opportunities do not exist. The fact of other selection criteria should not serve as excuse to avoid the difficult and often unglamorous task of scouring the countryside for profitable ventures.

[14] Hirschman, *op. cit.*, pp. 77–78.

The foreign-exchange criterion

Suppose project A is more profitable than project B, based on shadow prices measuring social return. But project B will earn or save more foreign exchange. Which should be selected? If the nation has a balance of payments deficit, should foreign exchange be a criterion in project evaluation? If so, how many pesos of foreign exchange saved by project B are equal to a peso of profit sacrificed by failure to select project A?

The extent to which foreign exchange becomes a criterion depends on whether one believes a balance of payments deficit is caused by the process of economic development itself or by improper monetary management and excessive inflation. I have argued the case for development with stability, or a close approximation thereof, in Chapter 7. To those who agree, the solution of a balance of payments problem depends more on the selection of a proper exchange rate than other aspects of national planning.

The process of development causes increased demand for capital imports. But this does not arise from a vacuum. A prior condition is increased demand for the consumer goods that capital will produce. The question of timing is all-important. A properly conceived development plan, based on aggressive search for profitable projects, may yield import substitutes that provide foreign exchange *before* the demand for capital goods is felt.

If development occurs with monetary stability, there is no *a priori* reason why it should call forth a balance of payments surplus or deficit. There will be a surplus if increased output of exports and import substitutes exceeds the increased demand for imported capital goods, and a deficit if the opposite is true. A persistent tendency toward one or the other will call for a revision in the exchange rate, possibly upward and possibly downward.

Suppose a deficit occurs despite monetary stability, and exchange depreciation is required. Exports will be encouraged and imports discouraged. But most important of all, the production of import substitutes will become more profitable, because competing imports are more expensive in local currency. New enterprises can then be selected according to the profitability criterion.

But, it may be argued, exchange depreciation will adversely affect the terms of trade. Demand for Latin American exports is inelastic. Any lowering of their price to foreigners will decrease the amount of foreign exchange realized, because the loss in receipts due to price fall would more than offset the gain due to increased sales.

This point would be well taken if exchange depreciations became general to all producers of any one primary product. In that case the dollar price would fall, and exporting nations would suffer. But if economic development occurs generally with stability, exchange depreciations become the exception rather than the rule, and appreciations may also occur. A single depreciating nation would probably not cause a decrease in the dollar price of exports, since competing suppliers would continue to offer at the same level. No Latin American country produces a high enough proportion of world output of any one commodity to exercise a monopoly. But exporters would benefit through higher prices in local currency. To the extent that their supply is elastic, they might expand sales and even gain foreign exchange for the nation.

All the theoretical considerations outlined above would lead to the conclusion that the foreign-exchange criterion has no place in project analysis and that total reliance should be placed on profitability. In practice, however, this is not so. Countries with balance of payments deficits cannot avoid considering whether or not a project will provide foreign exchange. To suggest that deficits should be corrected by monetary policy and exchange-rate adjustment does not excuse one from living in the real world where this does not always happen.

A persistent balance of payments deficit indicates an overvalued exchange rate. With such a rate, the social profitability of import substitutes and exports is greater than profitability to the entrepreneur. If, for example, the controlled rate is 100 pesos to the dollar but a realistic rate is 150, then an export selling for $1 yields only 100 pesos to the entrepreneur, but in terms of social benefit it is worth 150. Likewise an import substitute would be declared unprofitable because it yields only 100 pesos (and its costs are, say, 120 pesos) in competition with the import whose c.i.f. price is $1. But the social profitability of that import substitute is 30 pesos, for this is what it would yield (at a price of 150) if the peso were realistically valued.

One way to adjust for this discrepancy is to use a shadow price of foreign exchange—the realistic rate of 150 instead of the actual rate of 100—and at these prices the profitability of both the export and import substitute would increase. But this is simply a way of saying that the amount of foreign exchange earned is a criterion. Alternatively, application of the foreign-exchange criterion is one way of admitting that the local currency is overvalued, and the profitability criterion for export and import-substitute projects is to that extent inadequate.

Other criteria

The Economic Commission for Latin America lists six criteria for project selection: (1) net return, from the point of view of both the individual entrepreneur and the nation as a whole; (2) integrated development, or how the project will fit into the economic complex as outlined in macro-analysis; (3) stability and growth, or its susceptibility to "seasonal swings, international events, economic cycles and changes of other indices which reflect economic activity"; (4) balance of payments effects; (5) socioeconomic desirability, including the solution of human relations problems and geographic decentralization; and (6) experience and competition, including how the industry has fared in other areas under similar conditions. ECLA deems social profitability to be the most important of these tests and adds that the weight to be given to others depends on circumstances that vary with time and place. For example, the balance of payments criterion would presumably be more important the more serious the deficit, and socioeconomic desirability more important in countries where social inequities are greatest.[15]

Social projects

The profitability criterion does not apply to projects of a social nature, such as education and health. Measurement-minded economists have tried to put a money value on these, based on the marginal productivity of educated men over noneducated, of healthy people over those with malaria, or alternatively on how much it costs to raise a healthy and educated laborer. Such measurements confuse the objectives of economic development with their means, quite apart from the fact that they are usually matters of opinion anyway. The most practical way of assessing projects of a social value can only be a feeling for the situation—how much they are desired by the people and how capable the government is of providing them. The revenue sacrificed by devoting resources to education rather than industry can be measured, but the value of the education acquired is a matter of judgment that can only be made by one who is peculiarly sensitive to the aspirations of the people.

Housing, so often considered a means of bringing the fruits of development to the masses, has far greater potential to the economy than may be initially supposed. Presumably it fits under the fifth of ECLA's criteria listed above, that of socioeconomic desirability. The economic should be emphasized. If properly managed, a housing program can contribute to the saving habits of a nation. If a peasant is loaned $3,000 with which to build a house and if he must pay the debt in monthly installments at 2 per cent interest over thirty years, each payment amounts to $11.09. Now $11.09 is a substantial portion of the monthly income of many peasants, maybe all of it. In these cases a down payment should be made as a grant, thus reducing the debt burden. Or interest might be rescinded entirely, in which case the monthly repayment is

[15] *Manual on Economic Development Projects,* United Nations, New York, 1958, pp. 239–240.

reduced to $8.40. The ratio of loan to grant, and interest rate, can be decided according to local circumstances, for the project will have to be subsidized anyway.

Aside from the housing itself, the chief value of such a program is that the peasant learns to save. Not only is the monthly amortization genuine saving, which can be used to finance someone else's house, but the peasant can see that his saving is directly associated with an increase in his standard of living. Even if part of the cost is financed by a grant and even if interest is artificially low or zero, nevertheless the peasant has the dignity of knowing that his house has not been entirely financed by the beneficence of others. His own efforts are a contribution.

Housing is one of the principal activities of the Social Progress Trust Fund, established in 1961 with a United States appropriation of $500 million and operated by the Inter-American Development Bank. Latin American students have asked me whether the United States concern for housing is anything more than a reaction to the charge that foreign aid has not filtered down to the people. Has not Congress simply "written off" half a billion dollars as a small price for keeping the peasants from rebelling and preserving the *status quo*?

Call it this if you wish, but there is a positive as well as a negative side. The United States is still, as it always has been, interested in preserving political stability in Latin America. But it has finally dawned on the North American government that political stability is best assured not by military intervention and force but by the support of a peasantry whose land and houses are symbols of the stake *they* have in preserving the present order.

ECLA's criterion 5 is the basis for selecting a housing project. Even the profitability criterion falls into the background here, provided there is adequate finance. Here is an example of the inadequacy of market prices. Had the market mechanism assured social justice in the past, with rational and equitable income distributions, there would be little reason now to abandon the profitability criterion even in housing. Social inequities must be dispelled as rapidly as possible, but in the meantime, and subject to the limits of available financing, other criteria must override profitability in a few strategic types of project.

The role of interest

Marxists are more and more questioning whether interest is a social cost, to be considered along with others in profitability analysis. Marx himself argued that it belongs instead to surplus value, the "undeserved" payment to capitalists. Until recent years Communist planners studiously ignored interest in assembling priorities for the Soviet Union.

The close attention paid by Marx to social justice and his belief that the payment of interest was morally wrong blinded him and his Communist descendants to its role as a cost. Quite apart from its function in distributing the nation's output, interest equates time dimensions. It helps select the project that produces earlier. This "truth" has long been obvious to capitalist nations, but only within the last decade has the Soviet Union begun to see it as well.

Suppose two projects have the same "value" in the Marxist sense. The same number of labor hours is embodied in each, with all necessary adjustments for socially desirable labor and equation of skilled and unskilled. Over their lifetimes the projects will produce identical output at the same unit operating cost. But they use different technologies. Project A will start producing earlier than B and will maintain its lead.

Is not project A "obviously" superior to project B? By Marxist definitions it is not: they are alike. Strict adherence to the labor theory of value not only rubs out the distinction between scarce and abundant resources, but it also neutralizes the time factor. Yet there are many reasons why the nation as a whole would prefer the earlier-yielding venture, particularly if its output is a capital good whose head start would be an advantage that the later project could never recoup.

Because it is ideologically improper, planners in the Soviet Union do not use the term "interest." But in recent years they have begun to refer to the "coefficient of relative effectiveness," or the "recoupment period of capital," both of them euphemisms. The recoupment period is the length of time in which capitalistic methods produce a saving sufficient to pay their cost. A five-year period, for example, corresponds to an interest rate of 20 per cent. Projects with shorter recoupment periods (i.e., higher interest yields) are preferred over those with longer recoupment periods.

Two forces are afoot which may reduce the dispute over the labor theory of value to an academic matter only. In the first place, Karl Marx was a social philosopher with a keen insight into morality and justice, to which his theory was addressed. He was not a project analyst. Now that his followers have established a distributive system (communism) which to them meets the demands of justice, they feel free to drop the theory in those areas for which it was not intended. In the second place, the more developed capitalist countries have over time instituted a distribution system that meets most of the injustices that so rankled Marx. High income taxes on corporations and individuals, high inheritance taxes, social security, and all the regulations that mitigate the business cycle and prevent abuse of power are an integral part of the manner by which national product is shared. Only against this background of improved social justice, which is yet to be achieved in most of Latin America, can the "rightness" of classical cost principles be judged.

CONCLUSION

The science of economic planning provides the analyst with an array of implements, impressive, shiny, and subtle, often requiring the use of giant calculators and skill in linear programming and operations research. Macro-planning is done with equations based on the national income and flow-of-funds accounts and functional relationships empirically observed. They reveal the area of achievable goals and alternative policies designed to reach them. The mathematical instruments have been carried further, with the help of input-output tables, to pinpoint the sectors where development is required and to supply data useful to the selection criteria of micro techniques.

Simultaneously, the planner is armed with instruments of a micro nature by which to analyze specific projects. These are older, more tested, for they descend from centuries of experience in accounting, financial analysis, engineering economics, market research, and the like. They have been developed primarily in private enterprise but are applicable to government corporations as well. The profitability of a project lies at their core—possibly adjusted to social profitability—but there are other considerations as well.

There is no need for the two types of planning to conflict, and few planners admit that they do. Surely macro-plans can be checked against the results of project research and analysis. If they are inconsistent with each other, both can be examined for errors. Alternatively, macro-planning can help select the areas where projects are to be sought. Do they not complement each other?

There is evidence that in practice they do not, and this fact may be at the core of differences of opinion between economic planners in Latin America and their sources of funds, both in the private sector in Latin America and abroad.

First, Latin American literature reveals a widely held sentiment that centrally planned enterprises are more efficient and have a greater chance of success than those decided upon "haphazardly" by the market. It is believed they will integrate more closely in the total economic picture. In short, they will be more profitable. By sharp contrast, in the United States the feeling is strong that private enterprise is far more efficient and far more likely to yield a return than anything in which the government has a hand. The divergent opinions stem from differing experiences with private enterprise, which have been treated in earlier chapters. Attention is called here only to the impact of this divergence on the attitude toward planning.

Second, the relative importance that one places on capital in the development complex influences one's position on aggregate planning. Macro techniques depend heavily on the capital-output ratio, or the supposition that a given amount of capital is necessary to yield a given return. Any economist who believes that this ratio is distorted by its lack of attention to other factors, such as entrepreneurial ability, the general level of education, or its failure to account for technological change, is to that extent skeptical of the macro techniques that employ it. Few economists would deny that new capital is required for increased output, and few would deny that other factors are also responsible. But the weighting is not even. If the results of macro- and micro-analysis do not coincide, the analyst is usually prejudiced as to which is probably wrong.

Third, the rules of both macro- and micro-analysis are readily learned in textbooks. But there is a vast difference in their application. Macroanalytical exercises can be successfully completed without the selection of a single project. Calculations can be carried to the minutest detail, including amounts to be invested in every sector. But the proponents of micro techniques cannot analyze a project without finding it first. Herein lies the demanding task, which requires a knowledge of what to seek, the intelligence to recognize it when it is seen, and willingness to forgo physical comfort in the search. With all deference to macro-analysts, with all appreciation of their endowment in mathematical skills and recognition of the value of their efforts, nevertheless let me suggest that their whole job is easier than fulfilling the prerequisites to micro-analysis.

Fourth, the shortage of skill in finding profitable ventures combines with the existence of other criteria, including the whole array of macro techniques, to create a false feeling of achievement in a plan with no projects, or in projects that do not pass for profitability. While some of the latter—such as housing—must be selected for reasons of overriding social importance, nevertheless the economy can subsidize only so many of them. No nation—socialist or capitalist—can undertake a large number of ventures that do not cover their costs. This dictum applies not only to those selected for social reasons or for the foreign-exchange criterion but even to those deemed socially but not privately profitable.

In final analysis, have we—the economists of Latin America, the United States, and elsewhere—perhaps created a monster, in the form of sophisticated and theoretically desirable planning techniques, to which we pay great lip service but which we finally refuse to apply when the chips are down and the loan applications are in?

11 Revolution—Old and New

> Revolution is a mettlesome horse. One must either ride it or be trampled to death by it. The Hapsburg Monarchy and the Czardom have both been trampled to death within the last half century. But how did a revolutionary-minded Russian acrobat manage subsequently to vault into the saddle? He found the saddle vacant; so, by the date at which the present Russian rider lodged himself there, the original American rider must have dismounted. Can the United States recapture her revolutionary birthright? President Kennedy has proclaimed this as his ambition for her. Is the United States going to take the leap, or is she going to stall? Her destiny hangs on her choice; for to linger dismounted in the arena is to court death—especially in our day, when the world arena is rapidly contracting, so that the trampling horse is thundering round it in ever narrowing circles.[1]

TO HISTORIAN Arnold Toynbee, the crucial question of the Western Hemisphere is whether the United States can once again hold reins on the revolution that it abandoned when the youthful sheen had worn off. Lecturing at the University of Puerto Rico in 1962, Toynbee saw in the

[1] Arnold Toynbee, *The Economy of the Western Hemisphere,* London, Oxford University Press, 1963. Published in Spanish by University of Puerto Rico Press (Weatherhead Lectures at University of Puerto Rico, Lecture 3, February, 1962).

United States a dichotomy between a people weighted by vested interests and a President determined to lead them instead in the quest for social justice.

But the revolution that the United States "outgrew" was different from the one to whose leadership Mr. Kennedy would now aspire. Like the subsequent political independence of Latin America, that of the United States in 1776 was a landmark in the development of individualism and the freedom of man from domineering government. It occurred in the same year that Adam Smith wrote the *Wealth of Nations,* proclaiming the invisible hand by whose guidance man, if free, would serve his fellow men in his own interests.

In the succeeding century and a half, the paths of Latin America and the United States drew apart. Both witnessed a conflict between two types of capitalism—one invidious, in which man oversteps the bounds of decency to control the lives of others, and the other productive, in which man genuinely contributes to the well-being of the social unit in which he lives. The demarcation between them is unclear, and they are distinguished only by the relative preponderance of one. In the evolution of their respective histories, the invidious type came to dominate in Latin America, and the productive in the United States.

Capitalism was contained in the United States by limits to the abuse of freedom. The Civil War began the end of the primary-product, export economy of the South. Within the union, the Southern states shared the progress of the industrial colossus in the North. In a land where Indians were not abundant, labor shortage led to higher wages. The industrial economy depended for foodstuffs on Westward-moving farmers who tilled their own soil. These forces all led to decentralized government, and political power was spread among the many. The masses were strong enough to contain the excesses of oil monopolists and railroad magnates by the Interstate Commerce Act of 1887 and the Sherman Antitrust Law of 1890. Antibranch banking laws slowed the concentration of monetary power, and control over the banking system was transferred to the Federal Reserve in 1913. In the same year the Constitution was amended to permit an income tax, and high inheritance taxes were to follow. Only where wealth and political power are diffused will a democratic government vote to tax its people according to their means.

Unfortunately, the growing egalitarianism did not spread to Latin America. The pattern of landholdings inherited from the Spanish conquest, the abundance of Indians as cheap labor, the climate and barriers of geography, the specialization in primary products, the lack of political integration, the growth of self-willed military potentates, the constant struggles for political power—all militated against a system in which the rights of the weak would be protected.

The divergent evolution of capitalism was accompanied by different concepts of social justice. In Latin America, where wealth was gained by force and held by force, it was not the fault of the poor that they were oppressed. As the counterweight of revolution finally swings, social justice requires not only a redistribution of wealth but a rupture of the old institutions under which income is earned. These changes even command priority over economic growth, which in the past has served only to concentrate power in the few.

But in the United States, where wealth is attributed primarily to production, poverty has not been recognized as a sin of commission by the wealthy but a sin of omission by the poor. The poor have been deemed slothful, drunkards, unwilling to use the intelligence with which they were endowed. In this context, social justice has meant delivering unto each the product of his effort, no less and certainly no more. Egalitarianism was not sought as an end in itself. Its evolution has been incidental to a determination to preserve the system by which man is rewarded for his toil.

The two concepts of social justice were bound to conflict as the hemisphere became smaller. Morality is not universal but relates to the setting in which it grows. If business is subject to legal restraints and if other groups are strong enough to protect their interests, then the market mechanism and the profit motive are not immoral instruments of personal aggrandizement. But if the law is soft and mushy, and other interests are weak, then the same economic instruments cease to be moral.

In the United States it became acceptable for business to do everything within its legal power to earn profit, for public morality counted on the law and the counterweight of other blocs to hold it within reasonable proportions. If a loophole in the tax law made it possible for an industry to gain at the expense of others, it was moral for it to do so. By the same moral standard, the legislator's duty was to plug the loophole so that the practice could not continue. These checks and balances, North Americans believe, have provided not only the greatest freedom and the greatest restraint but also the greatest economic growth.

But North American businessmen misapplied the same morality in Latin America, where the checks and balances did not exist. They believed it was no fault of theirs if Latin American politicians were corrupt. If officials could be bribed, the businessmen would bribe them. To them the Latin American peasant did not "own" his mineral wealth, except in some formal sense of sovereignty that rested in his government. If the peasant did not control the government, that was his fault, and to him befell the consequences. If he did not himself extract the minerals, then they were forfeit, for it was "wicked" to leave them unused. Mineral wealth belonged to those with the genius to find it, the inventiveness and capital to take it out of the ground, and the means to buy it from whatever sovereign had power over the land.

The different experiences with morality help explain why the market mechanism is more respected as an economic arbiter in the United States than in Latin America. To North Americans, market prices are the only sensible means by which goods and services can be distributed, with due account for consumer preferences and the scarcity of resources. To many in Latin America, they are an instrument of oppression wielded by monopolies.

Let us now return to the question raised in Chapter 1 (page 10), of why economists who sincerely want to be objective nevertheless tend to divide along lines that belie their geographic origin. I cannot speak for Latin Americans on this, because I am not one. But I do believe that North American concepts of morality and social justice affect the degree to which we accept economic doctrine. They have influenced our receptivity to Latin American theories.

In the last fifteen years economic thought in Latin America has come of age. Before World War II it could hardly be said that Latin America possessed theories peculiarly her own; rather, she relied on products of European and North American thinking. But during the fifties a school of young economists, with Raul Prebisch as their acknowledged dean, has changed the face of Latin American economics. Since many in this school matured while associated with the Economic Commission for Latin America, a large part of their theory has become known as "the ECLA doctrine."

The new theories are by no means Marxist. But they do make penetrating incursions into classical (capitalist?) doctrine and are weighted on the side of State intervention. Their interpretation of terms of trade data supports protective commercial policies, planned integration, and international commodity agreements. They have been relatively tolerant of inflation and have prescribed State intervention to offset its undesirable effects. They have argued that balance of payments problems are inherent in economic development and controls are therefore necessary. Their views on the development process have supported macro-planning. All this has been outlined in earlier chapters.

This economic thought has not been well received in the United States. It has been widely criticized in professional journals as well as magazines, such as *Fortune,* aimed at the intelligent layman. In North American university circles as in Washington, it has become fashionable to criticize ECLA.

This adverse reaction has caused some disappointment among the Latin American theorists, plus the sentiment that we North Americans want to create the world in our own image. We are, of course, guilty of such parochialism. But this is not the only reason for our reluctance to accept the ECLA theories.

From the vantage point of many North Americans, ECLA's sin lies in assigning responsibility for underdevelopment primarily to occurrences in the outside world over which the Latin Americans have had little control. They have been buffeted by the terms of trade, helpless before the pricing policies of foreign enterprises and the vicissitudes of a business cycle generated abroad, and inflicted with inflation as an "undeniable" consequence of growth. Even where domestic weaknesses are recognized, they are dubbed "structural," as if to say "handed down by our ancestors and beyond the control of the present generation."

Considering our "capitalist ethic" background, it is not surprising that we should react adversely to this doctrine. Since earliest childhood, we have been brought up to judge people by their achievements and to damn them for their excuses. Man's duty is to control his environment, not cite it as an obstacle. The employee who blames his failures on his colleagues, or on circumstances, is the least likely to be promoted, *no matter how right he may be.*

I have talked with Latin American economists who are puzzled because the harder they try to help North Americans "understand" them, the greater the misunderstanding becomes. Usually they do not grasp that to these North Americans, ECLA's interpretation of history is a doctrine of weakness, and weakness is not sympathized with in the capitalist ethic.

It follows that North Americans deem "fanciful" the theories emanating from this doctrine, including the resigned acceptance of inflation, the "hope" that it will be cured in time as a substitute for the rigorous discipline of stabilization, and elaborate macro-planning as a substitute for the more difficult task of project selection. They question whether Latin Americans have really grasped what a "tough job" economic development is.

I would not be honest if I did not identify myself personally with much of this thought. Nevertheless, the very fact that North American attitudes are in a state of flux, with an ever-greater acceptance of collectivism, is (I believe) a confession that our approach to Latin American doctrines has been too dogmatic. We in the United States are gradually learning respect for the ideas of those whose material achievements are not as great as ours, prior lack of which has been a sore gap in our national character.

The Depression of the thirties marked a turning point in the North American concept of social justice. It was longer and more severe than any economic crisis the United States had ever experienced. For the first time in history large segments of the nation were crushed by a persistent misfortune that was obviously and conclusively not their individual blame. The economic theories of Keynes added intellectual bulk to the growing awareness that poverty was not, after all, the shame of the poor. The divergent paths in Western Hemisphere perspectives began to come together again.

A wave of social legislation swept the United States in the thirties. New laws gave strength to the labor movement, controlled the issuance of corporate stock, implanted monetary and fiscal weapons in the arsenal of economic policy, brought assistance to farmers and other primary producers, provided inexpensive housing to low-income groups, and established social security. In many ways the government intervened in the structure of market prices and traditional concepts of economic freedom. It even introduced planning for full employment.

The social revolution did not destroy the spirit of individualism or even move it far from center. Rather, it left the country with a fusion of two dogmas. The first is that solutions to economic and social problems are practical and deserved only if their primary impulse comes from those whose problems they are: Negroes in the southern United States, North American farmers, West Virginia miners, and Latin American countries in search of development. The other is a new recognition that failure to achieve is not always the fault of the disadvantaged. From this comes the moral obligation of the successful to elaborate programs by which the rights of others to income and opportunity are protected and facilitated.

This fusion of doctrines did not come suddenly, nor was it a rash reaction to specific inflammatory events. The United States did not recognize the moral obligations that gave rise to the Alliance for Progress until the domestic counterpart of each of the points in that Alliance had been carefully and elaborately fashioned over a period of three decades. But there were certain impulses—world-shaking events such as the cold war and the Cuban revolution—that caused the conscience and political awareness of the United States to spill into the international field in seeming sudden fashion.

Only against this backdrop can one understand the revival of the North American impulse to ride the revolutionary horse. It is a worthy steed to mount, and in three decades we are only half way up. But this is because it is not the same animal as before, and only now is it being broken in. The old revolution was designed to make the government weak and the individual strong. It was appropriate to its day, but that day has passed. The new revolution must strike a delicate balance. It must not restore the oppression of the past in a new guise, but it must curtail abusive liberties and free man to maximize his potential.

Index